Career Pathways and Professional Identities for Front-Line Workers in the Service Industries

Mark Peter Vitale
University of Phoenix, USA

A volume in the Advances in Hospitality, Tourism, and the Services Industry (AHTSI) Book Series

IGI Global
PUBLISHER of TIMELY KNOWLEDGE

Published in the United States of America by
IGI Global
Business Science Reference (an imprint of IGI Global)
701 E. Chocolate Avenue
Hershey PA, USA 17033
Tel: 717-533-8845
Fax: 717-533-8661
E-mail: cust@igi-global.com
Web site: http://www.igi-global.com

Library of Congress Cataloging-in-Publication Data

Names: Vitale, Mark, 1973- editor.
Title: Career pathways and professional identities for front-line workers in the service industries / Mark Vitale.
Description: Hershey, PA : Business Science Reference, [2024] | Includes bibliographical references and index. | Summary: "This publication is a unique synthesis of concepts presented for a collection of industries that have had little research of this nature conducted as of yet. The hospitality, restaurant and tourism industries feature hundreds of thousands of service-based frontline jobs that are rarely considered long-term careers by either employees or employers. With a deeper understanding of how strategic career pathways and cultures of professional identify can be integrated and applied within these disciplines, industry employers will be able to use this publication to develop proactive strategies to optimize their own operation, establish leadership-focused succession planning and minimize the cost impact of fluctuations in labor availability fluctuations"-- Provided by publisher.
Identifiers: LCCN 2023019962 (print) | LCCN 2023019963 (ebook) | ISBN 9781668425282 (hardcover) | ISBN 9781668425299 (paperback) | ISBN 9781668425305 (ebook)
Subjects: LCSH: Service industries--Vocational guidance. | Hospitality industry--Vocational guidance.
Classification: LCC HD9980.5 .C37 2023 (print) | LCC HD9980.5 (ebook) | DDC 338.4/7023--dc23/eng/20230501
LC record available at https://lccn.loc.gov/2023019962
LC ebook record available at https://lccn.loc.gov/2023019963

British Cataloguing in Publication Data
A Cataloguing in Publication record for this book is available from the British Library.
All work contributed to this book is new, previously-unpublished material.
The views expressed in this book are those of the authors, but not necessarily of the publisher.
For electronic access to this publication, please contact: eresources@igi-global.com.

Advances in Hospitality, Tourism, and the Services Industry (AHTSI) Book Series

Maximiliano Korstanje
University of Palermo, Argentina

ISSN:2475-6547
EISSN:2475-6555

MISSION

Globally, the hospitality, travel, tourism, and services industries generate a significant percentage of revenue and represent a large portion of the business world. Even in tough economic times, these industries thrive as individuals continue to spend on leisure and recreation activities as well as services.

The Advances in Hospitality, Tourism, and the Services Industry (AHTSI) book series offers diverse publications relating to the management, promotion, and profitability of the leisure, recreation, and services industries. Highlighting current research pertaining to various topics within the realm of hospitality, travel, tourism, and services management, the titles found within the AHTSI book series are pertinent to the research and professional needs of managers, business practitioners, researchers, and upper-level students studying in the field.

COVERAGE

- Service Management
- Casino Management
- Customer Service Issues
- Travel Agency Management
- Sustainable Tourism
- International Tourism
- Service Design
- Leisure & Business Travel
- Service Training
- Destination Marketing and Management

IGI Global is currently accepting manuscripts for publication within this series. To submit a proposal for a volume in this series, please contact our Acquisition Editors at Acquisitions@igi-global.com or visit: http://www.igi-global.com/publish/.

The Advances in Hospitality, Tourism, and the Services Industry (AHTSI) Book Series (ISSN 2475-6547) is published by IGI Global, 701 E. Chocolate Avenue, Hershey, PA 17033-1240, USA, www.igi-global.com. This series is composed of titles available for purchase individually; each title is edited to be contextually exclusive from any other title within the series. For pricing and ordering information please visit http://www.igi-global.com/book-series/advances-hospitality-tourism-services-industry/121014. Postmaster: Send all address changes to above address.

Titles in this Series

For a list of additional titles in this series, please visit: http://www.igi-global.com/book-series/

Experiences, Advantages, and Economic Dimensions of Pilgrimage Routes
Vítor João Pereira Domingues Martinho (ESAV, CERNAS-IPV Research Centre, Polytechnic Institute of Viseu, Portugal) João Augusto Guerra da Rocha Nunes (School of Education, Polytechnic Institute of Viseu, Portugal) Maria Lúcia de Jesus Pato (Agricultural S (IPV), 3chool (ESAV), and CERNAS-IPV Research Centre, Polytechnic Institute of Viseu, Portugal) and Liliana Andrade de Matos Castilho (School of Education, Polytechnic Institute of Viseu, Portugal)
Business Science Reference • © 2023 • 367pp • H/C (ISBN: 9781668499238) • US $240.00

Exploring Culture and Heritage Through Experience Tourism
Yashwant Singh Rawal (Parul Institute of Hotel Management, Parul University, India) Rupa Sinha (Amity Institute of Travel and Tourism, Amity University, India) Sankar Kumar Mukherjee (Amity Institute of Travel and Tourism, Amity University, India) and Debasish Batabyal (Amity Institute of Travel and Tourism, Amity University, India)
Business Science Reference • © 2023 • 348pp • H/C (ISBN: 9781668499573) • US $240.00

Sustainable Development Goal Advancement Through Digital Innovation in the Service Sector
Vipin Nadda (University of Sunderland, UK) Pankaj Kumar Tyagi (Chandigarh University, India) Rubina Moniz Vieira (St. Mary's University, London, UK) and Priyanka Tyagi (Chandigarh University, India)
Business Science Reference • © 2023 • 272pp • H/C (ISBN: 9798369306505) • US $275.00

Management and Practices of Pilgrimage Tourism and Hospitality
S.K. Gupta (Centre for Mountain Tourism and Hospitality Management, HNB Garhwal University, India) Lilibeth C. Aragon (College of International Tourism and Hospitality Management, Lyceum of the Philippines University, Philippines) Pankaj Kumar (Department of Tourism and Hospitality Management, Mizoram University, India) Madhurima S. (Department of Environmental Science, Mizoram University, India) and Rajesh Ramasamy (Department of Tourism and Hospitality Management, Mizoram University, India)
Business Science Reference • © 2023 • 264pp • H/C (ISBN: 9798369314142) • US $250.00

IGI Global
PUBLISHER of TIMELY KNOWLEDGE

701 East Chocolate Avenue, Hershey, PA 17033, USA
Tel: 717-533-8845 x100 • Fax: 717-533-8661
E-Mail: cust@igi-global.com • www.igi-global.com

Table of Contents

Section 3
Enabling Future State Career Satisfaction in Hospitality

Preface

Simultaneously disruptive and destructive, the COVID-19 pandemic eliminated millions of jobs overnight and changes global perspectives on thresholds for what was acceptable in a career. However, while the pandemic is the most visible (at least in recent years) catalyst for change in workplaces, it is not the only component of trends and paradigms that shape context for billions of people working across the planet. In fact, labor shortages were being reported throughout the 2010s in the United States and internationally and the Great Recession of 2009 was – at the time – had a great impact on employment. Employers were already reporting that they could not find enough employees who had the skills necessary to fill positions that they needed to achieve the work that was being developed (Gosslin, Scott, & Hall, 2020). For those that could be hired, employers would further discover that organizational citizenship was observed to be significantly less than in previous times (Hall, 2020). This manifested itself where in-demand employees would often stay in a role for a very short time before being lured away for a more lucrative offer at another employer (Scholz, 2017).

Throughout the latter half of the twentieth century, millions of workers have been displaced while others have become involuntarily part-time unemployed, hired on temporary employment contracts, or experienced a distinct and significant change in how they approached the traditional employment relationship between an individual and an employer (Jacobson, 1991). For many employees, the changes in working life witnessed over the past two decades have caused dissonance originating from feelings of insecurity concerning the nature and future existence of their jobs. Where it was once common and desired for an individual to remain with a single employer for nearly their entire career, it is increasingly more likely for employees – in many industries – to exhaust an employment relationship in eight years or less (Roskies & Louis-Guerin, 1990).

The COVID-19 pandemic exacerbated an already tenuous situation while also strengthening a low tolerance among workers for delayed gratification in terms of earning potential opportunities for engaging significant work and establishing an acceptable work-life balance. Between the United States government providing monetary subsidization via various channels to support (or, in some cases, replace) work-based income combined with isolating shelter-in-place directives, employees in the United States were given utility to embrace and enjoy personal pursuits and accomplishments. Perhaps only intended as a temporary measure, this potent intermix of financing and decision-making utility resulted in an emerging world no longer quite as willing to accept conditions for work as it had been prior to the 2020s (Hawley, 2018).

This isn't to say that work isn't pursued, desired, and embraced. Nothing could be further from the truth. Rather, work is pursued on one's terms and the scale of acceptance on a global scale for this perspective is something that has driven new dynamics on what type of work to pursue, when to pursue it and what benefits are truly being sought (Senbeto & Hon, 2020). For example, within the Fourth Industrial revolution, the "gig" economy refers to the dynamic where employers hire individuals as contractors to perform work rather than a traditional pathway as employees.

Contractors (former employees) now can work when they choose (as opposed to when they are scheduled by a manager), and this benefit allows them to maintain an acceptable work-life balance scheduling professional commitments secondary to those of a personal nature. A parent can now make sure to attend family commitments (such as school plays, baseball games and family gatherings) without any challenges since they are contractors working for themselves. A variant of this model, peer to peer branded business platforms such as Uber, Lyft, Door Dash, Instacart and VRBO, have rapidly gained acceptance and prominence in recent years by leveraging the integration of technology with the desire to control one's schedule (Josserand & Kaine, 2019).

The rise of coveted influencer status in society for content creators is yet another derivative of the dynamic born out of the fourth industrial revolution. Content creators document their life's choices through a personal lens capturing their experiences through videos and photographs before sharing their perspective with a global audience via social media distribution channels (Burbano, 2021). The evidence is clear that everyone is working just as hard as ever although the nature of work may be different than in years past. What is truly distinguishing of modern times, however, is a demand and a desire to work on one's own terms rejecting conventional norms and frameworks around employee and employer relationships (Koo, Curtis & Ryan, 2021). The tangible result: A labor shortage reported by businesses. Standing out among its peers, the tourism and hospitality sector is one of the most affected by changing and uncertain conditions brought about by economic, political, or other extrinsic factors that induce rapid, significant change (Hall, 2010).

THE CHALLENGES

While there has been much attention about a deepening crisis around the notion that there are more jobs than qualified employees (by definition, a labor shortage), the solutions that have emerged in the past decade appear to misdiagnose the fundamental issue. One of the last industries to become disrupted by 21st century technology and societal values, higher education has been focused on as the core element of significance that is driving the labor issues. Curriculum being taught to students in college is out of alignment with the needs of industry is an oft heard remark in popular and even in some academic literature. This is perceived to be caused by a lack of currency in curriculum stemming from a variety of reasons including a misunderstanding of what industry needs or a lack of integration of an industry's most recent technology (Koo et. al., 2021).

However, an emerging parallel to explain the labor shortage dynamic is that it is employers who are out of alignment with the societal needs and desires of a modern workforce. There is growing research that indicates that how organizations operate as it relates to attracting, engaging, and retaining talent has not changed from its traditional framework over the past century to align with more rapid changes occurring withing societal norms and values (Burbano, 2021). This is a complex model to track, as disparate cultures across the globe intermix traditional tenets with universally accepted values that are diffused through the internet and social media. With the deeper penetration to an individual level on a global scale than any prior mass media technologies, modern communication channels have carried homogenized elements to cultures that rarely interact outside of virtual context (Koo et. al., 2021).

Employers who offer a salary, medical benefits, and paid time off are now faced with an unprecedented array of materialistic and intrinsic demands. Materialistic options such as flexible scheduling practices, child-care options, unlimited personal time packages, complimentary perks (food, entertainment, etc.) are becoming increasingly common discussions around employee satisfaction conversations. Opportunities for intrinsic satisfaction as it relates to satisfaction on the job, reducing stress and burnout, acknowledging personal achievements, having opportunities to be involved in how work is planned (as opposed to just carrying out the work) are now being documented as significant and instrumental aspects of what is important to modern workers (Burbano, 2021; Koo et. al. 2021). The long-standing transactional nature of work where an employee does what is told to them in exchange for a paycheck is becoming more and more diluted and ineffective, as evidenced by the dissonance demonstrated by workers in 2023 who, when instructed by employers to relinquish remote work and return to a physical office location or else face discipline and termination, are choosing discipline and termination with increasing numbers (Bloom, 2022; Smith & Carpenter, 2023).

SEARCHING FOR A SOLUTION

Regardless of the crisis, downsizing or "rightsizing" (Hitt, Keats, Harback, & Nixon, 1994) appears to be the standard solution in organizational attempts at improving organizational effectiveness and reducing labor costs. Consequently, millions of jobs have been eliminated, and the negative consequences of unemployment are well documented (Jahoda, 1982). This is a cycle that is repeated often, but that doesn't mean that alternative pathways can't be followed. There are many problems in the hospitality industry, such as the lack of sense of achievement, lack of work vitality, low career loyalty, low sense of work responsibility and high turnover rate, which bring bad effects to the development of the staff in the hospitality industry and the hotel itself (Yao, Qiu, & Wei, 2019). These are not necessarily the result of intentional acts by hotel leadership but rather a function of how hotels operate. A challenge for leadership is how to use the limited resources available within the organization to motivate employees has become a major challenge faced by the managers in the hospitality industry.

At first glance, the key to addressing the core issues that are catalyzing the dissonance between employees and employers seems elusive, but only until a paradigm shift occurs. Fundamentally employees are saying they want to work on their own terms, and they want to be actively involved in making decisions about the nature, scope, and direction of their personal and professional efforts. For a work environment, this suggests that employees are looking for opportunities to have a greater organizational commitment, albeit in the desired environment. Increasing organizational commitment among employees can reduce turnover, but the various strategies and tactics that can be utilized will vary in required investment and skill that is needed to implement. That said, strategies for intervening should be approached as a partnership and occur at both the level of the employee and the organization (Frone, 2018).

Many conversations are already taking place within this space and have been occurring in significance for over a decade. Ideas that have been discussed across industry among many different countries include realizing shorter work weeks, providing life-support programs (such as complimentary childcare or meals), developing employee ownership programs, and offering upskilling initiatives aligned with milestone-defined, life-oriented long-term career pathways (Wong & Ko, 2009). This certainly supports employees, but what about employers – what is their benefit? Differentiating one's employment culture through innovative, intrinsic benefits allows an organization to become an employer of choice resulting in an optimized work culture: Decreased burnout, increased job satisfaction and less turnover (Davies, 2020). This has demonstrated to increase operating efficiency and profitability for organizations (Federman, 2009).

The engineering of an engaging and proactive work culture isn't just about aligning with employee needs. It also involves dynamics of an operation outside of daily interactions. Crisis management, and how an organization responds to external events of disruption, are found to be a key element in how an employee evaluates his or her employer from an organizational commitment perspective (Bajrami, Terzic, Petrovic, Radovanovic, Tretiakova, & Hadoud, 2021). Crisis response can also be integrated into existing employee engagement efforts as well. If an employer engages its employees to address the crisis thereby allowing the collective to determine what it will do in response, organizational-wide engagement can often become enhanced. By creating more challenging tasks, respecting the effort invested in doing the job and giving support to the employees to complete their tasks, these types of active responses from a company can increase employee commitment to the organization, even after the crisis which first catalyzed the behaviors has passed (Vahtera, Kivimaki & Pentti, 1997).

The shortages of employees willing to work, in the hospitality industry and in others, is an ongoing challenge that continues through 2023 and beyond. Workers are less interested in returning to pre-pandemic practices and have been finding alternative methods of financing their lifestyles that align with their selected values. These methods include government subsidizations (regularly available during the COVID-19 pandemic but are no longer as convenient to secure now that the government has declared the pandemic has concluded), engaging in peer-to-peer platform or contractor work where they have the ability and flexibility to schedule their own work hours independently, and retaining a remote work paradigm while refusing directives from employers to return to office. This perpetuates the dissonance between employers and employees and – at best – sustains the labor shortages that already exist in the industry. By focusing on the cause of the fundamental dissonance, the altering of the accepted framework for professional work, a more effective solution to attract and retain talent can be developed. Hotel operators and owners should invest in leadership training among their people leaders to equip this group of employees with tools, skills, and knowledge on how to create an effective and high-performing culture that reduces voluntary separation. Ensuring that trust is established and maintained, as well as engineering opportunities for employees to secure and acknowledge personal achievements in their work roles is critical to reducing turnover. The chapters in this book seek to better understand the different dimensions associated with the dissonance that is driving labor shortages while continually interpreting analytical results to provide practical applications of conceptual frameworks.

ORGANIZATION OF THE BOOK

The book is organized into eight chapters. A brief description of each of the chapters follows: Chapter 1 connects the notion of career attraction to a workforce that is seeking new parameters in how it makes choices regarding the pursuit of a career within the discipline of focus, the hospitality industry. The characteristics of a 21st century workforce that has endured seemingly endless global conflicts, political strife, and disruption from technological innovation are explored and analyzed. This chapter establishes demonstrates that much of what has been classically understood about what motivates employees in a working environment has been changed in the new millennium. The chapter sets the scene for discussions presented by various dimensions of understanding what workers in the hospitality industry are seeking and how leadership, to ensure success for their companies, need to focus on delivering satisfaction, engagement, and empowerment for workers.

Chapter 2 traces the origins of the hospitality industry from its earliest inceptions through modern times. While there are many unique and modern elements associated with 21st century life being addressed by the hospitality industry today, the essence of what it offers remains fundamentally unchanged throughout the centuries. Understanding the industry's journey is essential to framing the analysis and evaluation, as well as determining practical application, of the needs and motivation for those who work in hotels today. This chapter concludes by offering insight into traditional and innovative benefits that remain effective in increasing employee satisfaction while minimizing intent to voluntarily separate.

Chapter 3 focuses on a deep analysis of the motivational dimensions that lead an individual to accept and sustain employment at a hotel in the 21st century. This chapter evaluates concepts in practice such as societal benefits associated with working in a hotel, maintaining a work-life balance, and how internal or external driven changes can impact an operational framework from an employee's perspective. The overall purpose of this chapter is to provide a practical analysis of organizational commitment framed within the context of practical applicability for leaders seeking to reduce employee turnover.

Chapter 4 conducts an analysis of the dimensions and facets intrinsic for employees that are associated with job satisfaction within the 21st century hospitality industry. These dimensions include positive encouraging elements such as work culture, having fun on the job, empowerment and celebrating achievement. Negative, detracting elements that are reviewed in this chapter also include job insecurity, burnout, turnover intention, depersonalization, and stress. This chapter also provides evaluation and insight for practical leadership applicability seeking to enhance positive elements of satisfaction while minimizing negative ones.

Chapter 5 focuses its analytical lens on extrinsic events of a disruptive nature that impact organizational effectiveness in a negative fashion. The author explores the impact of the COVID-19 pandemic, easily the most single most significant disruptive event of the past 100 years, on the hospitality industry. From this exploration, common aspects of crisis management can be determined that are applicable to other types of disruptive events including economic fluctuations, terrorist attacks and political strife. The chapter concludes with an evaluation of the dimensions associated with the concept of organizational resilience, an identified area of strategic opportunity for the hospitality sector in general.

Chapter 6 conducts a qualitative study to identify behavioral models associated with how organizational commitment is established and sustained for employees working at a hotel front desk. The author presents a methodology of study that included interviewing multiple employees in three broad classifications of hotel operations: budget hotels, mid-range hotels and high-end hotels or resorts. Each interview is transcribed with an ensuing analysis for the discovery. The chapter, based on the sampling contained within the study methodology, shows that there are distinct characteristics associated with various demographics that are key elements for establishing and sustaining organizational commitment. The chapter concludes by identifying additional areas of future research.

Chapter 7 documents the background, methodology and results of a study conducted to better comprehend how dimensions and scope of trust that hotel employees have with each other, with their leaders and with their employer contribute to their overall job satisfaction. The study was originally conducted in 2020 with an exclusive South Korean demographic. In 2023, for this publication, the study was recreated in the United States with comparative results. The chapter concludes by identifying additional areas of research opportunity.

Chapter 8 concludes the journey with a synthesis of perspective regarding technological innovation and disruption within the context of the hospitality industry. The chapter explores the defined periods of industrial revolution that are acknowledged historically with a special focus on the current, and fourth, such event. A hallmark of the fourth industrial revolution is the gig economy, and this chapter evaluates parameters associated with that phenomenon in relation to the hospitality industry. The chapter also presents an explorative review of enculturation opportunities utilizing the Eastern concept of Guaxni and how it may prove beneficial for western societies. The chapter concludes with a review that frames the disruptive emergence of artificial intelligence (AI) technologies against the components of job satisfaction with predictive declarations regarding the impact such technologies may have on job insecurity and turnover intent moving forward.

Mark Peter Vitale
University of Phoenix, USA

REFERENCES

Bajrami, D. D., Terzic, A., Petrovic, M., Radovanovic, M., Tretiakova, T., & Hadoud, A. (2021). Will we have the same employees in hospitality after all? The impact of COVID-19 on employees' work attitudes and turnover intentions. *International Journal of Hospitality Management*, 94. PMID:34785836

Bloom, N. (2002). *The great resistance: Getting employees back to the office*. Institute for Economic Policy Research (SIEPR), Standford, CA. Retrieved January 19, 2023, from https://siepr.stanford.edu/publications/work/great-resistance-getting-employees-back-office

Burbano, V. C. (2021). Getting gig workers to do more by doing good: Field experimental evidence from online platform labor marketplaces. *Organization & Environment*, *34*(3), 387–412. doi:10.1177/1086026619846455

Davies, W. (2020, March 24). The last global crisis didn't change the world. But this one could. *The Guardian*. https://www.theguardian.com/commentisfree/2020/mar/24/coronavirus-crisischange-world-financial-global-capitalism

Federman, B. (2009). *Employee engagement: A roadmap for creating profits, optimizing performance, and increasing loyalty*. John Wiley & Sons.

Frone, M. R. (2018). What happened to the employed during the Great Recession? A U.S. population study of net change in employee insecurity, health, and organizational commitment. *Journal of Vocational Behavior*, *107*, 246–260. doi:10.1016/j.jvb.2018.05.001 PMID:31303656

Gossling, S., Scott, D., & Hall, C. M. (2021). Pandemics, tourism and global change: A rapid assessment of COVID-19. *Journal of Sustainable Tourism*, *29*(1), 1–20. doi:10.1080/09669582.2020.1758708

Hall, C. M. (2010). Crisis events in tourism: Subjects of crisis in tourism. *Current Issues in Tourism*, *13*(5), 401–417. doi:10.1080/13683500.2010.491900

Hall, C. M. (2020). Biological invasion, biosecurity, tourism, and globalisation. In D. Timothy (Ed.), *Handbook of globalisation and tourism* (pp. 114–125). Edward Elgar.

Hawley, A. J. (2018). Regulating labour platforms, the data deficit. *European Journal of Government and Economics*, *7*(1), 5–23. doi:10.17979/ejge.2018.7.1.4330

Jacobson, D. (1991). Toward a theoretical distinction between the stress components of the job insecurity and job loss experiences. In S. B. Bacharach (Ed.), *Research in the sociology of organizations* (Vol. 9, pp. 1–19). JAI Press.

Jahoda, M. (1982). *Employment and unemployment*. University Press.

Josserand, E., & Kaine, S. (2019). Different directions or the same route? The varied identities of ride-share drivers. *The Journal of Industrial Relations*, *61*(4), 549–573. doi:10.1177/0022185619848461

Koo, B., Curtis, C., & Ryan, B. (2021). Examining the impact of artificial intelligence on hotel employees through job insecurity perspectives. *International Journal of Hospitality Management*, *95*(1), 102763. doi:10.1016/j.ijhm.2020.102763

Roskies, E., & Louis-Guerin, C. (1990). Job insecurity in managers: Antecedents and consequences. *Journal of Organizational Behavior*, *11*(5), 345–359. doi:10.1002/job.4030110503

Scholz, T. (2017). *Uberworked and Underpaid: How Workers are Disrupting the Digital Economy*. Polity Press.

Senbeto, D. L., & Hon, A. H. (2020). The impacts of social and economic crises on tourist behaviour and expenditure: An evolutionary approach. *Current Issues in Tourism*, *23*(6), 740–755. doi:10.1080/13683500.2018.1546674

Smith, R. A., & Carpenter, J. (2023). We asked workers why they're not coming back to the office. *The Wall Street Journal*. Retrieved July 14, 2023, from https://www.wsj.com/articles/we-asked-workers-why-theyre-not-coming-back-to-the-office-186b7565

Vahtera, J., Kivimaki, M., & Pentti, J. (1997). Effect of organizational downsizing on health of employees. *Lancet*, *350*(9085), 1124–1128. doi:10.1016/S0140-6736(97)03216-9 PMID:9343499

Wong, S. C., & Ko, A. (2009). Exploratory study of understanding hotel employees' perception on work-life balance issues. *International Journal of Hospitality Management*, *28*(2), 195–203. doi:10.1016/j.ijhm.2008.07.001 PMID:32287852

Yao, T., Qiu, Q., & Wei, Y. (2019). Retaining hotel employees as internal customers: Effect of organizational commitment on attitudinal and behavioral loyalty of employees. *International Journal of Hospitality Management*, *76*, 1–8. doi:10.1016/j.ijhm.2018.03.018

Acknowledgment

The author would first like to acknowledge the support and assistance provided by his family during the development of this project.

The author would especially like to thank his mother for her ongoing encouragement to not only begin the research, analytical interpretation, conceptual thought leadership and actual writing required to complete this book, but she also provided near daily inspiration for the author on his journey. Without fail, she believed so strongly in her future state vision where this book already existed, the author was motivated to believe and act upon it as well.

Finally, the author wishes to acknowledge the valuable contributions of the reviewers regarding the improvement of quality, coherence, and content presentation of chapters throughout the peer evaluation process. The author highly appreciates their support and insight, which were essential to achieving the comprehensive quality of the final published narrative.

Section 1

Following a Calling: Working in the Hospitality Industry

The hospitality industry is volatile and more susceptible to crises and other extrinsic factors than many other industries. It is an industry where employees have little control over their schedules, few opportunities for forward advancement along a strategic career pathway or general ability to insulate against acts of involuntarily separation. Yet those who seek employment within the sector feel it is their calling to serve others in such a way. This section explores the dynamic of workers following a calling and what implications that has for more effective employee engagement. It traces the historical origins of the industry and engages a meta-analysis to discover dimensions and components of what is effective for attracting and retaining talent specific within hospitality.

Chapter 1
What Attracts Workers to an Industry?
The Impact of Following a Calling in Hospitality

ABSTRACT

This chapter reviews the dimensions of attraction that factor into workers making choices regarding pursuit of a career within a discipline of preference. Through the process of both professional experiences and extensive research conducted to prepare this publication, the author shares learned insight—balanced with a meta-analysis of recent literature—on what attracts individuals to the hospitality sector, profiles the characteristics of a 21st century hotel workforce, and explores the dimensions associated with front-line hospitality empowerment. The narrative concludes with an overview of the ensuing chapters within this publication and how each focus on a different impact of discovery around the idea nucleus of understanding the challenges, needs, and motivational opportunities for front-line hotel employees.

INTRODUCTION

A research initiative is a personal endeavor that takes place in a professional environment. It always starts with curiosity and at least one question (although one always hopes that there are several). Curiosity isn't an emotion that can be manufactured on demand. At its purest, it is an inquiry of passion that

DOI: 10.4018/978-1-6684-2528-2.ch001

resonates with a researcher on a fundamental level. The best research focuses on a topic, no matter how broad, that connects with a researcher on a personal and emotional level. That said, what is it about hotels that connects with the author of this study? Why makes a hotel special enough to be the focus of such attention?

From a young age, the author maintained a fascination with hotels. A hotel always seemed like an exciting and fun place. They were clean, populated by professional people who were smiling and happy, and they often featured bright colors, fun activities and adventures everywhere. Their architecture and design were often unique and distinct from normal everyday experiences like grocery stores or department stores. Granted, the vast majority of hotels visited by the author at a younger age were usually connected to a summer vacation experience, and leisure hotels are known for creating an extension of the fun times as a business strategy. What kid understands that context though? When you go on vacation and the first thing you see upon arrival is a magical happy place with food, color, music, games, contests, prizes, your own fluffy bed AND a fully stocked mini fridge with the best unhealthy snacks possible what is a young kid supposed to believe? Make no mistake, the learning phenomenon of primacy worked very effectively into the author's perceptions and the magic produced by hotels maintained an almost mythical quality from that point on.

As the author grew older and had opportunities to stay at hotels that weren't associated with an amusement park vacation, the broader perspective gained from the experience did not dilute the affinity for the profession. That fascination and affinity was leveraged into a front desk job early in the author's career. At the time of being hired, the job was thought of as nothing less than the very stuff that dreams are made of. As is often the case when one thinks they're fulfilling their dreams, every sugary happy and subjective mythical perception came crashing down as fast as can be possibly conceived. The hotel wasn't a magical place after all, it was just a place of employment like an office or retail store. After working at the hotel throughout the college years, the author left the hospitality industry after graduation and sought employment in industries not forever tainted by the rose-colored glasses of childhood.

And yet, the fascination for the industry didn't disappear and – if anything – it got stronger over time. The inquiry of how the industry manages to survive (or even thrive) has continued to be present throughout a variety of jobs, companies and industries (no hotels though…). In exploring the body of knowledge associated with hotel front-line employees, one finds that there's a lot of research which is relevant but very little that is focused exclusively on those guest services providing roles within the hotel industry itself. This publication is a part of the journey to better understanding what is needed by those who serve us when we stay at those outwardly magical establishments.

At its most basic, a hotel is a business that provides lodging for its customers for a defined period. A hotel, in the 21st century, though, is something more than the sum of its parts and while that definition is something that is appropriate for describing its function, a hotel can (and often is) more. A hotel can take on its own personality that reflects the characteristics of those that work there, of those that stay there and of the desires of those who own it. A hotel can create its own world within the universe that whisks its guests out of real life into that set up by the hotel.

Whether desired or not, a hotel can influence a guest using all five senses. There are hotels that utilize color, sound and smells to establish a context that illustrates the world it invites its guests into. Sometimes this is deliberate, as is the case with themed hotels connected to properties with casinos (such as in Las Vegas) or amusement parks (such as in Southern California or Central Florida). These themes are elaborate, strategic and permeate throughout all touchpoints for the hotel including how its staff conducts itself. The artistic design and engineering strategies required to establish such an elaborate creation, along with the training of people and investment of resources required for upkeep and maintenance, is truly phenomenal and not something that can be achieved without significant financial investment. It's understandable that many hotels forego such an extensive manipulation of the real world in their business development.

Even without creating a themed environment, hotels will portray a personality – even one that isn't intended or planned for. A hotel is a magical place in a way that a retail storefront, airport terminal or office can never be. It exudes personality – sometimes seedy and undesirable, sometimes high end and snobby, sometimes just a reflection of the community where it exists. It achieves this when other businesses cannot probably because a hotel offers its customers a place to unwind, relax and sleep – a refugee from the world. In doing so, the hotel becomes a unique character, interacting with each of its guests in both consistent and customized ways. It can happen in small ways, perhaps when a weary business traveler dons an in-room cotton robe after a challenging day of travel and work. A soft and luxurious comfort, however small, that sets that experience apart from every other evening. One of the simplest, yet most common ways, that a hotel establishes its microcosm world apart from the real one is that guests have their beds and their room cleaned.

Most adults are responsible for doing this themselves (at least part of the time) so having this service be provided immediately sets the experience of staying in a hotel apart from every day, normal existence. This is the foundation of the true service that a hotel offers.

A hotel cannot create its magic without a dedicated team of professionals to bring it to life. A hotel staff may be small with only a few employees on site charged with carrying out the operations of servicing guests. It can be large, numbering in the hundreds at any given time with a diverse variety of roles and tasks including the standard ones (front desk, bell hop, housekeeping), luxury service roles (spa technicians, lifeguards at a pool, banquet services and catering) and unique roles including a S'moreologist at the Paws Up resort in Montana (who assists guests in perfecting their s'more creation efforts through the development of a guest's roasting, toasting, melting and assembly skills) or a Certified Spookmaster at the Hilton New Orleans Riverside (whose job it is to develop strategies, stories and experiences using local folklore to scare guests silly).

Hotel staff can fully embody the theme of a favorite movie or cinematic experience (as is often the case at hotels connected to amusement parks) where they dress as fictional characters, speak in dialects that don't exist and conduct their behavior in line with expectations associated with the storyline they are representing. On the other end of the spectrum, a hotel employee can exist in a no-nonsense, task-based environment where they serve guests with a focus on efficiency and themed standardization for visual uniforms exists no further than a nametag.

Truly, the hotel industry is a diverse and exciting place with its vast extremes connected only by the purity of the fundamental purpose – to provide lodging. At first glance, these vastly different types of establishments might almost demand their own sub industries and classifications, and its true – different hotel types are considered to be different based on how they choose to execute that fundamental purpose of providing lodging. To that end, one might assume that this is a recent development and that the 20th and 21st centuries are responsible for reinventing the hospitality industry in such a number of different ways. A look at the history of the hospitality industry, however, reveals this to be anything but the truth. Hotels have existed for hundreds of years with a diverse array of offerings that all provide lodging for their guests, and while some were content to offer little more there are examples of others that embraced lavish excess in ways that match and dominate some of the best themed or luxury experiences of the modern world.

WHAT ATTRACTS WORKERS TO AN INDUSTRY

There are many ways for an individual to evaluate their own interests and determine optimal career choices, although pursuing options within fields of interest may not always be realistic or possible. That said, people choose a specific occupation not only to satisfy their basic needs but also to satisfy higher-level needs. Some individuals may even feel called to a specific line of work in order to serve others, leading to personal gratification. The term calling, in the secular context, has been defined as something that is prosocial in nature, carries personal meaning, and is prompted by something outside the individual (Dik and Duffy, 2009).

There is a practical distinction between having a calling and living a calling. A person may have a calling but may not be pursuing that calling in the line of work or career in which they currently are employed. In order to be living a calling, one must have a passion for the current work role in which one is employed, such that even in the face of obstacles, there is no other career that one would find more meaningful (Duffy, Duffy, Dik, Douglass, England, & Velez, 2018; Kaminsky and Behrend, 2015).

Serving others is a hallmark of the hospitality industry and may serve as strong a calling as for the industries. This is a theory for why employees in the hospitality industry can successfully transcend the poor working conditions and pay associated with many positions that result in low work-life balance, high work stress and low quality of life. While this is all prevalent in the industry, there is also a strong love and bond that employees find for themselves through what is perceived to be meaningful work (Ariza-Montes, Arjona-Fuentes, Han, & Law, 2018; Ariza-Montes, Hern´andez-Perlines, Han, & Law, 2019; Baker & Kim, 2020; Kusluvan, Kusluvan, Ilhan, & Buyruk, 2010; Sirgy, 2019).

Living a Calling

Living a calling is important to understand as this phenomenon has been linked to many positive work-related employee outcomes including person-environment fit (Xiao, Zhou, Wu, Zhang, Miao, Zhang, Peng, 2014), career commitment (Duffy, Douglass, Autin, & Allan, 2014), job satisfaction (Duffy, Bott, Allan, Torrey, & Dik, 2012), and life satisfaction (Allan, Autin, & Duffy, 2014). Moreover, employees' living a calling through work roles, demonstrate greater instances of self-worth and find work meaningful (Duffy et al., 2014).

Research has shown the presence of a calling positively influences well-being (Hirschi, Keller, & Spurk, 2018; Wrzesniewski, McCauley, Rozin, & Schwartz., 1997). Additional research has focused on how one's calling is related to career development (Duffy, Dik, & Steger, 2011); positive work attitudes (Duffy et al., 2014); and well-being (Duffy & Dik, 2013; Duffy et. al., 2011) across various occupations. From this, increased organizational commitment can emerge because of an employee's perceived insider status in an environment that they feel aligned with or affectionate for. Insider status as an informal role, represents employee's perception of their belonging in the organization and was shown to significantly influence both job performance, citizenship behaviors, (Hui, Lee, & Wang, 2015) and sense of overall well-being (Mor Barak, & Levin, 2002).

Furthermore, this paradigm taps into the notion that psychological empowerment as a formal role represents employees' intrinsic motivation. It does so through a variety of factors including an employee's perception of what the purpose of their role is, the self-image of the employee's competence, their level of self-determination, and observed (or perceived) degrees of impact that an employe has on the course of an agreed set of outcomes (Spreitzer, 1995). Competence refers to one's degree of confidence in his or her ability to perform tasks in a proficient and consistent manner associated with one's work role (Bandura, 1989; Spreitzer, 1995). Self-determination refers to the autonomy to initiate and regulate work behaviors (Spreitzer, 1995).

One of the major benefits of being an insider within an organization is access to status, information, and perks. That said, insiders are also expected to contribute more work and effort to an organization (Tsai, Horng, Liu, & Hu, 2015). When employees perceive themselves as insiders, they are likely to expect to receive more organizational support and recognition such as training, promotions, and rewards. It is not uncommon to find work cultures that consider insiders to be those who are self-motivated to acquire the knowledge and experience necessary to remain in that role (Tsai et al., 2015). It isn't just a matter of one's perception though. An employee's formal role within the hierarchy of an organization and the associated role expectations has also been shown to positively influence the expectations and assessments of hospitality employees (Corley, 2004; Kang & Busser, 2018).

Psychological Well-Being

Psychological well-being experienced at work was shown to influence motivation, commitment to work, and life quality (Ariza-Montes et al., 2019). A reduced level of social support due to the hierarchical nature of hospitality organizations and a lack of empowerment were cited as considerable reasons for decreased employee well-being (Ariza-Montes et al., 2018). Due to this diversity of perspective, academic scholars and industry experts have argued among themselves that the industry may not attract motivated and committed employees if it fails to promote psychological well-being (Ariza-Montes et al., 2019). The challenge of connecting tasks that can be considered menial or requiring low skill to a larger purpose of service with impactful outcomes is significant, but there is ample research to demonstrate that doing so can be an essential element in attracting and retaining talent in the hospitality industry.

Psychological well-being is steeped in the pursuit of finding meaning in one's life, which is a pivotal component of healthy mental processes and behavior (Steger, 2012). Evolving from the eudaimonic lens, which views well-being as realizing human potential through personal achievement, self-actualization, or self-positioning (Ryan & Deci, 2001), there is evidentiary support that meaning in life is associated with psychological well-being (Krok, 2015) in addition to the observable benefits to one's life while employed with a company (Spreitzer & Porath, 2012). Defined as "engagement with existential challenges of life" (Keyes, Shmotkin, & Ryff, 2002, p. 1007), psychological well-being is comprised of six dimensions: self-acceptance, positive relations with others, autonomy, environmental mastery, purpose in life, and personal growth (Page & Vella-Brodrick, 2009; Ryff, 1989; Zheng, Zhu, Zhao, & Zhang, 2015). Psychological well-being has been used to represent employees' overall well-being in an organization and has been shown to improve their mental health, ultimately leading to positive job outcomes such as job satisfaction and affective commitment (Zheng et al., 2015).

As important as it may be for psychological well-being, pursuing one's calling can sometimes be challenging and deemed out of reach. This is especially true if one is not compensated appropriately, or if the individual does not have direct access to financial resources needed to maintain a desired quality of life. Research has revealed that individuals with higher income and education levels are more likely to live their calling (Duffy & Autin, 2013; Duffy et al., 2012). In addition, organizational hierarchy has been identified as a significant moderator of employees' perceptions, attitude, and behavior in the workplace (Corley, 2004; Kang, and Busser, 2018; Kim, Murrmann, & Lee, 2009; Lu, Lu, Gursoy, Neale, 2016; Schminke, Cropanzano, & Rupp, 2002). It has been noted that the importance of employee access to high value opportunities in the form of education, income, work volition and employment as key antecedents to and components of living one's calling (Duffy et al., 2018). Ultimately, it has been suggested that living a calling be defined as something that is accomplished from an individual's positive experiences with their work (Duffy et al., 2014).

Operationally, an employee's cognitive assessment of their standing within the workplace is known as perceived insider status (Hui et al., 2015; Lapalme, Stamper, Simard, & Tremblay 2009). Perceived insider status represents employee's interpretation of the formal and informal organizational norms in this study, their role alignment with norms, which subsequently influences their cognitive state (i.e., psychological well-being). Kang, Cain, and Busser's 2021 study addresses perceived insider status and psychological empowerment as the attributes of a supportive hospitality work environment. Perceived insider status refers to an employee's assessment of the way an organization makes them feel needed, desired, and valued (Hui et al., 2015; Pearce & Randel, 2004; Stamper & Masterson, 2002). The desire to be recognized as an insider has been acknowledged in the management literature (Hui et al., 2015). Perceived insider status is underpinned by role theory, as an individual's self-identity is tied to their specific organization and subsequent formal and informal roles within that organization (Masterson & Stamper, 2003; Stamper & Masterson, 2002).

This study also examines these factors as mediators to understand the underlying mechanisms between living a calling and fulfilling an employee's psychological well-being. In the hospitality industry, where serving others is the foundation of the craft, it stands to reason that living a calling through one's line of work will result in enhanced organizational commitment and personal fulfillment because of the job. This concept is explored more in research that investigates role theory.

Role Theory with a Hotel

Role theory is one that seeks to provide a deeper understanding how the notion of one's fit within their role, the expectations associated with the role, any formal and informal influences associated with the role, and general levels of cognition required to perform tasks associated with the role in at least a level of average competency (Biddle, 1986). According to role theory, role identities provide the context for interpreting socially accepted norms (Biddle, 1986; Gordon, 1976). Linton (1945) proposed that each cultural norm, which includes the rights, obligations, and expectations of behavior for a role, impacts an individual's behavior and ultimately helps to explain and predict future behavior. Those who study role theory and are considered experts in the field have asserted that the more an individual connects with or internalizes a particular role, the more likely they are to assume that role as part of their identity (Ashforth. Kreiner, & Fugate, 2000). Role theory has been empirically used to examine the hierarchical and task-oriented social systems of an organization and the way formal and informal roles influence employees' role expectations. Accordingly, sociologists employ role theory to understand the ways in which people perceive their specific roles in both work and life settings, as well as to assess how the perception of those roles influences subsequent interactions and cognitive states (Biddle, 1986).

Role theory supports the understanding of empowerment explaining the social factors that promote individual expectations, their measurement, and the subsequent impact of those expectations on resulting cognitive state (Biddle, 1986). Due to the inseparability of the service encounter, in which the product (service provided to the customer) is simultaneously produced and consumed (Kotler, Bowen, Makens, & Baloglu, 2017), hospitality employees often find themselves in situations in which they must immediately respond to guests' needs, without the luxury of time to consult a superior, and therefore benefit from empowerment.

The interactional nature of roles in the workplace leads to individuals assuming certain formal roles (e.g., line-level employee, manager, director level and above), demonstrating the behaviors and actions expected of these roles and then identifying and being classified as a member of this position (Stryker, 1968). There is a multifaceted relationship between individuals' conceptualization of their own identity and the roles they assume at work (Ashforth et al., 2000; Stryker, 1968). The roles individuals fully immerse and participate in lead to greater self-worth, lower depression, and overall greater well-being (Marks & MacDermid, 1996). Even so, a calling may not be enough to overpower the negative influences of an out of balance lifestyle when it comes to fulfilling personal and professional needs.

One study that examined executive chefs found that work-life balance was essential to achieve life satisfaction, even when the chefs had a calling (Cain, Busser & Kang, 2018). In other words, the presence of a calling was not sufficient to engender life satisfaction on its own; rather, balance between work and life roles was essential in mediating the relationship. Another study of front-line hotel employees revealed that the presence of a calling significantly impacted career satisfaction and that knowledge sharing significantly mediated the relationship between having a calling and career satisfaction (Kaminsky et. al., 2015).

Employees living a calling engage more in their work and personal development relates to work and well-being such as work effort, career adaptability (Praskova, Hood, & Creed, 2014), and personal growth initiatives (Duffy et al., 2014). Psychological empowerment fosters an employee's greater meaning from their work and life, which is linked to greater psychological wellbeing (Krok, 2015). This becomes a major factor in their propensity to be more likely to endorse the empowerment fostered by an organization as well as also affect an employee's positive attributes at work such as psychological empowerment. Empowering employees to assume extra-role responsibilities and facilitate autonomous decision-making and problem-solving has been shown to promote intrinsic motivation to serve the customer (Deci & Ryan, 2004) and offer greater levels of customer service and satisfaction (Chiang & Hsieh, 2012).

What special considerations or dynamics are observed when one looks at the hospitality industry though? Is it the same regardless of the job or geographical location? Kim et al. (2009) studied hospitality employees in Korea and found that organizational hierarchy significantly moderated the relationship between role stress and job satisfaction. Additional research with a population in the United States from 29 mid-level to upscale hotels also found differences across organizational hierarchy for work engagement, job satisfaction and turnover intention (Lu et al., 2016). A more recent, yet still pre-pandemic, study on hospitality employees examined the impact of organizational hierarchy on psychological capital. This study found that the service climate had a greater influence on employee engagement for managers than for front line employees (Kang and Busser, 2018).

Kang et. al. (2001) provides empirical evidence of how living one's calling impacts hotel employees' psychological job outcomes across various levels of the organization, offering a better understanding of the interplay between living a calling, perceived insider status, psychological empowerment, and psychological well-being. The results of this study demonstrated that finding meaning through work by living a calling, feeling a sense of belonging, and perceived insider status were important for all employees but were most meaningful for front-line employees. Additionally, the impact of living a calling on an employee's perceived psychological empowerment was most important for those who were managers or directors and above. While perceived insider status and psychological empowerment were important mediators between living a calling and psychological well-being overall for hospitality employees, the impact of psychological empowerment on well-being was strongest for directors and above.

Kang et. al.'s 2001work is important not just in its findings but how it implemented several procedural remedies in its study to control method bias before data collection since self-administered surveys in a cross-sectional research design are often susceptible to common method bias (Podsakoff, MacKenzie, Lee and Podsakoff, 2003). These mitigating strategies included offering voluntary participation in the study where respondents were assured of complete anonymity and confidentiality to avoid social desirability bias. Respondents also received assurance that there were no right or wrong answers. To minimize the possibility of respondents knowing what was being tested, the question order was intermixed between independent and dependent variables, and filler items were included between variables. Further, a different cover story was used for each variable to create a psychological separation for respondents (Kang et al., 2021). As with all research, though, Kang et al.' study featured certain limitations inherent in its methodology primarily the utilization of a convenience sampling being employed to recruit the study participants. The results are not generalizable without additional validation and triangulation with the accepted body of knowledge.

Psychological well-being was found to significantly influence motivation and commitment in the hospitality industry (Ariza-Montes et al., 2019), and identifying positive influences on well-being is critical for employee success. Kang et. al. (2021) showed that living a calling is linked to positive cognitive assessments of work as well as newly identified its relationship to psychological well-being. One's perception of their role in an organization ultimately impacts the importance of these psychological job outcomes. socially constructed norms like the insider behavior expected of members of the organization influences employee perceptions of role empowerment.

Kang et. al. (2001) provides empirical evidence of how living one's calling impacts hotel employees' psychological job outcomes across various levels of the organization, offering a better understanding of the interplay between living a calling, perceived insider status, psychological empowerment, and psychological well-being. The results demonstrated that finding meaning through work by living a calling, feeling a sense of belonging, and perceived insider status were important for all employees but were most meaningful for line-level employees. Additionally, the impact of living a calling on employees' perceived psychological empowerment was most important for those who were managers or directors and above. While perceived insider status and psychological empowerment were important mediators between living a calling and psychological well-being overall for hospitality employees, the impact of psychological empowerment on well-being was strongest for directors and above.

Insider Status and Role Empowerment

In order for a hospitality employee at any level who is living a calling to enhance their psychological well-being, they must also perceive themselves as an insider and feel psychologically empowered. Living a calling influences employees' psychological well-being through employees' cognitive assessments of the supportiveness of the work environment (i.e., perceived insider status and psychological empowerment). For front line employees, living a calling and perceived insider status carried greater importance, whereas for managers, directors and above, psychological empowerment was more likely to enhance their psychological well-being.

This is critical information to have in terms of practical application within the hospitality industry. Leadership at a hotel management company must recognize how important it is for employees to have opportunities in the form of education, income and work volition in order to promote living a calling (Duffy et al., 2018). The findings of Kang et. al. (2021) revealed that living a calling was a vital element across all work groups that impacted psychological well-being. To increase employee's sense of living a calling, it is important for hospitality executives and managers to foster employees' recognition of their work as meaningful and increase employees' commitment to work (Duffy et al., 2014). Ultimately recommended practical strategies to achieve these desired outcomes can include (but are not limited to) offering a mentoring program and both experiential as well as didactic formatted job-related training (Jung & Yoon, 2016).

It is not out of the question to challenge the current format of hospitality staffing, especially in light of challenges that many companies experience with hiring qualified employees. Those who have expertise in this area have recently been expressing a need for the reevaluation of how hospitality jobs are designed and managed in order to alleviate the stressors that are characteristic of this industry (Ariza-Montes et al., 2018). It has been suggested that organizations develop and tailor strategies specific to the various roles within the organization to help promote greater psychological well-being across work groups rather than focus on consistency and standardization across the enterprise. Sales personnel have different jobs (and different key performance indicators) than food and beverage staff or rooms management staff. Why approach them all in a homogenized manner? Individualizing an approach to foster an environment of inclusivity and identifying person-organization fit would be beneficial approaches for hospitality managers to consider, particularly when hiring front-line employees. Perceived insider status carries great importance, particularly among this employee group (Ariza-Montes et. al. 2018).

Organizational inducements such as supervisor support and participative decision making are known to be significant conditions for employees to feel like insiders (Hui et al., 2015). Cultivating an inclusive work environment will increase employee well-being, which in turn will benefit the organization through higher levels of performance, greater career development and an increase in organizational citizenship behavior (Stamper and Masterson, 2002; Wei, Liu, Chen, & Wu., 2010).

For managers, and directors and employees with greater responsibility, the emphasis for engagement should be placed on increasing levels of psychological empowerment. According to Zhang & Bartol (2010), not all employees desire empowerment and often demonstrate a level of such desire based on their unique role identity. Psychological empowerment is driven by a role identity in which employees view empowerment as part of their work. Thus, hospitality organizations need to make sure managers are clearly aware of their roles as leaders, including their power and responsibility (Kang et. al., 2021). In addition, frequent communication between management and employees will enhance trust, which is fundamental in developing empowerment (Chiang & Jang, 2008). Additionally, promoting creativity and innovation, facilitating autonomous decision-making, and encouraging problem-solving among organizational leadership will enhance well-being (Deci & Ryan, 2004). Such feelings of autonomy and empowerment have been shown to lead to the ability to provide greater levels of customer service and satisfaction (Chiang & Hsieh, 2012). Transforming hospitality management and leadership practices to focus on enhancing cognitive states like well-being through formal and informal programs that promote employee development and cultivate a culture of inclusivity, will benefit employees, customers, and ultimately the organization (Kang et. al., 2021).

CONCLUSION

The remainder of the research effort captured within this publication continues to explore the ideas, themes, concepts, and dynamics associated with developing a culture of trust within a hotel to engage workers as well as better understanding the factors that contribute to organizational commitment. In doing so, both of the primary demographics identified above (younger workers seeking to engineer a successful career and retired workers looking to earn some "spending cash" while qualifying for a travel benefit that will allow them to reduce expenses associated with leisure travel) are explored in more depth.

First up in Chapter 2 of this publication is an informed essay that traces the extensive origins of the hospitality industry as well as presents an interpretation of the ideal characteristics, and associated needs, for a 21st century workforce in the service industry in general. Chapter 3 investigates the perspectives associated with intrinsic parameters and characteristics associated with individuals who are interested in working at a hotel as well as explores the dimensions of exhaustion, burnout and job satisfaction. Chapter 4 focuses on the concept of job insecurity and how it presents itself in a 21st century workforce within the hospitality sector. This chapter explores stress, burnout and turnover intention for front-line hotel employees while also evaluating how management can use practical tools such as communication, empowerment, and engagement to offset negative emotions associated with job insecurity. The discovery in these chapters is achieved via an extensive meta-analysis literature review. This synthesis of published industry material primarily explores the various dimensions of organizational commitment within a hotel environment although many other topics tangential to this core concept are explored at length. Classic, seminal work on employee engagement as well as newer publications that explored employees' response to more recent crises were analyzed in creating create a comprehensive narrative of discovery that focuses exclusively on front-line hotel employees.

The global onset of the COVID-19 pandemic catalyzed a new wave of research focused on hotel employees to better understand how a front-line, low wage-earning employee would react and exist within the parameters of such a significant crisis. Chapter 5 of this publication explores how external factors translate into psychological stimuli for hospitality workers. There is a specific focus on the recent dynamics associated with employment in a service industry during a worldwide crisis. While this availability of new research is truly amazing, creating a better understanding than ever before of what makes a hotel employee tick (so to speak), much of the research was conducted using foreign cultures. The international perspective enriches understanding of what drives this type of employee and how better to engage and enrich their working existence. From a domestic research perspective, though, one cannot simply apply the results of these studies to a situation within any other culture without first determining what sort of impact the differences in culture between a researcher's environment and that of the comparative study will cause. In some cases, it may be negligible, or it could produce a statistically different result.

Following the meta-analysis reviewing internal and external factors associated with an individual's job satisfaction and insecurity, Chapter 6 of this publication explores original qualitative research that explores the mindset of a front-line hotel employee. Through a series of conversations and interviews, multiple employees at various hotel properties revealed their thoughts and perspectives on a variety of topics established by the meta-analysis to have an impact on organizational commitment. The sampling for this study focused on front-desk hotel employees working at different classes of properties including budget properties, mid-range hotels and high-end resorts and convention hotels. In addition to relaying the results of focused interviews, this chapter also offers interpretation of the results and identifies some future opportunities for additional research.

Chapter 7 of this publication identifies a 2020 research study and re-validates its results with a sample of employees from a significantly different geographic location. The original quantitative study explored the dimensions of trust and organizational commitment for hotel employees and tested nine different hypotheses using a factor analysis. While the study was repeated exactly as it was originally conducted, the sample engaged front desk employees working a hotel located within one of several states in the Western United States as opposed to the original study's sample environment of South Korea.

Chapter 8 of this publication turns its attention and focus to future manifestations of an ideal workplace. This chapter reviews the tenets for each of the four industrial revolutions that are catalogued by western societies as continuums of work are traced during the past 200 years. Current areas of concern, such as artificial intelligence, are reviewed within the framework of how emerging technologies (and the perception of its capabilities) are influencing job security within the hospitality sector. Through a scan of international environments, this chapter also introduces eastern cultural characteristics (such as the Chinese concept of "guanxi") that present an area of opportunity for adoption by western businesses.

The fluid nature of the hospitality industry and how it can best engage its workforce is a broad and complex subject. There are many different avenues to explore and many different dimensions to frame research efforts; Most have been underrepresented in business research efforts. Compounding the issue is that any research that is conducted may not remain relevant for long due to the rapid changes being brought about by disruptive technology, a phenomenon common with many industries during this current fourth industrial revolution.

Opportunities of discovery consist of new, wholly original research as well as updating and revalidating prior studies to accommodate differences resulting from different locations or modernized context. As ideas and concepts are identified, studied, and validated, the hope for all current and future research in this space to continue to retain a practical framework alongside the conceptual content. While academic discovery is always critical, it is equally important for industry to apply what is discovered to strengthen its own operations. This publication is truly just the continuation of this journey of discovery, and – like the work that comes before it (and, most likely, comes after it,) this publication only scratches the surface of the opportunities that exist.

REFERENCES

Allan, B. A., Autin, K. L., & Duffy, R. D. (2014). Examining social class and work meaning within the psychology of working framework. *Journal of Career Assessment*, *22*(4), 543–561. doi:10.1177/1069072713514811

Ariza-Montes, A., Arjona-Fuentes, J. M., Han, H., & Law, R. (2018). Work environment and well-being of different occupational groups in hospitality: Job Demand–control–support model. *International Journal of Hospitality Management*, *73*, 1–11. doi:10.1016/j.ijhm.2018.01.010

Ariza-Montes, A., Hern'andez-Perlines, F., Han, H., & Law, R. (2019). Human dimension of the hospitality industry: Working conditions and psychological well-being among European servers. *Journal of Hospitality and Tourism Management*, *41*, 138–147. doi:10.1016/j.jhtm.2019.10.013

Ashforth, B. E., Kreiner, G. E., & Fugate, M. (2000). All in a day's work: Boundaries and micro role transitions. *Academy of Management Review*, *25*(3), 472–491. doi:10.2307/259305

Baker, M. A., & Kim, K. (2020). Dealing with customer incivility: The effects of managerial support on employee psychological well-being and quality-of-life. *International Journal of Hospitality Management*, *87*, 102503. doi:10.1016/j.ijhm.2020.102503

Bandura, A. (1989). Human agency in social cognitive theory. *The American Psychologist*, *44*(9), 1175–1184. doi:10.1037/0003-066X.44.9.1175 PMID:2782727

Biddle, B. J. (1986). Recent developments in role theory. *Annual Review of Sociology*, *12*(1), 67–92. doi:10.1146/annurev.so.12.080186.000435

Cain, L., Busser, J., & Kang, H. J. (2018). Executive chefs' calling: Effect on engagement, work-life balance and life satisfaction. *International Journal of Contemporary Hospitality Management*, *30*(5), 2287–2307. doi:10.1108/IJCHM-02-2017-0105

Chiang, C. F., & Hsieh, T. S. (2012). The impacts of perceived organizational support and psychological empowerment on job performance: The mediating effects of organizational citizenship behavior. *International Journal of Hospitality Management*, *31*(1), 180–190. doi:10.1016/j.ijhm.2011.04.011

Chiang, C. F., & Jang, S. (2008). The antecedents and consequences of psychological empowerment: The case of Taiwan's hotel companies. *Journal of Hospitality & Tourism Research (Washington, D.C.)*, *32*(1), 40–61. doi:10.1177/1096348007309568

Corley, K. G. (2004). Defined by our strategy or our culture? Hierarchical differences in perceptions of organizational identity and change. *Human Relations*, *57*(9), 1145–1177. doi:10.1177/0018726704047141

Deci, E. L., & Ryan, R. M. (2004). *Handbook of Self-determination Research*. The University of Rochester Press.

Dik, B. J., & Duffy, R. D. (2009). Calling and vocation at work: Definitions and prospects for research and practice. *The Counseling Psychologist*, *37*(3), 424–450. doi:10.1177/0011000008316430

Duffy, R. D., & Autin, K. L. (2013). Disentangling the link between perceiving a calling and living a calling. *Journal of Counseling Psychology*, *60*(2), 219–227. doi:10.1037/a0031934 PMID:23438413

Duffy, R. D., Bott, E. M., Allan, B. A., Torrey, C. L., & Dik, B. J. (2012). Perceiving a calling, living a calling, and job satisfaction: Testing a moderated, multiple mediator model. *Journal of Counseling Psychology*, *59*(1), 50–59. doi:10.1037/a0026129 PMID:22059426

Duffy, R. D., & Dik, B. J. (2013). Research on calling: What have we learned and where are we going? *Journal of Vocational Behavior*, *83*(3), 428–436. doi:10.1016/j.jvb.2013.06.006

Duffy, R. D., Dik, B. J., Douglass, R. P., England, J. W., & Velez, B. L. (2018). Work as a calling: A theoretical model. *Journal of Counseling Psychology*, *65*(4), 423–429. doi:10.1037/cou0000276 PMID:29999369

Duffy, R. D., Dik, B. J., & Steger, M. F. (2011). Calling and work-related outcomes: Career commitment as a mediator. *Journal of Vocational Behavior*, *78*(2), 210–218. doi:10.1016/j.jvb.2010.09.013

Duffy, R. D., Douglass, R. P., Autin, K. L., & Allan, B. A. (2014). Examining predictors and outcomes of a career calling among undergraduate students. *Journal of Vocational Behavior*, *85*(3), 309–318. doi:10.1016/j.jvb.2014.08.009

Gordon, C. (1976). Development of evaluated role identities. *Annual Review of Sociology*, *2*(1), 405–433. doi:10.1146/annurev.so.02.080176.002201

Hirschi, A., Keller, A. C., & Spurk, D. M. (2018). Living one's calling: Job resources as a link between having and living a calling. *Journal of Vocational Behavior*, *106*, 1–10. doi:10.1016/j.jvb.2017.12.001

Hui, C., Lee, C., & Wang, H. (2015). Organizational inducements and employee citizenship behavior: The mediating role of perceived insider status and the moderating role of collectivism. *Human Resource Management*, *54*(3), 439–456. doi:10.1002/hrm.21620

Jung, H. S., & Yoon, H. H. (2016). What does work mean to hospitality employees? The effects of meaningful work on employees' organizational commitment: The mediating role of job engagement. *International Journal of Hospitality Management*, *53*, 59–68. doi:10.1016/j.ijhm.2015.12.004

Kaminsky, S. E., & Behrend, T. S. (2015). Career choice and calling: Integrating calling and social cognitive career theory. *Journal of Career Assessment*, *23*(3), 383–398. doi:10.1177/1069072714547167

Kang, H. J., Cain, L., & Busser, J. A. (2021). The impact of living a calling on job outcomes. *International Journal of Hospitality Management*, *95*, 95. doi:10.1016/j.ijhm.2021.102916

Kang, H. J. A., & Busser, J. A. (2018). Impact of service climate and psychological capital on employee engagement: The role of organizational hierarchy. *International Journal of Hospitality Management*, *75*, 1–9. doi:10.1016/j.ijhm.2018.03.003

Keyes, C. L. M., Shmotkin, D., & Ryff, C. D. (2002). Optimizing well-being: The empirical encounter of two traditions. *Journal of Personality and Social Psychology*, *82*(6), 1007–1022. doi:10.1037/0022-3514.82.6.1007 PMID:12051575

Kim, B. C. P., Murrmann, S. K., & Lee, G. (2009). Moderating effects of gender and organizational level between role stress and job satisfaction among hotel employees. *International Journal of Hospitality Management*, *28*(4), 612–619. doi:10.1016/j.ijhm.2009.04.001

Kotler, P., Bowen, J. T., Makens, J., & Baloglu, S. (2017). *Marketing for Hospitality and Tourism*. Prentice Hall.

Krok, D. (2015). The role of meaning in life within the relations of religious coping and psychological well-being. *Journal of Religion and Health*, *54*(6), 2292–2308. doi:10.100710943-014-9983-3 PMID:25524414

Kusluvan, S., Kusluvan, Z., Ilhan, I., & Buyruk, L. (2010). The human dimension: A review of human resources management issues in the tourism and hospitality industry. *Cornell Hospitality Quarterly*, *51*(2), 171–214. doi:10.1177/1938965510362871

Lapalme, M., Stamper, C. L., Simard, G., & Tremblay, M. (2009). Bringing the outside in: Can "external" workers experience insider status? *Journal of Organizational Behavior*, *30*(7), 919–940. doi:10.1002/job.597

Linton, R. (1945). *The Cultural Background of Personality*. Appleton-Century-Crofts.

Lu, L., Lu, A. C. C., Gursoy, D., & Neale, N. R. (2016). Work engagement, job satisfaction, and turnover intentions: A comparison between supervisors and line-level employees. *International Journal of Contemporary Hospitality Management*, *28*(4), 737–761. doi:10.1108/IJCHM-07-2014-0360

Marks, S. R., & Macdermid, S. (1996). Multiple roles and the self: A theory of role balance. *Journal of Marriage and Family*, *58*(2), 417–432. doi:10.2307/353506

Masterson, S. S., & Stamper, C. L. (2003). Perceived organizational membership: An aggregate framework representing the employee-organization relationship. *Journal of Organizational Behavior*, *24*(5), 473–490. doi:10.1002/job.203

Mor Barak, M. E., & Levin, A. (2002). Outside of the corporate mainstream and excluded from the work community: A study of diversity, job satisfaction and well-being. *Community Work & Family*, *5*(2), 133–157. doi:10.1080/13668800220146346

Page, K. M., & Vella-Brodrick, D. A. (2009). The "what," "why" and "how" of employee wellbeing: A new model. *Social Indicators Research*, *90*(3), 441–458. doi:10.100711205-008-9270-3

Pearce, J. L., & Randel, A. E. (2004). Expectations of organizational mobility, workplace social inclusion, and employee job performance. *Journal of Organizational Behavior*, *25*(1), 81–98. doi:10.1002/job.232

Podsakoff, P. M., MacKenzie, S. B., Lee, J.-Y., & Podsakoff, N. P. (2003). Common method biases in behavioral research: A critical review of the literature and recommended remedies. *The Journal of Applied Psychology*, *88*(5), 879–903. doi:10.1037/0021-9010.88.5.879 PMID:14516251

Praskova, A., Hood, M., & Creed, P. A. (2014). Testing a calling model of psychological career success in Australian young adults: A longitudinal study. *Journal of Vocational Behavior*, *85*(1), 125–135. doi:10.1016/j.jvb.2014.04.004

Ryan, R. M., & Deci, E. L. (2001). On happiness and human potentials: A review of research on hedonic and eudaimonic well-being. *Annual Review of Psychology*, *52*(1), 141–166. doi:10.1146/annurev.psych.52.1.141 PMID:11148302

Ryff, C. D. (1989). Happiness is everything, or is it? Explorations on the meaning of psychological well-being. *Journal of Personality and Social Psychology*, *57*(6), 1069–1081. doi:10.1037/0022-3514.57.6.1069

Schminke, M., Cropanzano, R., & Rupp, D. E. (2002). Organization structure and fairness perceptions: The moderating effects of organizational level. *Organizational Behavior and Human Decision Processes*, *89*(1), 881–905. doi:10.1016/S0749-5978(02)00034-1

Spreitzer, G. M. (1995). Psychological empowerment in the workplace: Dimensions, measurement, and validation. *Academy of Management Journal*, *38*(5), 1442–1465. doi:10.2307/256865

Spreitzer, G. M., & Porath, C. (2012). Creating sustainable performance. *Harvard Business Review*, *90*(1), 92–99. PMID:22299508

Stamper, C. L., & Masterson, S. S. (2002). Insider or outsider? How employee perceptions of insider status affect their work behavior. *Journal of Organizational Behavior*, *23*(8), 875–894. doi:10.1002/job.175

Steger, M. F. (2012). Making meaning in life. *Psychological Inquiry*, *23*(4), 381–385. doi:10.1080/1047840X.2012.720832

Stryker, S. (1968). Identity salience and role performance: The relevance of symbolic interaction theory for family research. *Journal of Marriage and Family*, *30*(4), 558–564. doi:10.2307/349494

Tsai, C., Horng, J., Liu, C., & Hu, D. (2015). Work environment and atmosphere: The role of organizational support in the creative performance of tourism and hospitality organizations. *International Journal of Hospitality Management*, *46*, 26–35. doi:10.1016/j.ijhm.2015.01.009

Wei, L., Liu, J., Chen, Y., & Wu, L. (2010). Political skill, supervisor-subordinate guanxi and career prospects in Chinese firms. *Journal of Management Studies*, *47*(3), 437–454. doi:10.1111/j.1467-6486.2009.00871.x

Wrzesniewski, A., McCauley, C., Rozin, P., & Schwartz, B. (1997). Jobs, careers, and callings: People's relations to their work. *Journal of Research in Personality*, *31*(1), 21–33. doi:10.1006/jrpe.1997.2162

Xiao, W., Zhou, L., Wu, Q., Zhang, Y., Miao, D., Zhang, J., & Peng, J. (2014). Effects of person-vocation fit and core self-evaluation on career commitment of medical university students: The mediator roles of anxiety and career satisfaction. *International Journal of Mental Health Systems*, *8*(1), 8. doi:10.1186/1752-4458-8-8 PMID:24555701

Zhang, X., & Bartol, K. M. (2010). Linking empowering leadership and employee creativity: The influence of psychological empowerment, intrinsic motivation, and creative process engagement. *Academy of Management Journal, 53*(1), 107–128. doi:10.5465/amj.2010.48037118

Zheng, X., Zhu, W., Zhao, H., & Zhang, C. (2015). Employee well-being in organizations: Theoretical model, scale development, and cross-cultural validation. *Journal of Organizational Behavior, 36*(5), 621–644. doi:10.1002/job.1990

Chapter 2
A History of Hospitality and an Inventory of Characteristics:
The Hospitality Sector's 21st Century Workforce

ABSTRACT

This chapter discovers the historical origins of the hospitality industry and reviews development and progress through modern times, highlighting the key factors that are prioritized for 21st century markets. Crisis management for a hotel resulting from disruptive technology or external factors such as the COVID-19 pandemic are explored from the perspective of impact on an employee's psychological well-being and their job satisfaction. Next the chapter proposes opportunities to reinvent the traditional role of a hotel front-desk employee to better position those employees for success within a modern framework. The chapter concludes by identifying traditional and innovative benefits to offer a hotel workforce that will be effective in increasing satisfaction and reducing turnover.

A HISTORY OF HOSPITALITY

As far back as Ancient Greece starting at 800 BC, there are archeological reports of the first hotels where thermal baths were developed in villages designed for the weary to rest and recuperate from their travels. The Romans were also known to have developed lavish mansions throughout the empire

DOI: 10.4018/978-1-6684-2528-2.ch002

to accommodate travelers conducting business of the government as well as creating thermal baths in many locations including what is modern day England, Switzerland, and the Middle East (Cunliffe, 1969). These accommodations, while not always operating exactly like what one expects from a modern hotel, were the original sparks in the recorded history of the hospitality industry with their grand gestures of extensive and luxurious service. The next distinct historical examples are Caravanserais, which would become common among Middle Eastern routes throughout the Middle Ages, which provided a safe place to rest for caravans. Around the same period in Europe, monasteries and abbeys became the first, formal establishments that would offer refuge for any traveler. Ultimately independently operated Inns, along with hospitals and other enterprising service or retail trades began to appear along well travelled routes to support trading merchants, religious pilgrimages and crusading forces as more mobile tendencies and dynamics transformed societies (Andrews, 2007).

Historical experts often identify the beginning of the fifteenth century as the true start of the modern hospitality industry (Ivanoa, Ivanov, & Magnini, 2016). Around this time, the French, and the English each introduced laws separately that required any establishment providing lodging services to maintain a register. A proliferation of establishments offering services is observed during this century, with inns maintaining some similarities including access through a central point, a kitchen, bedrooms available for rent (usually situated around a courtyard), a kitchen and dining area and stables (Andrews, 2007). Signage was developed as inns created unique characteristics and selling points to stand out from the rest of the offerings. A familiar offering of distinguishing characteristics was touted then (as now) which included unique cuisine, soft pillows and beds and reasonable fares. France even published a guidebook for travelers that showcased all the hospitality choices along well-traveled routes as well as some along less traveled ones (Groth, 1986).

The industrial revolution of the 19th century saw a surge of transition within the developing hospitality industry to resemble operations more familiar to what modern guests anticipate today. With the development of cities, and of a wealthy upper class, hotels began to align their services with the needs of specific target audiences (Davidson, 2005). The emerging wealthy upper class that was prospering from the innovation of the age embraced properties that featured high-end staterooms with luxurious appointments and services. Hotels embraced architectural innovation of the day and the advent of the skyscraper and elevators allowed hotels to become larger and taller (Groth, 1986).

In the early 20th century during the post-war boom of the 1920s, the hotel industry enjoyed its second major phase of expansion as establishment and operations began to appear more prolifically across the world than at any other point in history (Davidson, 2007). Hotels built in cities were no longer just small buildings consisting of a few rooms. Now these grand skyscrapers were designed as architectural masterpieces, showcasing themselves as much art as a functional source of lodging (Wiste & Li, 2017). Hotels had historically been built where a concentration of people needing lodging already existed. During this period, though, hotels began to transition away from servicing an existing need to become a destination for travelers (Davidson, 2005). Now guests could choose to travel to a destination (featuring a hotel) rather than elect to use its services based on convenience because the property just happened to be on their way. In this period, hotels would begin to appear in remote areas throughout the world including the first ski resorts in the mountains of Switzerland as well as a proliferation of seaside resorts along the Mediterranean (Andrew, 2007).

The third major boom of the hospitality industry was observed to have begun in the late 1970s and continued into the 1980s (Gustin & Weaver, 1996). This period of construction and expansion was primarily in support of the business and conference traveler although other specific target markets were identified as well. The business traveler market was capitalizing upon expansion of airline service, itself benefiting in the United States from deregulation which caused an explosive boom of new routes and service lines (Kahn, 1988). It was during this period that rooms became more spacious, cuisine became a defining and distinguishing characteristic and integration with other service providers in the travel industry (such as airlines, cruise lines and tours) all occurred (Andrew, 2007). The first information systems specifically designed for supporting the hotel industry also appeared on the market during this period (Holijevac, 2003). Globalization trends that integrated the world's economies also drove a proliferation of international hospitality development. New counties represented new markets to travel to for both business and leisure travel purposes (Susskind & Verma, 2011).

The 21st Century has been rife with disruptive events for the hospitality industry including terrorist attacks, wars, economic meltdowns, political upheaval, and outbreaks of deadly novel viruses. All these events rippled through the global hospitality industry. In addition, advances in technology continue to disrupt the industry as well. In some cases, its technology is designed to optimize operational processes that had always been performed by a human resource. In other cases, it's technology that eliminates the need for lodging all together.

Cloud based applications (aka "apps") functioned as disruptive technology across most industries but appeared in the hospitality industry in a few ways that usually resulted in the significant reduction, if not complete elimination, of jobs. Where you once reserved hotel rooms either through a hotel specific agent or an independent travel agent, cloud-based app technologies if functionality and utility directly to the end user (Susskind & Verma, 2011). The elimination of part of its distribution network allowed initial online booking systems to offer significant discounts to encourage early adoption by consumers (Ogbeide, 2013). It worked so well that little more than a decade after its introduction, direct reservations by the consumer using the internet (initially on a laptop computer, but almost exclusively now on a mobile device) has become the dominant channel making all other channels go extinct. Apps also allow guests to check themselves into a hotel, select their room virtually, allow one's mobile device to function as a key to access a guest room and settle their bill and check themselves out at the end of a stay (Druce, 2007). The core function of the hotel has not changed in the face of technology. However, technology has significantly disrupted and altered how the hospitality sector provides its services to its consumers.

But disruption to operations is not the only upheaval technology has introduced into the world of hospitality. The proliferation of high-speed internet accessible through wireless connection has allowed the development of software which allows for real-time synchronous interactions with video, audio, and interactive functionality. While virtual meetings and video chats were available prior to the COVID-19 pandemic, there was still a sense pre-2020 that important business needed to be conducted face to face (Ivanoa et. al., 2016). With a deadly novel virus released in the wild, the virtual meeting industry was propelled to explosive growth in response to isolation directives across the globe. While such drastic and rapid change rarely maintains over time, global societies emerging from the pandemic in 2021 and 2022 continued to embrace remote options for personal and professional engagement. Early forecasts for the hospitality industry's post pandemic recovery incorrectly identified business travel as returning faster than leisure travel would. Ultimately it was the reverse that occurred: Leisure travel rebounded rapidly after a year of isolation while business travel in 2023 continues to lag its pre-pandemic activity (BLS, 2023). The reason? It's harder to replace leisure travel experiences with a virtual offering Wiste & Li, 2017). Business travel, on the other hand, can be effectively conducted through virtual means with appropriate upskilling (Susskind & Verma, 2011). And so it goes that conferences, business traveler focused hotels and even commercial retail space all continue to experience (at best) soft recoveries while leisure travel is booming and driving growth for the hospitality industry in revenue and hiring.

Technology disrupting the status quo and necessitating creativity, innovation and change for an industry is not a new phenomenon, nor is it exclusive to the hospitality industry. The culture driven by the proliferation of the internet has changed how life is lived, and hospitality was certainly no exception (Ogbeide, 2013). In addition to the reduction of demand for a specific market segment, another change felt in many industries is the uprise in popularity of peer-to-peer sharing networks. Borne from the ease of connecting people together online, peer-to-peer sharing networks developed from simply an exchange of information in their early days to a more formal platform offering commerce exchanges currently. For hospitality, this has most notably become apparent with the rise of branded apps such as AirBNB or VRBO which offers individuals an opportunity to directly provide commercial lodging services for a fee to other individuals. Commercial brands must contend with a fracturing of their market as new market segments that are interested in less standardized, commercial lodging offerings find alternatives to meet their interests and needs (Susskind & Verma, 2011).

While technology is certainly a salient and longitudinal array, it Is not uniquely aligned with the hospitality industry and, therefore, not one of focus for this study or this essay. Rather, turning the attention of the narrative at this point to how the hospitality industry has contended with staffing itself is a focus of discovery for this narrative. In doing so, it is discovered that the parameters associated with the development of the workers themselves are an interesting story.

Profile of a Hotel Front Desk Employee

The author's experience along with current research (which is explored throughout other chapters in this narrative via several comprehensive meta-analyses) reveals some interesting and surprising characteristics associated with employees who are working at a hotel front desk. First, and probably most importantly, is that there are fewer tenured employees in this role than ever before. This position wasn't one that traditionally retained employees in it for long periods of time mostly due to the fact that it's low paid, hourly, one that involves a lot of standing (most front desk associates do not sit on the job) and can be on the receiving end of customer aggression like any front-line service role can be. On top of that, the hospitality industry was one of the most impacted by the COVID-19 pandemic in that it completely shut down quickly with employees furloughed without much warning or separation renumeration. Unlike in other industries where workers were retained in a remote capacity, the hospitality sector did not adapt virtual practices for most of its front-line workforce. In addition, the hospitality industry is the last sector, according to the Bureau of Labor Statistics, to fully recover from the collapse of available jobs. As of March of 2023, there are still 350,000 fewer available jobs in hospitality than there were in February of 2020 (Bureau of Labor Statistics, 2023).

Although the six-month period from November 2022 through March 2023 saw significant additions of available jobs, those being hired were primarily new hires so the individuals filling these rolls (when they can be filled) are either younger workers or retired workers. The younger workers were the ones that revealed interest in career planning and hoping to make hospitality their sector of choice (Holijevac, 2003). The older, retired workers were not at all interested in career planning or career pathways and this was to be expected. The retired workers revealed an opportunity for the hospitality industry to attract workers during a period where there is great scarcity among the labor pool. This opportunity lies within a unique benefit, that is for hotel employees (even part-time ones) to have access to significantly discounted room rates when booking personal trips at other property locations within the hotel's branded network (Woodworth & Mandelbaum, 2010). Two very distinct areas of attraction for people filling the same job, but through extensive conversations with currently employed associates, a common thread did emerge about what links these disparate groups.

Employees who are engaged and excited about working at a hotel front desk rarely speak affectionately about the actual work they are performing. It isn't about checking people into their rooms, answering questions in person or on the phone, helping guests with their luggage or providing change (or any other myriad of tasks associated with a Front Desk associate role). What commonly seems to attract employees regardless of age or hotel type is that they are all interested in engaging their guests and helping to provide them with a great experience. In other words, this current generation of employees is mostly motivated by creating that special hotel magic for their guests. In fact, many spoke of their guests in a possessive sense, further reinforcing the idea that there is intrinsic value in providing service to a customer beyond the necessary functions in a hotel operations role. This is an encouraging perspective, because it distinguishes the value-add of a human being working in a hotel from the operational tasks which can (and have been) automated to varying extents.

Reimagining the Role of a Hotel Employee

With a reimagining of how to describe the role that a front-line employee fulfills at a hotel, it is important to reframe the duties of the job. It isn't about whether someone is a front desk person checking someone in and answering phones, a bell hop delivering luggage to a guest room or securing ground transportation for a guest, a server providing a guest with a beverage or meal or a housekeeping person cleaning a room. To be direct and honest, all those jobs can be automated and while the barrier of a significant upfront investment to do so exists, many companies and independent properties have already begun to implement automation solutions to some degree. This doesn't necessarily remove the need for employes to be staffing a hotel, but it does necessitate a redesign of what those roles look like. Why categorize employees by functional role? It seems less important now, especially considering employes aren't really married to their specific job duties. What seems to motivate employees is the opportunity to engage guests and take care of their needs during a stay. Why not reimagine your property level roles as Guest Ambassadors that can provide any function but are defined by the key metric of engineering a positive guest stay. There is limited precedence for some hotels transitioning its property level employees in this direction where you have three shifts each day of Guest Ambassadors who are trained on supporting various operations as well as being familiar with the automated tasks and how to ensure guests can access and enjoy them.

A career pathway that incorporates this reframed role would still frame it as an entry point, but with a focus on being proficient in a variety of industry transferrable skills including communication, critical thinking, situational analysis, problem solving and relationship management (Ford, McLaughlin & Newstrom, 2005). If this role is trusted to be empowered with guest satisfaction, then it also needs the authority to make decisions about how to resolve issues when service expectations are not met. This can be a challenging area for many companies because it involves loss of revenue, but that's looking at the situation from the wrong angle. When service expectations are not met, a company can (and often does) require a customer to pay for services rendered, regardless of the quality. The opportunity cost that isn't often discussed is what happens next? Will that customer be retained? It becomes less likely after forcing a dissatisfied customer to pay, but a smart hotelier will commit to a standard of service execution and refuse to accept revenue unless that standard has been met (Kahn, 1988).

Here's where it gets challenging – to operate in that manner and at scale, a company must be able to objectively articulate the standard of service execution in a quantifiable manner (Korsgaard, Schweiger & Sapienza, 1995). It isn't enough to say, for example, as a part of the hotel's quality service we greet you in a friendly manner you're your arrival. How does one turn that nicely expressed conceptual vision into a measurable performance indicator that a leader can coach to and hold accountable to? There isn't any one right way to do it, but one example might be to identify distance from an employee as a trigger to engage a guest. For example, a hotel could establish an expectation that anyone within your three-foot sphere of engagement will be greeted warmly with a smile and a request to provide service if needed (Mansour & Tremblay, 2016). Now you have established a standardized and objective expectation associated with a conceptual vision that is both measurable and coachable. If an associate is not engaging customers within that distance, a coaching session between associate and leader can easily speak to the area of opportunity in an objective manner (Tsaur Hsu & Lin, 2019).

Most hotel operations do not think in this manner, but that is a shortcoming on the part of the industry and not from a resulting lack of options. Six sigma quality measurements have been the standard in the manufacturing sector in defining quality output for decades. At a high level, this philosophy establishes measurable standards and then tracks data to illustrate what is occurring, where standards are being met and where areas of opportunity exist. Quality, as a term, transitions from being a conceptual marketing buzzword and becomes associated with a specific framework of metrics that define the accepted parameters associated with the vague notion of quality service (Zemke, Raines & Filipczak, 2000).

Adapting a six-sigma process to a service industry is not as challenging as it may appear on the front end, and – once again – the presence of automated technology is an element that is easily integrated into the process. After all, any technology-based automation will also have collected data related to its operation. Review of data indicating whether standards have been met is as simple as extracting the information from the system and analyzing it. Who would do that? Well, that's how career pathways work when aligned with integration of disruptive technology: A new role (like six sigma data analyst) is now identified as a need at the hotel, and it has a defined skill set required to perform the duties of the role. What if no one on staff has that skill set? No worries and no need to lay off people – those interested in the role can be upskilled to perform the job duties and transition into the role (Abou Kamar, 2014).

Back to six sigma, though, where would these quality standards come from? It seems apparent for a manufacturing process since there are physical products being created which can have measured elements connected to the six-sigma evaluation process. In a service industry like a hotel, though, it can be less apparent. What's needed are experts in the operations of the hotel to articulate quality in definable and measurable terms. Who would be these experts? One of the best options would be the front-line workforce and since what defines quality can change over time, this now identifies another new role that has a specific skill set which associates can be trained for and transitioned into (Zhao & Ghiselli, 2016).

Front line hotel employees that are passionate about providing a great experience for guests are going to be in the best position to define what that experience looks like functionally (Abou Kamar, 2014). Why is this strategy important? Because a common element that excites and engages front line hotel employees is the opportunity to be involved in a collaborative culture that focuses on providing exceptional service. An enterprising leader at a hotel doesn't have to do much searching to find a team of interested people that can provide expertise on business operations (Tsaur, et. al. 2019). The current team is in the best position to provide that expertise. The team also has a chance to function as a team, which provides intrinsic value and motivation so it's a win-win situation for sure.

A characteristic of the fourth industrial revolution is significant disruptive change in how business is conducted, and this phenomenon is observed in multiple industries (Wiste & Li, 2017). While the recommended proposal of encouraging a collaboration among front-line workers to drive the strategic redesign of property level positions seems misaligned to traditional methods of organizing business, it really is about creating an engaged workforce to enhance and strengthen organizational commitment.

This ultimately represents a significant paradigm shift for the hotel industry and successfully adopting such transformative change is often challenging and easily abandoned. A critical element of workforce development and engineering of career pathways is that a business should not maintain the expectation of completing this work by itself. There are multiple stakeholders within a career pathway, and all should come together collaboratively to engineer a solution and support one another with its execution. Potential stakeholders include the business itself, but also providers of necessary training and education. These could be third party companies, community colleges or universities. In addition, most communities within the United States have an active workforce development contingent that partners with local and federal government to implement Federal Department of Labor workforce development funds. These funds are earmarked by the federal government for the specific purpose of creating integrated career pathways that encompass education, experience, and training (Bureau of Labor Statistics, 2023). There is often a strong level of local experts governing the implementation of these funds and those experts should also be engaged as active stakeholders.

CONCLUSION

Why is this all important? For the business, it can help ensure continued longevity as organizations pivot to incorporate disruptive technology into an optimized and cost-effective operation. For an employee, it demonstrates that an employer is truly invested in his or her personal success, which is a key element of establishing, strengthening, and maintaining high levels of organizational commitment. For businesses facing extreme levels of staffing shortages, attracting employees becomes important but retaining employees becomes critical.

The current staffing shortages of the current decade are often discussed in such a way that makes them appear to be unprecedented, but the research throughout this publication demonstrates that is not truly the case. In fact, there have been disruptions to availability of labor following most major crises and market disruptions in the 21st century including following 9/11 and the Great Recession (Ivanoa et. al. 2016). After both events, it became more challenging for businesses to identify qualified and engaged talent to fill available jobs. With this awareness being a part of the existing knowledge base in hospitality research, it is surprising to learn how unexpected the most recent labor availability disruptions have been (Abou Kamar, 2014). This is a potential area of opportunity for future research to determine the degree of correlation between the intensity of impact of the crisis (as the independent variable) with the degree of ensuing disruption that occurs in availability of qualified labor (as the dependent variable). While more than a simple linear regression analysis may be called for, this may help hotel operations better understand how to predict the severity of an expected labor crisis depending on how intense the preceding disruption becomes. Anticipation of challenges and crises always allows for an organization to better prepare and survive.

One of the most often reported methods of surviving oscillations in labor availability, yet least utilized effectively, is the straightforward strategy of retaining the workers already employed with a company (Gustin & Weaver, 1996). When labor becomes scarce and organizations begin competing for workers, it is not unusual for companies to recognize that it is critical they provide expanded amenities, boost salaries and benefit packages, and relax surveillance / performance efforts to better retain employees. These modifications to a workplace culture may not always survive once the cyclical nature of labor markets reverses (Korsgaard et. al., 1995). Removing or reducing initiatives designed to retain employees when talent is readily available only serves to position a company in a negative light as far as its relationship with human capital is concerned If only an organization (hotel or otherwise) approached the retention of talent in a more consistent and proactive manner (Ford, et. al., 2005).

There are three basic strategies that a business must consider when attracting and retaining employees: First, have a well-defined role that offers fair compensation, an effective benefits package and connects to a career pathway of an employee's interest. Second, invest in ongoing learning and development associated with the employee's desired career trajectory and third engage the employee in decisions making that helps flatten then organizational structure demonstrating that the individual is a key element in the business' success (Gustin & Weaver, 1996).

The three strategies outlined above are fantastic if an employee is looking to develop a career, but research has revealed that there is potential for a retired population to be attracted to work on the front line of a hotel operation. Once retired, there are many individuals that wish to partake in leisure travel enjoying the freedom of not working day in and out. The issue many face is that they're now living on a fixed income and travel can be expensive (Zemke et. al., 2000). Here is where an employer really understanding what benefits will truly motivate one's working population can be beneficial. Part-time employees are often not eligible for benefits like health care or retirement planning since there is an associated cost to an employer for providing the benefit. It is somewhat questionable whether a retired population would be interested in either benefit, though, since a retired individual has access to Medicare coverage. Similarly, a 401K investment plan would be less attractive for a retired individual than someone still working full time because the former most likely can access any retirement savings (Woodworth & Mandelbaum, 2010). So, what benefit might attract a retired population then?

Many hotels provide their employees with the opportunity to make reservations at significantly reduced rates with sister properties throughout the hotel's branded network. In some cases, hotels provide this discount even outside of their brand network if marketing co-op arrangements exist with other brands (Andrew, 2007). This particular benefit doesn't cost the organization an actual expense like healthcare premiums or investing in a 401K portfolio. There may be some allocated costs on profit and loss statements associated with amortization of overhead expenses for housekeeping as well as costs that are applied on a per room basis, such as the cost of cleaning supplies and in-room amenities (Woodworth & Mandelbaum, 2010). While there is less opportunity to recover these amortized costs associated with a guest stay, there are additional costs such as food and beverage other services (depending on the property) that might earn revenue from such a guest. It is highly likely that any actual costs associated with such a reduced room rental rate are recovered through additional expenditures within a hotel where the guest is staying (Holijevac, 2003; Woodworth & Mandelbaum, 2010).

What's just as important is that this benefit can effectively attract a quality employee who is willing to work part time to earn access to this benefit (Zemke, 2016). There is some precedent for this population being recruited including the Wal Mart store greeter model as well as most non-profits that solicit retired individuals to work as volunteers. In both scenarios, a retired individual is expected to work a scheduled shift and perform certain duties at a defined standard. In other words, there is no difference conceptually than working at a hotel. There are some differences in tasks, of course, but this notion is no different than a volunteer docent at a museum being recruited, trained, and scheduled for work. The idea behind developing a professional environment that is engaging for someone in the retired phase of their life while providing both a paid wage and benefits to complement an interest in travel can truly open new opportunities for a hotel's staffing strategy.

REFERENCES

Abou Kamar, M. S. (2014). Six-Sigma application in the hotel industry: Is it effective for performance improvement. *Research Journal of Management Sciences*, *3*(12), 1–14.

Andrews, S. (2007). History of Hotels and Motels. In Introduction To Tourism and Hospitality Industry (reprint ed.). New Delhi: Tata McGraw-Hill Education.

Bureau of Labor Statistics. (2023). *Labor force statistics from the current population survey*. Available at: www.bls.gov/cps/electronically-mediated-employment.Html

Cunliffe, B. (1969). *Roman Bath*. Society of Antiquaries of London. doi:10.26530/20.500.12657/37345

Davidson, L. P. (2005). "A Service Machine": Hotel Guests and the Development of an Early-Twentieth-Century Building Type. *Perspectives in Vernacular Architecture*, *10*, 113–129. https://www.jstor.org/stable/3514344

Druce, C. (2007). Green Regime will Bring in the Business. *CatererSearch*. http://www.caterersearch.com/Articles/2007/10/25/316825/Green-regime-39will-bring-in-the-business39.htm

Ford, R. C., McLaughlin, F. S., & Newstrom, J. W. (2005). Creating and sustaining fun work environments in hospitality and service organizations. *Journal of Human Resources in Hospitality & Tourism*, *4*(1), 11–30. doi:10.1300/J171v04n01_02

Groth, P. (1986). Living Downtown: The History of Residential Hotels in the United States. University of California Press.

Gustin, M., & Weaver, P. (1996). Are hotels prepared for the environmental consumer? *The Cornell Hotel and Restaurant Administration Quarterly*, *20*(2), 1–14.

Holijevac, I. A. (2003). A vision of tourism and the hotel industry in the 21st Century. *International Journal of Hospitality Management*, *22*(2), 129–134. doi:10.1016/S0278-4319(03)00021-5

Ivanoa, M., Ivanov, S., & Magnini, V. (2016). *The Routledge Handbook of Hotel Chain Management*. doi:10.4324/9781315752532

Kahn, A. E. (1988). Surprises of Airline Deregulation. *The American Economic Review*, *78*(2), 316–322.

Korsgaard, M. A., Schweiger, D. M., & Sapienza, H. U. (1995). Building commitment, attachment, and trust in top management teams: The role of procedural justice. *Academy of Management Journal*, *3*(8), 60–84. doi:10.2307/256728

Mansour, S., & Tremblay, D. G. (2016). Workload, generic and work–family specific social supports and job stress: Mediating role of work–family and family–work conflict. *International Journal of Contemporary Hospitality Management*, *28*(8), 1778–1804. doi:10.1108/IJCHM-11-2014-0607

Ogbeide, G.-C. (2013). Perception of Green Hotels in the 21st Century. *Journal of Tourism Insights*, *3*(1), 1.

Susskind, A., & Verma, R. (2011). Hotel guests' reactions to guest room sustainability initiatives. *Cornell Hospitality Report*, *11*(6), 1.

Tsaur, S.-H., Hsu, F.-S., & Lin, H. (2019). Workplace fun and work engagement in tourism and hospitality: The role of psychological capital. *International Journal of Hospitality Management*, *81*, 131–140. doi:10.1016/j.ijhm.2019.03.016

Wiste, P. M., & Li, M. (2017). Component hotel: The continued evolution of urban hotel design in the 21st century. *International Journal of Hospitality and Event Management*, *1*(4), 325–332. doi:10.1504/IJHEM.2016.082165

Woodworth, R. M., & Mandelbaum, R. (2010). Seventy-Five Years of U.S. Hotel Revenues, Expenses, and Profits. *Cornell Hospitality Quarterly*, *51*(1), 20–26. doi:10.1177/1938965509356774

Zemke, R., Raines, C., & Filipczak, B. (2000). Generations at Work: Managing the Cash of Veterans, Boomers, Xers, and Nexters in Your Workplace. Amacom.

Zhao, X., & Ghiselli, R. (2016). Why do you feel stressed in a "smile factory"? Hospitality job characteristics influence work–family conflict and job stress. *International Journal of Contemporary Hospitality Management*, *28*(2), 305–326. doi:10.1108/IJCHM-08-2014-0385

Chapter 3
Why Work at a Hotel?
A Meta-Analysis of Attracting and Retaining Talent in the Hospitality Industry

ABSTRACT

This narrative analyzes dimensions associated with the choice to work at a hotel, specifically in a front desk operations role. The chapter details the motivational dimensions that lead to a decision to accept work. It also analyzes how non-monetary benefits associated with a job can provide significant value for an employee. Such benefits are primarily social in nature, such as connecting with colleagues and enjoying a fun culture. Other motivational drivers include capturing experience to pursue a career pathway. These alternative benefits factor into job motivation and can reduce an employee's intent to voluntarily separate. The chapter also analyzes ideal work-life balance models for hotel employees and the impact of change to an organizational framework for employees. The chapter concludes with a practical analysis of how an employer can address low organizational commitment among its employees by strategically impacting the effective of role-specific engagement thereby reducing intent to voluntarily separate.

DOI: 10.4018/978-1-6684-2528-2.ch003

INTRODUCTION: WHY DO PEOPLE WORK?

The question of why people work is one that can be traced back further than recorded human history and transverses the disciplines of psychology, social sciences, and economic theory. Ultimately, people work because they have skills that can provide value for another. By entering a transactional arrangement, money (or other goods of value) is exchanged for goods or services. As economies became more formal, and cash standards were adopted by governments, employment agreements were formalized and quickly became a global standard in industrialized and non-industrialized nations around the world.

Employment provides critical manifest (income, health benefits, and retirement benefits) and latent (time structure, social contacts, collective purpose, status and identity, and regular activity) resources (Jahoda, 1982). Affective organizational commitment is an important work attitude representing an "employee's emotional attachment to, identification with, and involvement in the organization" (Meyer & Allen, 1991, p. 67). High affective organizational commitment is important to employers because it predicts higher motivation and performance, and lower levels of counterproductive work behavior (Dalal, 2005; Mathieu & Zajac, 1990; Meyer, Stanley, Herscovitch, & Topolnytsky, 2002; Riketta, 2002).

This chapter explores the specific characteristics associated with being employed in the hospitality industry and the unique employment challenges and opportunities that a seasonal service-based sector provides. The narrative explores different facets of how work can be more effectively managed in the hospitality sector. Specific components of discovery include the specific elements of what attracts an employee to one type of role versus an another, the benefits of having fun at work and how that can be a strategic pathway for retaining talent, how exhaustion and burnout impact employees within a hospitality workforce, maintaining an effective work-life balance for hotel employees, the effects of organizational change on the levels of demonstrated commitment and practical strategies associated with impacting low organizational commitment and employees' job insecurity.

BACKGROUND

The Benefits of Hotel Employees Having Fun at Work

There are a series of negative emotions displayed by employees in a hospitality environment that have been identified and validated as significant issues by prior research (Cheng & O-Yang, 2018; Mansour & Tremblay, 2016). These emotions include the stress felt by an individual employee and the levels of burnout displayed by an individual employee (Zhao & Ghiselli, 2016). It can be concluded from this research that employers have areas of opportunity associated with managing strategic frameworks for employee working environments, both practical and psychological to reduce the impact of negative emotions on employee tenure. The COVID-19 pandemic introduced an unprecedent level of crisis into everyday life across the globe, which resulted in significant attention being attributed toward taking care of the mental well-being frontline employees (Pfefferbaum & North, 2020).

Hospitality organizations are challenged by high employee turnover (Ma & Qu, 2011), due to the unique nature of hospitality jobs such as long and irregulate hours, low levels of pay and high requirements on employee's emotions displayed at work (Hinkin & Tracey, 2010). There are opportunities to offset these issues, and better retain employees, if an employer will dedicate focus to also developing a fun, engaging, empowering and intrinsically enriching framework for employees to work (Xu, Wang, Ma, & Wang, 2020). An individual's interest in identifying and engaging in activities that bring joy and a sense of fun within the workplace is a significant component of how an employee perceives his or her well-being, affinity, and engagement with his or her employer and his or her specific role (Ford, McLaughlin, & Newstorm, 2005). This can, and should, be leveraged by leadership to engineer strategic pathways to accomplishing their own talent recruitment and retention goals.

It has been observed that for service-based work environment where employees are perceiving that coming to work is fun and that being at work affords them fun opportunities, the quality of service that they will – in turn – provide for customers will reflect these values. In other words, the experience of one's customers is likely to be increased if employees are feeling positive about their own working experience (Ford et al., 2005). While many employers in the hospitality industry focus on standard management practices of a transactional nature, a strategic re-organization of focus to purposely engineer and curate working environments reflective of a fun climate is encouraged. Fun is a difficult environment to establish artificially, so leaders within a hospitality environment should not just seek to establish this type of culture at a front-line level, but support making fun a priority throughout all levels of a corporation. This can be a difficult strategy to develop, but one of the universally effective starting points to strengthen fun throughout one's organization and integrate it into an organization's culture is to make changes to provide employees with utility for engagement where employees feel heard, recognized, and acknowledged (Liu, 2019).

There has been a trend in the last decade for academic researchers to place a focus on understanding the dynamics associated with employee positive psychology. One way this appears is through the leveraging of fun in the workplace, and creating a workplace culture that supports it. Fun can be used to create an energized and effective work environment (Michel, Tews, & Allen, 2019; Tews, Michel, & Stafford, 2013). Climate in a workplace refers to employees' shared perceptions of organizational events, procedures, and practices (Tsaur, Hsu, & Lin, 2019). McDowell (2004) defined fun climate at work as a type of organizational climate that supports fun at work. Michel et al. (2019) further explained that fun in the workplace is "characterized as aspects or features of the work environment that have the potential to promote positive emotional reactions such as enjoyment, amusement, and lighthearted pleasure in individuals" (p. 99).

There is precedent for interjecting this sort of thing into a workplace environment. There are many anecdotes where businesses reflect success with a strategic and purposeful creation of a culture of fun within an organization. While often associated with smaller, startup cultures, a fun working environment has also been established at several well-known service-based companies across a variety of industries. Such brands that have successfully created a unique culture of fun for employees include the Walt Disney Company, Marriot Hotels & Resorts, Southwest Airlines, Google and IBM (Karl, Peluchette, Hall-Indiana, and Harland, 2005; Michel et al., 2019). A more granular review of each of these organizations reveals that the specific elements are different from one organization to the next ultimately demonstrating that the components of a fun workplace climate can be diverse under a broadly constructed umbrella (Tews, Michel, & Allen, 2014). Regardless of the specific cultural differences, the broad construct encompassing what is thought of when a fun workplace is described offers similar beneficial outcomes regarding short- and long-term benefits for attracting and retaining talent (Michel et al., 2019).

In order to gain a deep understanding of workplace fun climate, a multiple-component concept of fun climate at work should be used. Xu et. al. (2020) researched the impact of three distinct components for a fun climate. These three components include having a culture that globally celebrates fun across all facets of work, formal and informal opportunities for employees to socialize and celebratory efforts for workers. The notion of a work life balance where a workplace encourages employees to socialize, celebrate and spend time with friends, family and colleagues outside of normal working environments is also a critical element of a sustainable fun workplace culture (McDowell, 2004). This can often be interpreted that a focus on work is reduced, although a healthy work-life balance can be established with the right support and focus. Doing so can depend on cultural values and norms that exist outside of a corporate environment. Employees from a collectivistic culture often display challenges in establishing an effective work-life balance that are not observed as significantly with employees that are accustomed to a more individualistic culture (Billing, Bhagat, Babakus, Srivastava, Shin, & Brew, 2014; Vaziri, Benson, Salazar Campo, 2019). A universal condition between both individualistic and collective cultures is that employees who are also parents display the most severe challenges in balancing work and life commitments while also resisting employer-based efforts at engineering activities that promote such a balance (Lu, Cai, & Gursoy, 2009). Netemeyer, Boles, and McMurrian (1996) defined work-family conflict (WFC) as "a form of inter-role conflict in which the general demands of, time devoted to, and strain created by the job interfere with performing family-related responsibilities" (p. 401).

Work-family conflict happens when employees' participation in the work role causes conflict for them in performing family-related responsibilities (Netemeyer et al., 1996), especially when employees are trying to achieve satisfactory or even perfect levels in both roles (Ling and Poweli, 2001). Employees in collectivistic cultures normally perceive more severe Work-family conflict than those in individualistic cultures (Billing et al., 2014; Ling and Poweli, 2001; Vaziri et al., 2019) due to their concerns over and frequent acceptance of criticism and comments from others about their imperfection in family roles.

Xu et. al.'s (2020) study argues that global fun at work could help employees gain positive psychological resources (Tsaur et al., 2019), resulting in employees' perception of less WFC. As determined from exploring and examining relationships maintained by employees associated with national cultural patterns and quality of life, Hofstede (1984) determined that employees in collectivistic nations will more naturally perceive quality of their life through the experiences of core elements maintained by the collectivistic culture. In such cultures, individuals will come together and mutually acknowledge significant events as an achievement for the collective whole as opposed to focusing on the accomplishment of any single individual within the collective (Hofstede & Bond, 1984). Triandis, Bontempo, Villareal, Asai, and Lucca (1988) summarized that collectivism is associated with collective coping in unpleasant life events, emphasis on harmony within ingroups, and actions that benefit ingroups. Wagner III (1995) determined that collectivism significantly strengthens cooperation in groups and promotes collaborative working environments, which can result in higher quality output with increased efficiency. Ultimately the work of all three (Hofstede and Bond, 1984; Triandis et al., 1988; Wagner III, 1995) reveals many that multiple elements of collectivistic cultural values are effective when invested in activities designed to motivate employees to engage in workplace social activities related to engineering and establishing a climate of fun within the workplace.

It helps to calibrate understanding of what is meant by the term Fun Climate and how it can be focused on. Focusing on fun climate at work in a collectivistic cultural context translates fun climate at work as a means for increasing employees' psychological capital and mental resources (Tsaur et al., 2019). This dynamic helps employees reduce their perceived WFC and increase their engagement and passion for servicing their customers at work. Schneider (1975) originally defined organizational climate as molar perceptions employees have of their workplace. Molar perceptions, as articulated by Schneider (1975), have "a psychological unity being based on actual or inferred events, practices and procedures that occur in the daily life of a system" (p. 473). McDowell (2004) explained that "a climate for fun would conceptually refer to employee perceptions of the practices and behaviors that get rewarded and supported with regard to fun in the workplace" (p. 31).

Taking this into consideration, a fun climate can be articulated definitively by establishing three, separate and distinct categorizations for evaluation. First, exploring the impact on individual and collective attitude occurs when individual personality components are faced with partaking in fun activities (Choi, Kwon, & Kim., 2013). Next, scholarly discovery associated with the outcome of an established climate of fun from both a theoretical and a practical dimension is critical (Michel et al., 2019; Tews, Michel, & Noe, 2017; Tsaur et al., 2019). Finally, perceiving a fun climate as not a singular and consistent standard, but a multi-dimensional construct where the different components, activities and outcomes for each dimension should be examined and analyzed (Tews et al., 2014)

A facet of work-family conflict can be found in time-based conflict. A time-based conflict is best defined as an ongoing psychological dissonance that exists for hotel employees because they perceive they always must weigh the importance of attending personal celebratory gathers that occur on weekends and holidays against their commitments to work (Mansour & Tremblay, 2016; Qu & Zhao, 2012; Zhao & Mattila, 2013). Another observed area of dissonance that can dilute a fun work culture is acting – either surface or deep. Surface acting, defined as individuals expressing emotional elements without integrity and in bad faith, requires employees to manage their own observable demeanor and interactions in such a way to appear as expected. Conversely, the opposite of surface acting is deep acting. Deep acting is where an employee believes that offering a certain observable action or emotion will ultimately achieve desired results and manufactures the response in good faith. This dynamic requires management of an employee's emotions where true responses are buried under manufactured ones (Becker & Cropanzano, 2015; Grandey & Cropanzano, 1999). This can be a problematic element for a culture as Xanthopoulou et al. demonstrated that there are different outcomes for the two types of acting. With deep acting, it was discovered that employees are modifying their own fundamental personal emotions and reactions, which can help employees improve work-related flow and reduce work exhaustion. Conversely, though, surface acting ultimately damages workflow and causes work exhaustion because employees are not focusing on modifying their own emotions and response – they are simply attempting to hide how they truly feel. This is especially destructive within the hospitality industry because a front desk employee's role often requires them to display welcoming and friendly interactions consistently throughout one's work shift (Zhao and Ghiselli, 2016). The opportunity for an organization is to recognize that reducing levels of deep acting and surface acting can be a power tool for leadership to support culture of fun at work.

Regardless of the origin of the dissonance, it is something that employers should seek to reduce. An employees' overall perception of a fun climate at work could help them reduce WFC based on the following reasons: First, psychological capital earned through fun climate can help employees face WFC. Positive emotions gained from a fun climate at work represent an increase of employees' psychological capital (Tsaur et al., 2019). The more psychological capital an employee has, the better the employee is able to navigate negative emotions in WFC

Second, a fun climate at work brings social support within a social network. In a collectivistic context, employees who experience fun climate have chances to share and exchange work and family experiences. The common dilemma of WFC shared and understood within a social network could be considered a ritual for collective healing, making each employee feel socially supported and helping them realize that they are not the only one combatting WFC.

Third, a fun climate at work provides informal learning to overcome WFC. Fun climate offers opportunities for employees to encounter experiences and information not shared during work hours, making it a perfect channel for informal learning (Tews et al., 2017). Fourth, family-friendly plans in fun climate could directly reduce WFC. Some activities and events in fun climate could be planned that welcome employees to bring their families, strengthening family members' understanding of and support for employees' work. The study by Hammer, Neal, Newsom, Brockwood and Colton (2005) also found that employees' WFC can be reduced through a family-friendly workplace.

Fun climate creates job satisfaction, which motivates employees to perform deep acting as social exchange. The whole mechanism of cultural values in a collectivistic context is based on social exchange (Hwang, 1987). When employees enjoy fun and perceive love from their employer and colleagues, they are more willing to invest in resources to perform better at work (Wang, Ryan, & Yang, 2019).

In accordance with the concept of congruent emotional states (Mesmer-Magnus, DeChurch, & Wax., 2012), a fun atmosphere experienced at a workplace is the same as what customers want to experience in hospitality service settings. When hotel employees enjoy a fun climate in their own workplace, they can easily perceive customers' desire for a fun atmosphere and naturally deliver fun to customers.

Through team-level emotional contagion in fun climate (Grandey & Cropanzano, 1999), employees gain both social and emotional support from colleagues to perform deep acting. Support from colleagues gained through fun climate is also an informal learning opportunity for employees to absorb personal successful stories about deep acting from senior employees (Tews et al., 2017).

Ultimately, when management demonstrates a solid comprehension of the cultural values and norms associated with the collectivistic culture as well as an individualistic culture, the pathways to integrate the benefits of each while developing and implementing a company-specific culture of fun become more accessible (Xu et al., 2020). Some of the ways to achieve this include providing opportunities for socializing with coworkers and celebrating at work.

In addition to engineering a fun environment for employees, an equally relevant challenge lies in sustaining the culture once it has been established. A fun work climate can be nurtured through global efforts such as offering opportunities for colleagues to socialize as well as to celebrate identified milestones and achievements consistently and positively. Leaders at hospitality organizations should establish and support the catalyzing of a fun climate at work through the support of activities that employees perceive as fun, relaxing and engaging. Fun activities that foster social interactions should be organized (Tsaur et al., 2019) within work teams and across different departments, although consistency and standardization of execution should be maintained as much as possible. Some examples of consistent milestones include celebrating employee birthdays and offering friendly competitive activities that integrate with work but also stand apart from it are effective ways to create fun at work. Regular team meetings and company arranged social hours are also excellent occasions for employees to connect with each other (Xu et. al., 2020).

To create a sustainable cultural set of norms and values around fun, the common efforts won't be sufficient; An organization needs to develop unusual and innovative methods. Orientations and training activities should also be designed with ample opportunities for social interactions (Brown, 2019), so that employees not only get to know the work and the place, but also get to know the people. Corporate achievements, individual's success and personal milestones should be celebrated. Acknowledging individual achievements and cheering for each other power the success-fun celebration-success cycle (Liu, 2019). It is worth noting that due to the irregular work hours in hotels, managers should keep inclusion in mind when organizing these activities and do not accidentally exclude disadvantaged groups of employees because the nature of implementation does not allow for participation. One such example of this occurring would be mothers with young families not being able to partake in social events (like a holiday party) because they were unable to secure or afford child-care. This situation is not limited to just females or even parents of young children. Family responsibilities of any type can often make it extremely difficult for employees to fully involve themselves in many kinds of fun activities, leading to different levels of perceived fun climate at work (Xu et. al., 2020).

Likewise, it is challenging to assemble all employees due to the nature of consistent operations at a hotel. Leveraging technology and social media as a platform of collaborative celebration yet which can be consumed asynchronously can also provide significant benefits (Akorede, 2018). An organizational structure that has fewer management layers has been demonstrated to be more effective in offering opportunities to provide effective social interactions among employees than a more traditional hierarchical organizational structure (Perry-Smith, 2006). The framework of an open-designed workspace has become especially popular with the opportunities it affords to both promote and facilitate transparent communication, collaboration, organizational citizenship and social interactions among employees. There are opportunities to benchmark outside of the hospitality industry. Organizations such as Google and Flight Center have been creatively designing their workplace to add fun elements (Akorede, 2018).

Job Motivation and Turnover Intentions

According to Kim (2015; 2018), job motivation was a factor that displayed a strong negative correlation when studied against an employee's turnover intentions. Kim's work demonstrated that an employee's intent to separate from an organization was less pronounced among workers who were motivated and engaged in their role and also perceived their job as source of learning and progress (Cimbaljević, Nedeljković-Knežević, Demirović-Bajrami, Dunjić, El Bilali, Rančić-DemirDemir, 2020).

Conversely, employees were more likely to develop an intent to separate from a role or an organization when they perceived a lack of forward momentum in developing their careers. This came about often when an employee performs the same monotonous tasks for an extended period where most of the time was spent on repetitive tasks without an opportunity to learn and apply new skills. Dysvik and Kuvaas (2010) concluded that an employee's motivation displayed the strongest negative correlation with turnover intentions when compared to other analyzed components of job satisfaction proving that intrinsic parameters associated with satisfaction is what would help the most when encountering challenging situations (Ryan & Deci, 2000).

In addition, age and gender were factors that positively correlated to an employee's satisfaction on the job along with motivation to excel. In general, older employees appear to be more satisfied with their jobs and did not exhibit similar pronounced intent to voluntarily separate from their employer when compared to their younger colleagues (Kipkebut, 2013). This phenomenon can be explained by noting that older employees are often more invested in effort and time as it relates to their role's responsibilities. It's also a possibility that this phenomenon is explained by the fact that opportunities for securing new employment are, in general, more limited for employees fifty and older than their colleagues. As a result, older employees are more comprehensive in reviewing whether to voluntarily separate from a role because newer opportunities are limited (Cimbaljević et. al., 2020).

Conversely, it is observed that employees under 50 are more likely to take risks in regard to career development and display more significant intent to voluntary separate in order to accelerate perceived upward mobility (Tanova & Holtrom, 2008). That said, a quixotic dynamic observed in the literature is that younger employees in the hotel industry also demonstrated significantly higher levels of organizational commitment which has been demonstrated to reduce turnover intention (Akova, Cetin, & Cifci, 2015). The identified rationale was mostly due to this population being relatively inexperienced and feeling that there are fewer job opportunities for their experience level. The research also indicated that on a localized level, female voluntary turnover rates may be lower compared to males (Akova et al., 2015). While larger-scale, global research showed that women's turnover rates were slightly higher compared with their male counterparts (Chen, Ayoun, & Eyoun, 2018) indicating that a diversity of cultural norms and values may significantly contribute to this behavior as well.

Bajrami Terzic, A., Petrovic, M., Radovanovic, M., Tretiakova, T., and Hadoud (2021) collected data in March and April 2020 among employees in the hospitality industry in Serbia, a time during which most of the countries worldwide were affected by the pandemic caused by COVID-19. All data was collected via a web-based survey and the Ito and Brotheridge (2007) scale was used to measure if employees perceive changes made in the organization during the pandemic as fair. The scale had four items, such as: "The steps that company took during the pandemic (e.g. salary reduction) were fair to me. Respondents expressed their opinion on a 5-point scale (1 = strongly disagree to 5 = strongly agree). Only 29% of the respondents agreed that changes in the organization that occurred because of the pandemic were fair.

Bajrami et al. (2021) assessed job satisfaction with its localized geographic survey using a 6-item scale developed by Iversen (1996). The scale was designed to measure how much employees will be satisfied with different aspects of their job when they return to work. Items like job content, degree of responsibility, and recognition for good performances were assessed on a 5-point scale (1 = very dissatisfied, 5 = very satisfied). The respondents think they will be the least satisfied with job content (28%), degree of the variation in the job (36%), and recognition for good performances (37%). A significant percentage of the respondents (27%) expressed neutral attitude, showing that they are not sure what their job will be like after the pandemic.

The measure of employees' turnover intentions included six items. Two items came from Folkman (1984) scale, but one was divided into multiple different factors: "I am planning to look for a new job during the next 12 months" to "I am planning to look for a new job during the next 12 months in tourism industry" and "I am planning to look for a new job during the next 12 months in some other industry, rather than tourism". Additional items were derived from Meyer and Allen's (1991) research including "It would be hard to find employment outside my organization" integrated with original items like "After the pandemic, I do not find working in tourism attractive anymore". This study had responses expressing their intention to leave the organization across a five-point Likert scale (1 = strongly disagree, 5 = strongly agree). The results of the study showed that a majority of respondents (44% in the tourism industry) agreed they are looking for or will look for a new job, but 62% agreed or strongly agreed that finding a new job won't be easy (Bajrami et. al., 2021). With further analysis, when the control variables are taken into consideration, the variables age and marital status are shown to have a significant impact on job motivation and turnover intentions. For older participants (40+) and employees with families, there is an inverse correlation with intent to leave a job. For younger participants or employees who are single, there was a positive correlation with intent to leave a job. Employees who are a part of a family unit are also shown to maintain a status as a provider necessitating continuous income as a critical aspect of choosing to work. This status reduces the propensity for employees to make quick or hasty decisions regarding career dynamics (Bajrami et. al., 2021).

When the significance of age was taken into consideration, it was discovered that there were two intrinsic effects of the COVID-19 pandemic which may serve as direct predictors of job motivation: Risk Taking and job insecurity. It was determined that risk taking behavior will not have a significant impact on job motivation. This is because employees believe measures that are erected in response to a crisis are most likely only temporary. While extended or open-ended changes could serve to be problematic, those that are clearly in response to external crises are adopted more readily. The impact on the health of an employee can often increase concerns around both mental and physical health which occurred during pandemic-era isolation, but unless provided with conflicting information employees understand these changes are temporary and they will not have long lasting impact on job motivation.

A further analysis of these dynamics suggest that complaints of this nature are often caused by the restrictions on movement, impossibility to see friends and family members or to go to work – if these restrictions do not exist, the impact on physical and mental health is removed or greatly reduced (Bajrami et. al., 2021).

Job insecurity, risk-taking behavior, and fairness of organizational changes showed to predict job satisfaction significantly, in a negative direction (Bajrami et. al., 2021). This result implies that an employees' perceived levels of insecurity regarding continuance of work, the concern that the company can be closed temporary (or even permanently) because of COVID-19, changes made in the organization during the pandemic or the expected changes after the pandemic can and will all negatively affect job satisfaction. Although risk taking behavior did not have a significant impact on job motivation, the results revealed that the proposed safety instructions and perceived health risks after the employees return to work can be an important predictor of job satisfaction. However, none of the control variables were found to act as significant predictors when it comes to job satisfaction (Bajrami et. al., 2021). This speaks to the resilience of employees.

In the Bajrami et. al., 2021 study, the regression model of turnover intentions marked the two effects of COVID-19 as job insecurity and fairness of organizational changes. These two variables are effective predictors when the results are adjusted for the significance of the variables marital status and age. Job insecurity perceived by the respondents proved to be a strong predictor of job motivation, job satisfaction and turnover intentions. An inverse correlation between job satisfaction and job insecurity is explained by the dynamic when employees are insecure about the future stability of their role, which ultimately reduces satisfaction with the role in the present.

There are conclusions from this synthesis of research to address the issue of lower job satisfaction prior to a decision is made to separate. For one, creating more challenging tasks, respecting the effort invested in doing the job and giving support to the employees to complete their tasks are all active responses from a company that can increase employee commitment to the organization. These types of behaviors have been measured to stimulate desire to stay, even after the economy and society recover from the crisis (Vahtera, Kivimaki and Pentti (1997). While there may be an increased interest in separating from an organization because of crisis management, Bajrami et. al., 2021 demonstrated that the majority of those in the hospitality industry who think of looking for a new job because of the pandemic are still interested in looking for it within the tourism industry. What this information ultimately tells us is that the crisis, no matter how severe, will not be as influential on an employee as to significantly reduce the attractiveness of tourism industry for employment. The management practices of a specific organization, however, is a different matter. It is proven that poor managerial decision-making can cause a feeling of job insecurity (Vahtera, Kivimaki, & Pentti, 1997).

One of the first things that can be done (and for relatively little money) is to address the matter of how a crisis, and its subsequent impact, makes everyone feel. In such a case, there needs to be a visible and active effort by employers to demonstrate to employees that their workplace is one where individuals are free to openly discuss matters related to health complaints, especially mental health problems, without any prejudice. Markovits, Boer, & van Dick (2014) highlighted those employees who still remained in their jobs after a crisis demonstrated lower motivation and job satisfaction when compared to before the crisis. The reason had little to do with the crisis itself but rather an employer's response to the crisis, and specifically whether layoffs occurred. Employees who remained sympathized with those who were let go, and remaining employees worried that something similar could happen to them demonstrating lower organizational commitment as a result.

Memory of layoffs isn't all that can impact organizational commitment. Many companies will collectively reduce salaries and benefits (like time off) in response to addressing business dynamics (like lower sales) occurring during and after a crisis. Changes in salary or vacation benefits that are perceived to be taking away value from the employee often serve as powerful motivators for an employee to leave an organization and find a new job (Elshaer & Saad, 2016). In uncertain and unpredictable situations (like a pandemic), the emotional intelligence, experiential knowledge and overall competencies of crisis management demonstrated by the management team of an organization can be crucial in both managing the business and keeping employees motivated to do their jobs.

Exhaustion and Burnout on the Job

Severe competition is unavoidable in the hospitality and tourism sector due to the growing numbers of firms (e.g., hotels, restaurants, resorts, tourism-related companies) across the globe (Trang, Lee & Han, 2019). Hotels often tend to make it obligatory for employees to deliver superb and extra services to guests to meet/exceed guest expectations (Limpantigul, Robson, Gould-Williams & Lertthaitrakul, 2013; Kim, Lee & Han, 2019)

Many firms, particularly in the hotel industry, pursue service excellence as the core strategy to survive in the increasingly competitive marketplace (Jeaheng, Al-Ansi, & Han, 2019). This desire can ultimately trigger a core response syndrome leading to a work exhaustion situation for employees, which is likely to result in a high turnover rate and absenteeism as well as a low job performance (Maslach, Schaufeli, & Leiter, 2001). Emotional exhaustion and reduced personal accomplishment among burnout constituents significantly affected turnover. These variables also strengthened the influence of trust in supervisor support on hotel employee turnover, acting as significant mediators.

Indeed, recent research asserted that many hotel workers often experience burnout symptoms, suffering emotional annoyance and psychological/mental stress (Choi, Mohammad & Kim, 2019; Sirqy, 2019). Such symptoms become more serious when the number of contacts with guests increases, when service complaints are processed, and when rotating shift works including night shift are frequent (Yu, Ariza-Montes, Hernández-Perlines, Vega-Muñoz, & Han, 2020). Two types of exhaustion can be observed on the job: Emotional exhaustion (Yu et. al., 2020) and Physical exhaustion (Karatepe & Uludaq, 2008).

Emotional exhaustion refers to when individuals demonstrate an emotionally drained feeling due to diverse interactions with people that do not fulfill or compliment an employee on a personal level. These interactions can result in a perceived or real environment of depersonalization (Han, Al-Ansi, Chung, Ngah, Ariza-Montes, & Vega-Muñoz, 2020).

Depersonalization indicates non-emotional and callous responses toward others needing services/care, treating them like impersonal objects (Leiter & Meechan, 1986). In addition, according to Yu et al. (2020), reduced personal accomplishment indicates a lack of individuals' feeling, interest, and concern about the goal attainment in the situation of working as well as with working in collaboration or tandem to others.

Emotional exhaustion, depersonalization, and reduced personal accomplishment are generally regarded as core dimensions of employee burnout (Karatepe & Uludaq, 2008). Burnout is described as a state of emotional, psychological/mental, and physical exhaustion derived from substantial involvement in demanding/challenging situations (Shih, Jiang, Klein, & Wang, 2013). When the demands of the job remain unfulfilled, the phenomenon of burnout will occur (Karatepe & Uludaq, 2008).

Burnout is also one of the reasons affecting employees quitting their current organization (Shih, et. al., 2013; Kim, Kim, & Hwang, 2015). Kim et al. (2015) examined job stress and its influence on employee responses and behaviors. Their empirical results revealed that employee burnout increases employees' negative attitude toward the hotel and boosts employee turnover rate. More recently, Yu et al. (2020) uncovered the fact that hotel employee burnout is the significant determinant of job satisfaction, turnover, and job performance. Han et. al. (2020) explored the intricate associations between trust-in-support factors and burnout dimensions and uncovered the possible influence of such relationships on employee turnover in the hotel context.

Research has demonstrated the importance of trust in support and its role in reducing the burnout phenomenon among hotel employees and explaining their voluntary turnover decision formation in a satisfactory manner. The prominent role of emotional exhaustion in increasing hotel employee turnover was identified. In addition, the association between trust in supervisor support and employee turnover was mediated by burnout factors (Han et. al., 2020).

The high turnover rate brings a considerable increase in costs as it induces expenses related to employee recruiting and training (De Clercq, Azeem, Haq & Bouckenooghe, 2020). Hotel entrepreneurs need to make every endeavor to reduce employees' emotional exhaustion in the workplace for the reduction in employee turnover rate. Shih et al. (2013) asserted that increasing employees' beliefs about the possible rewards from the company/managers and decreasing their workload can be essential in minimizing their emotional exhaustion.

One such opportunity for hotel management to achieve this outcome could be to deploy workplace green atmospherics. These physical design elements are identified as having a critical positive impact for employees' psychological stress relief and emotional exhaustion. It is accordingly essential to design and build a green workplace (e.g., green walls, fresh air, green items, green rest areas/spaces, natural scent, green interior/exterior). This effort can be an effective tactic for lowering emotional exhaustion, which eventually results in lessened turnover among hotel employees (Han & Hyun, 2019).

Work-Life Balance for Hotel Employees

Employees providing operational services at an organization have less flexibility with their work schedules than other classifications of employees. An employee hired to work at a cash register in a grocery store, for example, must be scheduled to work the majority of his or her hours during the times the store is open for customers to shop. The hotel industry has an added complexity in that some (if not all) of its customers need access to the hotel 24 hours a day and seven days a week due to the unique aspects of the lodging industry. Long working hours, shift duties and providing effective customer service for upset, demanding and difficult customers in hotels has become a phenomenon in the hospitality industry that most just assume is a required part of the job (Hsieh, Pearson, Chang, & Uen, 2004; Sarabahksh, Carson, & Lindgren, 1989). This stress from these situations often creates a demand on an individual to decide on the balance between work and family, and that decision can often favor work over family. People have difficulty working in different roles or even multiple roles (as a supervisor in work, a parent at home, a child helping elderly parents in a Chinese cultural context) which leads to stress (Grandey and Cropanzano, 1999).

This is a relevant issue to explore more comprehensively as there are many cases that suggest that work–life balance assists in retention, productivity, and the recruitment of good staff (Evans & Vernon, 2007; Pocock, 2005).

The very concept of work–life balance has an extensive development history that dates back to the eighteenth century. It is thought that the concept of work-life balance emerged as a result from the initiation of trade union development (Chartered Institute of Personnel and Development, 2007a). Work–life balance is defined as the perception that an individual has a significant measure of control in choosing when, where, and how they work. In addition, the individual maintains a strong perception that they are in receipt of the expected right to enjoy a fulfilled existence both on the job as well as in their personal lives and where being paid for one's work is aligned with experience and achievement as it relates to the mutual benefit of the individual, business, and society (Employers and work–life balance, 2008). However, due to ever changing social, economic, and legislative conditions in different countries, there is no universal consensus on a specific definition of work–life balance that encompasses all of the various iterations and instances that exist on a global scale.

Historically, much discussion about the concept was catalyzed by the presence of a greater number of women into the workforce and associated split duties between childcare and professional commitments becoming much more relevant. Dual income parents report that it is challenging being able to balance responsibilities for their professional commitments as well as those for their families. Employee satisfaction is enhanced and intent to separate from an organization is reduced when an organization incorporates specific benefits for workers that are universally accepted to assist and support employees with family related commitments, such as provisions for childcare, paid leave to take care of newborn babies or elderly parents or flexible work schedules (Pocock, 2005).

Childcare is not the only context where work-life balance as a viable concept discovered its origins. Working professionals providing care for aging and elderly parents (or similar) also becomes more of a factor in the 19th, 20th, and 21st centuries as several million people throughout the world are both working and serving as caregivers for elderly or disabled family members (Chartered Institute of Personnel and Development, 2007b).

The issue of mental well-being for oneself is also a point of discussion and ongoing exploration of strategies that an employer can use to encourage workers to assist workers with maintaining a work life balance that promotes one's mental well-being is critical. Part of this effort is to recognize that not all workers have the same needs and that there must be additional discovery associated with an employer's specific population demographics of its employees. This precedent already exists in that there have been multiple attempts to categorize employees' needs exclusively by broad groups classified by their age: Baby boomers, Generation X, Generation Y, Generation Z, etc. Ultimately, what this demonstrates is that using the broad term ''family-friendly'' is too narrow a term and can quickly – and easily - alienate employees in today's workplace environment (Chartered Institute of Personnel and Development, 2007b)

There are three types of work and life conflicts for employees that have been identified. These include time-based conflicts, strain-based conflicts, and behavior-based conflicts (Greenhaus & Beutell, 1985). While the potential for all three exists within the working environment of a hotel, the most prominent of the three in that specific context is often time-based conflicts. This is where time commitments and expectations are misaligned due to the actual number of hours spent working, and often have a significant relationship with work and life balance. It is a salient area for hospitality workers in that employees maintain less independence on scheduling work in this industry than in others (Duxbury, Higgins, & Lee, 1994). They are also more likely to have to work outside of traditional 9-5 hours of office work (Greenhaus & Beutell, 1985) where conflict with personal commitments becomes more likely (Gutek, Searle, & Klepa, 1991). A culture of long working hours in the hospitality industry is so typical and accepted as normal that many workers see early morning, weekend, or overnight working hours as normal and rarely question this practice even as it impacts their send of work/life balance (Gutek et. all, 1991). This affects both managers and front-line employees nearly equally and the issue of working long hours is one that research, and the published literature, continually focuses on. In this scenario, it isn't only the employees who are directly impacted by the scheduling issues but all workers in an organization eventually become aware of what is occurring. When one or more groups of employees are consistently being overworked, all workers start to be aware of the impact of heavy workloads and long working hours. This is a prime breeding area for burnout.

Empirical research on employee burnout has been extensively conducted in the hospitality industry especially to explain why both managers and front-line employees will suddenly voluntarily separate from their employer (Tabacchi, Krone, & Farber, 1990). Due to an ongoing chronic labor shortage in the hospitality industry, many aspects of how an employee perceives his or her environment become negatively boosted. The overload of specific role responsibilities, irregularly scheduled work shifts, extended work shifts and a lack of enhanced compensation to offset the changes all exacerbate considerable pressure over an extended time period translating into a nutrient rich environment for the incubation of burnout is higher in service industries. This occurs because one's job involves a high degree of interaction with clients (Vallen, 1993) and can be observed in either a front-line associate or a people leader. Human Resource Management International Digest published a study in 2002 which indicated that managers who suffer from burnout are relatively young, under 40 years of age, and, most likely, working in a service-based hospitality environment. A correlation of high burnout to high turnover was also recorded (Buick & Thomas, 2001). Prolonged overwork is neither healthy nor productive, and the impact is significant (Buick & Thomas, 2001).

Recognizing this challenge, and that the issue of time-based conflicts is a major contributor to work-life balance issues leading to burnout and acts of voluntary separation, larger hospitality organizations in the western world (such as the United States or the United Kingdom) are increasingly adopting sophisticated family-friendly practices to become an employer of choice (Davies, 2020). These efforts are not limited just to the west though.

The first SARS pandemic during the first decade of the 21st century occurred mostly in Asian countries and went largely unnoticed (as far as labor dynamics go) in the west. However, some of the dynamics associated with the first SARS pandemic mirror what was observed globally during the COVID-19 pandemic during the 2020s. For example, downsizing efforts in the aftermath of SARS caused employees to tolerate longer scheduled hours for job security reasons (Luk, 2006). Following the passing of the crisis and increasingly strong economic growth afterwards, Hong Kong reported the highest staff turnover resulting from voluntary separation that it had experienced in decades (HKIHRM, 2007a). Job vacancies and employee turnover rates continued to stay high in 2006 (HKIHRM, 2007b) and ultimately becoming a polarized situation where employees transition quickly from company to company in effect shopping around for better career prospects as well as pay and benefits. The similarities in dynamics between 2005 – 2006 and 2021 are 2023 are striking. This indicates that additional research into pre, during and post dynamics associated with the Asian hospitality markets during the first decade of the 2000s can provide valuable insight, especially when compared with similar data obtained from additional cultures during the period 2020 – 2023.

The Asian lodging industry was studied extensively by Hsieh et al. (2004) who investigated the perceptions of managers working in a hotel. Specifically, this study explored managers' perceptions on how their work and personal life cross-pollinate (or pollute) one another. The study incorporated an instrument created from research conducted by MacDermid Barnett, R., Crosby, F., Greenhaus, J.H., Koblenz, M., and Marks (2000). Four dimensions were reviewed and analyzed in these efforts including: 1) work interference with personal life (WIP), 2) personal life interference with work (PIW), 3) work enhancement of personal life (WEP) and 4) personal life enhancement of work (PEW). The WIP and PIW were measured by four conflicts: time-, strain-, energy-, and behavior-based conflict. While WEP and PEW were measured by five enhancements: time-, strain-, energy-, behavior- and support-based enhancements. Among all the demographic variables, however, only tenure at the employee's hotel was found to have significance connection to the perceived difficulty and success regarding work and personal life balance (Hsieh et al., 2004)

As a result of the Hseish et al. work in 2004, there are seven distinct factors that leadership can directly impact which significantly enhance one's perception of work / life balance within the hospitality industry (Wong & Ko, 2009). These include Factor 1: Enough time-off from work; Factor 2: Allegiance to work; Factor 3: Workplace support on family matters; Factor 4: Flexibility on work schedule and Factor 5: Life orientation. While the results of the study are empirical and significant, they are limited to the time of the study and the location of the sample (Hong Kong). There may be cultural differences identified if this study was to be repeated in a different location, although it is noted that Hong Kong does encompass both eastern and western cultural values and norms into its lexicon. The study also did not account for seasonality, which is a common factor for the entire hospitality industry.

For factor 1, Wong & Ko (2009) determined that hotel employees did not agree with the statement that they received insufficient time-off from work. Long working hours and a physically demanding work nature is accepted among employees as a fact of life in the hotel field. As more and more degree-holders enter the hotel work force, however, it has the potential to trigger a different perspective and expectations would similarly shift. It is determined that additional effort and attention should be invested in the result that the higher the level of education an employee receives, the higher agreement they had to the factor of enough time-off-work.

For factor 2, it becomes understood that the term family matters not only refer to conventional activities associated with the term, like childcare or family responsibilities, but also broader non-conventional definitions. The goal in this case is to ensure that required duties are taken care of but still allow the staff an opportunity to be flexibility with its schedule. A good management system is achieved through the design of a well-designed roster system and a re-design of job duties that encourages cooperation between departments aiming to facilitate a smooth handover of duties. For example, according to Wong & Ko (2009), a front-line front desk hotel employee ideally should be able to transition at the end of their shift with a minimal of effort with the next shift's employee seamlessly integrating into ongoing work matters. The exiting employee would be able to handover their duties to the next shift worker and leave on time on a normal business day instead of having to invest additional hours to help transition open issues from the prior shift. However, very often, line managers are the ones that can determine the success of organizational and operational policies, ultimately affecting how the implemented system performs. A negative and resentful underbelly culture may develop among associates as a direct result of behavior by leadership. Even more troubling, an environment perceived by employees to be unsupported by management is quickly cultivated and spread among team members. Obviously, the challenge of allowing an employee to adjust work shifts around desired free time blocks is somewhat organization- and role-specific, but even attempting to incorporate this dynamic into a department's work culture would require the department's leadership to maintain awareness on supervising flexibility and building up a bond of trust and cooperation (Wong & Ko, 2009).

With factor 3, the study determined that allegiance to work is an ideal outcome for employers in a workplace. Having a high level of allegiance implies the significant support and loyalty expressed by employees to the company, its mission, and its customers. Staff commitment and loyalty towards both their own role and duties, as well as the company as an overall entity, exert a bonding force to maintain work–life balance. An employee's sense of commitment is often directly impacted by a sense of job security and progress toward achieving career goals. Staff will be willing to work overtime when they are committed and understand the value associated with the additional investment of time. Another key finding is that when employees maintain a strong sense of positive affection toward their colleagues, they demonstrate higher levels of organizational citizenship even when allegiance toward other groups (like management) is not as strong. Staff allegiance is boosted positively by the presence of employee benefits that support family matters and are a powerful presence that can offset negative perceptions employees hold about other aspects of working for a company such as poor relationships with managers, less than desirable tasks or scheduling or concerns about compensation (Wong & Ko, 2009).

For factor 4, Wong & Ko (2009) describe how the four statements encompassed in this factor were unique in the hotel arena as a norm for shift workers who tend not to possess a complete discretion of control and choices in relation to their work schedule. It is understandable that a hotel job is part of a 24 hours a day, seven days a week operation (including holidays) and is highly labor intensive. Everyone is assigned to be present and on duty at a certain time slot per day. Even during holidays, staff are allocated into the roster for maintaining the service. This factor reveals the fact that hotel employees have limited flexibility in setting their own working schedule.

Factor 5 demonstrated that employees will demonstrate the highest levels of positive agreement when they are provided with an opportunity to express and pursue their personal interests or aspirations. The research demonstrates that all employees balance a need to fulfill other responsibilities in life beyond work and that conflicts (and, ultimately, strain) between personal and professional commitments will always. The work in this area of the study showcased that employees feel positive about their work when they are enjoying what is perceived to be quality time with their family. In a capitalist society, where economic activity is the principal channel, full-time work employment is by far the most common type of central life activity. Job–family conflicts are more frequent in these societies due to the oft prevalent nature of dual-income families and the exponential increase in demands on an employee's time such as career goals, childcare needs and commitments to care of the elderly (Wong & Ko, 2009).

These five factors were determined to exert a significant influence on the dependent variable, as shown in figure 2. Significance was determined using a multiple regression analysis with the statement, ''I feel my work–life is balanced in this job,'' as a dependent variable. The five factors outlined in previous paragraphs were classified as independent variables, each resulting in Beta variable value of greater than 0.05. Factors 1, 2, 3 and 4 exerted positive correlation with the dependent variable while factor 5 exerted a negative correlation with the dependent variable:

Figure 1. Theoretical model of Wong and Ko (2009) research

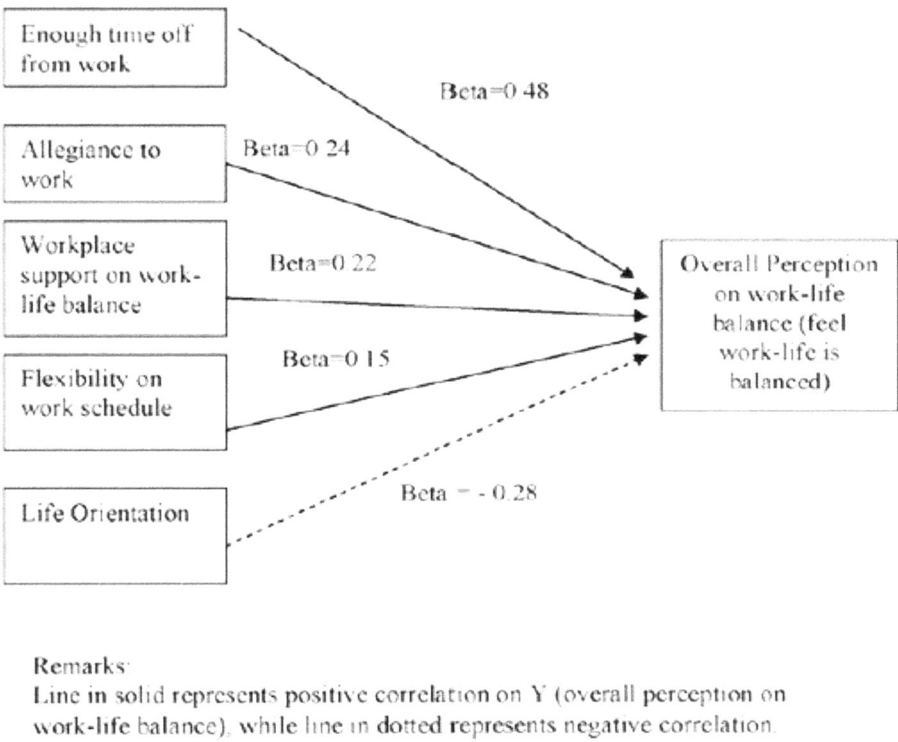

Wang and Ko's study demonstrated that the preference for employees falls within life orientation (factor 5) in general, employees are not perceiving that their existence reflects what is expected as ideal work—life balance. In other words, employees who look for personal aspiration will find their work and life not balanced. Factor 1: Enough time-off from work scored the highest beta value of 0.48. This result was interpreted to mean that if employees are provided, or scheduled, for an acceptable amount of time-off from work, they will perceive and accept that work and life will be more balanced. Employees that demonstrate allegiance to their employer (factor 3, beta = 0.24) will consider their work and life balanced. The support from the workplace (factor 2, beta = 0.22) is revealed to have a significantly positive impact on helping employees balance their work–life. Finally, the allowance of more flexibility on the work schedule (factor 4, beta = 0.15) will make employees feel that this is more alignment between work and personal life allowing them to better satisfy personal and professional commitments (2009).

This all provides valuable insight for managers in strategically looking to invest in a workplace environment that actively retains employees. There are three primary broad areas of strategic opportunity: First, actively listen to employees' concerns and appreciate their differences and needs. Second, optimize employee's free time through increased flexibility with work schedules and third, provide extensive workplace support on critical personal family matters of importance for employes.

For the first strategic area, an employer who limits its determination of its employees' needs to only information obtained through traditional methods of demographic profiling will most likely not be able to develop a working environment that effectively addresses the needs of its employees who are often working long hours as is the norm in the hotel industry. For an employer to address this, it is important to collect ideas, feedback, and suggestions from employees on a regular scheduled cadence and then visibly make practical changes and adjustments to the working environment as a result of the data collection. This promotes an open and more transparent management culture in the workplace. If such a dynamic solicitation of feedback is continuously utilized, it becomes a trusted and valuable method to obtain direct qualitative feedback from employees (Wong & Ko, 2009).

The second broad strategic area of free time and work schedule flexibility is a critical one. The dimension of time is perceived by employees to be one of paramount importance. The result of a significant and uncontrollable constraint (like a work schedule) imposed on employees' lives is often negatively perceived as a barrier to achieve desired work–life balance. The acknowledgement of the advocating of front-line hotel employees, particularly shift workers, toward amassing additional free time was clearly articulated on empirical grounds in Wong and Ko's study. There is a possibility of transforming daily hours and weekly hours into monthly hours or even annualized total (Wong & Ko, 2009). One such example of this might be a bid-based scheduling system based on tenure, performance or a combination of factors determined to be important to employees.

Hotels tend not to follow a bid system for schedules allowing hotel employes to submit formal requests for blocks of time where they'd like to be scheduled although this practice is found in many service-based industries like airline flight crews. The airline bidding system works primarily on a basis of fairness in that employees are provided with access based on a prioritization established exclusively on tenure. This is not the only method of ranking employees for the purpose of order of access – employee performance can be used as well, although it is a more complex framework than simply determining order of access based on tenure. As long as employees are ranked using the same method and this method is determined to be fair, a bid-system can often be successful for staffing practices in service-based organizations (Tabacchi et. al., 1990).

Associated with free time and work schedule is also the notion of a compressed work week. In Wang and Ko's study, it was discovered that this approach was successful in alleviating the problem of a time-based conflict and achieved a higher level of allegiance to work. There are also many other types of flexibility strategies that can be deployed in relation to time schedules. For instance, daily flextime, defining consistent hours for each of the three (or four) daily working shifts, allowing employees to work part-time and reserve hours, or even adopting HR policies to allow employees to trade off their salary in exchange for more free time, etc. Having a menu of options to allow employees an opportunity to select their own level of engagement with flexibility is a favored management mechanism is also an approach that would increase success in this area. If management could consistently empower employees to self-select the days off from work that they prefer or implement a perceived scheduling policy for rotating and trading work shifts for employees to accommodate personal needs when required, it would enrich and enhance organizational commitment significantly (Wong & Ko, 2009).

The third broad area of strategy, provide extensive workplace support on critical personal family matters of importance for employes, is no less critical for management to establish high commitment among employees and reduce burnout and voluntary separation. It is not as difficult as it is perceived to be for an employer to engineer, implement and sustain a framework to support family matters in the workplace. To do so will only require understanding the specific needs of employees, a basic system that outlines fair and equitable system of management for benefits (Marriott & Brown, 1997) and a consistent effort of implementation by leaders (Tabacchi et al., 1990). This can be manifested in several ways including on-site child care, providing meals for employees, extending benefits in an affordable manner to cover family members as well as an employee or offering special discounts via partnerships with external establishments that support employees in their personal lives (like having a co-op program where a hotel offers its employees a discount on purchases at a grocery store and the hotel offers the grocery store's employees a discount on reservations throughout its branded network) Through experience sharing, benchmarking and innovative thinking, stakeholders may further allow initiatives to emerge when appropriate. Of course, organizations and their needs change over time and an array of family support for employees should also be reviewed and refreshed in a consistent cadence (Tabacchi et. al., 1990).

The Effects of Organizational Change on Employee Commitment

Organizational change has been explained by Daft (2005) as a new idea or process being introduced in an organization which can be internal or external. Moran and Brightman (2001) described organizational change as an organization changing direction to keep up with the changing demands of customers. This is accomplished through structural and competency improvements (McLarney & Auila, 2020). The success of the change, as well as employees' acceptance of the change, can depend on how well managers of organizations manage the change process. If employees are not involved early in the change and lines of communication are not kept open throughout the change, it could result in unsuccessful implementation of the change (McLarney & Auila, 2020). It is important for managers to recognize how important employee commitment is to change organizations (Moran & Brightman, 2001).

Employee commitment has been described as an employee's positive relationship with the organization, department, or manager (Fedor, Caldwell, & Herold, 2006). Meyer and Allen (1990) further broke down employee commitment into three types: affective, continuance and normative. First is affective commitment, which is seen as being emotionally positive towards the organization. Employees who are affectively committed will strongly identify with the goals and values of an organization. Thus, the strongly committed employee wants to stay as a part of the organization. This employee remains with the company based on his/her own choice.

The second factor is continuance commitment, which is explained with reference to employees who believe they would be at a financial loss if they left the company. For example, they may lose economic benefits such as pension plans and social costs such as work friendships. This employee feels he/she has no choice but to remain with the company (Meyer & Allen, 1990).

The third and final component is normative commitment and is defined with reference to an employee who feels an obligation to stay with the organization because of strong relationships with the organization, supervisors and/or coworkers. These psychological bonds can be strong enough to convince an employee to stay at their current place of employment even if provided with substantially more lucrative offers (in terms of earnings, responsibilities and/or title) elsewhere (Aaron, 1999).

An employee's commitment to their organization can be easily influenced by factors such as relationship with co-workers and managers, rewards, conflicts, and efficiencies (Sofat, Kiran, & Kaushik, 2015). Meyer and Herscovitch (2001) point out that employees can also be committed to other factors such as change itself and leadership in the organization. Regardless of the specific factors in play at a specific company, increasing employee commitment can be key for organizations to be successful in implementing change and retaining employees. It is advisable that an employer focuses on building employee commitment early on in the relationship with its employees. This will help prepare employees for the inevitable changes that the organization may go through at any point (McLarney & Auila, 2020). These types of changes provide an opportunity for managers to engage employees for their input and can be implemented internally by managers as they are formal, planned and goal oriented (Sofat et al., 2015)

Internal changes are not the only type of change that can test the resilience of an employee's organizational commitment. External changes, as noted by Lunenburg (2010), can come in the form of a change in government laws and regulation, production and process innovation, marketplace shifts, labor market upheaval, and the internalization of business. Organizations may be mandated to comply with many of these external changes quickly, resulting in poor implementation and negative employee experience. Internal changes that can affect the organization have been explained by Pfeffer (1994) as employment policies, administrative processes, and people problems. Organizational changes have also been described as different change levers which simply refer to different areas of the organization, for example, technology, marketing, quality, cost strategy, managing people and leadership (Sofat et al., 2015). Fedor et al. (2006) posits that any changes that are closest to an employee's day-to-day routine than to work department changes seem to have more of an impact on the individual. In fact, most employees view any type of change in their department or their day-to-day job as an organizational change (McLarney &Auila, 2020).

It is easy to understand during times of change in an organization that there will be negative effects felt by employees (Maheshwari & Vohra, 2015). However, there can also be some positive effects (Hill, Seo, Kang, & Taylor,

2012). An increase in negative effects experienced by employees has been described by Lamsa and Savolaniem (2000) as stress, low morale, anxiety, loss of direction, lack of loyalty and lack of employee commitment. Positive effects that have been noted are increase in job satisfaction, regularity in work and motivation (Bennett & Durkin, 2000).

Whether change is from an external or an internal source, employees are likely to have concerns when one occurs. Concerns can be observed in many ways in employees: Through their physical and mental health complaints, changes in their everyday habits and their quality of work and personal life. Health-related symptoms may include fatigue, depression, digestive problems, back or neck pain, headaches, sleeping and concentration problems (Vandenberghe, De Keyser, Vlerick, and D'hoore, 2004). Changes in habits could include smoking, drinking alcohol, consuming sleeping or antidepressants addictions and changes in the attitude of employees (Vandenberghe et al., 2004). Quality of life that can be associated with health includes physical activity, physical health, mental health, energy, emotional well-being, social well-being, absence of pain, weight gain or loss and general health status (Ware & Sherbourne, 1992). Organizational changes can be challenging for employees in terms of adjustment and personal flexibility (Vandenberghe et al., 2004).

During times of change, employees may end up working longer hours to complete training and may support areas of the organization that may be short-handed. In doing so, they are usually not paying attention to their health and well-being which could lead to the above-mentioned physical and mental symptoms of stress (McLarney & Auila, 2020). These types of challenging situations could cause feelings of distress that employees may have difficulty adjusting to, until things return to normal (Vandenberghe et al., 2004). For example, even a change that could improve an employee's job could put new demands on adapting and create concerns of failure, adjustment, and uncertainty in the short term (Fedor et al., 2006). Conversely, major changes to an employee's individual job or insecurity of the job may induce more serious symptoms of stress over the long term. This could also lead to a decline in an individual's or collective's morale.

Morale, which has been defined as how an employee feels about the organization and his work environment (Lee, Vargo, & Seville, 2013), factors into how an employee perceives the work environment and the degree of commitment one maintains about their job, their duties, and their employer (McLarney & Auila, 2020). There are many factors that can affect an employee's morale such as motivation, job satisfaction, work meaningfulness, organizational commitment, and work pride (McKnight,

Ahmad, and Schroeder, 2001). Conditions in an organization that can cause low morale could be layoffs, high employee turnover, unclear expectations, contract disputes, change in leadership and lack of personal growth (Hui & Lee, 2000).

Negative reactions such as a decline in moral is explained by Coch and French (1948) mostly seem to come from poor change implementation. From an employee perspective, change results may not favor employees as much as it does the organization. If the result of the change can be demonstrated as benefiting the employee as much as the organization, uncertainty, fear of failure, loss of control and sense-making concerns can be eliminated (Coch & French, 1948). As can be expected, employees with higher commitment towards the organization tend to deal with stress better in times of organizational changes (McLarney & Auila, 2020). This is most likely true because they seem to understand the change and are willing to make it successful (Smollan, 2016)

A related concept to that of morals is that of job satisfaction. When job satisfaction is reviewed among employees in terms of regularity in work and motivation of employees in organizational change, morale and job satisfaction seem to be complementary. For example, increased motivation to do well could very well lead to increased job satisfaction and regularity at work (McLarney & Auila, 2020). The effects of change on employees can be strengthened through a few methods (Mathieu, Fabi, Lacoursière, & Raymond, 2015). According to Parish Cadwallader, and Busch (2008), employees who have quality relations with their managers have more desire to support changes within their organizations. For this reason, managers should make efforts to invest in their people through training, aligning salaries to performance, and gaining trust. Further, Parish et al. (2008) stated that organizations should have ways of assessing the approaches and emotions of employees on a regular basis to study how to develop and nurture employee relations.

So far, the conversation has focused on employes with high organizational commitment. What sort of behaviors can be expected when an employee demonstrates the opposite? Employees with low commitment will be absent from work more often, which will affect employee performance and can be costly to the organization (Sofat et al., 2015). Conversely, highly committed employees assist organizations in improving the performance of the organization by improving client relationships, communication within the organization and have a greater acceptance to embrace change (Wim & Gijs, 1998). Within this context, managers should be looking for ways to increase employee commitment by effectively managing the change process initiative (Yanti & Dahlan, 2017). There are three ways in which managers of organizations can increase employee commitment during organizational change. First, by strengthening employee's relationship with the organization, secondly, by improving employee's perception of the fairness of the change, and lastly by increasing the acceptance of change (Shah, Irani, & Sharif, 2017).

According to Kotter and Schelsinger, to have a successful change management initiative, reduction of employee resistance is crucial, (1979). Here employees are informed, engaged, trained, supported, and negotiated on differences prior to change process is initiated Judge, Thoresen, Pucik, and Welbourne (1999) argued that change can be concerning to employees because it makes them contemplate whether their personal alignment with the organization will be the same after the change initiative is implemented. Caldwell, Herold, & Fedor (2004) further claimed that the management must be aware that organizational changes may make employees question their relationship with the organization. An important factor that could have an impact on employees' reactions to change and consequently affect employee commitment could be the way that management treats and involves employees during the change (Fedor et al., 2006).

Managers have an opportunity to increase employee commitment and keep employees' reactions under control by effectively engaging employees as responses to changes are being developed and implemented. It may be equally important for managers to stay close to employees who have high levels of employee commitment as they will be the ones that are more likely to embrace change and be the leaders to champion change amongst their peers (Frone, 2018). Korsgaard, Schweiger, and Sapienza (1995) have further explained that if managers show openness and respect to employees' issues related to the change, it will result in positive employee reactions to that change. McLarney and Auila (2020) concluded that if employees have an opportunity to offer their suggestions, it will also have a positive effect on how the change is perceived. It gives them the feeling that their feedback will have an impact on the result of the change initiative. This will also help employees to perceive the change as impacting different parties in an equal and fair manner.

Employees' interpretation of the change, referred to as 'fairness of change', may influence employee commitment (Jones & Skarlicki, 2013). The fairness process also allows for reluctance experienced by employees to be mitigated in the change process. Degoey (2000) claimed that the practice of communicating the details about the change and collectively making sense of it amongst employees and managers, provides a stronger realization of its benefits. Employees may also consider the consequences of the change more personally to test its fairness. For example, improving a specific employee's working conditions to better their work life in their department will most likely lead to an increase in that employee's commitment to the change (Novelli, Kirkman, & Shapiro, 1995).

Iverson (1996) showed that the acceptance of organizational change by employees is positively associated with increases in commitment and can act as a determining factor in the change process. This increase in organizational commitment can only be accomplished if employees are involved early in the change initiative (Mowday, 1996). If the reasons why employees are resistant to change could be understood by managers and managed well, then resistance to change could be reduced. This in turn would lead to higher employee organizational commitment and employee participation (Sofat et al., 2015).

Meyer and Herscovitch (2001) describe an employee's commitment to change as "a mindset that binds an individual to a course of action deemed necessary for the successful implementation of a change initiative, and argued this mindset can reflect three dimensions. First, there is a desire to provide support for the change based on a belief in its inherent benefits (affective commitment to the change). Second, there is a recognition that there are costs associated with failure to provide support for the change (continuance commitment to the change). Finally, there is a sense of obligation to provide support for change (normative commitment to the change).

Madigan, Norton, & Testa (1999) also stressed how important work-life balance is to increasing employee commitment within an organization. The need for work-life balance has risen from the changing dynamics of the workforce. An example is the rise of single parent families and increased responsibilities in households where both parents are working (Yanti & Dahlan, 2017). Stum (2001) has described building employee commitment through a hierarchy of needs that includes: Psychological (including basic needs such as food, water, and shelter); Safety (encompassing a danger-free environment); Social – caring relationships; Esteem (described as dignity and individual importance); Self-actualization (following a sense of satisfaction and personal growth; and Work-Life Harmony (featuring a balance of work and personal life).

Within that framework, Madigan et al. (1999) suggested a list of best practices that could help with work-life balance such as flexible work options, shorter work weeks, job sharing, health and wellness programs, and personal leave. These types of work programs create a caring employee environment that helps employees balance work and life obligations, which in turn decreases stress and increases employee commitment.

While there are several complex socio-psychological factors that contribute to the matter of organizational commitment, the process of developing and sustaining motivated and committed employees is not expensive for organizations (Nelson, 1999). The theory of the 5 I's argues that to gain employee commitment, an organization must provide several dimensions of engagement. First is interesting work, which aims to keeping a portion of employee's job interesting and at the same time decreasing boredom caused by repetitive tasks. Second is information, where management provides employees with opportunities to know as much as they can about their jobs and thus allowing them to perform effectively in their positions. Employees also want feedback on how they are performing and how their contribution is part of the organization's success. Third is involvement, where leadership is active in including their employees in decision making to solve issues related to the employees' roles. This process of consulting and engaging employees leads to increased respect and employee commitment. Fourth is independence, which occurs by giving employees the opportunity to be innovative and imaginative in their roles rather than just completing tasks in a prescribed way and a feeling of being micromanaged. Fifth and finally is increased visibility, which comes about by providing employees chances to learn and develop by sharing their ideas and successes as part of reward and recognition amongst their peers and superiors. These five dimensions can be deployed with little to no expense on the part of an operation yet will yield significant return in employee morale, engagement, and organizational commitment.

How Can Employers Address Low Organizational Commitment?

Increasing organizational commitment among employees can reduce turnover, but the various strategies and tactics that can be utilized will vary in required investment and skill that is needed to implement. That said, strategies for intervening should occur at both the level of the employee and the organization (Frone, 2018).

At the level of organizations, perhaps the most important thing during recessions is that management provide communication that is timely, clear, and honest regarding the impact of economic downturns on the organization and the viability of jobs (Cameron, Freeman, & Mishra, 1993; Probst, 2005).

This is particularly important during periods of general economic decline because concerns about reemployment (employment insecurity) become more salient and add to the stress of job insecurity.

At the employee level, interventions may involve cognitive reappraisal techniques to reframe perceptions of employee insecurity to make them less detrimental (Lazarus & Folkman, 1984). For example, stresses related to realized and unrealized financial losses may require addressing financial management during economic declines Alternatively, an employer may invest in the development of desired skills or attributes to reduce the effects of employee insecurity. Shoss, Jiang, and Probst (2018) reported that high levels of employee resilience attenuated the association between job insecurity and several negative outcomes (e.g., emotional exhaustion and interpersonal counterproductive work behaviors).

Even if the hotel management invests in skill development, though, research has established that hotel employees may not realize the full benefit of such. This can occur because of inadequate or poorly executed development opportunities. In addition, intrinsic injustices such as low salaries, excessive workloads and long or unusual working hours may reduce (or completely cancel) the intended positive outcome of skill development outcomes (Cheng & O-Yang, 2018).

This is not to imply that training and investment in employee skill development is unwise. Rather, while it suggests that training to increase employee resilience may reduce the negative impact of job insecurity it must be looked at as a component in a larger strategy as opposed to a stand-alone effort (Probst, 2005). Likewise, employer-sponsored training to enhance work skills may attenuate the association between employment insecurity and adverse outcomes. While research has demonstrated this to be the case, general limitations with how that research was conducted raise the need for additional insight in this area. When conducting the study, the mediating and outcome variables were all obtained from self-reports. Although it is typically assumed that common method variance (CMV) can inflate observed associations relative to the true population associations, CMV can lead to deflated associations as well (Conway & Lance, 2010; Siemsen, Roth, & Oliveira, 2010). One way to address this limitation in additional studies include ensuring that the design of the any studies incorporated several procedural remedies to minimize the likelihood of CMV (Podsakoff, MacKenzie, & Podsakoff, 2012) such as:

- Assuring the confidentiality of responses and having participants consent to interviews while keeping a participant's employer secret from the interviewer and not include that information during the data collection process
- Building rapport with participants to enhance honest reporting
- Select measures, data collection items and response scales to minimize the cognitive demands of the survey
- Separate measures across multiple questionnaires
- Enhance response consistency by participants by conducting data collection efforts where interviewer and participant are in the same physical space, as opposed to over the telephone where prior responses physically unavailable and less likely to be available in short-term memory (Frone, 2018).

CONCLUSION

While the hotel industry has faced multiple crises that impacted its business model and dynamics in the industry's centuries long existence, the COVID-19 pandemic caused an unprecedented crisis in the 21st century to all industries on a global scale. Some of the hardest hit industries included service-based industries such as travel, tourism and lodging, the latter of which has been noted to be extremely sensitive to external shocks such as an epidemic (or pandemic). Hospitality especially observed suffered a sharp drop in demand (Chang, McAleer, & Ramos, 2020). The hotel industry experienced dramatic sales losses as occupancy rates have largely dropped due to social distancing and the drastic decline in the number of tourists (Sobieralski, 2020). Nearly immediately, the global hotel industry responded with a significant reduction of the number of employees in had maintained. While other service-based industries like the airlines encouraged its employees to take early retirement or enacted furloughs, hospitality separated permanently from its employees. More than three years after the pandemic officially began in the United States, the hospitality employment sector was the last sector to recover all the position it lost at the start of the pandemic in February 2020 as tracked by the Bureau of Labor Statistics (BLS, 2023).

However, the COVID-19 pandemic was not the only catalyst for this labor dynamic, although the pandemic was a significant enough global event that it does overshadow other observed elements. It Disruption as a result of rapid technological changes has continued to impact modern working environments. In addition to disruption due to technology, global economic fluctuations, armed conflicts and political insecurity also contribute to a lack of employment stability for the hospitality industry (Etehadi & Karatepe, 2019). Organizational restructuring and scale-downs that took place in the first 15 years of the 21st century have increased employees' perceptions of job insecurity, which can be defined as the subjective and unconscious perception of job loss (Niesen, Hootegem, Handaja, Battistelli, & De Witte, 2018). However, COVID-19 has aggravated this situation beyond what had been observed previously.

Job insecurity can spread among employees for two specific reasons (Mauno, De Cuyper, Tolvanen, Kinnunen, & M¨akikangas, 2014). First, changes in an organization caused by quantitative job insecurity, resulting from formal involuntary separation actions such as layoffs, downsizing, and mergers, often affect certain groups within the organization. This includes those groups' perceptions of job insecurity, which impact the overall work culture. Second, employees can interpret external threats or stressors in a similar fashion, and this can occur on an individual level or as a collective unit by employees of different divisions or companies. The conclusion in this case is that the phenomenon of job insecurity often acts as a significant stressor for employees (Gaunt & Benjamin, 2007) and maintains a negative correlative relationship with other factors associated with job attitudes impacting the psychological well-being of employees (De Witte, Vander Elst, De Cuyper, 2015; Tian, Zhang, & Zhou, 2014).

Job security is a complex phenomenon that features many different dimensions that are encompassed by the term. Simply, though, job security is described as the degree of fear acknowledged by an employee losing their current role and becoming unemployed (De Witte, et. al., 2014). An employee's psychological well-being is directly influenced by the degree of job insecurity being recognized by an employee (Nella, Panagopoulou, Galanis, Montgomery, & Benos. 2015; Inoue, Kawakami, Eguchi, and Tsutsumi, 2018). Job security is inversely correlated to an individual employee's motivation to engage in assigned tasks. Job engagement can be defined as a positive and fulfilling state for employees (Schaufeli, Salanova, Gonzalez-Roma, & Bakker, 2002). Overall, the higher one's job engagement, the more positive that individual's mental state is as it relates to their time at work. Employees that display high levels of job engagement can be a particularly important variable in performance, because these employes impact the level of realized organizational effectiveness, contribute to sustaining a productive work environment, and ultimately reduce employee turnover (Caplan & Whittemore, 2013).

In other research it has been determined that employees who display characteristics associated with higher job insecurity were much more likely to also display reduced levels of engagement and to put forth significantly less effort to achieve organizational goals. This is because these employees will ultimately end up spending less time and energy to complete the tasks associated with their roles (Greenhalgh & Rosenblatt, 1984). Lo Presti and Nonnis further determined that as an employee perceives greater levels of job insecurity, that employee will simultaneously display decreased emotional commitment to the role, to the organization and to the outcomes associated with the role. It has been observed that an employee with elevated job insecurity will ultimately commit to work in a more inconsistent manner (2012). Additionally, job insecurity is significantly associated with both job performance and job engagement in an inverse correlative relationship (Wang, Lu, & Siu., 2015). An employee's decreased levels of job engagement is a direct result of an employee's declining job insecurity (Karatepe, Rezapouraghdam, & Hassannia, 2020). An employee's engagement is directly hindered by declining job insecurity (Shin & Hur, 2020) and the physical, psychological, and mental energy of employees are all negatively impacted by increasing levels of job security which results in a negative trajectory for individual health (Karatepe et. al., 2020). This all ultimately produces significantly decreased levels of engagement and work output.

Given that job insecurity is a risk factor that induces employees to engage in harmful behaviors through negative psychological responses (Chirumbolo, 2015), Jung, Jung and Yoon's 2021 study sought to empirically investigate the effects of job insecurity on individuals employed by a hotel during the COVID-19 pandemic. These roles are not ones that could be easily conducted via a virtual engagement as hotels do not offer a service that can be duplicated in a virtual space and hotel employees are a critical and irreplaceable component to providing customer service and satisfaction during a customer's stay on a property (Ayse & Alexander, 2018). Another factor (and not one limited to just the COVID years) is that it is more common for front-line hotel employees to change jobs when experiencing increased workloads and/or changes to the work environment and culture (Kim et al., 2015). A voluntary separation typically occurs when an employee's motivation to leave a job is higher than one's motivation to complete the tasks associated with the current role. Anxiety over job security can lower job satisfaction and that directly impacts motivation and voluntary separation (Akgunduz & Eryilmaz, 2018). While not unique to COVID, the pandemic certainly provided an environment to culture such dynamics significantly.

As such, a generational cohort's response to specific workplace stimuli as it relates to perceived job insecurity is often found to be a combination of global generational experiences as well as one's primary experiences at their own workplace. According to the theory of cohorts, common values and opinions are formed and sustained among people in a group or cohort that is experiencing specifically similar events within a similar timeframe and, through homogeneity of experiences, develop similar emotional responses and perspectives associated with their experiences (Ryder, 1965). This can be observed both among workers at a company as well as on a more global scale among those in similar age ranges. When members of a generational cohort enter and complete school, enter job markets, and then retire at similar ages after living through similar global or national experiences at similar developmental stages, the collective response among people is often very similar (Kowske, Rasch, & Wiley, 2010). When this occurs, a generational cohort is often regarded as having similar tendencies in how it perceives and interprets historical events, daily engagements and expectations around work needs based on those various developmental stages (Duncan & Agronick, 1995).

For organizations to effectively manage its employees where generational spread exists in the workforce, it is important for leaders to understand that common values and opinions are formed among those who compose each generation (Ryder, 1965). Managing these various perspectives requires organizations and its leaders to better comprehend the diverse array of expectations, perceptions and behavioral characteristics associated with each generational cohort represented by the workforce (Kong, Wang, & Fu, 2015). Much exploration and discovery has been conducted during recent years in this area for hotel properties in Asia. For example, many hotel properties offering deluxe accommodations in Korea will often employ workers who fit age-wise into both Generations X (born between 1965 and 1980) and Generation Y (born between 1980 and 2000) (Eyoun, Chen, Ayoun, & Khliefat, 2020). This mixture of perspectives in the workplace requires that leaders understand the characteristics of these two generations in order to utilize cohort specific aspects to enhance productivity, morale and employee retention (Gursoy, Maier, & Chi., 2008). During the disruption in employment catalyzed by the COVID-19 Pandemic, Generation Y demonstrated a significantly higher level in job insecurity than what was observed in Generation X employees. The gaps in performance between the employees of different ages further illustrated that the negative impact of job insecurity was higher in Generation Y (Jung et. al., 2021).

There have been many studies dedicated to better understanding the impact of generational characteristics on job performance and job security. Much focus has been dedicated to the analysis of how job-related factors influenced and impacted one another, with work-related preferences, values, and attitudes inside of an organizational framework being of specific interest. These were all identified as variables of significance in better predicting employee responses to disruptive stimuli (Schuman & Scott, 1989; Park & Gursoy, 2012; Goh & Jie, 2019). The challenges of managing across multiple audiences with a vast array of differing needs is one that is readily observed in the hospitality industry as research has documented the significant gaps between generations working in organizations to be increasing as global populations remain in the workforce for longer period of their life (Cohen, 2002; Eisner, 2005; and Gursoy et al., 2008).

In reviewing generalized characteristics of these cohorts, literature has determined that those in Generation X have come of age as a part of a culture that values individualism and the pursuit of associated individual professional goals, materialistic acquisitions, competitive agendas, and valuing efficiencies in life as well as ample opportunities for professional growth (Zemke, Raines, & Filipczak, 2000). Conversely, those born into Generation Y experienced significant differences as they aged. Generation Y found itself as a culture valuing globalization and empiricism as well as transparency in communication and ethical conduct for collective benefit. However, Generation Y also values autonomy in its work and pursuing goals associated with self-actualization that often have little to do with professional commitments – in many cases they may be at odds with expectations around traditional professional activities designed to gain experience in a career. Generation Y has also been observed to maintain a strong level of self-centeredness with relatively high self-expression (Park & Gursoy, 2012). As an extension of this perspective, Generation Y was also found to focus its professional priorities on the environment surrounding a job and maintaining the expectation for self-expression and self-actualization to continue in a working environment (Chen & Choi, 2008). The threshold to voluntarily separate from an organization appears to be much lower for Generation Y because of this paradigm (Hurst & Good, 2009). Given that employees of Generation Y (and subsequent generations, who are increasingly exhibiting similar tendences with more extreme manifestations) will be the main resource of the hotel labor market in the future, a realignment of expectations for employees derived from systemic policies are needed to ensure that generational gaps do not derail management's attempts to engage its workforce and reduce turnover. Research has discovered that Generation Y demonstrates much more reduced levels of engagement than its predecessors once job insecurity begins to increase (Jung et. al., 2021). As such, there is empirical evidence to support the proactive engineering of a work environment where job insecurity is proactively minimized or extinguished.

As job insecurity increases, an employee's willingness to engage in the tasks associated with finding a new job also increases (Ashford, Lee, & Bobko., 1989.). The connective causative tissue between increasing employee turnover and increasing job security is well established (Arnold &Feldman, 1982) and the effects on an organization of individual job insecurity are significantly elevated when workers are faced with stress related to the future availability of their job (Staufenbiel & Konig, 2010). Ultimately, employee turnover intent is nearly consistently positively correlated with rising job insecurity, which is in turn nearly consistently positively correlated with rising stress. Reducing employee stress as it directly or indirectly relates to job insecurity is a first, critical step in leadership being able to successfully manage the workforce environment (Stiglbauer, Selenko, Batinic, & Jodlbauer., 2012).

When leadership addresses the reduction of turnover intent as a function of reducing job insecurity, the results are significant and often positive in nature (Mauno et. al., 2013). The employee's perception that his or her employer values not just his skills but his presence as an individual is one of the most powerful tools associated with reducing stress, job insecurity and turnover intent. However, while powerful, this perception of value is difficult to establish and even more challenging to sustain (Lee & Jeong, 2017). The challenge is worth the investment, however, as talent retention for effective and knowledgeable employees is a primary technique utilized to reduce expenses, especially in service-based companies like those in the hospitality sector (Akgunduz & Eryilmaz, 2018). This occurs because reduced job insecurity results in increased levels of confidence from employees to fulfill their basic needs establishing the perception of work and life balance (Urbanaviciute, Lazauskaite-Zabielske, Elst, De Witte., 2018). For example, if employees enjoy flexible scheduling that allows them to satisfy personal commitments, and an employee feels valued and respected at work, the desire to arrive late or leave early quickly evaporates (Karatepe et al., 2020).

While the levels of intent to separate voluntarily, or turnover intent, that are measured in an organization is an indicator of cultural deficiencies, there are other conclusions that can be derived from this information. The information can also be used in a predictive manner to better understand how employee perceptions of organizationally driven changes in job roles will be internalized and actualized (Brown & Peterson, 1993). With this ability, turnover intent can always be defined as the level of intent displayed by members of an organization where the intended outcome of abandoning their roles by quitting their current jobs (Meyer & Allen, 1984). In addition, there is a demonstrated positive causative relationship that exists between turnover intent and actual turnover rate where turnover intent can be acknowledged and utilized as a predictive factor for upcoming anticipated voluntary separation (Cotton & Tuttle, 1986), and turnover intent can thus be understood as a significant precursor to the actual rate of voluntary turnover (Cotton & Tuttle, 1996). The negative effect of voluntary turnover has been frequently discussed in the hospitality industry in terms of maintaining a competent workforce (Kim, Lee, & Carson, 2010), and employees' turnover intent can cause serious damage to an organization unless the organization takes preventive measures (S'ahin, 2011).

As established, the higher the positive engagement level for employees the lower the turnover intent and the lower levels of involuntary separation are observed by an organization. Within this model, positive employee engagement emerges as the most influential psychological variable in reducing the voluntary separation of employees (Jones & Harter, 2005; Rafiq, Wu, Chin, & Nassir, 2019; Shin & Jeung, 2019). Within this context, the individual and collective behaviors of employees are the most critical elements to an organization's success (Hughes & Rog, 2008), reinforcing the importance of investment in the workplace environment. Employees who are actively, enthusiastically, and positively engaged with their job and with their organization are found to have relatively low intent to leave their current organizations although this is a fluid status that becomes modified based upon direct interactions and indirect stimuli encountered by an employee. That said, there is empirical evidence in the literature that demonstrates that engagement with one's role and employer is sufficiently and closely related to reducing employee turnover intent (Erdil & Müceldili, 2014; Sibiya, Buitendach, Kanengoni, & Bobat, 2014).

The literature is clear – increasing engagement reduces turnover intent, but the practical challenge remains how this can be implemented and sustained effectively. Timms, Brough,, O'Driscoll, Kalliath, Siu, Sit, and Lo. (2015) posits that job engagement to reduce the turnover intent of employees can be engineered through small incremental changes in the work culture while Lu, Lu, Gursoy, & Neale (2016) determined that these changes include the employee having an opportunity to contribute to the success of the division or the organization which will ultimately increase personal satisfaction and thereby reduce turnover intent, even if additional hardships are experienced in one's personal or professional existence. Employee engagement can manifest in the form of satisfaction surveys, suggestion boxes or collaborative projects that are identified, selected, and developed with employee involvement (Casey & Sieber, 2016). Doing so is a key component of organizational sustainability. For example, a front desk team may collaboratively identify methods to objectively measure the quality of service offered and then further determine opportunities to enhance and enrich the daily work on the job. By aligning organizational goals with an employee's engagement on a personal level, the overall levels of turnover intent will be reduced (Babakus, Yavas, & Karatape, 2017).

Correlative relationships are important, but job insecurity, job engagement and turnover intent have also demonstrated an organic causal relationship that establishes a foundational model of theory to develop a deeper understanding how these factors associate with employees facing psychological responses to the workplace resulting in increased or decreased levels of job insecurity (Jung et al., 2021). This was evident during the COVID-19 pandemic as were two related and important practical implications for job insecurity: Perceptions of job insecurity and work environments engineered to minimize the impact of employees' insecurity.

The first implication ascertained that employees-maintained perceptions of job insecurity and that those perceptions significantly influenced both their degrees of engagement and desire to voluntarily separate. For employers, the practical application of this concept indicates that a working environment perceived as stable for employees over the long term and values their contributions is the ideal goal. Presenting employees with such a working environment will result in an increase in employee engagement and prevent the loss of a superior workforce (Jung et. al., 2021). As has been noted by many throughout this meta-analysis, the levels of job insecurity within the hospitality sector are significantly higher than in other sectors. This is caused by employees having to work long hours and the significant seasonality in business patterns often experienced by the entire industry. The sector is also sensitive to external factors, so events such as economic fluctuations or the COVID-19 pandemic have also served to heighten the level of job insecurity in the sector. This just reinforces that there are opportunities for leaders in the hospitality industry to positively influence the working environment through workers, but effective strategies will extend beyond standard compensation and benefit packages.

The second implication establishes that it's critically important for leaders to create and sustain working environments where employees can safely and enjoyably perform duties expected of their roles without experiencing anxiety about their employment status, remain safe while completing their tasks and become empowered on establishing future directional strategies for work. In addition, an ideal the working environment should allow leaders and employers to collaboratively establish autonomous and horizontally aligned organizational structures that encourage the expression of open thought, critical evaluation of current processes and identify areas of opportunity through mutual communication and respect (Jung et. al., 2021). The role of leadership in this environment is to engineer a culture that supports interconnectivity and transparency among all employees, regardless of role. This will help to ensure that intrinsic and extrinsic threats to the workplace are identified and satisfactorily addressed. This approach will ensure that employees do not begin to feel that leadership is disinterested or avoiding issues important to the workforce and is misaligned with their collective interests and need (Timms et al., 2015).

In the journey to reduce job insecurity for employees, leadership in the hospitality sector can take measures to encourage full team participation in a transparent decision-making process. Empowerment, where employees make decisions about the scope of their role or how their own jobs are conducted, is a challenging framework to implement and to sustain. It is a critical element of developing true engagement as a component of organizational culture. Through employee participation in the decision-making process, leaders will be able to truly share with employees the challenges that are facing an organization while encouraging ideas and perspectives that may otherwise be overlooked (Hurst & Good, 2009). There is little doubt that this will result in a better quality of decision to be made while enriching engagement among non-management employees. From the perspective of an organizational development framework, this open practice of engagement has been observed to enhance the transfer of information from prior eras of work into future ones. This can manifest itself through establishing effective internal record keeping for key workflows and product design, creating legacy projects and celebrations, and establishing formal mentoring opportunities that encourage personal development and professional growth. The oft observed result of such strategies are improved ways of increasing employee confidence and engagement while reducing negative emotions that support voluntary separation activities (Jung et al., 2021).

These discussed components are clearly much more advanced benefits than standard packages such as an annual vacation allowance or unpaid leave for medical reasons, benefits that only focus on tangible compensatory elements. Such compensatory benefits are so common across industries that they can no longer be considered meaningful or effective solutions for addressing the complex challenges facing workforce cultures in the 21st century hospitality industry (Jung et. al., 2021).

The best solution is for organizations to commit to providing offerings beyond standard components via custom and targeted employee investment strategies. Some examples of possible additive elements to an employee investment strategy could include a job-rotation system, unlimited paid time away from the office or onsite benefits such as cafeterias, exercise facilities or child-care options. Some employers may find that a critical need of their employees falls into transportation matters. Support through paid public transportation passes for those who may not have the means to travel from the workplace to home or to other locations where an employee maintains a commitment (such as a child's school or the grocery store) could be a critical strategy to reduce job insecurity. Such a custom evaluation of needs truly requires a willingness from both employees and managers to openly collaborate on what is needed and what types of resolution strategies are reasonable and sustainable (Jung et al., 2021).

Much valuable insight can be inferred from Jung et. al.'s work in 2021, including understanding the limitations associated with the study. Additional research beyond the South Korean market is needed to validate the developed model and the scope of employee age should be widened as well. In the study, there was not an equal sampling of Generation X and Generation Y employees which may skew the significance of generational characteristics in developing part or all of the model. Ultimately, Generation Y perceived job insecurity more seriously because its negative impact is relatively high for them, and they have fewer contextual references within to evaluate various stimuli associated with driving it. Generation Y are perceived to value job satisfaction over job insecurity as they focus on a challenging life in the 21st century which, in less than a quarter of its span, has witnessed domestic terrorist attacks, multiple wars, economic recession, perceived loss of constitutional freedoms and deadly viral outbreaks (Mohapatra, Saxena, Joshi, & Chaturvedi, 2017).

Of additional note is that the Jung et al 2001 study was cross-sectional meaning that the results cannot be accurately extrapolated over time increasing the need for additional longitudinal and comparative studies at different cultural levels to be conducted. The degree to which the COVID-19 pandemic influenced the outcomes of the study, or the uniqueness of the data because of the pandemic, are challenging to predict without additional analysis and exploration once more distance from the event has been realized.

REFERENCES

Aaron, C. (1999). Relationship among five forms of commitment: An empirical assessment. *Journal of Academy of Management Journal.*, *20*(3), 397–409.

Akgunduz, Y., & Eryilmaz, G. (2018). Does turnover intention mediate the effects of job insecurity and co-worker support on social loafing? *International Journal of Hospitality Management*, *68*, 41–49. doi:10.1016/j.ijhm.2017.09.010

Akorede, S. (2018). *Three things to learn from Google's workplace culture*. Retrieved from https://www.entrepreneur.com/article/317582

Akova, O., Cetin, G., & Cifci, I. (2015). The relation between demographic factors and the turnover intention in pre-opening hotel businesses. *Procedia: Social and Behavioral Sciences*, *207*, 377–384. doi:10.1016/j.sbspro.2015.10.177

Arnold, H. J., & Feldman, D. C. (1982). A multivariate analysis of the determinants of job turnover. *The Journal of Applied Psychology*, *67*(3), 350–360. doi:10.1037/0021-9010.67.3.350

Ashford, S. J., Lee, C., & Bobko, P. (1989). Content, causes, and consequences of job insecurity: A theory-based measure and substantive test. *The Academy of Management Annals*, *32*(4), 803–829.

Ayse, B. E., & Alexander, E. E. (2018). Alleviating job stress to improve service employee work affect: The influence of rewarding. *Service Business*, *12*(1), 121–141. doi:10.100711628-017-0340-y

Babakus, E., Yavas, U., & Karatepe, O. M. (2017). Work engagement and turnover intentions: Correlates and customer orientation as a moderator. *International Journal of Contemporary Hospitality Management*, *29*(6), 1580–1598. doi:10.1108/IJCHM-11-2015-0649

Bajrami, D. D., Terzic, A., Petrovic, M., Radovanovic, M., Tretiakova, T., & Hadoud, A. (2021). Will we have the same employees in hospitality after all? The impact of COVID-19 on employees' work attitudes and turnover intentions. *International Journal of Hospitality Management*, 94. PMID:34785836

Becker, W. J., & Cropanzano, R. (2015). Good acting requires a good cast: A meso-level model of deep acting in work teams. *Journal of Organizational Behavior*, *36*(2), 232–249. doi:10.1002/job.1978

Bennett, H., & Durkin, M. (2000). The effect of organizational change on employee psychological attachment: An exploratory study. *Journal of Managerial Psychology*, *15*(2), 126–147. doi:10.1108/02683940010310328

Billing, T. K., Bhagat, R., Babakus, E., Srivastava, B., Shin, M., & Brew, F. (2014). Work–family conflict in four national contexts: A closer look at the role of individualism–collectivism. *International Journal of Cross Cultural Management*, *14*(2), 139–159. doi:10.1177/1470595813502780

Brown, J. (2019). *Employee orientation: Keeping new employees on board.* Retrieved from https://www.thebalancecareers.com/employee-orientation-keeping-new-employees-on-board-1919035

Brown, S. P., & Peterson, P. A. (1993). Antecedents and consequences of salesperson job satisfaction: Meta-analysis and assessment of causal effects. *JMR, Journal of Marketing Research*, *30*(1), 63–77. doi:10.1177/002224379303000106

Buick, I., & Thomas, M. (2001). Why do middle managers in hotels burn out? *International Journal of Contemporary Hospitality Management*, *13*(6), 304–309. doi:10.1108/EUM0000000005968

Caldwell, S. D., Herold, D. M., & Fedor, D. B. (2004). Towards an understanding of the relationships between organizational change, individual differences, and changes in person-environment fit: Across-level study. *The Journal of Applied Psychology*, *89*(5), 868–882. doi:10.1037/0021-9010.89.5.868 PMID:15506866

Cameron, K. S., Freeman, S. J., & Mishra, A. K. (1993). Downsizing and redesigning organizations. In G. P. Huber & W. H. Glick (Eds.), *Organizational change and redesign* (pp. 19–65). Oxford University Press. doi:10.1093/oso/9780195072853.003.0002

Caplan, S., & Whittemore, R. (2013). Barriers to treatment engagement for depression among Latinas. *Issues in Mental Health Nursing*, *34*(6), 412–424. doi:10.3109/01612840.2012.762958 PMID:23805926

Casey, D., & Sieber, S. (2016). Employees, sustainability and motivation: Increasing employee engagement by addressing sustainability and corporate social responsibility. *Research in Hospitality Management*, *6*(1), 69–76. doi:10.2989/RHM.2016.6.1.9.1297

Chang, C. L., McAleer, M., & Ramos, V. (2020). A charter for sustainable tourism after COVID-19. *Sustainability (Basel)*, *12*(3671), 1–4. doi:10.3390u12093671

Chartered Institute of Personnel and Development. (2007a). *Trade Unions: a short history. Chartered Institute of Personnel and Development*. Retrieved February 4, 2022, from https://www.cipd.co.uk/subjects/empreltns/tradunin/tradunihist.htm?IsSrchRes=1

Chartered Institute of Personnel and Development. (2007b). Work–life balance: Who benefits? *Chartered Institute of Personnel and Development*. Retrieved February 4, 2022, from https://www.cipd.co.uk/subjects/wrkgtime/wrktmewrklfbal/worklifeba.htm?IsSrchRes=1

Chen, H., Ayoun, B., & Eyoun, K. (2018). Work-family conflict and turnover intentions: A study comparing China and U.S. hotel employees. *Journal of Human Resources in Hospitality & Tourism*, *17*(2), 247–269. doi:10.1080/15332845.2017.1406272

Chen, P. J., & Choi, Y. (2008). Generational differences in work values: A study of hospitality management. *International Journal of Contemporary Hospitality Management*, *20*(6), 595–615. doi:10.1108/09596110810892182

Cheng, J. C., & O-Yang, Y. (2018). Hotel employee job crafting, burnout, and satisfaction: The moderating role of perceived organizational support. *International Journal of Hospitality Management*, *72*, 78–85. doi:10.1016/j.ijhm.2018.01.005

Chirumbolo, A., & Areni, A. (2010). Job insecurity influence on job performance and mental health: Testing the moderating effect of the need for closure. *Economic and Industrial Democracy*, *31*(2), 195–214. doi:10.1177/0143831X09358368

Choi, H. M., Mohammad, A. A. A., & Kim, W. G. (2019). Understanding hotel frontline employees' emotional intelligence, emotional labor, job stress, coping strategies and burnout. *International Journal of Hospitality Management*, *82*, 199–208. doi:10.1016/j.ijhm.2019.05.002

Choi, Y. G., Kwon, J., & Kim, W. (2013). Effects of attitudes vs experience of workplace fun on employee behaviors: Focused on Generation Y in the hospitality industry. *International Journal of Contemporary Hospitality Management*, *25*(3), 410–427. doi:10.1108/09596111311311044

Cimbaljević, M., Nedeljković-Knežević, M., Demirović-Bajrami, D., Dunjić, M., El Bilali, H., & Rančić-DemirDemir, M. (2020). How do job-related constructs determine employee turnover? Serbian hotels example. *Journal of the Geographical Institute "Jovan Cvijic"*, *70*(2), 129–143.

Coch, L., & French, J. R. P. Jr. (1948). Overcoming Resistance to Change. *Human Relations*, *1*(4), 512–532. doi:10.1177/001872674800100408

Cohen, J. (2002). I/Os in the know offer insights on generation X workers. *Monitor on Psychology*, *33*(2), 66–67.

Conway, J. M., & Lance, C. E. (2010). What reviewers should expect from authors regarding common method bias in organizational research. *Journal of Business and Psychology*, *25*(3), 325–334. doi:10.100710869-010-9181-6

Cotton, J. L., & Tuttle, J. M. (1986). Employee turnover: A meta-analysis and review with implications for research. *Academy of Management Review*, *11*(1), 55–70. doi:10.2307/258331

Daft, R. L. (2005). Types of Planned Change. In R. L. Draft (Ed.), *Management* (6th ed., p. 387). Thomas South Western.

Dalal, R. S. (2005). A meta-analysis of the relationship between organizational citizenship behavior and counterproductive work behavior. *The Journal of Applied Psychology*, *90*(6), 1241–1255. doi:10.1037/0021-9010.90.6.1241 PMID:16316277

Davies, W. (2020, March 24). The last global crisis didn't change the world. But this one could. *The Guardian*. https://www.theguardian.com/commentisfree/2020/mar/24/coronavirus-crisischange-world-financial-global-capitalism

De Clercq, D., Azeem, M. U., Haq, I. U., & Bouckenooghe, D. (2020). The stress-reducing effect of coworker support on turnover intentions: Moderation by political ineptness and despotic leadership. *Journal of Business Research*, *111*, 12–24. doi:10.1016/j.jbusres.2020.01.064

De Witte, H., Vander Elst, T., & De Cuyper, N. (2015). Job insecurity, health and well-being. In J. Vuori, R. Blonk, & R. Price (Eds.), *Sustainable Working Lives. Aligning Perspectives on Health, Safety and Well-Being* (pp. 109–128). Springer.

Degoey, P. (2000). Contagious justice: Exploring the social construction of justice in organization. In B. M. Staw & R. I. Sutton (Eds.), Research in Organizational Behavior. JAI Press. doi:10.1016/S0191-3085(00)22003-0

Duncan, L. E., & Agronick, G. S. (1995). The intersection of life stage and social events: Personality and life outcomes. *Journal of Personality and Social Psychology*, *69*(3), 558–568. doi:10.1037/0022-3514.69.3.558 PMID:7562395

Duxbury, L., Higgins, C., & Lee, C. (1994). Work-Family Conflict: A Comparison by Gender, Family Type, and Perceived Control. *Journal of Family Issues*, *15*(3), 449–466. doi:10.1177/019251394015003006

Dysvik, A., & Kuvaas, B. (2010). Exploring the relative and combined influence of mastery approach goals and work intrinsic motivation on employee turnover intention. *Personnel Review*, *39*(5), 622–638. doi:10.1108/00483481011064172

Eisner, S. P. (2005). Managing generation Y. *S.A.M. Advanced Management Journal*, *70*(4), 4–15.

Elshaer, I. A., & Saad, S. K. (2016). Political instability and tourism in Egypt: Exploring survivors' attitudes after downsizing. *Journal of Policy Research Tourism Events.*, *9*(1), 3–22.

Employers and work–life balance. (2008). Work–Life Balance: Introduction. Employers for Work–Life Balance. *The Workfoundation*. Retrieved February 4, 2022, from http://www.employersforwork–lifebalance.org.uk/work/definition.htm

Erdil, O., & Müceldili, B. (2014). The effects of envy on job engagement and turnover intention. *Procedia: Social and Behavioral Sciences*, *150*, 447–454. doi:10.1016/j.sbspro.2014.09.050

Etehadi, B., & Karatepe, O. M. (2019). The impact of job insecurity on critical hotel employee outcomes: The mediating role of self-efficacy. *Journal of Hospitality Marketing & Management*, *28*(6), 665–689. doi:10.1080/19368623.2019.1556768

Evans, A., & Vernon, K. (2007). Work–Life Balance in Hong Kong: Case Studies. *Community Business.*

Eyoun, K., Chen, H., Ayoun, B., & Khliefat, A. (2020). The relationship between purpose of performance appraisal and psychological contract: Generational differences as a moderator. *International Journal of Hospitality Management*, *86*, 1–8. doi:10.1016/j.ijhm.2020.102449

Fedor, D. B., Caldwell, S., & Herold, D. M. (2006). The effects of organizational changes on employee commitment: A multilevel investigation. *Personnel Psychology*, *59*(1), 1–29. doi:10.1111/j.1744-6570.2006.00852.x

Folkman, S. (1984). Personal control and stress and coping processes: A theoretical analysis. *Journal of Personality and Social Psychology*, *46*(4), 839–852. doi:10.1037/0022-3514.46.4.839 PMID:6737195

Ford, R. C., McLaughlin, F. S., & Newstrom, J. W. (2005). Creating and sustaining fun work environments in hospitality and service organizations. *Journal of Human Resources in Hospitality & Tourism*, *4*(1), 11–30. doi:10.1300/J171v04n01_02

Frone, M. R. (2018). What happened to the employed during the Great Recession? A U.S. population study of net change in employee insecurity, health, and organizational commitment. *Journal of Vocational Behavior*, *107*, 246–260. doi:10.1016/j.jvb.2018.05.001 PMID:31303656

Gaunt, R., & Benjamin, O. (2007). Job insecurity, stress and gender. *Community Work & Family*, *10*(3), 341–355. doi:10.1080/13668800701456336

Goh, E., & Jie, F. (2019). To waste or not to waste: Exploring motivational factors of generation Z hospitality employees towards food wastage in the hospitality industry. *International Journal of Hospitality Management*, *80*, 126–135. doi:10.1016/j.ijhm.2019.02.005

Grandey, A. A., & Cropanzano, R. (1999). The conservation of resource model applied to work-family conflict and strain. *Journal of Vocational Behavior*, *54*(2), 350–370. doi:10.1006/jvbe.1998.1666

Greenhalgh, L., & Rosenblatt, Z. (1984). Job insecurity: Toward conceptual clarity. *Academy of Management Review*, *9*(3), 438–448. doi:10.2307/258284

Greenhaus, J. H., & Beutell, N. J. (1985). Sources of conflict between work and family roles. *Academy of Management Review*, *10*(1), 76–88. doi:10.2307/258214

Gursoy, D., Maier, T. A., & Chi, C. G. (2008). Generational differences: An examination of work values and generational gaps in the hospitality workforce. *International Journal of Hospitality Management*, *27*(3), 448–458. doi:10.1016/j.ijhm.2007.11.002

Gutek, B. A., Searle, S., & Klepa, L. (1991). Rational versus gender role expectations for work–family conflict. *The Journal of Applied Psychology*, *76*(4), 560–568. doi:10.1037/0021-9010.76.4.560

Hammer, L. B., Neal, M. B., Newsom, J. T., Brockwood, K. J., & Colton, C. L. (2005). A longitudinal study of the effects of dual-earner couples' utilization of family friendly workplace supports on work and family outcomes. *The Journal of Applied Psychology*, *90*(4), 799–810. doi:10.1037/0021-9010.90.4.799 PMID:16060797

Han, H., & Hyun, S. S. (2019). Green indoor and outdoor environment as nature-based solution and its role in increasing customer/employee mental health, well-being, and loyalty. *Business Strategy and the Environment*, *28*(4), 629–641. doi:10.1002/bse.2269

Han, H., Wei, Q., Al-Ansi, A., Chung, H., Ngah, A. H., Ariza-Montes, A., & Vega-Muñoz, A. (2020). A theoretical framework development for hotel employee turnover: Linking trust in supports, emotional exhaustion, depersonalization, and reduced personal accomplishment at workplace. *Sustainability (Basel)*, *12*(8065), 1–13. doi:10.3390u12198065

Hill, N., Seo, M. G., Kang, J., & Taylor, M. (2012). Building employee commitment to change across organizational levels: The influence of hierarchical distance and direct managers' transformational leadership. *Organization Science*, *23*(3), 758–777. doi:10.1287/orsc.1110.0662

Hinkin, T. R., & Tracey, J. B. (2010). What makes it so great? An analysis of human resources practices among Fortune's best companies to work for. *Cornell Hospitality Quarterly*, *51*(2), 158–170. doi:10.1177/1938965510362487

HKIHRM. (2007a). Hong Kong reports the highest staff turnover in Asia. Hong Kong Institute of Human Resource Management.

HKIHRM. (2007b). Job vacancy and employee turnover rates stayed high in 2006. Hong Kong Institute of Human Resource Management.

Hofstede, G. (1984). The cultural relativity of the quality of life concept. *Academy of Management Review*, *9*(3), 389–398. doi:10.2307/258280

Hofstede, G., & Bond, M. H. (1984). Hofstede's culture dimensions: An independent validation using Rokeach's value survey. *Journal of Cross-Cultural Psychology*, *15*(4), 417–433. doi:10.1177/0022002184015004003

Hsieh, Y. C., Pearson, T., Chang, H. C., & Uen, J. F. (2004). Spillover between work and personal life for lodging manager. *Journal of Human Resources in Hospitality & Tourism*, *3*(2), 61–83. doi:10.1300/J171v03n02_03

Hughes, J. C., & Rog, E. (2008). Talent management: A strategy for improving employee recruitment, retention and engagement within hospitality organizations. *International Journal of Contemporary Hospitality Management*, *20*(7), 743–757. doi:10.1108/09596110810899086

Hui, C., & Lee, C. (2000). Moderating effects of organizational-based self-esteem on organization uncertainty: Employee response relationships. *Journal of Management*, *26*(2), 215–232. doi:10.1177/014920630002600203

Hurst, J. L., & Good, L. K. (2009). Generation Y and career choice: The impact of retail career perceptions, expectations and entitlement perceptions. *Career Development International*, *14*(6), 570–593. doi:10.1108/13620430910997303

Hwang, K. K. (1987). Face and favor: The Chinese power game. *American Journal of Sociology*, *92*(4), 944–974. doi:10.1086/228588

Inoue, A., Kawakami, N., Eguchi, H., & Tsutsumi, A. (2018). Interaction effect of job insecurity and role ambiguity on psychological distress in Japanese employees: A cross-sectional study. *International Archives of Occupational and Environmental Health*, *91*(4), 391–402. doi:10.100700420-018-1288-5 PMID:29327214

Ito, J. K., & Brotheridge, C. M. (2007). Exploring the predictors and consequences of job insecurity's components. *Journal of Managerial Psychology*, *22*(1), 40–64. doi:10.1108/02683940710721938

Iverson, R. (1996). Employee acceptance of organizational change: The role of organizational commitment. *International Journal of Human Resource Management*, *7*(1), 122–128. doi:10.1080/09585199600000121

Jahoda, M. (1982). *Employment and unemployment*. University Press.

Jeaheng, Y., Al-Ansi, A., & Han, H. (2019). Halal-friendly hotels: Impact of halal-friendly attributes on guest purchase behaviors in the Thailand hotel industry. *Journal of Travel & Tourism Marketing*, *36*(6), 729–746. doi:10.1080/10548408.2019.1631940

Jones, D. A., & Skarlicki, D. P. (2013). How perceptions of fairness can change: A dynamic model of organizational justice. *Organizational Psychology Review*, *3*(2), 138–160. doi:10.1177/2041386612461665

Jones, J. R., & Harter, J. K. (2005). Race effects on the employee engagement: Turnover intention relationship. *Journal of Leadership & Organizational Studies*, *11*(2), 78–88. doi:10.1177/107179190501100208

Judge, T. A., Thoresen, C. J., Pucik, V., & Welbourne, T. M. (1999). Managerial coping with organizational change: A dispositional perspective. *The Journal of Applied Psychology*, *84*(1), 107–122. doi:10.1037/0021-9010.84.1.107 PMID:17227155

Jung, H. S., Jung, Y. S., & Yoon, H. H. (2021). COVID-19: The effects of job insecurity on the job engagement and turnover intent of deluxe hotel employees and the moderating role of generational characteristics. *International Journal of Hospitality Management*, *92*, 92. doi:10.1016/j.ijhm.2020.102703 PMID:33041428

Karatepe, O. M., Rezapouraghdam, H., & Hassannia, R. (2020). Job insecurity, work engagement and their effects on hotel employees' non-green and nonattendance behaviors. *International Journal of Hospitality Management*, *87*(May), 1–12. doi:10.1016/j.ijhm.2020.102472

Karatepe, O. M., & Uludag, O. (2008). Role stress, burnout and their effects on frontline hotel employees' job performance: Evidence from Northern Cyprus. *International Journal of Tourism Research*, *10*(2), 111–126. doi:10.1002/jtr.645

Karl, K., Peluchette, J., Hall-Indiana, L., & Harland, L. (2005). Attitudes toward workplace fun: A three-sector comparison. *Journal of Leadership & Organizational Studies*, *12*(2), 1–17. doi:10.1177/107179190501200201

Kim, B. C., Lee, G., & Carlson, K. D. (2010). An examination of the nature of the relationship between leader-member-exchange (LMX) and turnover intent at different organizational levels. *International Journal of Hospitality Management*, *29*(4), 591–597. doi:10.1016/j.ijhm.2009.10.025

Kim, J. (2015). What increases public employees' turnover intention? *Public Personnel Management*, *44*(4), 496–519. doi:10.1177/0091026015604447

Kim, J. (2018). The contrary effects of intrinsic and extrinsic motivation on burnout and turnover intention in the public sector. *International Journal of Manpower*, *39*(3), 486–500. doi:10.1108/IJM-03-2017-0053

Kim, J. J., Lee, Y., & Han, H. (2019). Exploring competitive hotel selection attributes among guests: An importance of performance analysis. *Journal of Travel & Tourism Marketing*, *36*(9), 998–1011. doi:10.1080/10548408.2019.1683484

Kim, S. S., Kim, J., & Hwang, J. (2015). The effects of mentoring on role stress, job attitude, and turnover intention in the hotel industry. *International Journal of Hospitality Management*, *48*, 68–82. doi:10.1016/j.ijhm.2015.04.006

Kipkebut, D. J. (2013). The effects of demographic characteristics on organizational commitment, job satisfaction and turnover intentions: The case of employees in Kenyan universities. *Journal of Organizational Human Behavior*, *2*(1), 20–33.

Kong, H., Wang, S., & Fu, X. (2015). Meeting career expectations: Can it enhance job satisfaction of generation Y? *International Journal of Contemporary Hospitality Management*, *27*(1), 147–168. doi:10.1108/IJCHM-08-2013-0353

Korsgaard, M. A., Schweiger, D. M., & Sapienza, H. U. (1995). Building commitment, attachment, and trust in top management teams: The role of procedural justice. *Academy of Management Journal*, *3*(8), 60–84. doi:10.2307/256728

Kotter, J., & Schelsinger, A. A. (1979). Choosing strategies for change. *Harvard Business Review*, *57*(2), 102–121. PMID:10240501

Kowske, B. J., Rasch, R., & Wiley, J. (2010). Millennials' (lack of) attitude problem: An empirical examination of generational effects on work attitudes. *Journal of Business and Psychology*, *25*(2), 265–279. doi:10.100710869-010-9171-8

Lamsa, A. M., & Savolainem, T. (2000). The nature of managerial commitment to strategic change. *Leadership and Organization Development Journal, 21*(6), 297–306. doi:10.1108/01437730010372822

Lazarus, R. S., & Folkman, S. (1984). *Stress, Appraisal, and Coping*. Springer Publishing Company.

Lee, A. V., Vargo, J., & Seville, E. (2013). Developing a tool to measure and compare organizations' resilience. *Natural Hazards Review, 14*(1), 29–41. doi:10.1061/(ASCE)NH.1527-6996.0000075

Lee, S., & Jeong, D. (2017). Job insecurity and turnover intention: Organizational commitment as mediator. *Social Behavior and Personality, 45*(4), 529–536. doi:10.2224bp.5865

Leiter, M. P., & Meechan, K. A. (1986). Role Structure and Burnout in the Field of Human Services. *The Journal of Applied Behavioral Science, 22*(1), 47–52. doi:10.1177/002188638602200107 PMID:10276302

Limpanitgul, T., Robson, M. J., Gould-Williams, J., & Lertthaitrakul, W. (2013). Effects of co-worker support and customer cooperation on service employee attitudes and behaviour: Empirical evidence from the airline industry. *Journal of Hospitality and Tourism Management, 20*, 23–33. doi:10.1016/j.jhtm.2013.05.004

Ling, Y., & Poweli, G. N. (2001). Work-family conflict in contemporary China: Beyond an American-based model. *International Journal of Cross Cultural Management, 1*(3), 357–373. doi:10.1177/147059580113006

Liu, A. (2019). Making joy a priority at work. *Harvard Business Review*. Retrieved from https://hbr.org/2019/07/making-joy-a-priority-at-work

Lo Presti, A., & Nonnis, M. (2012). Moderated effects of job insecurity on work engagement and distress. *TPM, 19*(2), 97–113.

Lu, L., Cai, R., & Gursoy, D. (2019). Developing and validating a service robot integration willingness scale. *International Journal of Hospitality Management, 80*, 36–51. doi:10.1016/j.ijhm.2019.01.005

Lu, L., Lu, A. C. C., Gursoy, D., & Neale, N. R. (2016). Work engagement, job satisfaction, and turnover intentions: A comparison between supervisors and line-level employees. *International Journal of Contemporary Hospitality Management, 28*(4), 737–761. doi:10.1108/IJCHM-07-2014-0360

Luk, C. Y. (2006). Work–life balance in Hong Kong's financial sector. *CSR Asia Weekly*, *2*(11). Retrieved May 5, 2022, from http://www.csr-asia.com/index.php?p=6001

Lunenburg, F. (2010). Approaches to managing organizational change. *International Journal of Scholarly Academic Intellectual Diversity*, *12*(1), 1–10.

Ma, E., & Qu, H. (2011). Social exchanges as motivators of hotel employees' organizational citizenship behavior: The proposition and application of a new three-dimensional framework. *International Journal of Hospitality Management*, *30*(3), 680–688. doi:10.1016/j.ijhm.2010.12.003

MacDermid, S. M., Barnett, R., Crosby, F., Greenhaus, J. H., Koblenz, M., & Marks, S. R. (2000). *The Measurement of Work/Life Tension: Recommendations of a Virtual Think Tank*. Alfred P. Sloan Foundation.

Madigan, M., Norton, J., & Testa, I. (1999). The quest for work life balance. *Rogers Media*. Available at https://www.benefitscanada.com/content/legacy/content/ 1999/html

Maheshwari, S., & Vohra, V. (2015). Identifying critical HR practices impacting employee perception and commitment during organizational change. *Journal of Organizational Change Management*, *28*(5), 872–894. doi:10.1108/JOCM-03-2014-0066

Mansour, S., & Tremblay, D. G. (2016). Workload, generic and work–family specific social supports and job stress: Mediating role of work–family and family–work conflict. *International Journal of Contemporary Hospitality Management*, *28*(8), 1778–1804. doi:10.1108/IJCHM-11-2014-0607

Markovits, Y., Boer, D., & van Dick, R. (2014). Economic crisis and the employee: The effects of economic crisis on employee job satisfaction, commitment and self-regulation. *European Management Journal*, *32*(3), 413–422. doi:10.1016/j.emj.2013.09.005

Marriott, J. W. Jr, & Brown, K. A. (1997). *The Spirit to Serve: The Marriott's Way*. Harper Business.

Maslach, C., Schaufeli, W. B., & Leiter, M. P. (2001). Job Burnout. *Annual Review of Psychology*, *52*(1), 397–422. doi:10.1146/annurev.psych.52.1.397 PMID:11148311

Mathieu, C., Fabi, B., Lacoursière, R., & Raymond, L. (2015). The role of supervisory behavior, job satisfaction and organizational commitment on employee turnover. *Journal of Management & Organization, 22*(1), 113–129. doi:10.1017/jmo.2015.25

Mathieu, J. E., & Zajac, D. M. (1990). A review and meta-analysis of the antecedents, correlates, and consequences of organizational commitment. *Psychological Bulletin, 108*(2), 171–194. doi:10.1037/0033-2909.108.2.171

Mauno, S., De Cuyper, N., Tolvanen, A., Kinnunen, U., & M¨akikangas, A. (2014). Occupational well-being as a mediator between job insecurity and turnover intention: Findings at the individual and work department levels. *European Journal of Work and Organizational Psychology, 23*(3), 381–393. doi:10.1080/1359432X.2012.752896

McDowell, T. (2004). *Fun at work: Scale development, confirmatory factor analysis, and links to organizational outcomes* [Unpublished doctoral dissertation]. Alliant International University, San Diego, CA.

McKnight, D. H., Ahmad, S., & Schroeder, R. G. (2001). When do feedback, incentive control and autonomy improve morale? The importance of employee-management relationship closeness. *Journal of Managerial Issues, 13*(4), 466–482.

McLarney, C., & Aujla, S. (2020). The Effects of Organizational Change on Employee Commitment. *The IUP Journal of Organizational Behavior., 19*(1), 7–22.

Mesmer-Magnus, J. R., DeChurch, L. A., & Wax, A. (2012). Moving emotional labor beyond surface and deep acting: A discordance–congruence perspective. *Organizational Psychology Review, 2*(1), 6–53. doi:10.1177/2041386611417746

Meyer, J. P., & Allen, N. J. (1984). Testing the 'side-bet theory' of organizational commitment: Some methodological considerations. *The Journal of Applied Psychology, 69*(3), 372–378. doi:10.1037/0021-9010.69.3.372

Meyer, J. P., & Allen, N. J. (1990). The measurement and antecedents of affective, continuance and normative commitment to the organization. *Journal of Occupational Psychology, 63*(1), 1–18. doi:10.1111/j.2044-8325.1990.tb00506.x

Meyer, J. P., & Allen, N. J. (1991). A three-component conceptualization of organizational commitment. *Human Resource Management Review*, *1*(1), 61–89. doi:10.1016/1053-4822(91)90011-Z

Meyer, J. P., & Herscovitch, L. (2001). Commitment in the workplace: Toward a general model. *Human Resource Management Review*, *11*(3), 299–326. doi:10.1016/S1053-4822(00)00053-X

Meyer, J. P., Stanley, D. J., Herscovitch, L., & Topolnytsky, L. (2002). Affective, continuance, and normative commitment to the organization: A meta-analysis of antecedents, correlates, and consequences. *Journal of Vocational Behavior*, *61*(1), 20–52. doi:10.1006/jvbe.2001.1842

Michel, J. W., Tews, M. J., & Allen, D. G. (2019). Fun in the workplace: A review and expanded theoretical perspective. *Human Resource Management Review*, *29*(1), 98–110. doi:10.1016/j.hrmr.2018.03.001

Mohapatra, A. K., Saxena, A., Joshi, D., & Chaturvedi, N. (2017). Does job security matter for generation Y? A behavioral analysis. *Pacific Business Review International*, *10*(5), 92–98.

Moran, J., & Brightman, B. K. (2001). Leading organizational change. *Career Development International*, *6*(2), 111–118.

Mowday, R. T. (1996). Reflections on the study and relevance of organizational commitment. *Human Resource Management Review*, *8*(4), 387–401. doi:10.1016/S1053-4822(99)00006-6

Nella, D., Panagopoulou, E., Galanis, N., Montgomery, A., & Benos, A. (2015). Consequences of job insecurity on the psychological and physical health of Greek civil servants. *BioMed Research International*, *2015*, 1–9. doi:10.1155/2015/673623 PMID:26557687

Nelson, B. (1999). *Low cost ways to build employee commitment.* Nelson Motivation Inc. Available at https://www.inc.com/articles/1999/12/16412.html

Netemeyer, R. G., Boles, J. S., & McMurrian, R. (1996). Development and validation of work–family conflict and family–work conflict scales. *The Journal of Applied Psychology*, *81*(4), 400–410. doi:10.1037/0021-9010.81.4.400

Niesen, W., Hootegem, A. V., Handaja, Y., Battistelli, A., & De Witte, H. (2018). Quantitative and qualitative job insecurity and idea generation: The mediating role of psychological contract breach. *Scandinavian Journal of Work and Organizational Psychology.*, *3*(1), 1–14. doi:10.16993jwop.36

Novelli, L. Jr, Kirkman, B. L., & Shapiro, D. L. (1995). Effective implementation of organizational change: An organizational justice perspective. In C. L. Cooper & D. M. Rousseau (Eds.), *Trends in Organizational Behavior* (Vol. 2, pp. 15–36). Wiley.

Parish, J. T., Cadwallader, S., & Busch, P. (2008). Want to, need to, ought to: Employee commitment to organizational change. *Journal of Organizational Change Management*, *21*(1), 32–52. doi:10.1108/09534810810847020

Park, J., & Gursoy, D. (2012). Generation effects on work engagement among US hotel employees. *International Journal of Hospitality Management*, *31*(4), 1195–1202. doi:10.1016/j.ijhm.2012.02.007

Perry-Smith, J. E. (2006). Social yet creative: The role of social relationships in facilitating individual creativity. *Academy of Management Journal*, *49*(1), 85–101. doi:10.5465/amj.2006.20785503

Pfeffer, J. (1994). *Competitive Advantage Through People*. Harvard Business School Press. doi:10.2307/41165742

Pfefferbaum, B., & North, C. S. (2020). Mental health and the Covid-19 pandemic. *The New England Journal of Medicine*, *383*(6), 510–512. doi:10.1056/NEJMp2008017 PMID:32283003

Pocock, B. (2005). Work–life 'balance' in Australia: Limited progress, dim prospects. *Asia Pacific Journal of Human Resources*, *43*(2), 198–209. doi:10.1177/1038411105055058

Podsakoff, P. M., MacKenzie, S. B., & Podsakoff, N. P. (2012). Sources of method bias in social science research and recommendations on how to control it. *Annual Review of Psychology*, *63*(1), 539–569. doi:10.1146/annurev-psych-120710-100452 PMID:21838546

Probst, T. M. (2005). Economic stressors. In J. Barling, E. K. Kelloway, & M. R. Frone (Eds.), *Handbook of work stress* (pp. 267–297). Sage. doi:10.4135/9781412975995.n11

Qu, H., & Zhao, X. (2012). Employees' work–family conflict moderating life and job satisfaction. *Journal of Business Research*, *65*(1), 22–28. doi:10.1016/j.jbusres.2011.07.010

Rafiq, M., Wu, W., Chin, T., & Nasir, M. (2019). The psychological mechanism linking employee work engagement and turnover intention: A moderated mediation study. *Work (Reading, Mass.)*, *62*(4), 615–628. doi:10.3233/WOR-192894 PMID:31104045

Riketta, M. (2002). Attitudinal organizational commitment and job performance: A meta-analysis. *Journal of Organizational Behavior*, *23*(3), 257–266. doi:10.1002/job.141

Ryan, R. M., & Deci, E. L. (2000). Self-determination theory and the facilitation of intrinsic motivation, social development, and well-being. *The American Psychologist*, *55*(1), 68–78. doi:10.1037/0003-066X.55.1.68 PMID:11392867

Ryder, N. B. (1965). The cohort as a concept in the study of social change. *American Sociological Review*, *30*(6), 843–861. doi:10.2307/2090964 PMID:5846306

S'ahin, F. (2011). The effect of gender on the relationship between leader-member exchange and intention to quit. *Ege Academic Review*, *11*(2), 277–288.

Sarabahksh, M., Carson, D., & Lindgren, E. (1989). Hospitality managers' stress and quality of life: Recommendations for change. *Hospitality Education & Research Journal*, *13*(3), 239–245. doi:10.1177/109634808901300324

Schaufeli, W. B., Salanova, M., Gonzalez-Roma, V., & Bakker, A. B. (2002). Burnout and engagement in university students. *Journal of Cross-Cultural Psychology*, *33*(5), 464–481. doi:10.1177/0022022102033005003

Schneider, B. (1975). Organizational climates: An essay. *Personnel Psychology*, *28*(4), 447–479. doi:10.1111/j.1744-6570.1975.tb01386.x

Schuman, H., & Scott, J. (1989). Generations and collective memories. *American Sociological Review*, *54*(3), 359–381. doi:10.2307/2095611

Shah, N., Irani, Z., & Sharif, A. (2017). Big data in an HR context: Exploring organizational change readiness, employee attitudes and behaviors. *Journal of Business Research*, *70*(3), 366–378. doi:10.1016/j.jbusres.2016.08.010

Shih, S. P., Jiang, J. J., Klein, G., & Wang, E. (2013). Job burnout of the information technology worker: Work exhaustion, depersonalization, and personal accomplishment. *Information & Management*, *50*(7), 582–589. doi:10.1016/j.im.2013.08.003

Shin, I., & Jeung, C. W. (2019). Uncovering the turnover intention of proactive employees: The mediating role of work engagement and the moderated mediating role of job autonomy. *International Journal of Environmental Research and Public Health*, *16*(5), 1–16, 843. doi:10.3390/ijerph16050843 PMID:30857145

Shoss, M. K. (2017). Job insecurity: An integrative review and agenda for future research. *Journal of Management*, *43*(6), 1911–1939. doi:10.1177/0149206317691574

Sibiya, M., Buitendach, J. H., Kanengoni, H., & Bobat, S. (2014). The prediction of turnover intention by means of employee engagement and demographic variables in a telecommunications organization. *Journal of Psychology in Africa*, *24*(2), 131–143. doi:10.1080/14330237.2014.903078

Siemsen, E., Roth, A., & Oliveira, P. (2010). Common method bias in regression models with linear, quadratic, and interaction effects. *Organizational Research Methods*, *13*(3), 456–476. doi:10.1177/1094428109351241

Sirgy, J. M. (2019). Promoting quality-of-life and well-being research in hospitality and tourism. *Journal of Travel & Tourism Marketing*, *36*(1), 1–13. doi:10.1080/10548408.2018.1526757

Smollan, R. K. (2016). The personal costs of organizational change: A qualitative study. *Public Performance & Management Review*, *39*(1), 223–247. doi:10.1080/15309576.2016.1071174

Sobieralski, J. B. (2020). COVID-19 and airline employment: Insights from historical uncertainty shocks to the industry. *Transportation Research Interdisciplinary Perspectives*, *5*(100123), 1–9. doi:10.1016/j.trip.2020.100123 PMID:34173453

Sofat, K., Kiran, R., & Kaushik, S. (2015). Management of organizational change and its impact on commitment: A study of select Indian IT companies. *International Global Business and Management Research Journal.*, *7*(3), 69–87.

Staufenbiel, T., & Konig, C. J. (2010). A model for the effects of job insecurity on performance, turnover intention, and absenteeism. *Journal of Occupational and Organizational Psychology*, *83*(1), 101–117. doi:10.1348/096317908X401912

Stiglbauer, B., Selenko, E., Batinic, B., & Jodlbauer, S. (2012). On the link between job insecurity and turnover intentions: Moderated mediation by work involvement and well-being. *Journal of Occupational Health Psychology*, *17*(3), 354–364. doi:10.1037/a0028565 PMID:22746370

Stum, D. L. (2001). Maslow revisited: Building the employee commitment pyramid. *Strategy and Leadership*, *29*(4), 4–9. doi:10.1108/10878570110400053

Tabacchi, M. H., Krone, C., & Farber, B. (1990). A support system to mitigate manager burnout. *The Cornell Hotel and Restaurant Administration Quarterly*, *31*(3), 32–37. doi:10.1177/001088049003100310

Tanova, C., & Holtom, B. C. (2008). Using job embeddedness factors to explain voluntary turnover in four European countries. *International Journal of Human Resource Management*, *19*(9), 1553–1568. doi:10.1080/09585190802294820

Tews, M. J., Michel, J. W., & Allen, D. G. (2014). Fun and friends: The impact of workplace fun and constituent attachment on turnover in a hospitality context. *Human Relations*, *67*(8), 923–946. doi:10.1177/0018726713508143

Tews, M. J., Michel, J. W., & Noe, R. A. (2017). Does fun promote learning? The relationship between fun in the workplace and informal learning. *Journal of Vocational Behavior*, *98*, 46–55. doi:10.1016/j.jvb.2016.09.006

Tews, M. J., Michel, J. W., & Stafford, K. (2013). Does fun pay? The impact of workplace fun on employee turnover and performance. *Cornell Hospitality Quarterly*, *54*(4), 370–382. doi:10.1177/1938965513505355

Tian, Q., Zhang, L., & Zou, W. (2014). Job insecurity and counterproductive behavior of casino dealers: The mediating role of affective commitment and moderating role of supervisor support. *International Journal of Hospitality Management*, *40*, 29–36. doi:10.1016/j.ijhm.2014.03.005

Timms, C., Brough, P., O'Driscoll, M., Kalliath, T., Siu, O. L., Sit, C., & Lo, D. (2015). Flexible work arrangements, work engagement, turnover intentions and psychological health. *Asia Pacific Journal of Human Resources*, *53*(1), 83–103. doi:10.1111/1744-7941.12030

Trang, H. L. T., Lee, J. S., & Han, H. (2019). How do green attributes elicit pro-environmental behaviors in guests? The case of green hotels in Vietnam. *Journal of Travel & Tourism Marketing*, *36*(1), 14–28. doi:10.1080/10548408.2018.1486782

Triandis, H. C., Bontempo, R., Villareal, M. J., Asai, M., & Lucca, N. (1988). Individualism and collectivism: Cross-cultural perspectives on self-ingroup relationships. *Journal of Personality and Social Psychology*, *54*(2), 323–338. doi:10.1037/0022-3514.54.2.323

Tsaur, S.-H., Hsu, F.-S., & Lin, H. (2019). Workplace fun and work engagement in tourism and hospitality: The role of psychological capital. *International Journal of Hospitality Management*, *81*, 131–140. doi:10.1016/j.ijhm.2019.03.016

Urbanaviciute, I., Lazauskaite-Zabielske, J., Elst, T. V., & De Witte, H. (2018). Qualitative job insecurity and turnover intention: The mediating role of basic psychological needs in public and private sectors. *Career Development International*, *2*(3), 274–290. doi:10.1108/CDI-07-2017-0117

US Bureau of Labor Statistics. (2023). *Labor force statistics from the current population survey*. Available at: www.bls.gov/cps/electronically-mediated-employment.Html

Vahtera, J., Kivimaki, M., & Pentti, J. (1997). Effect of organizational downsizing on health of employees. *Lancet*, *350*(9085), 1124–1128. doi:10.1016/S0140-6736(97)03216-9 PMID:9343499

Vallen, G. K. (1993). "Organizational climate and burnout. *The Cornell H.R. AQ*, (February), 54–59.

Vandenberghe, C., De Keyser, V., Vlerick, P., & D'hoore, W. (2004). Organizational changes, employee stress, and customer satisfaction: Emergence of the flexihealth concept. *Belgian Science Policy*, *46*, 8–19.

Vaziri, H., Benson, G. S., & Salazar Campo, M. (2019). Hardworking coworkers: A multilevel cross-national look at group work hours and work–family conflict. *Journal of Organizational Behavior*, *40*(6), 676–692. doi:10.1002/job.2361

Wagner, J. A. III. (1995). Studies of individualism-collectivism: Effects on cooperation in groups. *Academy of Management Journal*, *38*(1), 152–173. doi:10.2307/256731

Wang, H. J., Lu, C. Q., & Siu, O. L. (2015). Job insecurity and job performance: The moderating role of organizational justice and the mediating role of work engagement. *The Journal of Applied Psychology*, *100*(4), 1249–1258. doi:10.1037/a0038330 PMID:25402953

Wang, Y. C., Ryan, B., & Yang, C. E. (2019). Employee brand love and love behaviors: Perspectives of social exchange and rational choice. *International Journal of Hospitality Management*, *77*, 458–467. doi:10.1016/j.ijhm.2018.08.009

Ware, J. E., & Sherbourne, D. (1992). The MOS 36-Items Short-Form Health (SF36): Conceptual Framework and Item Selection. *Medical Care*, *30*(6), 473–483. doi:10.1097/00005650-199206000-00002 PMID:1593914

Wim, J. N. M., & Gijs, B. (1998). Employee commitment in changing organizations: An exploration. *Journal of European Industrial Training*, *22*(6), 243–248. doi:10.1108/03090599810224701

Wong, S. C., & Ko, A. (2009). Exploratory study of understanding hotel employees' perception on work-life balance issues. *International Journal of Hospitality Management*, *28*(2), 195–203. doi:10.1016/j.ijhm.2008.07.001 PMID:32287852

Xu, S., Wang, Y., Ma, E., & Wang, R. (2020). Hotel employees' fun climate at work: Effects on work-family conflict and employee deep acting through a collective perspective. *International Journal of Hospitality Management*, *91*, 102666. doi:10.1016/j.ijhm.2020.102666 PMID:32934433

Yanti, S., & Dahlan, J. (2017). The effects of organizational culture, leadership behavior, and job satisfaction on employee organizational commitment. *Journal of Positive Management*, *8*(4), 80–96. doi:10.12775/JPM.2017.132

Yu, J., Ariza-Montes, A., Hernández-Perlines, F., Vega-Muñoz, A., & Han, H. (2020). Hotels' eco-friendly physical environment as nature-based solutions for decreasing burnout and increasing job satisfaction and performance. *International Journal of Environmental Research and Public Health*, *17*(17), 6357. doi:10.3390/ijerph17176357 PMID:32882825

Zemke, R., Raines, C., & Filipczak, B. (2000). Generations at Work: Managing the Cash of Veterans, Boomers, Xers, and Nexters in Your Workplace. Amacom.

Zhao, X., & Ghiselli, R. (2016). Why do you feel stressed in a "smile factory"? Hospitality job characteristics influence work–family conflict and job stress. *International Journal of Contemporary Hospitality Management*, *28*(2), 305–326. doi:10.1108/IJCHM-08-2014-0385

Zhao, X., & Mattila, A. S. (2013). Examining the spillover effect of frontline employees' work–family conflict on their affective work attitudes and customer satisfaction. *International Journal of Hospitality Management*, *33*, 310–315. doi:10.1016/j.ijhm.2012.10.001

Section 2
Engineering Organizational Effectiveness: Factors Associated With Job Satisfaction

Job satisfaction is a complex continuum of multiple dimensions resulting from the interaction of employee's intrinsic facets with one another, as well as reacting to various positive and negative extrinsic stimuli. This section reviews and evaluates these dimensions independently, first investigating intrinsic factors that drive job satisfaction and then exploring extrinsic factors that have a negative impact on organizational effectiveness.

Chapter 4
A Meta-Analysis of Intrinsic Factors That Drive Job Satisfaction:
Effective Talent Management in the Hotel Industry

ABSTRACT

This narrative evaluates the dimensions associated with job satisfaction for hotel employees in the 21st century. The extensive literature review and meta-analysis explores the various facets encompassing job satisfaction and job insecurity including depersonalization, stress, burnout, and turnover intention for hotel workers with a focus on front desk employees. The analysis reviews the impact of work environment and work culture as it correlates to job satisfaction and job insecurity, determining an engaging, empowering, and fun culture often offsets negative emotions associated with front desk work at a hotel. The chapter also provides an assessment of how an employee receiving negative career feedback can correlate with negative career outcomes, and how leadership can utilize career pathways to increase employee retention. Finally, the chapter identifies practical tactics to utilize within a hotel operation to reduce voluntary separation by offering targeted benefit packages while also keeping employes engaged, satisfied, and excited about their roles.

DOI: 10.4018/978-1-6684-2528-2.ch004

INTRODUCTION: UNDERSTANDING JOB INSECURITY IN THE 21st CENTURY

In literature, much has been discussed around what causes job insecurity but additional insight into the nature of job insecurity and how it influences employee behavior is needed. While the 21st century has seen a significant volume of external crises that impact work, the truth is that disruption of this nature has been occurring for a much longer period of time. Since the late 1970s, economic recessions, industrial restructuring, technological change, and intensified global competition have dramatically changed the nature of work (Howard, 1995). While some of the intensities of these changes have been lost to generational paradigms, it is important to understand the phenomenon of job insecurity beyond current events, as significant as those may appear to be at the time they occur (Sverke & Hellgren, 2002).

Job insecurity only occurs in the case of involuntary job loss (Greenhalgh & Rosenblatt, 1984). Hartley, Jacobson, Klandermans, & Van Vuuren (1991) argued that the construct, in its most general sense, reflects the discrepancy between the level of security a person experiences and the level he or she prefers. It would be meaningful to make a distinction between at least two different aspects of job insecurity: Quantitative and qualitative insecurity. Quantitative job insecurity is similar to the global conceptualizations of the construct. Qualitative job insecurity pertains to perceptions of potential loss of quality in the employment relationship, such as deterioration of working conditions, demotion, lack of career opportunities, decreasing salary development, and concerns about person–organization fit in the future.

Long-term, ominous job insecurity is likely to have severe consequences for an employee's overall life situation in that economic and other highly valued aspects of life will be perceived as threatened (Ashford, Lee, & Bobko, 1989; Hartley et al., 1991). Job insecurity is associated with impaired well-being (Barling & Kelloway, 1996; Hartley et al., 1991; Jick, 1985). Physical health complaints, mental distress, and work-to-leisure carry-over increase proportionately with the level of job insecurity (e.g. Ashford et al., 1989; Lim, 1996; Mattiasson, Lindgarde, Nilsson, & Theorell, 1990; Noer, 1993)

Throughout the latter half of the twentieth century, millions of workers have been displaced while others have become involuntarily part-time unemployed, hired on temporary employment contracts, or experienced "a fundamental and involuntary change in their sets of beliefs about the employing organization and their place in it" (Jacobson, 1991, p. 2). For many employees, the changes in working life we have witnessed over the past two decades have caused feelings of insecurity concerning the nature and future existence of their jobs (Hartley, et. al., 1991). Individuals who once experienced safe and long-term employment now, to an increasingly larger extent, face insecure employment conditions (Roskies & Louis-Guerin, 1990).

As noted by several commentators (e.g. Gowing, Kraft, & Campbell Quick, 1998; Howard, 1995; Pfeffer, 1998; Rifkin, 1995), working life has been subject to dramatic change over past decades. In this context, job insecurity has emerged as an important construct. There are several reasons for this development: intensified global competition has forced organizations to cut production costs and become more flexible; periods of economic recession have led to widespread organizational closure with unemployment and growing insecurity in its wake; new technologies have paved the way for less labor intensive production and also restricted the employment alternatives of less skilled workers; the rapid industrial restructuring from manufacturing to service production has called into question employees' view of the stability of their employers; and a belief in the market-driven economy has changed government policies and in many countries resulted in relaxations of employment legislation (Davy, Kinicki, & Scheck, 1997; Greenhalgh & Rosenblatt, 1984; Hartley et al., 1991; Sparrow, 1998).

This chapter explores the specific characteristics associated with understanding intrinsic factors that employees maintain which influence their levels of satisfaction and security around their employed role. The narrative explores different facets of what makes job security in the 21st century unique, reflects on how leadership in a hospitality industry can more effectively manage the job insecurity of employees, how psychological factors of stress, burnout and turnover intention align within front-line hotel employees, fostering work engagement among different levels of employees in the hospitality industry, reviewing the impact of job insecurity and work engagement on employee behaviors in a hotel working environment and the impact that negative feedback about one's hospitality career has on their employment outcomes.

BACKGROUND

Regardless of the crisis, downsizing or "rightsizing" (Hitt, Keats, Harback, & Nixon, 1994) appears to be the standard solution in organizational attempts at improving organizational effectiveness and reducing labor costs. Consequently, millions of jobs have been eliminated, and the negative consequences of unemployment are well documented (Jahoda, 1982). Research has also demonstrated that the success or failure of any downsizing strategy is essentially determined by the reactions of the survivors in the organization (Kozlowski, Chao, Smith & Hedlund, 1993). There is also substantial evidence to suggest that the nature of work has changed dramatically for those who remain employed. Employers in virtually every industrialized nation of the world are moving, in varying degrees, toward increased flexibility in how they staff their organizations (Klein Hesselink & van Vuuren, 1999; Sparrow, 1998). Organizational striving for functional and numerical flexibility has resulted in demands for new types of skills as well as in changes in employment contracts. Most notably, organizations have shown increased interest in employing workers on the basis of short or fixed term contracts rather than on the basis of implicit long-term contracts (McLean Parks, Kidder, & Gallagher, 1998; Sverke, Gallagher, & Hellgren, 2000). In addition, downsizing survivors have to do more with fewer resources, their work-load increases, and uncertainty regarding task performance is likely to be prevalent (Burke & Nelson, 1998; Hartley et al., 1991).

Following a layoff or downsizing event, job security for those remaining employed at the organization drops to its lowest point. Job insecurity has consistently been found to associate with reduced levels of work attitudes such as job satisfaction. Ashford et al. (1989) showed that employees who felt insecure about their future employment were more dissatisfied with their jobs compared to those who perceived their future job situation as more secure. Similar results have been obtained in a number of studies (e.g. Davy et al., 1997; Hartley, Israel, & House, 1991; Heaney et al., 1994; Rosenblatt & Ruvio, 1996). In a similar vein, perceived insecurity concerning one's future role in the organization may also make the employee less inclined to remain with the organization. Job insecurity, like any stressor, could lead to a withdrawal response as manifested in, for example, higher levels of turnover intention (Arnold & Feldman, 1982; Brockner, 1988; Burke & Nelson, 1998; Davy et al., 1997; Dekker & Schaufeli, 1995; Hartley et al., 1991).

The relationship between job insecurity and employee reactions may not be as clear-cut as implied though (Sverke and Hellgren, 2002). First, not all studies have found that job insecurity in fact is related to impaired work attitudes and well-being. Moreover, even where the findings are congruent the magnitudes of relationships differ substantially between studies. Greenhalgh and Rosenblatt (1984) introduce the distinction between what would become known as quantitative and qualitative insecurity. They noted that the aspect reflecting concerns about continued employment might be the most important of the factors. Although a loss of valued job features certainly represents an aspect of job insecurity "inasmuch as it involves losing the job as the affected employee currently knows it", it is likely that this threat is "less severe because organizational membership—and all that such membership means to the individual—is not lost" (p. 441).

In their model of job insecurity, presented below in Figure 4.1, Greenhalgh and Rosenblatt (1984) postulated that individual differences could be expected to moderate the relationship between the experience of job insecurity and the employee's reactions to it.

Figure 1. Greenhalgh and Rosenblatt (1984) integrated model of jos insecurity

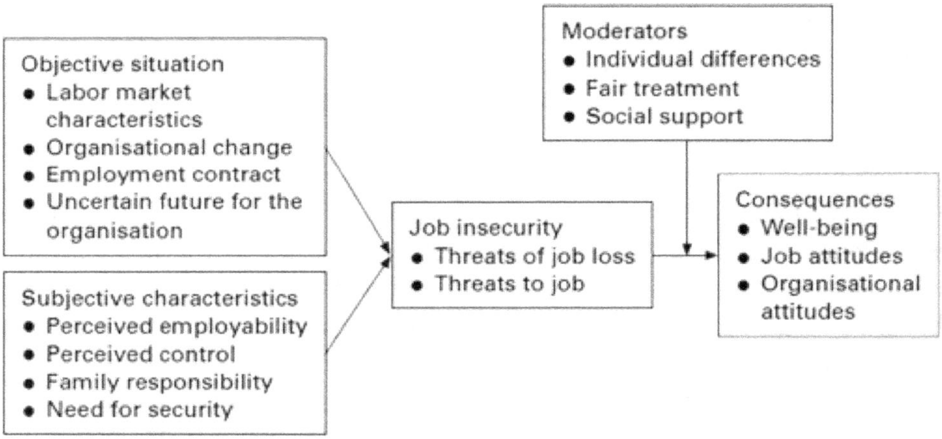

Individuals report higher job satisfaction when they have an opportunity to provide input into factors associated with the objective situation, such as how a company or a department makes decisions (Konovsky & Folger, 1987). Participation (i.e. being kept informed and involved over the course of the crisis or the downsizing) was associated with improved job satisfaction and well-being as well. Participation has also been shown to moderate the effects of role stress among hospital employees (Pozner & Randolph, 1980). It is likely that employees feel a sense of control over the situation when they have an opportunity to influence the decisions being made. Barling and Kelloway (1996) found that control perceptions had positive direct effects on various health indicators and work attitudes, and in addition, moderated the effects of job insecurity on physical health. Tetrick and LaRocco (1987) reported that control predicted perceived stress and job satisfaction and moderated the relationship between these variables.

The area of factors that may moderate the negative effects of job insecurity certainly represents a fruitful direction for further research. Even if individual differences, fair treatment of employees in layoffs, and social support do nothing about the stressor itself, that is, they do not change the

insecure employment situation into a more favorable one, they all may have beneficial effects for the individual if they prevent the most negative reactions from occurring. Given that employees' reactions to uncertainties in a given organizational context are of fundamental importance from both the occupational health and managerial perspectives (Matteson & Ivancevich, 1987), moderators of job insecurity take on double importance (Svercke and Hallgren, 2002).

In terms of how the negative effects of job insecurity can be reduced in a practical manner, there are three areas of moderators that appear to be especially important. These moderators are individual differences, fairness perceptions, and social support (Abildgaard, Neilsen, & Sverke, 2018). Organizations can take measures to prevent the most negative impact of job insecurity from occurring by, for instance, providing accurate information, enhancing communication, supplying retraining for alternative employment, and training their employees in how to cope with the stress created by job insecurity (Hartley et al., 1991; Heaney et al., 1994; Kets de Vries & Balazs, 1997).

Exploring How to Manage Job Insecurity

There is a growing focus in the literature on how restructuring, mergers, and layoffs may contribute to increased job insecurity and posing a threat to psychological well-being among employees (Kieselbach, Armgarth, Bagnara, Elo, A.-L., Jefferys, Joling, & Rogovsky, 2009; Wiezer Nielsen, Pahkin, Widerszal-Bazyl, de Jong, Mattila-Holappa, & Mockałło., 2011). It has even been argued that stable jobs are becoming the exception rather than the rule (Allvin, Mellner, Movitz, & Aronsson, 2013). With organizations being forced to adapt to globalization, restructuring has become inevitable (Rosa, 2013), often leading to job insecurity and decreased well-being among employees (de Jong et al., 2016).

To manage job insecurity and promote well-being and employee health, organizational-level interventions have been proposed as a solution (De Witte, Vander Elst, & De Cuyper, 2015). Organizational-level interventions are here defined as "planned, behavioral, theory-based actions that aim to improve employee health and well-being through changing the way work is designed, organized and managed" (Nielsen, 2013, p. 1030). Field experiments (Schweiger & Denisi, 1991) and other studies (as well as this own meta-analysis) have shown that the negative effects of specific aspects of the change process can be reduced by involving employees in proactively implementing changes (Sverke, Hellgren, Näswall, Göransson, & Öhrming, 2008) or participative decision making (Probst, 2005). Recent studies have documented that both quantitative job insecurity (De Witte, 2005; Sverke, Hellgren, & Näswall, 2002) and qualitative job insecurity have negative effects, such as poor well-being, low commitment to the organization, and high levels of depressive symptoms (De Witte, De Cuyper, Handaja, Sverke, Näswall, & Hellgren, 2010; Vander Elst, Richter, Sverke, Näswall, De Cuyper, & De Witte, 2014).

Organizational-level interventions have been found to be effective for reducing sickness absenteeism (Semmer, 2011), enhancing job satisfaction (Nielsen, Fredslund, Christensen, & Albertsen, 2006), improving social support and decision latitude, and reducing demands (Bambra, Egan, Thomas, Petticrew, & Whitehead, 2007). Together, these studies support the notion that interventions may be an effective means of reducing the organizational and psychological problems caused by restructuring.

The conceptual foundation of the intervention in Abildgaard et. al.'s 2018 study was based on employee participation, in the form of employees' active involvement in the planning and implementation of an intervention and its related activities. This type of participation builds on the premise that utilizing a highly participatory design (Nielsen & Randall, 2012) and focusing on both adverse and positive aspects of work (Demerouti, Bakker, Nachreiner, & Schaufeli, 2001; Schaufeli & Bakker, 2004) will encourage the development of problem-solving skills and enable employees to maintain or increase their resources for addressing problematic issues (Nielsen, 2013). Employees must be involved in the planning, assessment, implementation, and evaluation of the activities to attain the desired positive outcomes and learn from the intervention (Nielsen & Randall, 2012). In addition, letting participants prioritize which issues to work on creates ownership and makes it more likely that improvements in working conditions are achieved (Holman & Axtell, 2015). To sustain this participatory process, the intervention has to be highly systematic and transparent and include a detailed, context-specific risk assessment as well as priority-setting and action planning – to some extent inspired by British Risk Management approach (Cox, Griffiths, Barlowe, Randall, Thomson, & Rial-Gonzalez, 2000).

Participating in the decision-making procedure regarding change processes is likely to result in the organizational change being implemented in a way that produces a less dramatic increase in job insecurity (Probst, 2005b). Participation itself is potentially a type of collective coping strategy (Kuo, 2013), which can further manage job insecurity during restructuring, even if restructuring efforts are still deployed. A proactive approach to restructuring appears to outbalance job insecurity during organizational change (Sverke et al., 2008).

Abildgaard et. al.'s study identified that when employees are actively engaged in collaboratively developing restructuring efforts, these action plans were viewed as positive and were thought to have led to improvements in the cases where they had been implemented. Similarly, the impact of the action plans and the opportunity to work with them were often seen as temporary, and the impact of the intervention was viewed as a manifestation of a general cultural change towards better planning and consideration of colleagues' feelings (2018).

Job insecurity and restructuring were perceived as substantial problems and that these issues, according to the program theory developed by managers and employees, were to be addressed through action plans, such as more consistent information sharing and personal development feedback during restructuring. That said, the 2018 Abildgaard et. al. study was based on a single organization (a national postal service) and while the results appear to be generalizable, the study took place within a specific context without any calibration for other professional environments. In addition, an actual reduction in job insecurity may sometimes be too ambitious a goal even though one was observed in the study's outcome. Organizations should set themselves up for greater success by instead establishing a lesser or slower increase in job insecurity as a more realistic goal for an intervention of this nature.

The Role of Stress, Burnout, and Turnover Intention in Front-Line Hotel Employees

The hotel industry is facing a labor shortage in developed countries as well as emerging markets (Kim, Um, Kim, and Kim, 2016). The total turnover rate in the hospitality industry was 27.6 percent in 2014 in China alone (Chen, Wang, & Tang, 2016) and high throughout the rest of the world as well – even before the COVID-19 pandemic shut down the hospitality industry (Wen, Zhou, Hu & Zhang, 2020). Hotel employees also face many challenges while performing their jobs (Kim et al., 2015). Facing a strenuous workload, frequent changes of circumstances, lack of performance feedback and low pay, they are easily irritated and exhausted, which in turn affects their behavior and may lead to resignation (Kim Paek, Chang, & Lee, 2012).

One critical challenge faced by front-line employees in the hotel industry is role stress. Long hours of operation, polychronic behaviors, a high demands-low resources job model and little feedback result in high levels of stress and burnout (O' Neill & Davis, 2011). Over time, role stress and burnout cause poor job performance and high turnover intention. A reasonable and tolerable level of stress can generate positive effects, such as higher motivation, a competitive edge and a dynamic working atmosphere (Beehr & Newman, 1978).

Conversely, excessive stress that causes burnout has negative impacts for both organizations and individuals. This argument is in line with the challenge-hindrance theory of work stressor (Cavanaugh, Boswell, Roehling, & Boudreau, 2000), which suggests that challenge stressors may produce positive emotions, even though employees may feel stressed. On the contrary, hindrance stressors are often associated with egregious or undesirable constraints, job demands and work circumstances, causing negative outcomes. Challenge stressors may produce positive emotions, even though employees may feel stressed (Montani, Courci, & Vandenberghe, 2017). This can be referred to as role stress.

Kahn, Wolfe, Quinn, Snoek, and Rosenthal (1964) introduced the concept and development process of role stress, arguing that role stress is the result of communication and interaction between role senders and receivers. When studying the overload of factors within one's role, it produces some different opinions. It is a complex dimension to describe in a simple factor analysis. According to some scholars (e.g., Cooper & Marshall, 1976; Jung, Yoon, & Kim, 2012), role overload is regarded as a quantitative factor, while role conflict and ambiguity are qualitative factors. Others believe that role overload consists of both quantitative and qualitative overload (Kelly and Barrett, 2011).

Role theory states that when the expectations and requests of an employee are inconsistent, he/she may feel stressful, become dissatisfied, and perform less efficiently. Therefore, role conflict can be seen as the result of conflicting expectations imposed on individuals (Rizzo, House, & Lirtzman, 1970). Role theory states that role ambiguity refers to a lack of necessary information required for a given position, which may lead to a person being discontented with his role, experiencing anxiety and misrepresenting reality. Role stress has a two-dimensional structure consisting of conflict and ambiguity that is often defined as a three-dimensional structure consisting of role conflict, ambiguity, and overload (Abdel-Halim, 1981; Schaubroeck, Cotton & Jennings, 1989). Some scholars believe that role overload is a part of role conflict (Coverman, 1989), while others regard role overload as a separate dimension (Peterson et al., 1995). According to Jones et al. (2007), role overload is a sensation that job requirements are overpowering relative to usable capabilities and resources. Moreover, the effect of role overload appears to be subsumed by role stressors and is conceptually different from two other stressors: role conflict and ambiguity (Singh, 1993). Role overload affects employee well-being negatively. As employees become overloaded, their physical and psychological health may decline. Other unfavorable outcomes of role overload include low organizational commitment, high absenteeism, and turnover intention (Jones, Chonko, Rangarajan, & Roberts, 2007; Mulki, Jaramillo, & Locander, 2008; Huang, Wellman, Ashford, Lee, & Wang, 2017).

Conversely, Freudenberger - who proposed the burnout concept - believes it has two aspects: Physical and behavioral symptoms (1974). Physical symptoms refer to the individual's perceived state of fatigue and depletion, and behavioral symptoms mean that it is difficult to control emotions, eventually leading to poor performance. Burnout is defined as the serious psychological and physical symptom resulting from continuous stressful and frustration at work (Maslach & Jackson, 1984). Burnout results from three factors: emotional exhaustion, depersonalization, and lack of self-efficacy (Densten, 2001).

Front-line employees in the hotel industry often experience extensive workloads as a common feature of their job and can display signs of burnout resulting from all three factors. During very busy hours, they sometimes cannot complete every task well because of too much work or time limits, and then role overload may occur. Thus, role overload is an independent assessment considering the specific work of frontline employees in the hotel industry (Wen et. al., 2020). Burnout occurs more commonly among hotel employees who serve many customers but have difficulties coping with excessive emotional and communication demands as well as long-term frustration because of limited emotional resources (Teoh, Wang, & Kwek, 2019).

Role conflict and role overload are found to influence burnout and job satisfaction directly, while role overload is found to be a precursor to depersonalization (Bacharach, Bamberger, & Conley, 1991). Job stressors are found to be positively related to emotional exhaustion among hotel employees (Darvishmotevali, Arasli, & Kilic, 2017). Employees who have work overload and work-family conflicts are more likely to experience emotionally exhausted; and high levels of emotional exhaustion may result in employee withdrawal intentions (Karatepe, 2013).

When hotel employees experience excessive role stress and cannot obtain the resources to relieve it, they will consider coping with the depressed situation with turnover (Wen et. al. 2020). Burnout strongly affects work outcome variables, and the combined impact of burnout and role stress is more obvious while burnout plays a strong intermediary role between stress variables and work outcome variables (Singh, 1993).

Leadership in a hotel operation has a clear interest in creating a positive service climate as a way to improve employee attitudes, behaviors and performance has increased. Service climate refers to an employee's individual perceptions of the events, practices, procedures, and behaviors that are rewarded, supported, and expected in a customer service setting (Schneider et al., 1998). According to the definition, service climate is different from general climate because it is a strategical goal for improving service quality (Schneider, White, & Paul, 1998).

Front-line employees in the hospitality industry are also under serious role stress, which exerts detrimental impacts on employees and hospitality organizations. Accumulated employees stress may cause burnout, which manifests as various physical, behavioral, and psychological symptoms. Stress indirectly affects turnover intent through burnout, revealing that stressed employees do not choose to resign immediately unless they suffer from a high level of burnout. However, it is important to recognize that Stress does not directly lead to turnover. An appropriate and tolerable level of stress may not generate negative effects (Beehr & Newman, 1978). It is only once an individual's threshold for absorbing stress that behavioral triggers may lead to burnout and/or voluntary separation from an organization. Service climate is an important linkage when converting organizational resources and management concept to practical performance (Lin & Liu, 2016). Wen et. al. (2020) defined this model, which is featured in Figure 4.2:

Figure 2. Model of stress, burnout, and turnover intention for hotel front-line employees
Source: Wen et al. (2020)

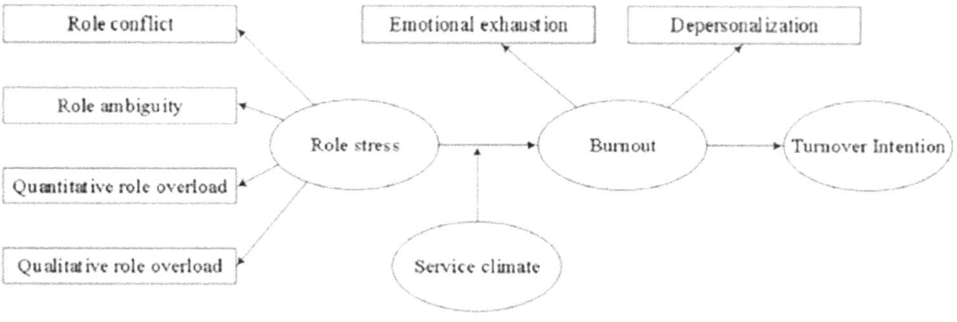

The importance of a good service climate for front-line hotel employees cannot be underestimated. A service climate has been demonstrated to significantly reduce the negative effect of role stress on burnout (Wen et. al., 2020). Both hindrance and challenge stressors lead to burnout but the interaction between hindrance stressors and service climate has a negative effect on burnout, while the interaction between challenge stressors and service climate is not significantly related to burnout (Karatepe & Uludag, 2008). Researchers agree that challenge stressor may not necessarily be bad while hindrance stressor is often detrimental (Cavanaugh et al., 2000). What this indicates is that improving service climate as an intervention to alleviate the negative effects of role stress is only effective when the stressors are hindrance. This demonstrates that there is a solution to mitigate the negative effect of hindrance stressor by creating a positive service climate (Wen et. al. 2020).

Conflicts and work overload are endemic among hotel front-line employees. Most of the frontline employees are in a stable working group. They identify with the rationality of their job and have clear ideas about their responsibilities. The main reason behind role conflict is that people's requirements and expectations vary with who they are as individuals. Superiors should define the kinds of duties of employees when they allocate assignments and try to eliminate extra work as much as possible to reduce the feelings of role conflict (Wen et. al., 2020).

That said, it is perfectly normal for employees to interpret an environment in different ways, with some feeling jaded, which leads to resignation and has a negative effect on service quality (Karatepe and Uludag, 2008). Even more important to realize is that front-line employees do their routine jobs regularly, receive poor pay, and often feel a sense of emotional exhaustion. Therefore, managers need to address the range of emotions in their staff. A variety of extracurricular activities, training and competition can be organized to avoid negative impacts on both the employees and enterprises. Besides, many hotel employees are uncertain about the value of their jobs, which also happens in other industries and is related to changing social values. Most front-line employees are young, with more than half of them under the age of 28, and they have not yet developed a clear career plan. Thus, more career planning should be provided to help front-line employees gain thorough insights into the hotel business and find their own career paths (Karatepe and Uludag, 2008; Wen et. al., 2020).

There are clear strategic opportunities for creating an enriched service environment for front line employees, but a word of caution about exuberance in doing so needs to be provided. Management being too aggressive about developing and implementing career planning and training solutions can also create pressure on employees to complete more work (Wen et. al., 2020). Pressure is a double-edged sword. A certain amount of pressure may stimulate the enthusiasm of employees, push them to complete tasks and realize their career goals (Karatepe and Uludag, 2008). Conversely, too much pressure may discourage them from trying their utmost in their work. It is not role stress but burnout that directly leads to turnover (Fogarty, Singh, Rhoads, & Moore, 2000) and this is an important distinction for leadership in a hotel to understand.

Hotel managers proceed to reduce turnover intention in two directions. Hotels need to reduce employees' perception of pressure to decrease burnout. Training programs on how to monitor and regulate emotional exhaustion as well as depersonalization could be offered to front-line employees. As a result of training programs, employees may learn more about self-regulation strategies. Participation in management, social support and other factors can also regulate the relationship between role stress and its dependent variables (Lin and Liu, 2016).

Hotels can improve the organizational service climate through communication, incentive schemes, service quality and corporate responsibility plans. Hotels can provide training to help front-line employees expand their knowledge. At the same time, hotels should reflect professional attitudes and high standards regarding training employees. In addition, hotels need to offer employee assistance programs, which may contribute to relieving stress and helping employees to reach high service performance. Moreover, hotels are advised to encourage communication between employees and their superiors and colleagues to express stressful and negative emotions, and share work skills and suggestions, provide psychological consultations to eliminate stress. Finally, hotels can give their employees opportunities to participate in social activities while promoting healthy lifestyles to help them develop a positive attitude to life. When employees have turnover intentions, hotels should not only seek reasons from their employees, but reflect whether they provide a good service to their employees. This helps a hotel learn and add additional dimensions to future efforts, ultimately increasing the impact of its actions while reducing turnover (Wen et. al, 2020).

Fostering Work Engagement in the Hospitality Industry

There are many problems in the hospitality industry, such as the lack of sense of achievement, lack of work vitality, low career loyalty, low sense of work responsibility and high turnover rate, which bring bad effects to the development of the staff in the hospitality industry and the hotel itself (Yao, Qiu, & Wei, 2019). These are not necessarily the result of intentional acts by hotel leadership but rather a function of how hotels operate. A challenge for leadership is how to use the limited resources available within the organization to motivate employees has become a major challenge faced by the managers in the hospitality industry. Therefore, it is necessary to explore the impact of organizational inducement on employee engagement. One area to explore further is the employee's relationship with their organization, or Employee Organization Relationship (EOR).

EOR content includes two aspects: what employers expect employees to contribute to the organization and what incentives employers will use to motivate employees to make these contributions (Hom, Tsui, & Wu, 2009; Wang, Tsui, & Zhang, 2003). Based on these aspects, Jia, Shaw, and Tsui (2014) label the incentives and investments provided by the organization as organizational inducements, which are defined as the actions that the organization provides to its employees to motivate them to demonstrate the attitudes and behaviors that the organization expects to see, including material rewards and developmental rewards. Material rewards refer to the material remuneration that the organization gives to its employees, including salary, performance rewards, welfare, and so on. Developmental rewards refer to the organization's training or assistance for employees' growth and development, including providing a supportive work environment, training, and career development; participating in decision making, fair treatment, respect, and care; and so on (Jia et al., 2014).

According to social exchange theory, the purpose of organizational inducements is to receive reciprocal returns from employees, promote employees' positive attitudes and behaviors (including organizational commitment, job satisfaction, organizational citizenship behavior, employee performance, and similar) as well as reduce negative attitudes and behaviors (including behaviors like tardiness, absenteeism, turnover intentions, and turnover rate). Doing so will result in organizational performance improvements. Work engagement is one of the outcomes of organizational expectations (Yao et. al., 2020).

Kahn argues that work engagement is the self-control of organizational members when combining themselves with their work roles, which has the three levels of engagement: Physical, cognitive, and emotional (1990). Maslach, Schaufeli, and Leiter treat the range from work engagement to job burnout, the two-extreme states, as a three-dimensional continuum that consists of the following factors: Energy, involvement, and efficacy (2001). Schaufeli et al. (2004) believe that the two states are not simply direct opposites, but that both are interconnected and relatively independent of the psychological state. They define work engagement as a positive, fulfilling emotional and cognitive state associated with work that includes 3 dimensions: vigor, dedication, and absorption.

Vigor refers to outstanding energy and toughness, a willingness to work using one's own efforts, not easily fatigued, perseverance in the face of difficulties, and so on. Dedication is a strong engagement in work with a purpose and a high degree of enthusiasm and the feeling of being proud and inspired. Absorption is the state of being fully engaged, and it feels like time is passing too fast during work (Schaufeli, Salanova, Gonzalez-Roma, & Bakker, 2002).

Understanding this environment is important as it has been demonstrated that work engagement can negatively impact absenteeism and turnover as well as positively impact job satisfaction, organizational commitment, and job performance (Karatepe, Beirami, & Bouzari, 2014). Work engagement can also improve individuals' subjective well-being and physical health (Little, Simmons, & Nelson, 2007). According to social exchange theory (Blau, 1986), the relationship between employees and organizations is a kind of social exchange. If an organization provides regular material investments in its employees and considers for employees' career development, the employees will perceive that the organization appreciates their value, will be willing to establish strong relationships with the organization, and will take positive actions to feedback the organization.

An organization's material and developmental inputs are strong signals to the employees that the organization is concerned about human capital and hope that employees work actively to improve their service capacity and productivity. However, the above relationships can also be influenced by individual differences (such as exchange ideology) and the external environment (perceived job alternatives) (Yao et. al., 2020). Exchange ideology, a key exchange orientation, is an individual's attitude toward the relationship between work effort and organizational rewards (Eisenberger, Huntington, & Hutchison, 1986); employees with a high level of exchange ideology are more rational and self-motivated. Witt (1991) found that exchange ideology has a moderating effect on many social exchange relationships in organizations.

There are some additional factors of importance to consider in evaluating: Job embeddedness and organizational inducement (Yao et. al., 2019). Job embeddedness is a force that prevents an individual from leaving a job (Yao, Lee, & Mitchell., 2004). The higher the embedding level, the less likely it is for employees to leave their jobs (Mitchell, Holtom, & Lee, 2001), and job embeddedness reflects individual inertia and the attachment to their work environment (Hom et al., 2009). Organizational inducement can increase the work engagement of employees, which is consistent with social exchange theory (Blau, 1964). That is, the organization provides a high level of material and developmental rewards, which are exchanged for the employees' high work engagement. In this process, job embeddedness plays a mediating role, and again it shows that the positive actions taken by the organization can increase the linkage between the organization and employees, increase employees' costs of leaving the organization, and ultimately affect employees' work attitudes and behaviors (Bambacas & Kulik, 2013; Hom et al., 2009; Tian, Cordery, & Gamble, 2016). Xinhua. Shih-Shuo, Yeh., Tai-Ying, and Tzung-Cheng developed a model to explain the interchange between work engagement, organizational inducement, and job embeddedness while factoring in influences from exchange ideology and job alternatives (2020) that is featured in Figure 3 below:

The Xinhua et. al. (2020) model proposed several hypotheses explaining interactions among the various factors identified in figure 2.8, most of which were supported. The first hypothesis (H1) stated that organizational inducement has positive relationship to employees' work engagement. The second hypothesis (H2) determined that job embeddedness will mediate the effect of organizational inducements on employees' work engagement. The third hypothesis (H3) identified that exchange ideology will positively moderate the positive relationship between organizational inducements and job embeddedness: The relationship will be stronger when employees' exchange ideology is high (vs. low). The fourth hypothesis (H4) explored the notion that exchange ideology will positively moderate the positive relationship between organizational inducements and work engagement: The relationship will be stronger when employees' exchange ideology is high (vs. low). The fifth hypothesis (H5) ascertained that job alternatives will negatively moderate the influence of job embeddedness on employees' work engagement. In other words, the more job alternatives perceived to be available by an employee, the weaker the influence of job embeddedness on employees' work engagement. The sixth hypothesis (H6) postulated that exchange ideology will positively moderate the indirect positive effects of organizational inducements on employees' work engagement via job embeddedness: The indirect positive effect will be stronger when employees' exchange ideology is high (vs. low). The seventh and final hypothesis (H7) identified that Job alternatives will negatively moderate the indirect positive effects of organizational inducements on employees' work engagement via job embeddedness: The indirect positive effect will be stronger when employees' perceived job alternatives are less (vs. more).

Figure 3. Research model exploring the relationship between organizational inducement and work engagement
Source: Xinhua et al. (2020)

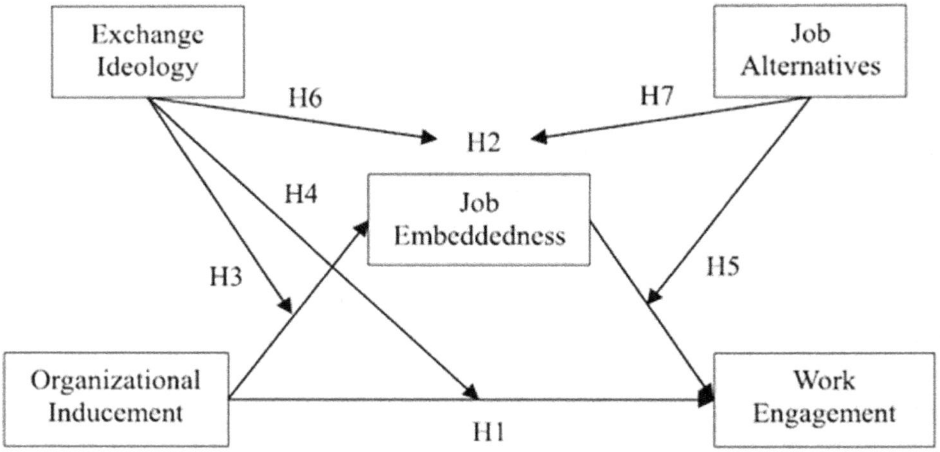

Xinhua et. al.'s study determined that of the stated hypotheses, the only one not supported by the results of the research was H7 (2020). Ultimately, this research demonstrates that the employees' exchange ideology can positively moderate the impact of organizational inducement on job embeddedness and work engagement, indicating that employees' individual exchange ideology plays an important role in employees' organizational relationships (Shore & Coyle-Shapiro, 2003). In addition, the employees' perceived job alternatives negatively moderate the effect of job embeddedness on work engagement, indicating that the external job market and environment can affect employees' work choices and work attitudes to some extent (Huang et al., 2017). In short, it is determined that the mediating role of job embeddedness can be moderated by the employees' exchange ideology but not perceived job alternatives (Xinhua et. al., 2020).

Practical applications of this discovery for management in a hotel environment are numerous. While giving the employees material rewards and developmental rewards, the organizations need to also consider employees' exchange ideology and the external job alternatives. The degree of exchange ideology has a direct impact on the success of social exchange, while external job alternatives can provide a wider option for social exchange (Xinhua et. al., 2020).

In addition, the organizations need to provide employees not only with competitive remuneration, good health insurance and housing subsidies, but also with developmental rewards. The developmental rewards, such as the fair treatment of employees, full empowerment, encouragement to participate in decisions-making, career development opportunities, and respect for employees' personal dignity, are at least as important as material rewards. These actions directly influence employees' work engagement and also indirectly increase the employees' work engagement by enhancing employees' job embeddedness (Huang et. al., 2017; Xinhua et al., 2020) In addition, the idea of teamwork can also be used (Tian et al., 2016) to help employees plan their careers, enable them to work in a more efficient way, enhance their connections with other employees, improve their skills and job matching, and increase the material and psychological costs of job turnover (Xinhua et. al., 2020).

The Impact of Job Insecurity and Work Engagement on Behaviors in a Hotel Working Environment

The unpredictable economic situation, mergers, downsizing, outsourcing, acquisitions, use of robots, automation and artificial intelligence, and other types of structural changes threaten employees' job security and give rise to uncertain employment conditions (Shin & Jeung, 2019; Sverke et al., 2002). Job insecurity which refers to the threat of unemployment or the fear of losing the current job in the future is considered a hindrance stressor that thwarts employees' personal growth and development (Staufenbiel & Konig, 2010).

In a work environment where employees have the fear of potential job loss, management is unable to retain employees who are high on work engagement (Karatepe, Rezapouraghdam, & Hassannia, 2020). Vigor, dedication, and absorption are the dimensions representing work engagement (Schaufeli, Bakker, & Salnova, 2006). Employees who feel energetic, are enthusiastic about their job, and are engrossed in their work report positive attitudinal and behavioral outcomes (Ibrahim, Suan, and Karatepe, 2019). However, it has been shown that job insecurity erodes work engagement and engenders detrimental outcomes such as nonattendance behaviors and counterproductive work behaviors (Bosman, Rothmann, & Buitendach, 2005; Etehadi & Karatepe, 2019; Sverke, Låstad, Hellgren, Richter, & Näswall, 2019). Non-attendance behaviors (i.e., tardiness and absenteeism) are generally considered those that are undesirable in a work environment (Karatepe et. al., 2020) as they directly lead to higher turnover (Krausz, Koslowski & Eiser, 1998), which is an unresolved and significant issue in the hotel industry (Chen & Ayoun, 2019) that is primarily triggered by job insecurity (Akgunduz & Eryilmaz, 2018).

Job insecurity is a hindrance stressor that impedes individuals' learning orientation, personal growth, and development. It also erodes the social element of business sustainability. Employees who worry about the possibility of future job loss may not accomplish their work goals (Karatepe et. al., 2020). Hindrance stressors have the potential to thwart employees' learning efforts, growth, and development. Such stressors impede their progress toward the accomplishment of goals (Crawford, LePine, & Rich, 2010). Threat-rigidity thesis suggests that employees demonstrate habituated responses in a threat situation (Niesen, De Witte, & Battistelli, 2014). These responses can imply withdrawal behaviors. Employees who feel insecure about their job may be willing to display (frequent) absences from work. Not surprisingly, job-insecure employees may feel demoralized to deal with tasks effectively at work. Such avoidance can result in absenteeism (Karatepe et. al., 2020).

Job insecurity erodes employees' motivation to have full concentration on their work (Akgunduz & Eryilmaz 2013). This is due to the fact that such employees have already lost their trust in the organization regarding the provision of a stable employment (Etehadi & Karatepe, 2019). Job security, which is a social sustainability practice leads to better job performance and quality of work life (Zuo, Jin & Flynn, 2012). Job insecurity, as a hindrance stressor, impedes employees' learning efforts and thwarts their growth and development. Under these conditions, such employees exhibit work engagement at low levels while employees having a trusting and loyal relationship with the employer are high on work engagement (Staw, Sandelands, &Dutton, 1981). A front-line hotel employees' cognitive appraisal of the threat of job loss in the future in the company will almost always lead to lower work engagement, which is an emotional response to job insecurity and can be significant in its ripple effects across other aspects of an employee's relationship with (or performance for) his or her employer (Niesen et. al, 2014). At this point, the phenomenon of threat-rigidity appears, which highlights an employees' propensity to respond in a way that is aligned with the perceived intensity of a threat. The response Is defined in its dimensions of type and strength and will aways be dictated by how severe a threat is perceived, independent of how significant a threat actually exists (Staw et. al., 1981). As threat-rigidity thesis proposes, employees display habituated responses under uncertainty surfacing from the threat of job insecurity (Niesen et al., 2014). Job-insecure hotel employees exhibit diminished work engagement threat-rigidity theory (Niesen et al., 2014). These are employees who worry a lot about their job security in the company and display habituated responses in the form of reduced work engagement and nonattendance intentions. Simply put, the presence of job insecurity will almost always give rise to low levels of work engagement and leadership should maintain a vigil for it as well as continually develop and deploy employee relations strategies to proactively diffuse its inception (Karatepe et. al., 2020).

The Impact of Negative Career Feedback and Career Outcomes

In the career domain, career feedback, which refers to information regarding individuals' career goal progress and goals (Hu, Creed, and Hood, 2016), has been linked to a range of career-related outcomes. Negative career feedback has been shown to be related to greater career distress (Creed, Wamelink, & Hu, 2015), disengagement from career goals, and lowering of career expectations (Hu, Creed, & Hood, 2017). Negative feedback can elicit an identity disturbance, which, in turn, can lead to implementing adaptive career strategies and actions (Hu, Hood and Creed, 2018). In particular, feedback indicating discrepancies between the person's current state and their career goals, where it is felt that goals are unsuitable or unattainable, can elicit reconsideration and self-reflection on the current goal choice. This, in turn, can trigger career exploration activities, such as gathering further information related to possible selves and career options (Anderson & Mounts, 2012).

Career exploration and career goal shifting are important for young adults to develop a career identity and to facilitate progress toward their future career, especially when facing setbacks (Anderson & Mounts, 2012). Young people who are able to explore their career possibilities are likely to have fewer difficulties in making a commitment to a career path (Xu, Hou, & Tracey, 2014), and, after graduation, might stay in a job for career satisfaction rather than financial obligations (Anderson & Mounts, 2012).

In addition, those young people who are able to disengage from unsuitable/unattainable career goals and find other meaningful goals are likely to avoid experiencing repeated failures and frustrations, and, consequently, increase their likelihood of success in their future career (Wrosch, Scheier, Miller, Schulz, & Carver, 2003).

Following career identity control theory, the goal of the Hu et. al.'s 2018 study was to examine how negative career feedback related to these two important activities: career exploration and goal shifting. Career exploration is an adaptive strategy for young adults, which is related positively to person-job fit, career-related engagement (Creed, Tilbury, Buys, & Crawford, 2011), and meaningful work life (Flum & Blustein, 2000). The model Hu et. al. (2018) developed was to test the relationships between negative feedback, career exploration and career goal setting. The model was only tested in a specific collectivist setting including young people from different universities and colleges in China. It is determined that while the findings are valid from the Hu et. al. (2018) study, the findings would need to be confirmed by repeating the study in different cultures, especially western ones. The tested model is featured in figure 4.4 below:

In young adults, career exploration can be triggered by a number of factors. For example, normative events such as graduation and entering the job market stimulate realistic and operational thoughts, and, thus, enable exploration of possible selves and environment opportunities and barriers (Anderson & Mounts, 2012). In addition, career exploration can also be initiated in response to an identity crisis or disturbance (Anderson & Mounts, 2012;

Kerpelman, Pittman, & Lamke, 1997). That is, when perceiving information that indicates discrepancies between the person's current state (e.g., goal progress, abilities, values) and goals (e.g., aspirations), they might try to eliminate the discrepancies by adjusting or consolidating their self-perceptions and career goals by exploring possible selves and career options.

Figure 4. The relationship between negative feedback, career exploration and career goal setting
Source: Hu et al. (2018)

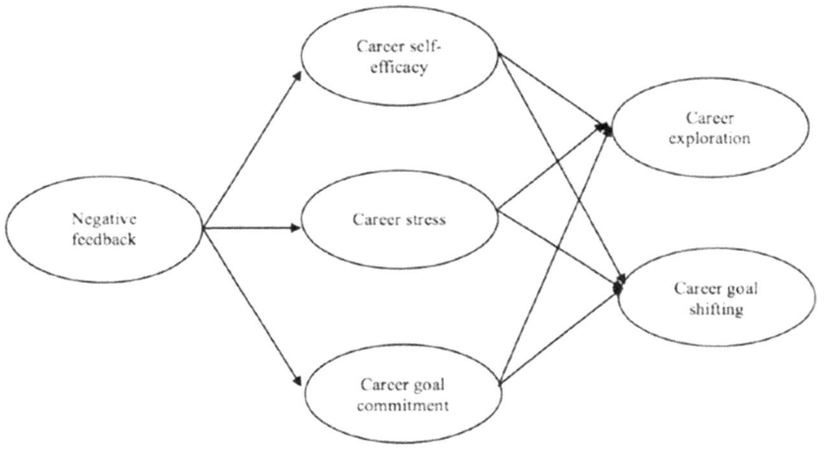

In addition to career exploration, young people can also switch to other career goals in the face of negative feedback (Bandura, 1991; Carver & Scheier, 1990; Latham & Locke, 1991; Lent, Ireland, Penn, Morris, & Sappington, 2017; Wrosch et al., 2003). This process includes identifying alternative meaningful goals, imbuing value and meaning to those goals, and taking action to reach them (Wrosch et al., 2003). Career goal shifting is highly adaptive, as engaging with other meaningful career goals can help young people reduce psychological distress when it is elicited by past goal failures and prevent them from feeling aimless after goal abandonment (Wrosch et al., 2003).

CONCLUSION

Anderson and Mounts (2012) were the first to test career exploration as an outcome elicited by negative career feedback. However, in their experimental design, all participants received the same-level of manipulated negative feedback, whereas career exploration was not controlled prior to the experiment. This means that no direct evidence was provided for the link between negative feedback and career exploration. Hu et al. (2018) hypothesized that negative feedback would be related to greater career exploration and operationalized negative career feedback as three different factors: Feedback on progress being made toward the goal, on whether goals were suitable and compatible with the person's personal qualities, and on whether improvements were needed to achieve the goal (Hu et al., 2016).

Hu et. al. (2017) tested career goal shifting (operationalized as an intention to engage with a lower career goal) as an outcome of negative career feedback. They provided evidence that young people who received more negative feedback reported a greater likelihood to pursue a less challenging career goal at a later time. However, young people can engage with a new goal without necessarily lowering their expectations in the same domain; they can also switch to a new career path such as from being a doctor to a psychologist (Wrosch et al., 2003). When confronted with feedback that indicates unsatisfactory progress or unsuitable or unattainable goals, young adults are likely to re-evaluate their capabilities for achieving their future career goals (i.e., lower their self-efficacy), feel anxious and frustrated about their goal choice (i.e., experience career stress), and be less motivated when pursuing the current goals (i.e., reduce their commitment).

Previous literature has demonstrated that negative career feedback related to lower career self-efficacy and greater career stress (Creed, Wamelink, & Hu et. al., 2017; Hu et al., 2018). In addition, negative feedback was found to relate to a greater likelihood of withdrawing effort and commitment from current career goals, implying that negative feedback might be related to lower career goal commitment (Hu et. al., 2017). Negative affect, such as career anxiety about decision-making, can elicit career exploration and career goal adjustment so as to reduce the disturbance (Anderson & Mounts, 2012; Kerpelman et al., 1997). Young people undertook more exploratory activities when they perceived their career goals to be important to them (Anderson & Mounts, 2012), suggesting a positive relationship between commitment and career exploration (Hu et. al., 2018).

Negative feedback on goal suitability and improvements needed is related to greater career goal shifting, suggesting that young people are more likely to take adaptive actions of switching their effort and commitment to an alternative goal when perceiving that their current goals are unsuitable or unattainable (Hu et al., 2018). Negative feedback on progress is related to less goal shifting. The component of feedback on progress that is independent of the other two feedback types (i.e., that is unrelated to feedback that referred to an unsuitable/unrealistic goal) directly points out improvements needed to regulate behaviors to achieve the goal, such as exerting more effort. This might focus the person's attention on the current goal and, thus, lower their interest in shifting to another goal (Hu et al., 2017)

Feedback on progress and on improvements needed were related to less career exploration, suggesting that young people were less likely to gather information about their possible selves and career options in the face of negative feedback indicating a lack of progress and strategies to improve. more negative feedback on progress initiates more engagement and effort in progressing the current career goals, rather than prompting the exploration of, and engagement in, other goals. Meanwhile, negative feedback is related to greater career stress, indicating that young people were more likely to experience anxiety and uncertainty about their career future when confronted with negative feedback (Hu et. al., 2018).

In addition, feedback on goal suitability and improvements needed is related to lower goal commitment. Feedback on goal suitability contributes 50% of the variance to goal commitment. This means that these two types of feedback, especially feedback indicating a goal misfit, might de-motivate young adults in pursuing their current goals, which is reasonable, as the feedback indicates that the current goals are inappropriate and/or unattainable (Hu et. al., 2018). Negative relationships exist between feedback on progress and goal suitability and career self-efficacy. This indicates that young people might lower their self-beliefs about their career capacity when perceiving feedback that indicates a lack of progress and goal misfit (Hu et. al., 2017). Finally, when negative feedback and the other self-regulatory processes ware controlled, self-efficacy was related positively to career exploration as expected. This means that when the young adults felt more competent in achieving career goals, they were more likely to engage in career exploration activities (Hu et. al., 2018).

Career goal commitment and career stress carries the effects of feedback on goal suitability and improvements to career goal shifting. This suggests that, when the young people receive negative feedback about their goal suitability and improvements needed, they are more likely to experience greater anxiety about their goal choice, lower their commitment to the current goal, and, potentially, switch their commitment to another goal. In contrast, when they perceived feedback that more effort and engagement were needed to reach the goal, they were more likely to commit to the goal, and, thus, less likely to shift to another goal (Hu et. al., 2018). Career self-efficacy does, however, mediate between negative feedback on progress and career exploration. When confronted with feedback indicating a lack of progress, young people experience lower self-confidence in their general career capacity, which, in turn, makes them less active in career exploration activities (Hu et. al., 2017).

Because front-line positions in a hotel operation are often filled by younger individuals who are only beginning (or yet to start) their career development, the importance of leadership investing time, effort, and mentorship activities on supporting employees in this type of initiative is critical. Although engagement in another career goal could be adaptive when current career goals are unsuitable, career counsellors need to help young people evaluate whether this is the best strategy in their own case. Understanding the person's underlying self-regulation processes will also be helpful in this evaluation. In particular, counsellors (or those trained in career development coaching) can help young people identify the type of negative feedback they are receiving (Shin et al., 2019).

Feedback indicating goal misfit and a lack of strategies is related to less goal commitment and more career stress, with, in turn, engagement in another goal (Hu et. al, 2018). In this situation, counsellors are encouraged to facilitate the client to assess the credibility of the feedback via, for example, seeking more feedback from different, available sources, reflecting on how they interpret and process the feedback (e.g., whether they might be overly focused on the negative part of the feedback), identifying the barriers that hinder their progress in goal pursuit, and identifying resources that could be employed to overcome these barriers (Anderson and Mounts, 2012).

If the goal is still considered attainable, specific strategies to improve an employee's current state need to be offered. If the goal is indeed not suitable or attainable for the person, helping them set a more appropriate goal and preventing them from repeated failures is a crucial task (Creed et. al., 2015). Career exploration is a necessary and beneficial step before people set a new goal (Wrosch et. al., 2003). When confronted with negative feedback, however, young people became less active in career exploration, partially because they experienced less self-confidence in their career abilities. It is important at this stage to support young people in the restoration of self-efficacy while collaboratively engaging in discovery of how skills, interests and career possibilities align leading to optimized decision making about individual development and milestone goals regarding career choices.

REFERENCES

Abdel-Halim, A. A. (1981). Effects of role stress-job design-technology interaction on employee work satisfaction. *Academy of Management Journal*, *24*(2), 260–273. doi:10.2307/255840

Abildgaard, J. S., Nielsen, K., & Sverke, M. (2018). Can job insecurity be managed? Evaluating an organizational-level intervention addressing the negative effects of restructuring. *Work and Stress*, *32*(2), 105–123. doi:10.1080/02678373.2017.1367735

Akgunduz, Y., & Eryilmaz, G. (2018). Does turnover intention mediate the effects of job insecurity and co-worker support on social loafing? *International Journal of Hospitality Management*, *68*, 41–49. doi:10.1016/j.ijhm.2017.09.010

Allvin, M., Mellner, C., Movitz, F., & Aronsson, G. (2013). The diffusion of flexibility: Estimating the incidence of low-regulated working conditions. *Nordic Journal of Working Life Studies*, *3*(3), 99–116. doi:10.19154/njwls.v3i3.3013

Anderson, K. L., & Mounts, N. S. (2012). Searching for the self: An identity control theory approach to triggers of occupational exploration. *The Journal of Genetic Psychology*, *173*(1), 90–111. doi:10.1080/00221325.2011.573027 PMID:22428377

Arnold, H. J., & Feldman, D. C. (1982). A multivariate analysis of the determinants of job turnover. *The Journal of Applied Psychology*, *67*(3), 350–360. doi:10.1037/0021-9010.67.3.350

Ashford, S. J., Lee, C., & Bobko, P. (1989). Content, causes, and consequences of job insecurity: A theory-based measure and substantive test. *The Academy of Management Annals*, *32*(4), 803–829.

Bacharach, S. B., Bamberger, P., & Conley, S. (1991). Work-home conflict among nurses and engineers: Mediating the impact of role stress on burnout and satisfaction at work. *Journal of Organizational Behavior, 12*(1), 39–53. doi:10.1002/job.4030120104

Bambacas, M., & Kulik, T. C. (2013). Job embeddedness in China: How HR practices impact turnover intentions. *International Journal of Human Resource Management, 24*(10), 1933–1952. doi:10.1080/09585192.2012.725074

Bambra, C., Egan, M., Thomas, S., Petticrew, M., & Whitehead, M. (2007). The psychosocial and health effects of workplace reorganization: A systematic review of task restructuring interventions. *Journal of Epidemiology and Community Health, 61*(12), 1028–1037. doi:10.1136/jech.2006.054999 PMID:18000123

Bandura, A. (1991). Social cognitive theory of self-regulation. *Organizational Behavior and Human Decision Processes, 50*(2), 248–287. doi:10.1016/0749-5978(91)90022-L

Barling, J., & Kelloway, K. E. (1996). Job insecurity and health: The moderating role of workplace control. *Stress Medicine, 12*(4), 253–259. doi:10.1002/(SICI)1099-1700(199610)12:4<253::AID-SMI710>3.0.CO;2-2

Beehr, T. A., & Newman, J. E. (1978). Job stress, employee health, and organizational effectiveness: A facet analysis, model, and literature review. *Personnel Psychology, 31*(4), 665–669. doi:10.1111/j.1744-6570.1978.tb02118.x

Blau, P. M. (1964). Justice in social exchange. *Sociological Inquiry, 34*(2), 193–206. doi:10.1111/j.1475-682X.1964.tb00583.x

Blau, P. M. (1986). *Exchange and power in social life* (2nd ed.). Routledge.

Bosman, J., Rothmann, S., & Buitendach, J. H. (2005). Job insecurity, burnout and work engagement: The impact of positive and negative affectivity. *SA Journal of Industrial Psychology, 31*(4), 48–56. doi:10.4102ajip.v31i4.199

Brockner, J. (1988). The effects of work layoffs on survivors: Research, theory, and practice. In B. M. Staw & L. L. Cummings (Eds.), *Research in organizational behavior* (Vol. 10). JAI Press.

Burke, R. J., & Nelson, D. (1998). Mergers and acquisitions, downsizing, and privatization: A North American perspective. In M. K. Gowing, J. D. Kraft, & J. C. Quick (Eds.), *The new organizational reality: Downsizing, restructuring, and revitalization* (pp. 21–54). American Psychological Association. doi:10.1037/10252-001

Carver, C. S., & Scheier, M. F. (1990). Origins and functions of positive and negative affect. *Psychological Review*, *97*(1), 19–35. doi:10.1037/0033-295X.97.1.19

Cavanaugh, M. A., Boswell, W. R., Roehling, M. V., & Boudreau, J. W. (2000). An empirical examination of self-reported work stress among U.S. managers. *The Journal of Applied Psychology*, *85*(1), 65–74. doi:10.1037/0021-9010.85.1.65 PMID:10740957

Chen, H., & Ayoun, B. (2019). Is negative workplace humor really all that "negative"? Workplace humor and hospitality employees' job embeddedness. *International Journal of Hospitality Management*, *79*(May), 41–49. doi:10.1016/j.ijhm.2018.12.010

Chen, J., Wang, L., & Tang, N. (2016). Half the sky: The moderating role of cultural collectivism in job turnover among Chinese female workers. *Journal of Business Ethics*, *133*(3), 1–12. doi:10.100710551-014-2395-1

Cooper, C. L., & Marshall, J. (1976). Occupational sources of stress: A review of the literature relating to coronary heart disease and mental ill-health. *Journal of Occupational Psychology*, *49*(1), 11–28. doi:10.1111/j.2044-8325.1976.tb00325.x

Coverman, S. (1989). Role overload, role conflict and stress: Addressing consequences of multiple role demands. *Social Forces*, *67*(4), 965–982. doi:10.2307/2579710

Cox, T., Griffiths, A., Barlowe, C., Randall, R., Thomson, L., & Rial-Gonzalez, E. (2000). Organisational interventions for work stress: A risk management approach. *HSE Contract Research Report*, *286*, 68.

Crawford, E. R., LePine, J. A., & Rich, B. L. (2010). Linking job demands and resources to employee engagement and burnout: A theoretical extension and meta-analytic test. *The Journal of Applied Psychology*, *95*(5), 834–848. doi:10.1037/a0019364 PMID:20836586

Creed, P., Tilbury, C., Buys, N., & Crawford, M. (2011). The career aspirations and action behaviours of Australian adolescents in out-of-home-care. *Children and Youth Services Review*, *33*(9), 1720–1729. doi:10.1016/j.childyouth.2011.04.033

Creed, P. A., Wamelink, T., & Hu, S. (2015). Antecedents and consequences to perceived career goal–progress discrepancies. *Journal of Vocational Behavior*, *87*, 43–53. doi:10.1016/j.jvb.2014.12.001

Dai, Y., Zhuang, W., & Huan, T. C. (2019). Engage or quit? The moderating role of abusive supervision between resilience, intention to leave and work engagement. *Tourism Management*, *70*, 69–77. doi:10.1016/j.tourman.2018.07.014

Darvishmotevali, M., Arasli, H., & Kilic, H. (2017). Effect of job insecurity on frontline employee's performance: Looking through the lens of psychological strains and leverages. *International Journal of Contemporary Hospitality Management*, *29*(6), 1724–1744. doi:10.1108/IJCHM-12-2015-0683

Davy, J. A., Kinicki, A. J., & Scheck, C. L. (1997). A test of job security's direct and mediated effects on withdrawal cognitions. *Journal of Organizational Behavior*, *18*(4), 323–349. doi:10.1002/(SICI)1099-1379(199707)18:4<323::AID-JOB801>3.0.CO;2-#

de Jong, T., Wiezer, N., de Weerd, M., Nielsen, K., Mattila-Holappa, P., & Mockałło, Z. (2016). The impact of restructuring on employee well-being: A systematic review of longitudinal studies. *Work and Stress*, *30*(1), 91–114. doi:10.1080/02678373.2015.1136710

De Witte, H. (2005). Job insecurity: Review of the international literature on definitions, prevalence, antecedents and consequences. *SA Journal of Industrial Psychology*, *31*(4), 1–6. doi:10.4102ajip.v31i4.200

De Witte, H., De Cuyper, N., Handaja, Y., Sverke, M., Näswall, K., & Hellgren, J. (2010). Associations between quantitative and qualitative job insecurity and well-being. *International Studies of Management & Organization*, *40*(1), 40–56. doi:10.2753/IMO0020-8825400103

De Witte, H., Vander Elst, T., & De Cuyper, N. (2015). Job insecurity, health and well-being. In J. Vuori, R. Blonk, & R. Price (Eds.), *Sustainable Working Lives. Aligning Perspectives on Health, Safety and Well-Being* (pp. 109–128). Springer.

Dekker, S. W. A., & Schaufeli, W. B. (1995). The effects of job insecurity on psychological health and withdrawal: A longitudinal study. *Australian Psychologist*, *30*(1), 57–63. doi:10.1080/00050069508259607

Demerouti, E., Bakker, A. B., Nachreiner, F., & Schaufeli, W. B. (2001). The job demands-resources model of burnout. *The Journal of Applied Psychology*, *86*(3), 499–512. doi:10.1037/0021-9010.86.3.499 PMID:11419809

Densten, I. L. (2001). Re-thinking burnout. *Journal of Organizational Behavior*, *22*(8), 833–847. doi:10.1002/job.115

Eisenberger, R., Huntington, R., Hutchison, S., & Sowa, D. (1986). Perceived organizational support. *The Journal of Applied Psychology*, *71*(3), 500–507. doi:10.1037/0021-9010.71.3.500

Etehadi, B., & Karatepe, O. M. (2019). The impact of job insecurity on critical hotel employee outcomes: The mediating role of self-efficacy. *Journal of Hospitality Marketing & Management*, *28*(6), 665–689. doi:10.1080/19368623.2019.1556768

Flum, H., & Blustein, D. L. (2000). Reinvigorating the study of vocational exploration: A framework for research. *Journal of Vocational Behavior*, *56*(3), 380–404. doi:10.1006/jvbe.2000.1721

Fogarty, T. J., Singh, J., Rhoads, G. K., & Moore, R. K. (2000). Antecedents and consequences of burnout in accounting: Beyond the role stress model. *Behavioral Research in Accounting*, *12*, 31–67.

Freudenberger, H. J. (1974). Staff burn-out. *The Journal of Social Issues*, *30*(1), 159–165. doi:10.1111/j.1540-4560.1974.tb00706.x

Gowing, M. K., Kraft, J. D., & Campbell, Q. J. (Eds.). (1998). *The new organizational reality: Downsizing, restructuring, and revitalization.* American Psychological Association. doi:10.1037/10252-000

Greenhalgh, L., & Rosenblatt, Z. (1984). Job insecurity: Toward conceptual clarity. *Academy of Management Review*, *9*(3), 438–448. doi:10.2307/258284

Hartley, J., Jacobson, D., Klandermans, B., & van Vuuren, T. (1991). *Job insecurity: Coping with jobs at risk.* Sage.

Heaney, C. A., Israel, B. A., & House, J. S. (1994). Chronic job insecurity among automobile workers: Effects on job satisfaction and health. *Social Science & Medicine*, *38*(10), 1431–1437. doi:10.1016/0277-9536(94)90281-X PMID:8023192

Hitt, M. A., Keats, B. W., Harback, H. F., & Nixon, R. D. (1994). Rightsizing building and maintaining strategic leadership: A long-term competitiveness. *Organizational Dynamics*, *23*(2), 18–32. doi:10.1016/0090-2616(94)90066-3

Holman, D., & Axtell, C. (2015). Can job redesign interventions influence a broad range of employee outcomes by changing multiple job characteristics? A quasi-experimental study. *Journal of Occupational Health Psychology*, *21*(3), 284–295. doi:10.1037/a0039962 PMID:26641482

Hom, P. W., Tsui, A. S., Wu, J. B., Lee, T. W., Zhang, A. Y., Fu, P. P., & Li, L. (2009). Explaining employment relationships with social exchange and job embeddedness. *The Journal of Applied Psychology*, *94*(2), 277–297. doi:10.1037/a0013453 PMID:19271791

Howard, A. (1995). *The changing nature of work*. Jossey-Bass.

Hu, S., Creed, P. A., & Hood, M. (2017). Career goal revision in response to negative feedback. *Journal of Counseling Psychology*, *64*(3), 335–345. doi:10.1037/cou0000193 PMID:28165259

Hu, S., Hood, M., & Creed, P. A. (2018). Negative career feedback and career outcomes: The mediating roles of self-regulatory processes. *Journal of Vocational Behavior*, *106*, 180–191. doi:10.1016/j.jvb.2018.02.002

Huang, G.-H., Wellman, N., Ashford, S. J., Lee, C., & Wang, L. (2017). Deviance and exit: The organizational costs of job insecurity and moral disengagement. *The Journal of Applied Psychology*, *102*(1), 26–42. doi:10.1037/apl0000158 PMID:27618406

Ibrahim, S. N. H., Suan, C. L., & Karatepe, O. M. (2019). The effects of supervisor support and self-efficacy on call center employees' work engagement and quitting intentions. *International Journal of Manpower*, *40*(4), 688–703. doi:10.1108/IJM-12-2017-0320

Jacobson, D. (1991). Toward a theoretical distinction between the stress components of the job insecurity and job loss experiences. In S. B. Bacharach (Ed.), *Research in the sociology of organizations* (Vol. 9, pp. 1–19). JAI Press.

Jahoda, M. (1982). *Employment and unemployment*. University Press.

Jia, L., Shaw, J. D., Tsui, A. S., & Park, T.-Y. (2014). A social-structural perspective on employee organization relationships and team creativity. *Academy of Management Journal*, *57*(3), 869–891. doi:10.5465/amj.2011.0147

Jick, T. D. (1985). As the axe falls: Budget cuts and the experience of stress in organizations. In T. A. Beehr & R. S. Bhagat (Eds.), *Human stress and cognition in organizations: An integrated perspective* (pp. 83–114). Wiley.

Jones, E., Chonko, L., Rangarajan, D., & Roberts, J. (2007). The role of overload on job attitudes, turnover intentions, and salesperson performance. *Journal of Business Research*, *60*(7), 663–671. doi:10.1016/j.jbusres.2007.02.014

Jung, H. S., Yoon, H. H., & Kim, Y. J. (2012). Effects of culinary employees' role stress on burnout and turnover intention in hotel industry: Moderating effects on employees' tenure. *Service Industries Journal*, *32*(13), 2145–2165. doi:10.1080/02642069.2011.574277

Kahn, R. L., Wolfe, D. M., Quinn, R. P., Snoek, J. D., & Rosenthal, R. A. (1964). *Occupational Stress: Studies in Role Conflict and Ambiguity*. John Wiley & Sons.

Kahn, W. A. (1990). Psychological conditions of personal engagement and disengagement at work. *Academy of Management Journal*, *33*(4), 692–724. doi:10.2307/256287

Kahneman, D. (2011). *Thinking, Fast and Slow*. Doubleday.

Karatepe, O. M. (2013). The effects of work overload and work-family conflict on job embeddedness and job performance: The mediation of emotional exhaustion. *International Journal of Contemporary Hospitality Management*, *25*(4), 614–634. doi:10.1108/09596111311322952

Karatepe, O. M., Beirami, E., Bouzari, M., & Safavi, H. P. (2014). Does work engagement mediate the effects of challenge stressors on job outcomes? Evidence from the hotel industry. *International Journal of Hospitality Management*, *36*, 14–22. doi:10.1016/j.ijhm.2013.08.003

Karatepe, O. M., Rezapouraghdam, H., & Hassannia, R. (2020). Job insecurity, work engagement and their effects on hotel employees' non-green and nonattendance behaviors. *International Journal of Hospitality Management*, *87*(May), 1–12. doi:10.1016/j.ijhm.2020.102472

Karatepe, O. M., & Uludag, O. (2008). Role stress, burnout and their effects on frontline hotel employees' job performance: Evidence from Northern Cyprus. *International Journal of Tourism Research, 10*(2), 111–126. doi:10.1002/jtr.645

Kelly, T., & Barrett, M. (2011). The leading causes and potential consequences of occupational stress: A study of Irish trainee accountants. *Irish Accounting Review, 18*(2), 31–55. doi:10.52399/001c.27033

Kerpelman, J. L., Pittman, J. F., & Lamke, L. K. (1997). Toward a microprocess perspective on adolescent identity development: An identity control theory approach. *Journal of Adolescent Research, 12*(3), 325–346. doi:10.1177/0743554897123002

Kets de Vries, M. F. R., & Balazs, K. (1997). The downside of downsizing. *Human Relations, 50*(1), 11–50. doi:10.1177/001872679705000102

Kieselbach, T., Armgarth, E., Bagnara, S., Elo, A.-L., Jefferys, S., Joling, C., & Rogovsky, N. (2009). *Health in Restructuring: Innovative Approaches and Policy Recommendations (HIRES)*. Universität Bremen.

Kim, J. (2015). What increases public employees' turnover intention? *Public Personnel Management, 44*(4), 496–519. doi:10.1177/0091026015604447

Kim, S. M., Um, K. H., Kim, H. Y., & Kim, Y. H. (2016). Hospital career management systems and their effects on the psychological state and career attitudes of nurses. *Service Business, 10*(1), 87–112. doi:10.100711628-014-0257-7

Kim, T. T., Paek, S., Chang, H. C., & Lee, G. (2012). Frontline service employees' customer-related social stressors, emotional exhaustion, and service recovery performance: Customer orientation as a moderator. *Service Business, 6*(4), 503–526. doi:10.100711628-012-0164-8

Klein Hesselink, D. J., & van Vuuren, T. (1999). Job flexibility and job insecurity: The Dutch case. *European Journal of Work and Organizational Psychology, 8*(2), 273–293. doi:10.1080/135943299398366

Konovsky, M., & Folger, R. (1987). Relative effects of procedural and distributive justice on employee attitudes. *Representative Research in Social Psychology, 17*, 15–24.

Kozlowski, S., Chao, G., Smith, E., & Hedlund, J. (1993). Organizational downsizing: Strategies, interventions and research implications. In C. L. Cooper & I. T. Robertson (Eds.), *International review of industrial and organizational psychology* (Vol. 8, pp. 263–332). Wiley.

Krausz, M., Koslowsky, M., & Eiser, A. (1998). Distal and proximal influences on turnover intentions and satisfaction: Support for a withdrawal progression theory. *Journal of Vocational Behavior*, *52*(1), 59–71. doi:10.1006/jvbe.1996.1565

Kuo, B. C. H. (2013). Collectivism and coping: Current theories, evidence, and measurements of collective coping. *International Journal of Psychology*, *48*(3), 374–388. doi:10.1080/00207594.2011.640681 PMID:22335198

Latham, G. P., & Locke, E. A. (1991). Self-regulation through goal setting. *Organizational Behavior and Human Decision Processes*, *50*(2), 212–247. doi:10.1016/0749-5978(91)90021-K

Lent, R. W., Ireland, G. W., Penn, L. T., Morris, T. R., & Sappington, R. (2017). Sources of self-efficacy and outcome expectations for career exploration and decision making: A test of the social cognitive model of career self-management. *Journal of Vocational Behavior*, *99*, 107–117. doi:10.1016/j.jvb.2017.01.002

Lim, V. K. G. (1996). Job insecurity and its outcomes: Moderating effects of workbased and nonwork-based social support. *Human Relations*, *2*(2), 171–194. doi:10.1177/001872679604900203

Lin, Y. T., & Liu, N. C. (2016). High performance work systems and organizational service performance: The roles of different organizational climates. *International Journal of Hospitality Management*, *55*, 118–128. doi:10.1016/j.ijhm.2016.04.005

Little, L. M., Simmons, B. L., & Nelson, D. L. (2007). Health among leaders: Positive and negative affect, engagement and burnout, forgiveness and revenge. *Journal of Management Studies*, *44*(2), 243–260. doi:10.1111/j.1467-6486.2007.00687.x

Maslach, C., & Jackson, S. E. (1984). Burnout in organizational settings. *Applied Social Psychology Annual*, *5*, 133–153.

Matteson, M. T., & Ivancevich, J. M. (1987). *Controlling work stress: Effective human resource and management strategies*. Jossey-Bass.

Mattiasson, I., Lindgarde, F., Nilsson, J. A., & Theorell, T. (1990). Threat of unemployment and cardiovascular risk factors: Longitudinal study of quality of sleep and serum cholesterol concentration in men threatened with redundancy. *BMJ (Clinical Research Ed.)*, *301*(6750), 461–466. doi:10.1136/bmj.301.6750.461 PMID:2207398

McLean Parks, J., Kidder, D. L., & Gallagher, D. G. (1998). Fitting square pegs into round holes: Mapping the domain of contingent work arrangements onto the psychological contract. *Journal of Organizational Behavior*, *19*(S1), 697–730. doi:10.1002/(SICI)1099-1379(1998)19:1+<697::AID-JOB974>3.0.CO;2-I

Mitchell, T. R., Holtom, B. C., Lee, T. W., Sablynski, C. J., & Erez, M. (2001). Why people stay: Using job embeddedness to predict voluntary turnover. *Academy of Management Journal*, *44*(6), 1102–1121. doi:10.2307/3069391

Montani, F., Courcy, F., & Vandenberghe, C. (2017). Innovating under stress: The role of commitment and leader-member exchange. *Journal of Business Research*, *77*, 1–13. doi:10.1016/j.jbusres.2017.03.024

Mulki, J. P., Jaramillo, J. F., & Locander, W. B. (2008). Effect of ethical climate on turnover intention: Linking attitudinal and stress theory. *Journal of Business Ethics*, *78*(4), 559–574. doi:10.100710551-007-9368-6

Nielsen, K. (2013). Review article: How can we make organizational interventions work? Employees and line managers as actively crafting interventions. *Human Relations*, *66*(8), 1029–1050. doi:10.1177/0018726713477164

Nielsen, K., Fredslund, H., Christensen, K. B., & Albertsen, K. (2006). Success or failure? Interpreting and understanding the impact of interventions in four similar worksites. *Work and Stress*, *20*(3), 272–287. doi:10.1080/02678370601022688

Nielsen, K., & Randall, R. (2012). The importance of employee participation and perceptions of changes in procedures in a teamworking intervention. *Work and Stress*, *26*(2), 91–111. doi:10.1080/02678373.2012.682721 PMID:22745519

Niesen, W., De Witte, & Battistelli, A. (2014). An explanatory model of job insecurity and innovative work behavior: insights from social exchange and threat rigidity theory. In Contemporary Occupational Health Psychology: Global Perspectives on Research and Practice (vol. 3). John Wiley & Sons Limited.

Noer, D. (1993). *Healing the wounds: Overcoming the trauma of layoffs and revitalizing downsized organizations*. Jossey-Bass.

O' Neill, J. W., & Davis, K. (2011). Work stress and well-being in the hotel industry. *International Journal of Hospitality Management*, *30*(2), 385–390. doi:10.1016/j.ijhm.2010.07.007 PMID:23794780

Pfeffer, J. (1998). *The human equation: Building profits by putting people first*. Harvard University Press.

Pozner, B. Z., & Randolph, W. A. (1980). Moderators of role stress among hospital personnel. *The Journal of Psychology*, *105*(2), 215–224. doi:10.1080/00223980.1980.9915154 PMID:7400988

Probst, T. M. (2005). Economic stressors. In J. Barling, E. K. Kelloway, & M. R. Frone (Eds.), *Handbook of work stress* (pp. 267–297). Sage. doi:10.4135/9781412975995.n11

Rifkin, J. (1995). *The end of work: The decline of the global labor force and the dawn of the post-market era*. Putnam.

Rizzo, J. R., House, R. J., & Lirtzman, S. I. (1970). Role conflict and ambiguity in complex organizations. *Administrative Science Quarterly*, *15*(2), 150–163. doi:10.2307/2391486

Rosa, H. (2013). *Social acceleration: A new theory of modernity*. Columbia University Press. doi:10.7312/rosa14834

Rosenblatt, Z., & Ruvio, A. (1996). A test of a multidimensional model of job insecurity: The case of Israeli teachers. *Journal of Organizational Behavior*, *17*(S1), 587–605. doi:10.1002/(SICI)1099-1379(199612)17:1+<587::AID-JOB825>3.0.CO;2-S

Roskies, E., & Louis-Guerin, C. (1990). Job insecurity in managers: Antecedents and consequences. *Journal of Organizational Behavior*, *11*(5), 345–359. doi:10.1002/job.4030110503

Schaubroeck, J., Cotton, J. L., & Jennings, K. R. (1989). Antecedents and consequences of role stress: A covariance structure analysis. *Journal of Organizational Behavior*, *10*(1), 35–58. doi:10.1002/job.4030100104

Schaufeli, W. B., & Bakker, A. B. (2004, May). with burnout and engagement: A multi-sample study. *Journal of Organizational Behavior*, *25*(3), 293–315. doi:10.1002/job.248

Schaufeli, W. B., Bakker, A. B., & Salanova, M. (2006). The measurement of work engagement with a short questionnaire: A cross-national study. *Educational and Psychological Measurement*, *66*(4), 701–716. doi:10.1177/0013164405282471

Schaufeli, W. B., Salanova, M., Gonzalez-Roma, V., & Bakker, A. B. (2002). Burnout and engagement in university students. *Journal of Cross-Cultural Psychology*, *33*(5), 464–481. doi:10.1177/0022022102033005003

Schneider, B., White, S. S., & Paul, M. C. (1998). Linking service climate and customer perceptions of service quality: Test of a causal model. *The Journal of Applied Psychology*, *83*(2), 150–163. doi:10.1037/0021-9010.83.2.150 PMID:9577232

Schweiger, D. M., & Denisi, A. S. (1991). Communication with employees following a merger: A longitudinal field experiment. *Academy of Management Journal*, *34*(1), 110–135. doi:10.2307/256304

Semmer, N. K. (2011). Job stress interventions and organization of work. In J. C. Quick & L. E. Tetrick (Eds.), *Handbook of occupational health psychology* (pp. 299–318). American Psychological Association.

Shin, I., & Jeung, C. W. (2019). Uncovering the turnover intention of proactive employees: The mediating role of work engagement and the moderated mediating role of job autonomy. *International Journal of Environmental Research and Public Health*, *16*(5), 1–16, 843. doi:10.3390/ijerph16050843 PMID:30857145

Singh, J. (1993). Boundary role ambiguity: Facets, determinants, and impacts. *Journal of Marketing*, *57*(2), 11–31. doi:10.1177/002224299305700202

Sparrow, P. (1998). The pursuit of multiple and parallel organizational flexibilities: Reconstituting jobs. *European Journal of Work and Organizational Psychology*, *7*(1), 79–95. doi:10.1080/135943298398970

Staufenbiel, T., & Konig, C. J. (2010). A model for the effects of job insecurity on performance, turnover intention, and absenteeism. *Journal of Occupational and Organizational Psychology*, *83*(1), 101–117. doi:10.1348/096317908X401912

Staw, B. M., Sandelands, L. E., & Dutton, J. E. (1981). Threat rigidity effects in organizational behavior: A multilevel analysis. *Administrative Science Quarterly*, *26*(4), 501–524. doi:10.2307/2392337

Sverke, M., Gallagher, D. G., & Hellgren, J. (2000). Alternative work arrangements: Job stress, well-being and pro-organizational attitudes among employees with different employment contracts. In K. Isaksson, C. Hogstedt, C. Eriksson, & T. Theorell (Eds.), *Health effects of the new labour market* (pp. 145–167). Plenum.

Sverke, M., & Hellgren, J. (2002). The nature of job insecurity: Understanding employment uncertainty on the brink of a new millennium. *Applied Psychology*, *51*(1), 23–42. doi:10.1111/1464-0597.0077z

Sverke, M., Hellgren, J., & Naswall, K. (2002). No security: A meta-analysis and review of job insecurity and its consequences. *Journal of Occupational Health Psychology*, *7*(3), 242–264. doi:10.1037/1076-8998.7.3.242 PMID:12148956

Sverke, M., Låstad, L., Hellgren, J., Richter, A., & Näswall, K. (2019). A meta-analysis of job insecurity and employee performance: Testing temporal aspects, rating source, welfare regime, and union density as moderators. *International Journal of Environmental Research and Public Health*, *16*(14), 1–29. doi:10.3390/ijerph16142536 PMID:31315198

Teoh, M. W., Wang, Y., & Kwek, A. (2019). Coping with emotional labor in high stress hospitality work environments. *International Journal of Contemporary Hospitality Management*, *28*, 883–904.

Tetrick, L. E., & LaRocco, J. M. (1987). Understanding, prediction, and control as moderators of the relationships between perceived stress, satisfaction, and psychological well-being. *The Journal of Applied Psychology*, *72*(4), 538–543. doi:10.1037/0021-9010.72.4.538 PMID:3680098

Tian, A. W., Cordery, J., & Gamble, J. (2016). Staying and performing: How human resource management practices increase job embeddedness and performance. *Personnel Review*, *45*(5), 947–968. doi:10.1108/PR-09-2014-0194

Wang, D., Tsui, A. S., Zhang, Y., & Ma, L. (2003). Employment relationships and firm performance: Evidence from an emerging economy. *Journal of Organizational Behavior*, *24*(5), 511–535. doi:10.1002/job.213

Wen, B., Zhou, X., Hu, Y., & Zhang, X. (2020). Role stress and turnover intention of front-line hotel employees: The roles of burnout and service climate. *Frontiers in Psychology*, *11*, 36. doi:10.3389/fpsyg.2020.00036 PMID:32082216

Wiezer, N., Nielsen, K., Pahkin, K., Widerszal-Bazyl, M., De Jong, T., Mattila-Holappa, P., & Mockałło, Z. (2011). *Exploring the link between restructuring and employee well-being*. Central Institute for Labour Protection-National Research Institute.

Witt, L. A. (1991). Exchange ideology as a moderator of job attitudes-organizational citizenship behaviors relationships. *Journal of Applied Social Psychology*, *21*(18), 1490–1501.

Wrosch, C., Scheier, M. F., Miller, G. E., Schulz, R., & Carver, C. S. (2003). Adaptive self-regulation of unattainable goals: Goal disengagement, goal reengagement, and subjective well-being. *Personality and Social Psychology Bulletin*, *29*(12), 1494–1508. doi:10.1177/0146167203256921 PMID:15018681

Xinhua, G. (2020). Does organizational inducement foster work engagement in hospitality industry? Perspectives from a moderated mediation model. *Journal of Hospitality and Tourism Management*, *43*, 259–268. doi:10.1016/j.jhtm.2020.04.010

Yao, T., Qiu, Q., & Wei, Y. (2019). Retaining hotel employees as internal customers: Effect of organizational commitment on attitudinal and behavioral loyalty of employees. *International Journal of Hospitality Management*, *76*, 1–8. doi:10.1016/j.ijhm.2018.03.018

Yao, X., Lee, T. W., & Mitchell, T. R. (2004). Job embeddedness: Current research and future directions. In R. Griffeth & P. Hom (Eds.), *Understanding employee retention and turnover* (pp. 153–187). Information Age.

Zuo, J., Jin, X.-H., & Flynn, L. (2012). Social sustainability in construction-an explorative study. *International Journal of Construction Management*, *12*(2), 51–63. doi:10.1080/15623599.2012.10773190

Chapter 5
A Systematic Review of Extrinsic Factors That Destroy Organizational Effectiveness:
How Hotels Can Withstand Disruptive Events

ABSTRACT

This narrative analyzes factors external to a hotel operation that correlate negatively with organizational effectiveness. The COVID-19 pandemic of 2020 is the most significant global event of this type to have occurred in the past 100 years, with hotel operations around the planet experiencing a near complete elimination of business. The pandemic revealed that the hotel industry is unprepared to survive a crisis of this magnitude. The chapter details phases of recovery from any crisis, as well as strategies to encourage solution-generating effort from all employees. This chapter also reviews how events such as the COVID-19 pandemic, economic recessions, and other crises can affect the mental health of employees and how leaders can proactively dilute the impact of negative external stimuli. The chapter concludes by analyzing dimensions of organizational resilience and an evaluation of how the hotel industry has an opportunity to strategically enrich its practices in this area.

DOI: 10.4018/978-1-6684-2528-2.ch005

INTRODUCTION: JOB INSECURITY AND EXTERNAL DISRUPTIVE EVENTS

Day to day interactions on the job for front line hospitality associates are not the only source of burnout. External factors on a national, and sometimes global, scale that are often out of control for employees (like an economic recession) can also impact emotional exhaustion and burnout. This can sometimes lead to increased levels of voluntary separation and turnover. Job and employment insecurity partially mediated the association of the recession with physical health and fully mediated its association with mental health. Job insecurity, but not employment insecurity, partially mediated the association of the recession with affective organizational commitment (Frone, 2018).

A study showed that the 1974–1975 recession observed in the United States economy was associated with a net increase in job insecurity (Tausig & Fenwick, 1999). Tausig and Fenwick's panel study of the 1974–1975 U.S. recession found a statistically significant, though small, net increase in job insecurity from 1973 (prerecession period) to 1977 (post-recession period) among the employed. The results underscore the importance of research that furthers our understanding of how macroeconomic events affect those who remain employed, and that takes a broad view of employee insecurity regarding continuity of employment (Frone, 2018).

Job insecurity represents the perceived likelihood of involuntarily losing one's current job (Cheng & Chan, 2008; Chung & van Oorschot, 2011; Probst, 2005; Shoss, 2017; Sverke, Hellgren, & Naswall, 2002). Research shows that job (in)security is an important predictor of employee well-being and work-related attitudes (Shoss, 2017). Moreover, several models of job insecurity propose that it is a direct outcome of macroeconomic fluctuations in society (Probst, 2005; Shoss, 2017), though little research has directly tested this assertion.

An association between recession and job insecurity identifies that an experienced or anticipated primary stressors such as a loss of income or employment as a result of a recession can lead to a proliferation of secondary stressors, which can manifest as increased concern and emotional exhaustion related to being out of work (Pearlin and Bierman, 2013).

This chapter explores the specific characteristics associated with understanding how job insecurity can be caused by external factors as well as opportunities that the hospitality sector must prepare and proactively address these situations. The narrative explores how the COVID -19 global pandemic, the most significant disruptive event of the past 100 years, impacted hotel organizations and their employees. It also determines phases of recovery from a crisis (not just a global pandemic) as well as how the pandemic created unique opportunities for the entire hospitality sector to strategically navigate a post-pandemic future of uncertainty. The chapter will also review how the pandemic impacted employees, the affect it had on their mental health and job satisfaction before offering insight into how these observed behavioral characteristics can be better managed when future events occur to increase resilience and adaptability of the hotel, its employees and the entire sector.

BACKGROUND

In addition to job insecurity, a related concept is that of employment insecurity. Whereas job insecurity represents concerns about involuntarily losing one's current job, employment insecurity represents the perceived likelihood of not finding comparable new employment in the event of job loss (Cheng, Huang, Li, & Hsu, 2011; Chung & van Oorschot, 2011; Cottini & Ghinetti, 2018). Employment insecurity can result from external factors, such as a recession causing companies to reduce the number of positions they are hiring for (Muffels & Wilthagen, 2013). It can also result from intrinsic concerns that manifest in a belief (perceived or real) that an individual does not have the proper skills, characteristics or personality to secure new employment (Kuhnert & Vance, 1992).

Job insecurity and employment insecurity can manifest in populations who retain employment, but have observed involuntary separations occurring in their organization, in their industry or in other industries (Cheng, Huang & Hsu, 2011; Cotti & Ghinetti, 2018). Those who remain employed see media reports about mass layoffs, decreases in the number of available jobs, and increasing rates of long-term unemployment. They also see the reemployment struggles of laid-off family members, friends, neighbors, or coworkers and internalize those negative emotions applying them to potential envisioned personal future outcomes (Mathieu & Zajac, 1990).

Downsizing, permanent layoffs, and jobless recoveries that occur during modern recessions may have a broad influence on work environments and place high demands on the employed because productivity gains result from more output from fewer workers (Cottini & Ghinetti, 2018). Moreover, the dynamics of modern recessions may broadly affect perceptions of insecurity regarding continuity of employment. Several models of stress suggest that a recession represents a primary macroeconomic stressor that increases exposure to secondary stressors at work, which then undermine employee health and work attitudes (Burgard & Kalousova, 2015; Pearlin & Bierman, 2013; Probst, 2005; Shoss, 2017; Tausig, 2013). These secondary stresses potentially can undermine the health and work attitudes of the employed when employers reduce workforce as a result of an economic downturn.

This phenomenon is one that is not limited to either recent times or a single geography. Frone (2018) collected data from workers in the United States prior to and during the 2008 Recession. That research concluded that the recession was associated with a net decrease in physical and mental health and affective organizational commitment.

Using a repeated cross-sectional study of civil servants in Northern Ireland, Houdmont, Kerr, and Addley (2012) found that the 2008 Recession was associated with net increases in work demands, role ambiguity, coworker interpersonal conflict, and with net decreases in job control, coworker support, and participation in change at work.

Earlier economic fluctuations have been associated with similar impact. Using national panel data, Tausig and Fenwick (1999) reported that the 1974–1975 U.S. recession was associated with net increases in work demands, job insecurity, lack of promotions, inadequate pay, psychological distress, and life dissatisfaction.

Frone's more recent research (2018) replicated the finding for job insecurity focused on two goals. The first was to assess net population change in job and employment insecurity, physical and mental health, and affective organizational commitment. The second goal was to explore job and employment insecurity as parallel mediators of the associations between the Great Recession and the health and affective organizational commitment outcomes within the working population of the United States. It is the first study to show that a recession was also associated with net increases in employment insecurity.

Frone collected data from two national surveys of U.S. workers, one of which occurred before the 2008 recession (N = 2354) and one during the 2008 recession (N = 2322). The results show that the 2008 recession was associated with a net increase in both job and employment insecurity, though the increase in employment insecurity was 3.4 times larger than the increase in job insecurity. The increase of 7.8 percentage points in the prevalence of job insecurity during the recession represented an additional 10.9 million job-insecure U.S. workers, whereas the increase of 22.1% percentage points in the prevalence of employment insecurity represented an additional 30.9 million employment-insecure U.S. workers.

Frone also reported that the increase of 5.6 percentage points in the prevalence of poor physical health during the recession represented an additional 7.8 million physically unhealthy U.S. workers, and the increase of 3.6 percentage points in the prevalence of poor mental health during the recession represented an additional 5.0 million mentally unhealthy U.S. workers (2018).

COVID 19 Crisis and the Hospitality Industry

Economic downturns such as recessions are not the only externally imposed disruptive factor that could produce the type of mental health phenomenon in hospitality workers as described in the previous section. The COVID-19 pandemic of 2020 is also responsible for instigating disruptive events translating into significant changes in the business. In a review of data outlining monthly numbers of available jobs by sector prepared by the United States Bureau of Labor Statistics, it becomes clear that the COVID-19 pandemic was one of the most disruptive and damaging events to occur to the hospitality industry during the past century. Not since the second world war had the entire global hospitality industry experienced such rapid contraction of employees as a result of vaporizing market demand for tourism products. With significant impact to both the supply and demand channels of the hospitality industry, millions of workers across the globe in this sector were faced with potentially devastating hardships (Martins, Riordar & Dolnicar, 2020).

During mid-March of 2020, global travel reduced drastically at a meteoric rate as travel bans between countries (and sometimes even within countries) were imposed within fewer than 30 days. While air travel was shut down in an attempt to halt the spread of infectious diseases, the airline industries in the United States would eventually receive significant cash infusion from the US Government. The hospitality industry domestically and abroad would not receive any sector-specific financial support from any government and – as a result – is now considered the most significantly impacted sector because of the pandemic (World Bank, 2020). The reality facing the hospitality industry by late March of 2020 were booking cancellations nearing 100%. Organizations that operate hotels found themselves in a situation of extended empty occupancy while looking to the future with uncertainty (Gossling, Scott, & Hall, 2020). According to the World Tourism Organization (WTO), in fewer than two months by May 2020 major restrictions included a 98% decline in international arrivals worldwide. Also in May 2020, recorded hotel occupancy was observed to be at the lowest levels in nearly a century with European hotels reporting 13% occupancy, African hotels reporting 14% occupancy, South and Central American hotels reporting 15% occupancy, the United States faring a bit better with 33% occupancy and the Middle East, Asia and Pacific market hotels reporting a 36% occupancy (UNWTO, 2020).

While this may seem like an unprecedented event, outbreaks of deadly diseases that impact economic dynamics are not a new phenomenon. The epidemic diseases that started with the 1900s have created social, cultural, and economic effects as well as health problems and deaths (Ozbay, Sarijski, Ceylan, & Cakmak, 2021). While the outbreaks had created their effects within the time they occurred, these effects – especially in the economy – continued after the outbreak had completely ended. The main epidemics that have had a significant impact on the tourism industry are Ebola, SARS, and COVID-19. The economic effects of flu outbreaks remained lower than Ebola, SARS, and COVID-19. Flu outbreaks have shown their effects mostly on social life (Ammon, 2002). Among the flu outbreaks, swine flu was the disease that most affected the economy and tourism activities. While the disease primarily affected the agriculture and transportation sector, it caused the cancellation of holiday and airline reservations in Mexico and the USA (McKibbin, 2009).

Even without a global pandemic, the tourism and hospitality sectors are one of the most vulnerable industries operating today due to the increased number of severe natural and human-made crises that result in enormous financial loss to the sector (Kim, Kim, Lee, & Tang, 2020; Dube, Nhamo, & Chikodzi, 2020). The modern world simply provides more dissenting factors for a seasonal, service-based industry like hospitality including global political unrest, armed conflict between formal governments and organized factions that do not represent a country and economic fluctuations. Even though there are clearly many potentially devastating events which can occur anywhere and affect tourism activity everywhere, it is important to note that the tourism industry can never fully anticipate the timing or full impact of such threats (Ritchie, 2008). If predictability isn't a realistic outcome for the tourism industry, crisis management must be. When reviewing how prepared hotel organizations are to respond to and thrive in a crisis environment, a significantly large number of hospitality organizations both outright fail to predict a crisis and do not undertake any preventive measures that will help dilute the crisis' impact upon business operations or revenue (Wang and Ritchie, 2010).

The hotel industry's response to the Covid-19 crisis cycle can be categorized into four stages. The emergency began when the World Health Organization (WHO, 2020) declared the new disease a global pandemic, which caused hotel revenues to shrink drastically. Next came a period of short-term adaptation to the emergency. As consumers in Europe and the United States began to consumer information about the crisis and make decisions about next steps, they slowed down their travel plans and became cautious about the location and the type of accommodation where they chose to stay. This occurred equally for both business and leisure travel (McKinsey, 2020).

The third phase was longer-term planning to adapt to changed circumstances amid great unknown circumstances. With little to no information about how the virus was transmitted, how it infected its hosts, how people could protect themselves against infection and what to do once infected, immediate recovery from this downturn was difficult to navigate by most industries, the hospitality sector being one of the most impacted (McKinsey, 2020).

By early 2023, with information and interventions (both pharmaceutical and non-pharmaceutical) widely available, the United States Bureau of Labor Statistics began documenting large month over month gains of hiring occurring in the hospitality sector. By late 2020, a fourth phase of recovery was identified where more emphasis on planning for an eventual upturn and economic recovery was defined that would also, ideally, describe lessons learned and strategies to protect business during a future, similar crisis (McKinsey, 2020). According to the March 2023 United States Bureau of Labor Statistics Job Report released in April 2023, the Hospitality Leisure and Hospitality sector reported 16,577,000 positions. This is 368,000 fewer positions than the industry reported in February 2020 indicating that the sector is nearing the end of its fourth phase of recovery (US Bureau of Labor Statistics, 2023).

The crisis was the direct cause of millions of jobs in the hospitality sector disappearing overnight and not returning for nearly three years. The individuals who lost those jobs in 2020 were, by and large, not prepared for the evaporation of regularly earned income and quickly qualified for poverty status (Jones & Comfort, 2020). Employees who witnessed their careers and the industry they had been employed in disintegrate at best experienced extremely high levels of job insecurity and physical and psychological risks associated with it. Even as jobs began to return to the hospitality industry, the employees who filled those jobs were oftentimes not the employees who watched the industry collapse earlier (Bajrami, Terzic, Aleksandra, Marko, Radovanovic, Tretiakova & Hadoud, 2021). One perspective to analyze in relation to COVID- 19 is to express the impact of the pandemic through the levels of perceived job insecurity by employees, health complaints incurred during isolation, risk-taking behavior observed at workplaces when revenue stopped being realized and organizational changes employers made to maintain solvency without business. This study developed the following model to better understand employee level work-related attitudes (job motivation and job satisfaction) and turnover intentions of the employees in hospitality industry within this framework:

This model was a synthesis of many layers of research that had been previously conducted. Perceived job insecurity was marked as one of the most stressful moments in the career of every employee (Reisel, Probst, Chia, Maloles, Konig., 2010). Employees' subjective perception of a possibility to lose their job was recognized in the literature as quantitative job insecurity (De Witte, Vander Elst, & De Cuyper, 2015). Previous research showed that job insecurity was negatively associated with job satisfaction and motivation leading to undesirable employees' behavior and responses (Reisel et al., 2010). In hospitality,

Figure 1. Theoretical model of research
Source: Barjami et al. (2021)

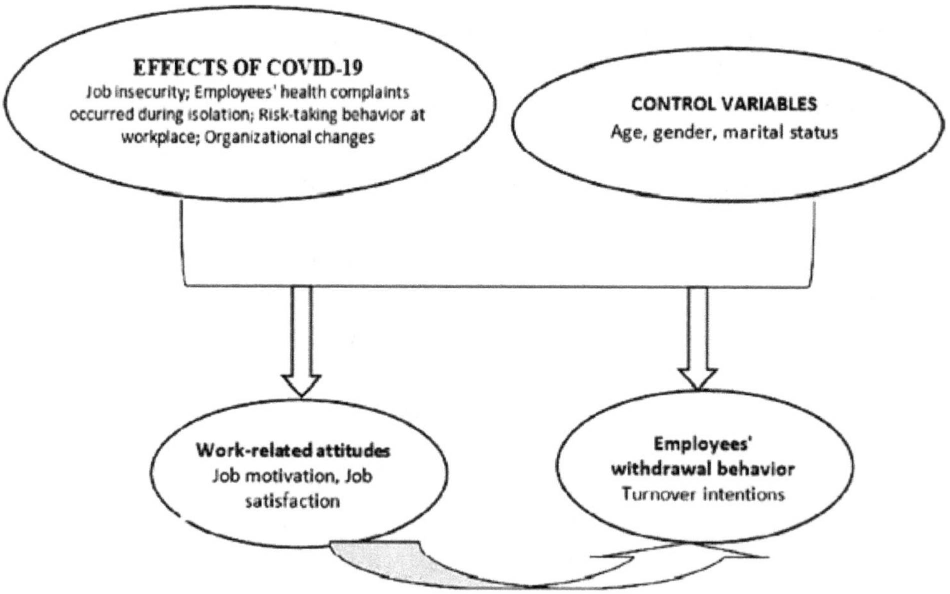

A high level of job insecurity that is maintained by a hotel employee will nearly always translate into reduced levels of job satisfaction for either an employee or a collective group (Vujičić, Jovičić, Lalić, & Cvejanov, 2014). The phenomenon is explained as an employee's job insecurity catalyzing an accelerated development of one's desire to voluntarily separate from an employer. The underlying psychological rationalization of this dynamic is that employees perceive this action as one of the most effective techniques to deal with the stress they experience caused by uncertainty if they would be remaining employed in the future (Artz & Kaya, 2014). Job insecurity and turnover intentions were positively correlated, demonstrating that the more intense feelings of insecurity an employee maintained about his or her current job, the more he or she would also think about voluntarily separating from the organization (Lee & Jeong, 2017). Shropshire and Kadlec (2012) and Akgunduz and Eryilmaz (2018) identified that both an employee's perceived job insecurity and burnout were the most significant and relevant factors which increased the development of turnover intentions in the hospitality sector. In addition, employees in the hospitality sector under duress often maintained thoughts about changing careers and exiting the sector altogether (Shropshire & Kadlec, 2012).

Hospitality employees' reaction to the COVID-19 crisis can be better understood by studying their reaction to earlier crises that impacted the industry. Research done before and throughout the crisis like Great Recession showed that job insecurity was significantly increased, while job satisfaction was reduced and this situation lasted for as many as several years after the recession had been finished (Ünsar, 2011).

Established patterns of job insecurity that existed in the hospitality industry prior to 2020 were shatted by the global crisis caused by COVID-19. The perceptions that emerged from the crisis were elevated to more extreme levels with employees no longer able to draw upon familiar context to predict the duration and scope of impact because of the crisis. Of course, this phenomenon was not exclusively observed in the hospitality sector but was a widespread dynamic through many service industries indicating that there are common traits from sector to sector. Unsafe workplace conditions as well as exposure to dangerous working conditions was one of the most common reasons for thinking about leaving a job among various service industries such as airline employees, healthcare workers (Wen, Zhou, Hu, & Zhang., 2020), grocery store employees and commercial truck drivers (Smith, 2018). For those employees that did not leave their job, the unpredictable and dangerous situation presented by the pandemic led them to ignore, or improperly implement, established safety parameters. This was done in hopes of retaining their job by elevating their employer's perception of contributed value (Storseth, 2006).

If not laid off, employees in the hospitality sector found themselves working in a high-risk environment during the COVID-19 pandemic due to risk of contracting a novel virus, second only to the risk faced by healthcare practitioners (Chinazzi, Davis, Ajelli, Gioannini, Litvinova, & Merler, 2020). Furthermore, the escalating nature of global panic induced by the threat of uncontrolled disease spread was accompanied by the implementation of strict safety measures throughout the world. While designed to help keep people healthy, these new safety restrictions caused additional anxiety and frustration (Mao, He, Morrisson, & Coca-Stefaniak 2020), especially among the workers in the service-providing sector. It often fell to the front-line workers to enforce these new restrictions and rules, which were often not agreeably embraced by the public.

Recent research on the impact of COVID-19 highlighted that isolation contributed to the feelings of loneliness, pessimism, anger and confusion resulting in higher blood pressure (O'Neil, Nicholls, Redfern, Brown, & Hare 2020), reduced life satisfaction (Li, Yang, Zhao, Zhi, Wang, Liu, Bi, & Zhao, 2020), or even caused mental deterioration (Godinic, Obrenovic, & Khudaykulov, 2020). Additional research focused on employees returning to work after their absence (caused by illness or other involuntary reasons) showed that they were most concerned whether they would be as productive as before (Soeker, Wegner, & Pretorius, 2008). Going back to work after a justified absence (due to an illness or some other problem) was mostly seen as a way to increase employees' quality of life and as some type of therapy (Steiner, Cavender, Main, & Bradley, 2004). The workplace represented a sense of normalcy for employees and in many cases a return was desired greatly (Peteet, 2000). The speculation because of this work is that mental health issues caused by isolation during the COVID-19 pandemic may not reflect negatively as independent factors on job motivation and job satisfaction. It is also felt that these will not encourage employees to consider leaving the organization (O'Neil et al. 2020).

An employee, however, will not necessarily trade safety for a desired return to normalcy. As Folkman (1984) pointed out, events that employees have not encountered before, but might be perceived as threatening (as in this case COVID-19), can cause different reactions in the workplace and require a longer period of adjustment.

This is also not to say that a company or its leadership will get a free pass by employees following a crisis like the COVID-19 pandemic. Many of the known parameters associated with change are still valid. The perception of implemented or planned organizational changes reflects employees' evaluation of the fairness of changes carried out by the management (Emen, 2020).

Herscovitch and Meyer (2002) expressed an opinion that organizational changes caused fear among employees because they were not sure how these changes would affect them. Organizational changes reduced the level of job satisfaction and job motivation of those who remained at work, especially if those changes were perceived as unfair and reflected carelessness of the management (Schouteten, Van Der Vleuten, 2013). Efforts in 2023 by several large companies such as The Walt Disney Company, J.P. Morgan Chase and Apple to force employees to return to work in an office, which have been met with such negative engagement by employees, could be a result of the concepts discussed in this chapter.

Phases of Recovery From a Crisis

Recovering from a crisis is essential and research has demonstrated that effective crisis management is an important determinant that affects hotel sustainability (Wang and Ritchie, 2010; Jayawardena, Tew, Lu, Tolomiczenko, & Gellatly, 2008; Milojevic & Katsadze, 2020). Crisis management in a tourism environment encompasses many components including identifying measures of containment, accepted techniques to quickly and effectively respond to a crisis while proactively minimizing impact on the guest experience (Wang and Ritchie, 2010).

Much of prior research, and those labeled as industry specialists, have focused attention on the prevention of crises. A review of available literature reveals that there are nearly no studies that have analyzed additional steps of crisis management, namely how organizations can effectively contain the impact of a crisis on business as well as mitigate recovery efforts once the crisis has passed (Barton, 1994). An additional drawback of previous studies in tourism crisis management is that studied situations have been largely confined to a specific geographic location - e.g., Hurricane Katrina, heat waves in Europe, Mozambique floods, a series of earthquakes and massive tsunamis, terrorism attacks and political instability (Nelson & Nesmith, 2003; Pforr & Hosie, 2008). Regardless of limitations, research in this area is essential for industry. Crisis management literature suggests that learning from past events is essential to maintaining positive business dynamics and retaining employees. The less prepared a hospitality business is for a crisis, the less likely that its workers will not be impacted – either through involuntary separation or emotional exhaustion. The hotel business should implement crisis plans before, during and after its occurrence (Coombs & Laufer, 2018).

As observed historically when hotel operations are preparing for recovery from a crisis, several key recovery strategies related to sales and marketing are traditionally emphasized and prioritized. As a component of these revenue-generating efforts, operations focused protocols are highlighted within marketing communications that guarantee guests' safety, regardless of the type of specific crisis being experienced. Crises have encompassed outbreaks of infectious diseases, terrorist attacks, economic downturns or similar (Chien & Law, 2003).

More recent research has been conducted to better analyze the hotel industry's response to the Covid-19 Crisis. Heredia-Colaco and Rodrigues (2021) built a survey instrument to conduct a cross-sectional study comprised of four assessments made between April and June 2020 representing hoteliers from for different classification of international hospitality establishments: city center hotels, resort hotels, bed and breakfasts, and conference hotels.

This research revealed insight into how a hotel business perceives its initial ability to effectively prepare for, operate throughout and recover from a global crisis like the Covid-19 Pandemic. During the first two studies, in respect to the major key strategies to prepare for the anticipated upturn at the end of the pandemic, an unequivocal majority of the hoteliers across those included in the sample initially prioritized special cleaning programs to accommodate consumers' health and safety concerns at the start of the crisis. This indicates that the priority was focusing on the operation. The remaining strategies focused on marketing and sales to drive business although these were in place to a significantly lesser extent. Strategies included the offer of long-term vouchers for bookings, the redesign of sales and marketing strategies to attract new markets or segments, the creation of special offers and packages and the introduction of offers and incentives focused to generate revenues from targeting local markets. Hoteliers anticipated that domestic business travel would recover quicker than domestic leisure travel or any type of international travel. Hoteliers' interest in investing in the upskill of the workforce to meet future demands was the lowest of all priorities across all four classifications (Heredia-Colaco & Rodigues, 2021).

As the crisis continued, study 3 revealed that hotel companies (regardless of their type of operation) increasingly began to invest substantially in marketing and sales strategies to attract new markets or segments, or in the creation of special offers and packages aimed at the domestic leisure market. Although initially thought to be less of a factor in recovery than domestic business travel, the opposite turned out to be true. A significant shift in market segmentation focus to prioritize offers and incentives aimed at attracting business from local demographics was observed frequently after the start of the pandemic to appeal to the domestic travel market. Another developing trend involved organization leadership identifying areas of opportunity where upskilling of the incumbent workforce to meet modified future demands gained relevance and prominence, especially among resorts, bed and breakfasts and conference hotels. However, it also remained the least focused-on opportunity.

In Study 4, the key recovery strategies used by hotels were more balanced across the three property types (excluding conference hotels) with the creation of special offers and packages, as well as redesign of sales and marketing strategies gaining more relevance. This may be an indication of why no significant differences were observed when examining the impact of travel market segment on consumer concerns and business recovery expectations, since hoteliers across all property types were behaving similarly when preparing for recovery. In regard to focusing on investing in developing their employees' skills, only one of the four categories (conference hotels) showcased a significant increase in utilizing this strategy. It remained the least focused on strategy in City Center Hotels, Resort Hotels and Bed and Breakfasts. Conference hotels' interest in developing employee skills appears to have been the result of reimagining their own business model. Since domestic business travel lagged in recovery compared to domestic leisure travel, and conference hotels were not historically set up to service that segment of the hospitality market, the research concluded that these properties were less likely to effectively pivot and service a leisure market without reskilling its employees. (Heredia-Colaco & Rodigues, 2021).

Other types of external crises can trigger similar responses in workers as what was revealed in the years following the onset of the COVID-19 pandemic. It is established that a recession is associated with lower levels of affective organizational commitment. The increase of 5.5 percentage points in the prevalence low organizational commitment during the 2008 – 2009 recession represented an additional 7.7 million uncommitted U.S. worker (Frone, 2018). Given the importance of affective organizational commitment to employers (Dalal, 2005; Mathieu & Zajac, 1990; Meyer, Stanley, Herscovitch, & Topolnytsky, 2002; Riketta, 2002), this increase in the proportion of uncommitted U.S. workers during a recession and its aftermath is significant.

How the COVID-19 Pandemic Creates an Uncertain Future for the Hospitality Industry

Transformative moments are often repeated as milestone historical events that are discussed across many generations moving forward after the event has long since concluded (Hall, Scott and Gössling, 2020). In December 2019, coronavirus (COVID-19) emerged in the Wuhan city of China, and since then, it has been spread to almost 210 countries around the world (Hui, Azhar, Madani, Ntoumi, Kock, Dar, Ippolito, Mchugh, Memish, & Drosten 2020). Researchers and experts have argued that the COVID-19 pandemic presents a transformative moment or opportunity that will change the world (Davies, 2020; Gills, 2020; Mair, 2020; Politico, 2020). McKinsey and Company (2020) suggest that the pandemic is not only a health crisis of immense proportion but that it is also an imminent restructuring of the global economic order because of the economic impact of virus suppression, potentially including the nature of international tourism as an economic and social phenomenon. Nevertheless, that things will change for the better or that economic development, including tourism, will become more sustainable, is not a foregone conclusion (Kozul-Wright & Barbosa, 2020; Mair, 2020). This is concerning as the tourism industry has a vital role in the global economy (Sundaram, 2019).

As Buranyi (2020) observed in relation to the COVID-19 response, many wealthy nations have not only pursued their own national strategies for public health but have also withdrawn from the globalized world of diplomacy and trade that they themselves set up. Aggressive nationalism has become normalized, as Lawrence Gostin, director of the WHO Collaborating Center on National and Global Health Law, stated "All the previous rules about global norms, public health and understanding of what's expected in terms of an outbreak has crumbled … None of us know where this is leading" (Buranyi, 2020, p.7).

Uncertainty around the severity of the long-lasting impact for a novel deadly viral outbreak can challenge society in unprecedented ways (Hall et. al., 2020). Wolfe et al. (2007) reports that infectious diseases, as a leading cause of human morbidity, mortality, and societal apprehension, have long exerted important selective forces on politics, society, the economy, and human's attitudes to nature, as well as the human genome. Therefore, the transformational actions and possibilities of modern pandemics are nothing new, they perhaps just seem that way because it is affecting the developed world and generations who have either not been exposed to, or otherwise just forgotten given access to antibiotics and modern medicine, the impacts of pandemic and the essential role of mobility within them.

Despite medical and public health advances, the threat of pandemics has been gradually increasing since the latter half of the twentieth century. The main reasons for this can be found in the context of globalization and global change which required travel and tourism as an integral component (Burkle, 2006; Hall, 2020; Allen, Murray, Zambrana-Torrelio, Morse, Rondinini, Marco, Breit, Olival, & Daszak, 2017). Several processes have come together to increase pandemic risk.

First, humanity is now more urbanized than it has ever been with over half of the world's population living in urban centers showcasing high densities of population. The greater concentration of people has increased the potential for diseases to be spread by contact and proximity (Hall, 2020).

Second, these urban centers are now more interconnected than ever before because of transport connectivity via plane, train, shipping and road. A passenger, and therefore a disease, can now travel from one urban center to another, from one side to the other side of the world in a day. Travel and tourism are critical for carrying disease and disease vectors (Browne, St-Onge Ahmad, Beck, & Nguyen-Van-Tam, 2016), and pandemics have major impacts on tourism given the role of nonpharmaceutical interventions (NPI), such as quarantine and border control (Ryu Gao, Wong, Shiu, Xiao, Fong and Cowling., 2020).

Third, the requirements of such a dramatically increased population for housing and food have resulted in the destruction of previously undeveloped landscapes where novel viruses are thought to often emerge and transfer into a human population via a zoonosis event (Devaux, Mediannikov, Medkour, & Raoult, 2019; Mossoun, Pauly, Akoua-Koffi, Couacy-Hymann, Leendertz, Anoh, Gnoukpoho, Leendertz, & Schubert, 2015; Myers, Gaffikin, Golden, Ostfeld, Redford, Ricketts, Turner, & Osofsky, 2013). This can lead to certain geographic locations becoming associated (fairly or otherwise) with a zoonosis event. The association of a disease with place, even generally with respect to outbreaks, can then have substantial effects on destination image. For example, even though Ebola has been limited to a small number of African locations, tourism to other parts of the continent has been negatively affected purely by them being "African" and associated with increased risk (Maphanga & Henama, 2019; Novelli, Burgess, Jones, & Ritchie, 2018; WTTC, 2018).

From an economic development perspective, a location that engages in tourism as a part of its economy needs to be able to respond effectively to a crisis associated with a viral outbreak. Of course, as was observed with the COVID-19 pandemic, this would appear to be a more challenging prospect than many may have previously thought. The capacity for a destination to respond to pandemics has been framed in terms of the stages of a disaster, which also highlights the extent to which destinations and industry may learn from prior pandemic or other disaster experiences and adapt accordingly (Hall & Prayag, 2020). Significantly, the systems approach highlights that how destination and industry responds is also affected in the long-term by competing destinations and businesses. This may have implications for recovery trajectories as some destinations may deliberately position themselves in low-cost terms, with little concern for externalities (e.g., introducing a second wave into the resident population), in order to try and increase visitor numbers and employment possibilities as soon as possible. Others, such as Hawaii (McAvoy, 2020), may continue to attempt to restrict arrivals and hotel reservations to reduce the potential of a second wave of infections or, like Singapore, introduce new third party audited cleaning standards to rebuild traveler trust (Singapore Tourism Board, 2020).

Ultimately, as both recent and historic pandemics have demonstrated, an outbreak like COVID-19 may provide an impetus for individuals to transform their travel behaviors in both the short and (possibly) the near term. However, transformation of the entire tourism system is extremely difficult (Hall et. al., 2020). Pandemics are unlike many other disasters and crises that tourism has experienced. Although, as with any other disaster related tourism attention-issue cycle, consumer and industry confidence will rise and fall in relation to media reporting on the impacts of COVID-19 (Gossling et al., 2021).

As observed during the period 2021 – 2023, most countries pursued a tourism reboot after reversal of shutdowns had occurred in other industries. Promotional campaigns by tourism entities encouraged people to travel locally and regionally to stimulate the economy while maintaining continued vigilance on precautions to support Covid-19 surveillance and safety. There was an uneven recovery as some markets were aligned with early phases of restarting tourism, although there were many false starts that occurred across the world and at different times as well. This was primarily due to the emergence of new variants with the ability to evade previously achieved immunity (through prior infection or vaccination) which held the potential to impact a society's safety and health.

Early predictions of recovery placed an emphasis on saving local restaurants, trips focused on o reconnecting with loved ones, essential business travel, and parks and nature tourism where physical distancing can be accomplished.

Seniors' tourism was predicted to be discouraged or restricted because of vulnerability to Covid-19. Sports and events tourism was predicted to remain shut down until a vaccine is developed and widely deployed, a timeline estimated to be 12-18 months (Liu, Zhou, Li, Garner, Watkins, Carter, L. Smoot, Gregg, Daniels, Jervey, & Albaiu, 2020). Many of these early predictions were observed during the two years following Liu's 2020 study, although early predictions did not incorporate the significant variability of infectious capability that was observed in an iterative process and continues through 2023 and beyond.

COVID-19's quick spread triggered nations to make decisions regarding their economics that have been unprecedented in modern times. The mass unemployment caused by the industry spanning rapid shutdown of economies in many leading outbound tourism countries had a negative ripple effect against international travel for cost, risks of a subsequent waves of infection, and likely patriotic messages to rebuild the domestic economy (Hall, et. al. 2020).

The latter includes the promotion of domestic tourism as a tool by some governments to reduce leakage from the national economy and to bolster regional centers and rural economies. Such a policy focus may have the unintended outcome of creating new sustainable tourism trajectories with positive implications for lower emissions, place-based economic development and travel and tourism practices. Critically, the depth and length of the recession/depression will be the main driver of such socio-economic change. However, the domestic focus on tourism is likely to only be temporary while constraints on mobility remain in place. Pandemics are clearly an important issue for society and tourism, even if many of their potential threats and the actions needed to manage them have either been ignored or forgotten by the public, industry and politicians at large (Hall et. al. 2020). Resilience research tells us that drivers for transformation and change can move up and down the different panarchical levels of the tourism system (Hall, Prayag, & Amore, 2018). This means that in some locations, individuals, businesses and communities will seek to transform and change the way in which tourism and hospitality is conducted (Nunn, 2020; Tourism From Zero, 2020).

While many official organizations including individual governments and multi-national organizations (such as the World Health Organization) have declared that the COVID-19 crisis has transitioned from a pandemic to an endemic in 2023, although there is little agreement on the significance of that classification. Changes to tourism because of COVID-19 will be uneven in space and time, with some tourism operations reverting to pre-2020 dynamics. Others have maintained adopted practices in part or full. While some destinations will undoubtedly reconsider the nature of their tourism industry, others may continue to focus more on local and more sustainable forms of tourism. As was observed in 2021 and forward, even without substantial institutional and governmental interventions, the juggernaut that is tourism (domestic and international) will roll on. For many destinations and governments, especially those with authoritarian tendencies, the focus on tourism will be business-as-usual. Furthermore, there are not enough stakeholders in the tourism sector that question the sustainability of success defined by growth in visitor numbers or increases in material consumption to expect transformational change driven from within. The resilience of growth in international tourism numbers and the capacity of tourism to rebound from crisis has long been recognized (Hall et. al., 2020).

The Impact of the COVID-19 Pandemic on Employee Withdrawal Behavior in the Hospitality Industry

The president of the World Travel and Tourism Council stated that COVID-19 has tremendously affected the hospitality and tourism industry. The hospitality industry was attempting to survive during the early years of the global pandemic (Dayour, Adongo, Amuquandoh, & Adam, 2020). The hotels were suffering from financial crises (Gossling et al., 2021). Moreover, the hotel industry would contract drastically as most of the hotels face financial crises due to COVID-19 (Gossling et al., 2021). In that regard, the influence of COVID-19 has caused business closures due to cash inflows (Hall et al., 2020). While much of the sector has recovered, researching the dynamics that occurred in 2020 separated from knowledge of recovery will provide greater understanding for how to optimize responses to future crises.

Organization management has applied alternative strategies to cope with the financial crises as the current economy's situation worsens due to the pandemic (Dube et al., 2020). Downsizing strategies such as layoff of all part-time employees, reducing staff salaries and ending employees' contracts have sparked feelings of anxiety, stress and depression (Ashford, Lee, & Bobko, 1989; Elshaer & Saad, 2017; Kaushal & Srivastava, 2021). The organization's downsizing has caused adverse employee outcomes such as job performance (Agyeiwaah, Dayour, & Zhou, 2021; Latack, Knicki, & Prussia, 1995). In addition to that, employees are stressed out about the organization's continuity (Greenhalgh & Rosenblatt, 1984) as well as more current psychological impacts associated with the severity of the crisis and uncertainty around how it can be resolved (Hall, et. all, 2020).

With the increase in downsizing events occurring within the hotel industry, employees become stressed either because of the fear of being laid off or unclear job descriptions. In addition to that, restructuring the workforce caused an increase in job insecurity among employees, resulting in employees' withdrawal behavior (Ghaderi, King & Hall, 2021). Previous studies have revealed that employees' behaviors and attitudes are affected by job insecurity. Employees withdraw when they doubt their jobs (Karatepe et al., 2020). Job insecurity causes a decrease in trust. Depression, stress, anxiety, job dissatisfaction affect employees' mental health, well-being and aggravate absenteeism; thus, employee turnover has increased (Chirumbolo & Areni, 2010; Hellgren, Sverke, & Isaksson, 1999; Jiang & Lavaysse, 2018; Karatepe, Rezapouraghdam,& Hassannia, 2020).

In this context, there is a need to examine employees' perceptions regarding their job withdrawal. Workers' mental health is quite vital for work efficiency, and it also helps the organization to maintain sustainability. COVID-19 affects employees' mental and psychological health, which causes higher nervousness and depression, including isolation and frustration (Ahmed, Ahmed, Aibao, Hanbin, Siyu, & Ahmad, 2020; Lai & Wong, 2020; Sarfraz, Shah, Fareed, & Shahzad, Xiang, Yang, Li, Zhang, Zhang, Cheung, & Ng, 2020). Employee wellness is considered a vital source of productivity and effectiveness (Berry, Mirabito, & Baun, 2010; Jiang & Wen, 2020; Mirabito & Berry, 2015). Occupational health's effectiveness is vital for employee's wellness.

Hurrell, Nelson, & Simmons (1998) have defined workplace stressors as a work environment that decreases employees' well-being and health. Stress is a common human reaction in a working environment when faced with challenging or threatening situations (Keskin, Akgun, Ayar, & Kayman, 2016). Workplace stressors lead to negative behavior among individuals (Vranjes, Baillien, Vandebosch, Erreygers, De Witte., 2018). Researchers have highlighted several stressors common within the workplace environment, including the pace of work, emotional workload, varied work, skill use, social support, role conflict, role ambiguity, participation and autonomy (Notelaers, De Witte, Van Veldhoven, and Vermunt. 2007).

Workplace stress in significant amounts can manifest in ways other than withdrawal. Stress can sometimes become aggression. Barling, Dupre, & Kelloway (2009) described workplace aggression as any physical or verbal behavior to cause harm directed toward another employee. According to

Neuman and Keashly (2004), verbal aggression includes several behaviors like being yelled at or verbally threatening someone. Physical aggression contains behaviors like being attacked with a weapon, being hit or slapped by someone. The inclusion of this knowledge is from the perspective that it should always be an organization's goal to ensure a safe and calm workplace for its employees. Knowing that mitigation of stress can reduce, or eliminate, the potential for aggression should be motivation for organizations to invest in stress reducing preventative measures as opposed to working through a crisis associated with workplace violence, shootings, or other criminal acts. Mitigation efforts can help maintain lower level of stress manifestation, like withdrawal behavior, which – while not ideal in isolation – is preferable to other manifestations of stress.

Rosse and Hulin (1985) defined withdrawal behavior as acts leading to the psychological or physical distance between the work environment and employees. Workplace behavior includes turnover and absenteeism (Dalton & Todor, 1993). Work withdrawal behavior consists of an employee's psychological and behavioral withdrawal from the workplace (Lehman & Simpson, 1992). Withdrawal behavior is not one behavior but several behaviors, containing multiple behaviors (Liu. Yuan, Zhang, & Hu, 2019).

The COVID-19 pandemic presents some additional unique considerations that may contribute to withdrawal behavior. Employees can be worried about their health if any physical infection symptoms appear (Desclaux, Badji, Ndione, & Sow, 2017). The study suggests that employees' depression, anxiety, and stress have been increased due to high COVID-19 worry, which will affect an individual's routine life as this outbreak continues (Ahmed et al., 2020).

The new norm of avoiding social interactions during the COVID-19 pandemic combined with maintaining a balance between professional and personal needs and stressful psychological effects triggered counterproductive work behaviors (Malik, Sinha & Goel, 2020). Hospitality industries adhered to hierarchical downsizing and restructuring strategies due to increased competition and opened economies due to globalization, which has given rise to factors like job insecurity, increased turnover rate and job dissatisfaction in employees. Researchers have investigated that workplace aggression is the source of job stressors. Research has shown that job stress, lack of commitment and job dissatisfaction lead to workplace withdrawal behavior (Peachey, Burton, & Wells, 2014).

The hospitality industry is considered aggressive because of the intensive workload, long working hours and pressure to maintain a reputation through high-quality work within a short period. Researchers have found that an aggressive work climate causes to increase in the turnover rates in employees (Mohsin. Lengler, & Kumar, 2013; Yang, Wan, Fu, 2012). It has been observed that layoffs and downsizings directly affect aggression due to the COVID-19 pandemic. Studies have suggested that during the COVID-19 pandemic, the downsizing organizations have significantly caused stress and anxiety for managers (Graf-Vlachy, Sun, & Zhang, 2020). Workplace withdrawal behavior is strongly related to financial need (Van Hoye, Saks, Lievens, & Weijters, 2015). The pandemic's anxiety and financial insecurity have caused workplace stress, leading to workplace aggression and employees' withdrawal behaviors. Based on the transactional model of stress (Lazarus & Folkman, 1984), employees act to cope with such events when exposed to stressful events.

From an employee perspective, other aspects contributed to observed withdrawal behaviors. Employees reported a lack of organizational commitment and job satisfaction due to workplace aggression. Moreover, employees engaged in withdrawal behavior-related activities are more dissatisfied (Elrehail, Harazneh, Abuhjeeleh, Alzghoul, Alnajdawi, & Ibrahim, 2019; Kanfer, Wanberg, & Kantrowitz, 2001). Workplace aggression and stress cause employees to transfer to another job or leave the organization. Employees also found that connecting with perceived peers (peers defined by either sociological or demographical means) by using a social media network also helped address rising levels of stress and associated. withdrawal behaviors.

Researchers have found that using social media, surfing the internet are often used to reduce stress and anxiety (Kiraly, Potenza, Stein, King, Hodgins, Saunders, Griffiths, Gjoneska, Billieux, & Brand, 2020). Researchers have investigated that to cope with work stress, workers participate in cyberloafing activities to alleviate stressful work conditions (Pindek, Krajcevska,& Spector, 2018). Cyberloafing acts as a coping strategy that distracts employees from the stressful experience to handle the demands of stressful events (Lazarus &Folkman, 1984. Psychological withdrawal means an employee's mental escape from work (Lehman & Simpson, 1992). For example, employees are engaged in personal matters at the workplace instead of doing their work-related activities. Social activities can help to reduce stress, and it leads employees to cyberloafing (Lehman & Simpson, 1992). Cyberloafing works as an emotion focused coping mechanism that serves as a psychological detachment from workplace aggression. The employees would engage in cyber loafing and use the internet for non-work-related activities to cope with the stress, which would buffer the detrimental effects of aggression on withdrawal behaviors (Khawaja, Sarfraz, Rashid, & Rashid, 2021).

This all maintains the potential to be devastating to any industry's workplace environment. However, the hospitality industry is particularly susceptible to the issues being explored in this section. Hospitality industries have higher fixed costs. They are prone to instabilities in the market, such as foodservice and lodging service sectors (Dimitropoulos, 2018), as many industries are going toward downsizing of employees to cut the cost in employee reduction layoffs (Kaushal & Srivastava, 2021). Due to downsizing, the employees are facing work stressors and heavy workloads. Distress about job insecurity among employees and changing organizational policies are associated with negative emotions (Kiefer, 2005). Researchers have also shown increased levels of boredom and anger quarantined because of lockdown situations (Xiang et al., 2020). Moreover, experiencing a stressful workplace climate may increase job stress in employees (Vigoda, 2000).

Khawaja et. al. determined that employees' perception of COVID-19 worry, and job insecurity is the primary reason that would trigger stress and aggression, leading to employees' withdrawal behavior. Their study collected data from frontline employees working in the hospitality sector located in the Punjab province of Pakistan. While the results are valid, the study did not calibrate its outcomes for cultures outside of the geographic and cultural location where the study was conducted. That said, there appear to be similarities. Employees' cyberloafing can reduce stress and withdrawal behavior, which – in turn - lessens the positive impact of aggression on withdrawal behavior. COVID-19 worry moderates the impact of workplace stressors on withdrawal behavior positively. The center of this study was establishing the relationship between Aggression and external sources of stress (like COVID-19), stress emerging from the workplace, the impact of withdrawal behavior, and the impact of cyberloafing (2021). This model appears as figure 2.7:

In the above figure, the first hypothesis (H1) postulated that aggression mediates the relationship between workplace stressors and withdrawal behavior. The second hypothesis (H2) ascertained that Cyberloafing moderates the relationship negatively between aggression and withdrawal behavior. Finally, the third hypothesis (H3) theorizes that COVID-19 worry moderates the relationship positively between workplace stressors. All these hypotheses were accepted with significant values as a part of the study, which demonstrated that employees' perception of COVID-19 worry, and job insecurity is the primary reason that would trigger stress and aggression, leading to employees' withdrawal behavior. Employees' cyberloafing can reduce stress and withdrawal behavior, lessen the positive impact of aggression on withdrawal behavior. COVID-19 worry moderates the impact of workplace stressors on withdrawal behavior positively (Khawaja et. al., 2021).

Figure 2. Theoretical model of employee withdrawal behavior
Source: Khawaja et al. (2021)

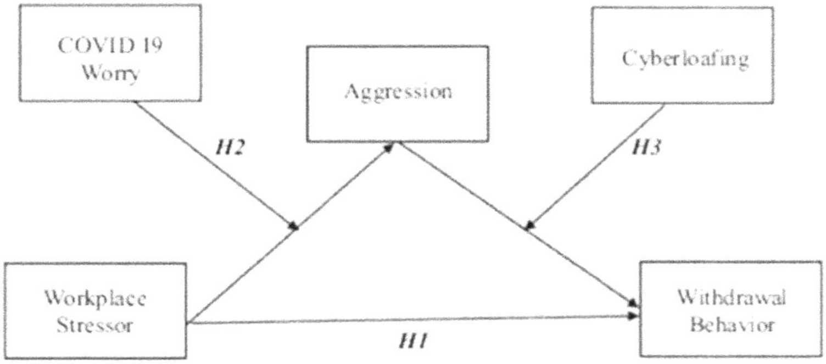

Leadership in a hotel environment should help manage a health emergency for its employees by creating a workplace environment that focuses on identifying locales of stress as well as associated coping mechanisms. Even before the pandemic, most organizations restricted employees' cyberloafing activities because they consider cyberloafing a harmful behavior. This restrictive behavior can lead to negative morale. When such a policy is deployed, organizations have neglected the positive effects of cyberloafing. Cyberloafing can be a mechanism for micro-breaks, and it can manage workplace stress and aggression at work, especially during COVID-19. Organizations and managers should consider the positive impact of cyberloafing when implementing policies for cyberloafing (Khawaja et. al., 2021).

In addition, there are several strategies that can be implemented to keep employees away from the stress and worries of losing their job. Organizations should create an alternative plan to layoffs or downsizing by utilizing the firm's emergency funds to keep paying employees' salaries or pivot company operations to replace lost revenues with new products less impacted by a pandemic-related shutdown. Leadership should also act instantly to employees' needs and ensure that COVID-19 standard operating procedures are followed. Training programs should be introduced to protect employees from deadly viruses via emails, newsletters, internal social networks, and the provision of protective equipment. These initiatives would aid employees in sustaining their job performance during this pandemic (Khawaja et al., 2021). Finally, employees should be involved in developing the pandemic recovery plan with the management. According to previous studies, employees who are involved in the firm's strategic reflection feel safer and secure (Pham, Thanh, Tuckova, & Thuy 2020; Vinodkumar & Bhasi, 2010).

The Impact of the COVID-19 Pandemic on Perceptions and Sentiments of Tourism Employees

It is a truism that with the COVID-19 pandemic, the global tourism community is facing its largest disruptive crisis since World War II and the inception of modern-day travel throughout the past century (Hunt, 2020). Amidst the health pandemic and economic fallout due to COVID-19, tourism and hospitality industries are one of the hardest struck due to several interrelated factors, including travel restrictions, national lockdowns, business closures and the subsequent impact on lives and livelihoods. The COVID-19 pandemic caused a 22% drop in international tourist arrivals during the first quarter of 2020 and the crisis at the time was projected to further deteriorate to a decline of at least 60% by year's end.

According to the recent World Economic Outlook (International Monetary Fund, 2020), tourism-dependent island economies are likely to face significant economic contraction in 2020 with lingering recessionary effects throughout 2021. The combination of high economic dependency on and high employment concentration in tourism makes any nation with a low economic profile extremely vulnerable to external shocks (Peterson, 2019). Based on previous tourism research (Emen, 2020; Evans & Elphick, 2005; Hajibaba, Gretzel, Leisch, & Dolnicar, 2015; Santana, Hall, Timothy, & Duval, 2003; Vargas-Sanchez, 2018), recent COVID-related studies (Carnevale & Hatak, 2020; Martins et al., 2020; Ozdemir, 2020; Sharma, Thomas, & Paul, 2021; Sigala, 2020), and postmodern behavioral economic theory (Ackerlof & Shiller, 2009; Kahneman, 2011; Katona, 1975; Manolis, Meamber, Winsor, & Brooks, 2001), this study proposes that the well-being of tourism employees, that is, the self-perception and sentiments of tourism employees, is disproportionately affected by the COVID-19 crisis as compared to non-tourism employees. This study hypothesizes that the experienced well-being of tourism employees, in comparison to non-tourism employees, is significantly more negatively affected by the COVID-19 crisis.

International tourism and the hospitality industry are a significant engine of job creation as well as a driving force for economic growth and development (UNWTO, 2020).

The tourism and hospitality service industries depend on the work and well-being of their employees to build a connection with their visitors and guests. It is important to ensure that these employees are healthy, motivated, and positive in their jobs. Their emotionally demanding jobs are often challenging as tourism is one of the most vulnerable industries during crisis times (Santana, et al., 2003; Vargas-Sanchez, 2018). Even during the best of times, the tourism and hospitality industries are not guaranteed to be successful or easy for the employees that work in them (Emen, 2020).

In terms of consumer sentiments, Katona (1975) focuses on the perceptions and expectations that drive discretionary purchases, which are shaped by the uncertainty of current employment and income levels and the uncertainty of future employment and income prospects. An increase in discretionary spending is indicative of optimism, whereas precautionary savings signal pessimism. According to Katona (1975), it is the affective component that propels collective waves of optimism and pessimism in a society, which influences spending habits of consumers. Previous studies indicate that health and income are significantly related to experienced well-being (Killingsworth, 2021; Miret, Caballero, Olaya, Koskinen, Naidoo, Tobiasz-Adamczyk, Leonardi, Haro, Chatterji, & Ayuso-Mateos, 2017; Wolf, Metzing, & Lucas, 2019). Recent COVID impact studies suggest that the loss of income, unemployment and increasing COVID health concerns have a profound impact on experienced well-being of tourism employees (Carnevale & Hatak, 2020; McGuire, Germain, & Reynolds, 2021; Ozdemir, 2020) and their consumption sentiments and habits (Martin et al., 2020).

Unlike subjective well-being that includes general life satisfaction, experienced well-being is narrowed to a specific referenced period, for example, a traumatic event and posttraumatic cognitive and emotional responses. Thus, experienced well-being is measured through momentary assessments of affect to episodical assessments over a specific time frame (Diener, 2009; Fleche and Smith, 2017; Kahneman and Krueger, 2006). Research suggests that negative episodes and related affective states may have a larger impact than positive events and feelings of optimism, which ultimately could affect general life satisfaction and societal well-being (Miret et al., 2017; Sharma et al., 2021).

Research also indicates that experienced wellbeing is strongly related to the immediate work environment, including job responsibility, personal enrichment, fringe benefits, work stress, employment image, health conditions and exposure to work hazards (Diener, 2009; Kahneman & Krueger, 2006; McGuire et al., 2021). These factors are akin to Herzberg's two-factor theory of motivation, which include both intrinsic and extrinsic components that change the way that work is perceived (Herzberg, Mausner, & Bloch Snyderman, 2005; Lundberg Gudmundson, & Andersson, 2009). Experienced well-being underscores the importance of the subjective construction of social realities (Berger & Luckmann, 1966) and is integral to employee engagement, which is one of the key determinants of service quality and customer value in the tourism industry (Heskett, Jones, Loveman, Sasser, & Schlesinger 2008)

Much research has been done in the area of dealing with crises in the tourism industry, but these crises have primarily been focused on terrorist attacks and financial crisis. The scope and size of these crises have been, however, relatively more regionalized with less systemic impacts for tourism (Evans & Elphick, 2005; Hajibaba et al., 2015). The COVID-19 pandemic is indeed unprecedented in modern times, in its scope and duration. According to the UNWTO (2020), past crises have shown tourism's capacity to rebound strongly and quickly after external shocks. While that dynamic was repeated, unique aspects of the pandemic (such as the sequential emergence of multiple, immunity dodging variants over the next three years) tempered the rate of recovery (BLS, 2023).

This resilience underscores the importance of adaptive capacities in tourism's internal business operations and service delivery system. Value is created by satisfied, loyal and productive employees (Heskett et al., 2008). Employee engagement stems largely from high-quality support services, learning capabilities and transformational leadership that empower employees to provide quality experiences to guests. Including employees in decision-making, providing them with (continuous) learning and advancement opportunities, as well as workplace redesign and lateral communication are essential in nurturing a healthy work environment. Employee well-being and engagement will become even more important in a post-pandemic tourism economy of shifting tourism demands and visitor (health quality) needs (Martin et al., 2020; McGuire et al., 2021; Sharma et al., 2021; Sigala, 2020; UNWTO, 2020).

One lesson learned is that during crisis situations, it is important to ensure communication and flexibility in strategy to keep employees and other stakeholders abreast of situations and to keep them feeling safe and secure

(Evans & Elphick, 2005). That said, employees in the tourism industry face a certain level of work stress in their jobs regardless of any external crisis. This stress can cause employees a certain amount of personal stress in their home life as well as organizational distress and turnover (Deery & Jago, 2009; Ross, 2005).

Tourism jobs are transitory in many places in the world and people do not tend to stay in them for lifetimes or even long term in many cases (which is part of the problem). Part of the reason for the low commitment levels are the long hours, less than desirable working conditions, emotional labor and exhaustion among employees. Organizations that communicate effectively with employees tend to eliminate some stress in the workplace as they help employees' well-being (Deery & Jago, 2009; Ross, 2005). Employees tend to assess the organizational justice in their workplace, and when they perceive the workplace to be fair and just, they do not feel as much stress (Deery &Jago, 2009; Ross, 2005).

These studies demonstrate results illustrating that tourism employee perceptions are significantly more negative and their concerns about the future are significantly more pessimistic, especially in terms of financial and economic conditions and outlook. As frontline workers, tourism employees are generally more exposed to the virus contagion and consequently experience a significantly greater threat to their personal health and safety. In the wake of the tourism fallout and travel lockdown, tourism employees are also more concerned about their employment, income and their household finances. Behavioral economic theory (Ackerlof & Shiller, 2009; Kahneman, 2011; Katona, 1975) show that sentiments and confidence explain behavior particularly during episodes of economic shocks and crisis.

The tourism and hospitality service industries depend on the work and motivation of their employees to build a connection with their visitors and guests. It is important to ensure that these employees are motivated and positive in their jobs. Tourism employees perceived overall lower experienced well-being. Experienced well-being also is related to employee engagement, which tourism employees have shown that they are unlikely to be engaged in times of crisis due to relatively high levels of uncertainty and pessimism. Moreover, employee engagement stems largely from high-quality support services, learning capabilities and transformational leadership that empower employees to provide quality experiences to guests (Peterson & DiPietro, 2021).

The tourism industry, even when there is no global pandemic, creates an environment that is associated with a wide range of risks (Chew & Jahari, 2014; Deery & Jago, 2009; Ross, 2005; Santana et al., 2003). Whereas tourism is usually associated with relaxation and positive memories, crises evoke negative thoughts, anxieties and fears and it does so for both tourists and for employees. Likewise, concerted policy actions are recommended for investing in skills development and reskilling of tourism employees (Peterson & DiPietro, 2021).

It is important that employees are trained in some of the advanced skills that will be needed as changes to the tourism environment will play a more critical role following crisis situations. Moreover, the importance of employee engagement and transformational leadership is primal to pivot toward recovery and resilience of the tourism industry. Ultimately, providing more open communication and professional development opportunities would help employees feel more a part of the team and therefore be more willing to work in these types of jobs. Providing improved benefits may increase optimism during downturns in the economy, helping employees to save for a "rainy day" fund or vacation time to mitigate the inevitable tough times as well (Peterson & DiPietro, 2021).

The Impact of the COVID-19 Pandemic on an Organization's Capital

Thus far, the focus of industry research has been almost exclusively on front-line employees, and the greatest talent shortages exist with that pool of employees (Filimonau, Derqui & Matute, 2020). However, the relationship of a hotel with its customers is a critical element of the operation and a further investigation of how this relationship is impacted by an event like the COVID-19 pandemic is as significant as understanding the needs of the front-line team.

The long(er) term impacts of COVID-19 are yet implicit but likely to be exemplified by the diminished consumer demand for hospitality services in the foreseeable future due to health and hygiene precautions (Dube et al., 2020). Coupled with the need to decrease operational capacity in order to follow the newly established social distancing rules (Hancock, 2020), this will reduce the long-term profitability of hotels, thus undermining the viability of their traditional business models (Gössling et al., 2021). There are speculations that the hotel sector will shrink significantly in the result of the pandemic, thus outlining bleak prospects for its current and future investors and employees (Taylor, 2020).

One of the main negative long term implications of COVID-19 for the hotel business is likely to be in the reduced attractiveness of hospitality occupations (Baum & Hai, 2020). Irregular and/or seasonal working patterns (Lee & Way, 2010) coupled with a relatively low pay (Wan, Wong, & Kong, 2014) have already discouraged many prospective employees from up-taking hotel jobs in the past. This has positioned staff recruitment and retention as a major challenge for hotel management in a pre-pandemic world (McGinley, Hanks, & Line, 2017). The need for many hotels to put their employees on a furlough scheme (in the case of many developed countries) and/or make them redundant (in the case of many developing economies) in the time of the pandemic, may have presented hotel jobs as being highly insecure whilst positioning employment within the hotel sector as being fragile to external disruptions (Sogno, 2020). This perceived insecurity and fragility may negatively affect future recruitment of hotel staff (Mao et al., 2020).

Additionally, top managerial positions in hotels have been difficult to fill with knowledgeable, effective, and high-quality candidates long before the pandemic (Birdir, 2002). This is attributed to the lack of assigned to the unwillingness of senior executives to work in the sector which offers limited scope for creativity and provides limited training (Wong and Pang, 2003) but, concurrently, requires significant levels of personal commitment, interpersonal communication, teamwork, and stress resistance (Kichuk, Brown, & Ladkin, 2019). The current and future measures adopted by hotels against the pandemic may have been determined by the levels of their organizational resilience. In simple terms, organizational resilience explains business preparedness to crises and disasters which provides scope for adequate predictive and adaptive algorithms or mechanisms to be put in place for prompt recovery (Filimonau & De Coteau, 2020; Lee, Vargo, & Seville, 2013; Nguyen, Inamura, & Luchi, 2017).

Corporate social responsibility (CSR) highlights the need for hotels, in addition to conserving the environment, to look after their customers, employees and local communities (Levy & Park, 2011). This need becomes especially prominent in the time of crises and disasters which exposes vulnerability of these categories of stakeholders (Henderson, 2007). From the perspective of senior hotel managers, past CSR practices adopted by their hotels may, therefore, influence their perceived job security and, subsequently, impact on their organizational commitment. This is confirmed in a recent study by Mao et al. (2020) who demonstrated the positive effect of CSR on self-efficacy, hope, resilience, and optimism of tourism employees in China during the COVID-19 outbreak and showcased the inter-linkages between job satisfaction of staff and an organizational response to the pandemic.

The concepts of organizational resilience and CSR in the hotel sector, alongside the measures taken by specific hotel businesses to reduce the negative effect of COVID-19 on their customers and employees, are closely related to the organizational 'capital' paradigm. This is because the capacity of any organization to adapt to crises and disasters and future organizational planning for such external disruptions requires a careful allocation of (physical, financial, and labor) resources alongside their prioritization in critical times (McManus et al., 2008).

Likewise, the success of implementing CSR practices in hotels is underpinned by resource availability (Filimonau & De Coteau, 2020). Resource constraints can, at least partially, explain, for example, why CSR practices are predominantly adopted by larger, chain-affiliated, hotels whilst smaller, independent and/or family-run, hotel businesses often fail to demonstrate genuine engagement with the CSR agenda (Gilfillan, 2018). The current and future resources available to an organization describe this organization's 'capital', thus linking all these concepts/paradigms together (Leonidou, Leonidou, Fotiadis, & Zariti, 2013).

Brown, Rovins, Feldmann-Jensen, Orchiston, and Johnston (2019) distinguish between six types of organizational capital, namely economic, social, human, physical, natural, and cultural. It is argued that some of these capital types overlap. For instance, cultural capital represents a logical product of social and human capital where the social networks created by an organization and the skills of its employees offer adequate resources for disaster planning and management (Filimonau and De Coteau, 2020). Regardless of any possible overlaps, Brown et al. (2019) claim that a truly integrative, multi-capital, perspective is necessary when designing a disaster management framework for hotels. This is because all capital types become critical for hotel businesses to plan, prepare, adapt and recover from external disruptions (Jiang, Ritchie, & Verreynne, 2019).

A link between CSR practices adopted by hotels and their organizational resilience was established. Arguably, this is a key finding of this study which shows that hotels should be investing in CSR to improve their chances to withstand future crises and disasters. This is in line with Mao et al. (2020) who showcased this connection by highlighting the role of CSR practices in enhancing job satisfaction and improving work productivity of tourism employees. Given that staff is a cornerstone of human capital of any organization (Brown et al., 2019), which exerts direct influence on its resilience, as discussed earlier, hotels should more pro-actively engage in CSR considering future disastrous events, such as climate change, for example.

Senior managers in larger hotels were found to have lower levels of organizational commitment. This can be attributed to the vertical management structure of such hotels, as per above, which is a known job demotivator (Giudici & Filimonau, 2019). The flat structures of smaller hotels can, therefore, be seen as more attractive. A more 'humane' touch in the form of more personalized/sympathetic human resources management (Carnevale and Hatak, 2020) and staff empowerment may increase organizational commitment of senior hotel managers in larger organizations in the times of crisis.

Perceived job security was directly linked to organizational commitment of hotel managers and larger hotels demonstrated lower levels of organizational resilience (Filimonau et. al., 2020). This can be partially attributed to the relative 'bulkiness' and 'inflexibility' of such organizations where vertical, hierarchical, management structures can slow down the flows of information, thus restricting knowledge exchange across various levels of decision-making and, potentially, reducing the positive effect of larger organizational capital (Hodari & Sturman, 2014). This is partially confirmed by the fact that the larger hotels in the studied sample with the better adoption of CSR practices showcased higher than average levels of organizational resilience. In theory, this may suggest that CSR may at least partially offset the negative impact of inflexible and bulky hotel management structures.

A Post-Pandemic Model of Tourism and Hospitality Workforce Resilience

COVID-19 has proven to be at least, if not more, disruptive to global tourism and hospitality than World War II (Hunt, 2020). Workers in these industries are hardest hit (Remeikis, 2020) because few of them had continuous employment contracts before the pandemic, instead relying on non-standard and contingent arrangements including self-employment, subcontracting, and casual work. Non-standard workers typically lack entitlements such as annual, sick and careers leave (Markey & McIvor, 2018). Of all hospitality workers, 65% are non-standard workers (Gilfillan, 2018).

A hallmark of the 4th industrial revolution is the aspect of employees maintaining contract status instead of full-time employment, in essence calling it "the gig economy." Non-standard work is becoming more common around the world, with workers engaged as necessary without a guarantee of ongoing employment (Markey & McIvor, 2018). The relatively recent emergence of online on-demand (De Stefano, 2016) and peer-to-peer trading platforms (Dolnicar, 2019) provide additional non-standard working opportunities (Stewart & Stanford, 2017). In hospitality and tourism, online platforms such as Uber Eats and Airbnb arrange such 'gigs'. Platform workers, as opposed to casual employees, are not employees and unable to access associated benefits or protections (Goods, Veen, & Barratt, 2019).

While that may appear to be undesirable, from an employee standpoint there are benefits associated with a gig lifestyle. The flexibility of non-standard forms of work minimizes risks for employers and can benefit some workers, especially those with competing engagements such as education or caring responsibilities (Markey & McIvor, 2018), and those unable to secure permanent employment (Kaine & Josserand, 2019). Non-standard work also offers an entry point into the local workforce for migrants (Duncan, Scott, & Baum, 2013). However, non-standard work is also associated with insecurity and income instability, which can negatively affect mental health and increase gaps within society (Robinson, Martins, Solnet, & Baum, 2019).

To explain this phenomenon, Martins et. al. (2020) created a sector-mobility model based on sector-transferable skills versus specialized skills, which is detailed in figure 5.3:

The following key insights from the COVID19 pandemic have informed the Martins et. al. (2020) model:

1) Non-standard work arrangements, even with safety-net loading, do not offer sufficient protection in the case of a pandemic when workers earn no income for extended periods of time.
2) Pandemics affect sectors differently. Non-essential services suffer most, while essential services experience increased demand. The workforce needs to shift quickly and dramatically. During COVID-19, for example, supermarkets desperately needed additional workers, while other sectors went into hibernation.
3) In pandemics, one of two characteristics are valued in workers: High-level narrow expertise in critical areas, like intensive care and vaccine development (Humphrey & Nash, 2020); or transferrable skills facilitating worker mobility from hibernating to emergency sectors of the economy. During COVID-19, for example, tourism workers transferred to supermarkets (McIlvaine, 2020).

Figure 3. Sector-mobility model based on sector-transferable skills versus specialized skills
Source: Martins et al. (2020)

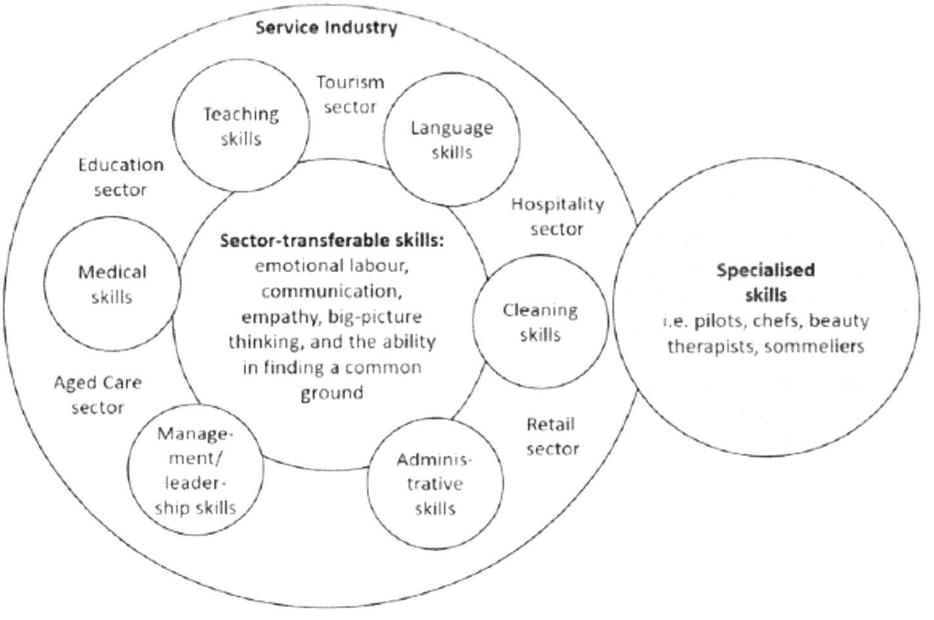

4) Pandemics are expected to become more common in the future (World Economic Forum, 2019). Economic sectors need to be more resilient as they are rebuilt post-COVID19.

This model is based on the notion of skills transferability within and across service sectors (Baum, 2002; Riley, 2004). It offers employers increased levels of flexibility, ensures a higher level of income security for workers, and is more likely to cover demand in emergency areas during a pandemic. The service industry includes many sectors that workers can move across (Baum, 2002; Riley, 2004). A worker is considered sector-mobile if they have skill sets that transfer across sectors.

The tourism and hospitality sectors, for example, require much of their workforce to have a high level of soft or interpersonal skills (Elshaer & Marzouk, 2019). These skills rely on the emotional labor of workers, including face-to-face contact with the public and the ability to produce an emotional state in another person thus requiring the control of emotional activities (Huang, Chen, Liu, 2017). These are complemented by other interpersonal skills such as communication, empathy, big-picture thinking, and the ability to find a common ground (Elshaer & Marzouk, 2019). Such skills are just as important in call centers across a range of different sectors, as they are for supermarket workers; they are sector transferable. In a sector-mobile world, transferable skills are increasingly valuable as they give workers the flexibility to move between different sectors following demand and capitalizing on available opportunities. The transferability of skills is currently undervalued by employers, workers, and trainers alike (Snell, Gekara, & Gatt, 2016).

Both flexibility and income security matter to workers. Within this community, registered sector-mobile workers can move between employers and sectors based on demand. Contractually, there are different options. Workers could be engaged as contractors with the ability to frequently change workplace or sector when required. Whilst this provides flexibility and security due to the maximized employment options, entitlements, protections, and benefits are not ensured. Alternatively, workers could be employed by organizations and borrow from low to high demand sector employers for a limited time for a fee. Such an arrangement opens the possibility for continuous entitlements, protections, and benefits. Another option would be for a central administering entity to employ all registered sector-mobile workers, which are then deployed to different employers (Martins et. al., 2020).

In terms of training for a post-COVID-19 model of tourism and hospitality workforce resilience, universities and registered training operators would need to provide generalized training in sector-transferable skills. Once graduated, service industry workers have their credentials recognized to enter any service sector. If additional training is required, workers can learn sector- and even role-specific skills. Reconceptualizing the service industry as a services industry community will allow workers with sector-transferable skills to move between service sectors to improve their employment opportunities and increase income security. Whilst sector- and role-specific training may still be required, the recognition of sector-transferable skills will ensure workers are sufficiently equipped to do their job. Workforce resilience is not only critically important in the context of pandemics and economic crises, but also contributes to addressing the increased use of technology and automation for service workforces moving forward (Martins et. al., 2020).

Resilience in the Hospitality Industry

The onset of the COVID-19 pandemic, as well as the economy oscillations and extreme staffing shortages that followed have demonstrated the significant need for organizations to address external dynamics in a manner that ensures continued livelihood. In study after study of how various economic sectors are affected by different types of crises, it is discovered that the hospitality and tourism sectors are nearly always the earliest – and often most severely – impacted. The hospitality and tourism sectors are unofficially recognized by other industries as an early warning indicator that a global crisis of significance is emerging (Glaesser, 2006).

There are nine types of changes that the tourism industry faces (Melian-Alzola, Fernandez-Monroy, & Hidalgo-Penate, 2020). These include changes related to competitors such as the appearance of new hotels, changes in the competitor's offer or in its pricing policy or similar (Faulkner,2001; Johansen, Johansen, & Weckesser, 2016). Second would be a change to a hotel's customers including servicing new types of tourists or responding to changes in demand (March, Saurí, & Llurdés, 2014). Third is a change to intermediaries that provide services within the hotel's hospitality offerings like tour operators or bankruptcy, mergers and/or alliances between travel agencies (Faulkner, 2001; Johansen et al., 2016); Fourth is a change in suppliers of guests such as new airlines, changes to existing airline services, change in laundry services, etc. (Faulkner, 2001; Johansen et al., 2016); Fifth encompasses other partners and/or external agents such as the creation of tourism clusters or changes in professional associations (Faulkner, 2001; Tsai & Chen, 2010, 2011); Sixth reveal economic context that may result from new economic alliances between countries, changes in currencies or changes in economic cycles Faulkner, 2001; Hall, 2010). Seven are the type of changes associated with dynamics in the political-legal context like the regulation of holiday homes, regulation for tourism rehabilitation, new taxes, etc. (Faulkner, 2001; Hall, 2010). The eighth type of change is associated with technological context such as social networks, hotel management software, online commerce, cloud-based applications driving peer-delivery networks (Johansen et al., 2016). Finally, the ninth classification of change that impacts the hospitality industry are the changes associated with environmental context such as environmental impact, climate change or natural disasters (Faulkner, 2001; Hall, 2010).

In the last decade, repeated incidents of disruptive crises have exposed weaknesses inherent in hospitality and tourism industry that has catalyzed interest in developing two categories of strategic resilience: Destination location resilience and organizational resilience (Orchiston, Prayag, & Brown, 2016). Destination location resilience speaks to maintaining guest experience (inclusive of safety) during a crisis, operational response procedures when facing a crisis and ensuring employee safety and security throughout the duration of the crisis (Prayag, 2018). The second category is Organization resilience, which encompasses the proactive business development, cost management, operational parameters and investment practices that are followed to help an organization withstand a crisis (Filimonau & De Coteau, 2019). If an organization is not prepared to respond to a crisis or an emergency prior to the crisis occurring, the communities it serves will rarely respond appropriately to the crisis either (Lee et. al., 2013). For the hospitality industry, this potentially impacts organizations that provide service to hotels (such as food and beverage vendors), employees of the hospitality industry and guests of the hospitality industry. When one considers how many large tourist destination drivers have developed communities in response to needed infrastructure, the impact of poor resilience becomes significant and widespread increasing the significance of proactive planning (Attila, 2016). With this perspective in mind, leaders in the hospitality industry need to adopt an approach to enterprise management that incorporates resiliency tactics and strategies. Leaders at hospitality organizations must be prepared to react when changes occur, but also to conduct environmental scans to anticipate, identify and address challenges and maximize opportunities (Brown, Orchiston, Rovins, Feldmann-Jensen, & Johnston, 2018; Tibay, Miller, Chang-Richards, Egbelakin, Seville, and Wilkinson, 2018).

Within this framework, it is important to note that hotels can develop a competitive advantage by being agile and adaptive to change, although the industry has been less then effective at both throughout its entire existence (Melian-Alzolz, et. al., 2020). A change is a challenging event (incremental or extraordinary situation) which can generate both

threats and opportunities. There are three distinct perspectives of resilience that can be considered. First, resilience is considered from the ecological perspective. This perspective measures the degree of ability for an organizational system to absorb the impact from a crisis with as little change to its structure, identity or functions as possible. The second perspective looks at resilience from an adaptive approach. In this perspective, an organization or a system endures the impact of a change without losing its ability to effectively manage its resources. Finally, the third perspective embraces an engineering approach. This perspective measures the speed at which an organization or a system returns to its pre-crisis state of operation following the impact of a crisis (Sabatino, 2016).

An alternative interpretation of crisis response interprets the act of resilience against the framework of an organization's systems, economics and associated communities. Within this interpretative model, an organization's successful response to a crisis should be measured in the degree of adaptation and change that a company undergoes to reach a new functional state. In this model, organizational resilience involves developing processes, policies, structures and resources to cope with extended periods of adverse conditions. Similarly, economic resilience in this model encompasses the organization's ability to assemble resources to protect against harm or loss. Finally, community resilience in this model focuses on an organization comprehensively addressing the needs of all its stakeholders within a crisis scenario (Brown et. al., 2018).

Complimenting this perspective, Duchek, Raetze, and Scheuch (2019) demonstrate that te degree of resilience displayed by an organization is the demonstrated result of a company's ability to recover itself after a crisis has occurred. The degree of success enjoyed by an organization can only be evaluated after disruption has occurred and views resilience as a dynamic process involving how a company operationally and economically effectively deals with situations of an adverse nature before, during and after they have occurred. Within Duchek et al.'s model, resilience emerges as a targeted outcome resulting from organizational processes that were implemented that enable reaching that state. Seville, Brunsdon, Dantas, Le Masurier, Wilkinson, and Vargo (2008) consider organizational resilience as the capability to survive, and potentially even grow and prosper, in times of crisis. Similarly, Ruiz-Martin, López-Paredes, and Wainer (2018) argue that resilience means achieving continuous adjustment to the challenging conditions faced by the organization, while being reinforced.

There are two distinct categories of resilience that manifest for both people and organizations. The first is that resilience can be defined as reactive capabilities that a person or an organization demonstrate after a disruption has been encountered. An example would be an individual modifying his or her personal expenditure budget following being laid off from work unexpectedly. The second type of resilience is associated with capabilities that are developed proactively by a person or an organization to prepare for the future, as of yet not occurring disruptions. An example of this type of resilience would be an individual who prepares a personal expenditure budget that allocates a portion of all revenue into a savings or emergency use fund (Kamalahmadi & Parast, 2016).

In this exploration it is important to distinguish between resilience and crisis management, which are two distinct yet related phenomenon. From this perspective, resilience refers to the capacity of an organization or an individual to adequately cope with an extraordinary or incremental event of disruption while crisis management represents the decisions, actions and ultimately outcomes that emerge from decisions made as a part of resilience (Prayag, 2018). To this end, resilience can be perceived as more than just demonstrations of resistance or acts of adaptation. Resilience involves an individual or an organizational collective adopting a proactive attitude when processing changes and taking steps to anticipate future changes and even attempting to leverage change for one's benefit. Successful resilience can require a full renewal of spirit, attitude, values and processes to be effective (Bouaziz & Hachicha, 2018). Finally, resilience can be thought of from two additional perspectives: First, it is certainly the capacity for reactive affect when faced with disruptive events. However, it can also be considered a proactive, strategic effort that anticipates future disruption and aligns resources and tactics to optimize the situation prior to disruptive events occurring (Gilly, Kechidi, & Talbot, 2014). The practical application in this sense is for leaders and employees to become proficient with integrating resilience strategies into personal and professional activities. As this is not a common element of organizational cultures in the hospitality industry (Kamalahmadi & Parast, 2016) seeking out training and opportunities to become proficient with this skill set is a critical point of training efforts for human resources management strategies.

For an organization to be resilient, it must also be fully aware of the limitations of its capabilities. Ultimately a resilient system is not one that displays invulnerability when exposed to disruptive change. Vulnerability simply refers to the degree of exposure or sensitivity displayed to the impact of disruptive events rather than a more commonly held definition implying immunity from disruptive events (Bec, McLennan, and Moyle, 2018). To become truly resilient, an organization or an individual can assess their vulnerability to truly understand what decisions and actions should be taken to increase resilience (Calgaro, Lloyd, and Dominey-Howes, 2014). There is no one standard tool to conduct this assessment as there are multiple pathways an organization or an individual can adopt to measure vulnerability. These include assessing potential impact for probable disruptive events as well as an evaluation of internal resources available for utilization in the event of a disruptive event. For example, a business can understand how much liquidity it needs to operate daily and then decide how many days of reserve cash it wants to keep on hand should revenue intake cease. An organization can also identify critical resources, needs and processes that it must maintain to continue regular operations in the event of a crisis so that should a disruptive event occur, it can smoothly transition its focus to deploying those elements while pausing other items that were not identified as critical (Wolf, Hinkel, Hallier, Bisaro, Lincke, Ionescu, & Klein, 2013).

This comprehensive internal assessment is a critical element of an effective forward-looking strategy as well since resilience incorporates an organization's ability to be ability and pivot in the face of disruption. In exploring the relationship between the variables of agility versus resilience, the literature identifies that agility encompasses an organization's ability to continue operating even when faced with unexpected disruptive events leading to daily challenges and changes (Duchek 2020). There are three dimensions in measuring resilience that have been observed: robustness, integrity and agility (Bouaziz & Hachicha, 2018). Lengnick-Hall and Beck (2009) suggest that resilience is a precursor, and often a predictor, to an organization achieving strategic stability.

Agility, as either a standalone dimension or a facet of resilience, measures the speed that an organization can transition its own processes, policies and behaviors in an accelerated manner. For example, when the COVID-19 pandemic forced the cessation of face-to-face activities, businesses that were able to transition their operations into a virtual framework were considered more resilient than those that were not able to do so. Among businesses that did transition to a virtual framework, those that did so quickly were considered more agile than those that took a longer period to establish the new operational paradigm (Duchek, 2020). In general, when faced with the COVID-19 pandemic crisis, the hospitality industry did not reveal strengths in either resilience or agility (Bajrami et. al., 2021).

Melian-Alzola et. al. (2020) created an advanced framework for measuring organizational resilience that combines different measurement and conceptualization approaches of organizational resilience building upon earlier work created by Lee et. al, 2013. This model is presented as Figure 5.4 below:

In this model, disruptive situations are first identified and aligned with predictors of resilience, considering the nine types of changes, and measuring three attributes of each: impact, frequency and predictability (Melian-Alzola et.al., 2020). This model can be deployed practically in analyzing contextual relevancy for organizations when it considers resilience preparations and enable leaders within the hospitality sector to develop a framework for upskilling its employees to identify potential events of disruption, evaluate an organization's current state of resilience and agility and develop policies and tactics to address changes catalyzed by disruptive events. Training in this skillset, practicing the skills and proactively preparing for likely disruptive events can be challenging but will also position organizations and their employees to be successful at managing both day to day crisis as well as more significant disruptive events (Lee et al., 2013).

Figure 4. Model of hotel resilience
Source: Melian-Alzola et al. (2020), Lee et al. (2013)

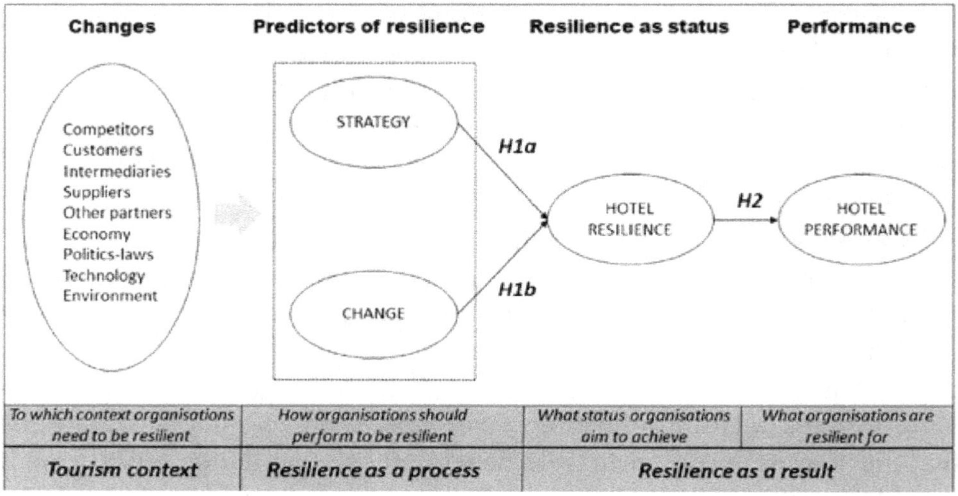

This model is dependent upon integration of prior efforts into current evaluation processes for success. A critical skill associated with successful resilience is the ability to extract meaning and organizational processes from prior mistakes or failures (Patriarca, Di Gravio, Costantino, Falegnami, & Bilotta., 2018). Implied in highlight the importance of learning from past failures and successes to promote stronger organizational resilience. Creative management of unexpected or disruptive events is most observed when experiential learning about past events is available among employees. This speaks to the importance of an organization reducing its turnover and another benefit of investing in strategies designed to achieve that dynamic. Nearly as effective is engaging employees in either simulated or actual crisis management efforts. After all, it isn't enough to simply maintain the proverbial institutional history. It is incumbent upon an organization to also call upon its employees with experience (who many not be emlpoyed in a leadership role) to participate in decisions regarding plans and strategies that respond to the impact of a disruptive event (Al-Ayed, 2019; Bouaziz & Hachicha, 2018; Brown et al., 2019; Lengnick-Hall, Beck, & Lengnick-Hall, 2011). There are multiple examples in the literature that demonstrate the ability of a hotel management team to be effective at motivating their employees during a crisis is often a combination of that team's experience with the organization (or the industry) and the organizational culture's degree of resilience (Ivkov, Blešić, Janićević, Kovačić, Miljković,, Lukić, Sakuls, 2019).

CONCLUSION

Most organizations describe their culture as one that supports innovation, but an actual innovative environment indeed (as well as name) will almost always enhance organizational resistance to disruptive events as the fundamental skills associated with innovative practices develop similar capabilities to those associated with risk or crisis management efforts (Sabahi & Parast, 2020). This is an area of true opportunity within the hospitality and tourism sectors, where researchers have identified few examples of empirical evidence that organizations make any concerted effort to focus on developing themselves in a resilient manner (Verreynne, Williams, Ritchie, Gronum, & Betts, 2019). Successfully resisting a disruptive event is not the only benefit associated with innovative skills. Innovation and effective change management are critical elements for an organization to progress and survive as external factors change (Morais-Storz, Platou, & Norheim, 2018). This is another area of opportunity for the hospitality sector, which tends to be somewhat risk adverse (Sabahi & Parast, 2020). Another important dimension to promote organizational resilience is cultural innovation (Rahi, 2019) which is a precursor for the successful adoption of most advanced quality management models (Marwa, 2012). The key to developing resilience lies not in one's predictive cognition, but rather in upskilling leaders to be more effective managers who utilize tools, techniques and paradigms that not just promote accountability and production but also continuous improvement, reflection, empathy and collaborative techniques (Verreynee et. al., 2019).

Based on the impact, frequency and predictability of the nine different types of reviewed and analyzed change (competitors, customers, intermediaries, suppliers, other partners and/or external agents, economic situation, political-legal issues, technological development and environmental factors), hotels have demonstrated that frequent change is often related more to customer interactions (primarily) and development of technology (secondarily) as opposed to strategic efforts (Sabahi & Parast, 2020) . These changes are perceived as having a high level of impact and therefore supported by the sector. It has been determined that the outcomes associated with changes brought about by customer interactions are more predictable than those that are catalyzed by technological change (Melian-Alzoa et. al., 2020). On the other hand, economic, political-legal and environmental changes present low levels of frequency and predictability and are considered a higher risk for an organization to undertake even as it is observed that disruptive events of this type produce a medium to high level of impact for an organization (Marwa, 2012). This ultimately demonstrates that hotels should develop strategic actions to increase its own resilience and, as part of a corporate social responsibility plan, also improve the resilience of organizations that contribute complementary services such as ground transportation, entertainment and dining options that service the hotel's guests (McManus, Seville, Vargo, & Brunsdon, 2008).

Regarding the dimension of change, hotels that wish to excel should make effort to consistently promote employee development around creativity, continuous improvement, and innovation. To this end, it is suggested the incorporation of quality models that promote continuous improvement (Marwa, 2012) and a culture of innovation as suggested by Rahi (2019). In the research model presented in figure 5.4 by Melian-Alzola (2020), hotel resilience measures the degree to which the hotel is in continuous equilibrium in a changing context. The scale of resilience predictors explains almost 60% of hotel resilience (Melian-Alzola, 2020; Lee et. al., 2013). This is a clear area of opportunity, and – ironically – the least risky option for the hospitality sector. In developing resilience and adaptability among its employees, hotel organizations will increase the likelihood of being positioned for success to endure disruptive events as they occur.

REFERENCES

Ackerlof, G., & Shiller, R. (2009). *Animal Spirits: How Human Psychology Drives the Economy, and Why It Matters for Global Capitalism*. Princeton University Press.

Agyeiwaah, E., Dayour, F., & Zhou, J. Y. (2022). How does employee commitment impact customers' attitudinal loyalty? *Journal of Hospitality and Tourism Insights*, *17*(1), 1–30. doi:10.1108/JHTI-09-2020-0169

Ahmed, M. Z., Ahmed, O., Aibao, Z., Hanbin, S., Siyu, L., & Ahmad, A. (2020). Epidemic of COVID-19 in China and associated psychological problems. *Asian Journal of Psychiatry*, *51*, 102092. doi:10.1016/j.ajp.2020.102092 PMID:32315963

Akgunduz, Y., & Eryilmaz, G. (2018). Does turnover intention mediate the effects of job insecurity and co-worker support on social loafing? *International Journal of Hospitality Management*, *68*, 41–49. doi:10.1016/j.ijhm.2017.09.010

Al-Ayed, S. I. (2019). The impact of strategic human resource management on organizational resilience: An empirical study on hospitals. *Verslas: teorija ir praktika*, *20*(1), 179–186.

Allen, T., Murray, K. A., Zambrana-Torrelio, C., Morse, S. S., Rondinini, C., Di Marco, M., Breit, N., Olival, K. J., & Daszak, P. (2017). Global hotspots and correlates of emerging zoonotic diseases. *Nature Communications*, *8*(1), 1124. doi:10.103841467-017-00923-8 PMID:29066781

Ammon, C. E. (2002). Spanish flu epidemic in 1918 in Geneva, Switzerland. *Eurosurveillance*, *7*(12), 190–192. doi:10.2807/esm.07.12.00391-en PMID:12631986

Artz, B., & Kaya, I. (2014). Job insecurity and job satisfaction in the United States: The case of public sector union workers. *Industrial Relations Journal*, *45*(2), 103–120. doi:10.1111/irj.12044

Ashford, S. J., Lee, C., & Bobko, P. (1989). Content, causes, and consequences of job insecurity: A theory-based measure and substantive test. *The Academy of Management Annals*, *32*(4), 803–829.

Attila, A. T. (2016). The impact of the hotel industry on the competitiveness of tourism destinations in Hungary. *Journal of Competitiveness*, *8*(4), 85–104. doi:10.7441/joc.2016.04.06

Bajrami, D. D. (2021). Will we have the same employees in hospitality after all? The impact of COVID-19 on employees' work attitudes and turnover intentions. *International Journal of Hospitality Management*, 94.

Barling, J., Dupre, K. E., & Kelloway, E. K. (2009). Predicting workplace aggression and violence. *Annual Review of Psychology*, *60*(1), 671–692. doi:10.1146/annurev.psych.60.110707.163629 PMID:18793089

Barton, L. (1994). Crisis management: Preparing for and managing disasters. *The Cornell Hotel and Restaurant Administration Quarterly*, *35*(2), 59–65. doi:10.1177/001088049403500219

Baum, T. (2002). Skills and training for the hospitality sector: A review of issues. *Journal of Vocational Education and Training*, *54*(3), 343–364. doi:10.1080/13636820200200204

Baum, T., & Hai, N. T. T. (2020). Hospitality, tourism, human rights and the impact of COVID-19. *International Journal of Contemporary Hospitality Management*, *32*(7), 2397–2407. doi:10.1108/IJCHM-03-2020-0242

Bec, A., McLennan, B., & Moyle, C. L. (2018). Resilient and sustainable communities. *Sustainability (Basel)*, *10*(12), 4810. doi:10.3390u10124810

Berger, P. L., & Luckmann, T. (1966). *The Social Construction of Reality: A Treatise in the Sociology of Knowledge*. Anchor Books.

Berry, L., Mirabito, A.M., & Baun, W. (2010). What's the hard return on employee wellness programs? *Harvard Business Review, 88*, 1-9.

Birdir, K. (2002). General manager turnover and root causes. *International Journal of Contemporary Hospitality Management*, *14*(1), 43–47. doi:10.1108/09596110210415123

Bouaziz, F., & Hachicha, Z. S. (2018). Strategic human resource management practices and organizational resilience. *Journal of Management Development*, *37*(7), 537–551. doi:10.1108/JMD-11-2017-0358

Brown, N. A., Orchiston, C., Rovins, J. E., Feldmann-Jensen, S., & Johnston, D. (2018). An integrative framework for investigating disaster resilience within the hotel sector. *Journal of Hospitality and Tourism Management*, *36*, 67–75. doi:10.1016/j.jhtm.2018.07.004

Brown, N. A., Rovins, J. E., Feldmann-Jensen, S., Orchiston, C., & Johnston, D. (2019). Measuring disaster resilience within the hotel sector: An exploratory survey of Wellington and Hawke's bay, New Zealand hotel staff and managers. *International Journal of Disaster Risk Reduction*, *33*, 108–121. doi:10.1016/j.ijdrr.2018.09.014

Browne, A., St-Onge Ahmad, S., Beck, C. R., & Nguyen-Van-Tam, J. S. (2016). The roles of transportation and transportation hubs in the propagation of influenza and coronaviruses: A systematic review. *Journal of Travel Medicine*, *23*(1), tav002. doi:10.1093/jtm/tav002 PMID:26782122

Buranyi. (2020, April 10). The WHO v coronavirus: Why it can't handle the pandemic. *The Guardian*. https://www.theguardian.com/news/2020/apr/10/world-health-organization-who-vcoronavirus-why-it-cant-handle-pandemic

Burgard, S. A., & Kalousova, L. (2015). Effects of the Great Recession: Health and well-being. *Annual Review of Sociology*, *41*(1), 181–201. doi:10.1146/annurev-soc-073014-112204

Burkle, F. M. Jr. (2006). Globalization and disasters: Issues of public health, state capacity and political action. *Journal of International Affairs*, *59*(2), 231–265.

Calgaro, E., Lloyd, K., & Dominey-Howes, D. (2014). From vulnerability to transformation: A framework for assessing the vulnerability and resilience of tourism destinations. *Journal of Sustainable Tourism*, *22*(3), 341–360. do i:10.1080/09669582.2013.826229

Carnevale, J. B., & Hatak, I. (2020). Employee adjustment and well-being in the era of COVID-19: Implications for human resource management. *Journal of Business Research*, *116*, 183–187. doi:10.1016/j.jbusres.2020.05.037 PMID:32501303

Cheng, G. H. L., & Chan, D. K. S. (2008). Who suffers more from job insecurity? A meta-analytic review. *Applied Psychology*, *57*(2), 271–303. doi:10.1111/j.1464-0597.2007.00312.x

Cheng, Y., Huang, H. Y., Li, P. R., & Hsu, J. H. (2011). Employment insecurity, workplace justice and employees' burnout in Taiwanese employees: A validation study. *International Journal of Behavioral Medicine, 18*(4), 391–401. doi:10.100712529-011-9152-y PMID:21380932

Chew, E. Y. T., & Jahari, S. A. (2014). Destination image as a mediator between perceived risks and revisit intention: A case of post-disaster Japan. *Tourism Management, 40*, 382–393. doi:10.1016/j.tourman.2013.07.008

Chien, G. C., & Law, R. (2003). The impact of the Severe Acute Respiratory Syndrome on hotels: A case study of Hong Kong. *International Journal of Hospitality Management, 22*(3), 327–332. doi:10.1016/S0278-4319(03)00041-0 PMID:32287842

Chinazzi, M., Davis, T. J., Ajelli, M., Gioannini, C., Litvinova, M., Merler, S., Pastore y Piontti, A., Mu, K., Rossi, L., Sun, K., Viboud, C., Xiong, X., Yu, H., Halloran, M. E., Longini, I. M. Jr, & Vespignani, A. (2020). The effect of travel restrictions on the spread of the 2019 novel coronavirus (COVID-19) outbreak. *Science, 368*(6489), 395–400. doi:10.1126cience.aba9757 PMID:32144116

Chirumbolo, A., & Areni, A. (2010). Job insecurity influence on job performance and mental health: Testing the moderating effect of the need for closure. *Economic and Industrial Democracy, 31*(2), 195–214. doi:10.1177/0143831X09358368

Chung, H., & van Oorschot, W. (2011). Institutions versus market forces: Explaining the employment insecurity of European individuals during (the beginning of) the financial crisis. *Journal of European Social Policy, 21*(4), 287–301. doi:10.1177/0958928711412224

Coombs, W. T., & Laufer, D. (2018). Global crisis management–current research and future directions. *Journal of International Management, 24*(3), 199–203. doi:10.1016/j.intman.2017.12.003

Cottini, E., & Ghinetti, P. (2018). Employment insecurity and employees' health in Denmark. *Health Economics, 27*(2), 426–439. doi:10.1002/hec.3580 PMID:28868624

Dalal, R. S. (2005). A meta-analysis of the relationship between organizational citizenship behavior and counterproductive work behavior. *The Journal of Applied Psychology, 90*(6), 1241–1255. doi:10.1037/0021-9010.90.6.1241 PMID:16316277

Dalton, D. R., & Todor, W. D. (1993). Turnover, transfer, absenteeism: An interdependent Perspective. *Journal of Management*, *19*(2), 193–219. doi:10.1177/014920639301900202

Davies, W. (2020, March 24). The last global crisis didn't change the world. But this one could. *The Guardian.* https://www.theguardian.com/commentisfree/2020/mar/24/coronavirus-crisischange-world-financial-global-capitalism

Dayour, F., Adongo, C. A., Amuquandoh, F. E., & Adam, I. (2021). Managing the COVID-19 crisis: Coping and post-recovery strategies for hospitality and tourism businesses in Ghana. *Journal of Hospitality and Tourism Insights.*, *4*(4), 373–392.

De Stefano, V. (2016). "The rise of the "just-in-time workforce": On-demand work, crowdwork and labor protection in the "Gig Economy." *Comparative Labor Law Journal, 37*(3), 471-504.

De Witte, H., Vander Elst, T., & De Cuyper, N. (2015). Job insecurity, health and well-being. In J. Vuori, R. Blonk, & R. Price (Eds.), *Sustainable Working Lives. Aligning Perspectives on Health, Safety and Well-Being* (pp. 109–128). Springer.

Deery, M., & Jago, L. (2009). A framework for work-life balance practices: Addressing the needs of the tourism industry. *Tourism and Hospitality Research*, *9*(2), 97–108. doi:10.1057/thr.2009.4

Desclaux, A., Badji, D., Ndione, A. G., & Sow, K. (2017). Accepted monitoring or endured quarantine? Ebola contacts' perceptions in Senegal. *Social Science & Medicine*, *178*, 38–45. doi:10.1016/j.socscimed.2017.02.009 PMID:28192745

Devaux, C. A., Mediannikov, O., Medkour, H., & Raoult, D. (2019). Infectious disease risk across the growing human-non human primate interface: A review of the evidence. *Frontiers in Public Health*, *7*, 305. doi:10.3389/fpubh.2019.00305 PMID:31828053

Diener, E. (2009). Subjective well-being. In E. Diener (Ed.), Social Indicators Research Series: Vol. 37. *The Science of Well-Being*. Springer. doi:10.1007/978-90-481-2350-6_2

Dimitropoulos, P. E. (2018). Profitability determinants of the Greek hospitality industry: the crisis effect. In Innovative Approaches to Tourism and Leisure. Springer.

Dolnicar, S. (2019). A review of research into paid online peer-to-peer accommodation: Launching the Annals of Tourism Research curated collection on peer-to-peer accommodation. *Annals of Tourism Research*, *75*, 248–264. doi:10.1016/j.annals.2019.02.003

Dube, K., Nhamo, G., & Chikodzi, D. (2020). COVID-19 cripples global restaurant and hospitality industry. *Current Issues in Tourism*, 1–4.

Duchek, S., Raetze, S., & Scheuch, I. (2019). *The role of diversity in organizational resilience: A theoretical framework.* Business Research. doi:10.100740685-019-0084-8

Duncan, T., Scott, D. G., & Baum, T. (2013). The mobilities of hospitality work: An exploration of issues and debates. *Annals of Tourism Research*, *41*, 1–19. doi:10.1016/j.annals.2012.10.004

Elrehail, H., Harazneh, I., Abuhjeeleh, M., Alzghoul, A., Alnajdawi, S., & Ibrahim, H. M. H. (2019). Employee satisfaction, human resource management practices and competitive advantage: The case of Northern Cyprus. *European Journal of Management and Business Economics*, *29*(2), 125–149. doi:10.1108/EJMBE-01-2019-0001

Elshaer, A. M., & Marzouk, A. M. (2019). *Labor in the tourism and hospitality industry: skills, ethics, issues, and rights.* CRC Press. doi:10.1201/9780429465093

Elshaer, I. A., & Saad, S. K. (2017). Political instability and tourism in Egypt: Exploring survivors' attitudes after downsizing. *Journal of Policy Research in Tourism, Leisure & Events*, *9*(1), 3–22. doi:10.1080/19407963.2016.1233109

Emen, J. (2020). Hospitality industry facing potentially devastating coronavirus impact. *Barron's*. Available at: https://barrons.com/articles/hospitality-industry-facing-potentially-devastatingcoronavirus-impact-01584118579

Evans, N., & Elphick, S. (2005). Models of crisis management: An evaluation of their value for strategic planning in the international travel industry. *International Journal of Tourism Research*, *7*(3), 135–150. doi:10.1002/jtr.527

Faulkner, B. (2001). Towards a framework for tourism disaster management. *Tourism Management*, *22*(2), 135–147. doi:10.1016/S0261-5177(00)00048-0

Filimonau, V., & De Coteau, D. (2020). Tourism resilience in the context of integrated destination and disaster management (DM2). *International Journal of Tourism Research*, *22*(2), 202–222. doi:10.1002/jtr.2329

Filimonau, V., Derqui, B., & Matute, J. (2020). The COVID-19 pandemic and organisational commitment of senior hotel managers. *International Journal of Hospitality Management*, *91*, 102659. doi:10.1016/j.ijhm.2020.102659 PMID:32904709

Folkman, S. (1984). Personal control and stress and coping processes: A theoretical analysis. *Journal of Personality and Social Psychology*, *46*(4), 839–852. doi:10.1037/0022-3514.46.4.839 PMID:6737195

Frone, M. R. (2018). What happened to the employed during the Great Recession? A U.S. population study of net change in employee insecurity, health, and organizational commitment. *Journal of Vocational Behavior*, *107*, 246–260. doi:10.1016/j.jvb.2018.05.001 PMID:31303656

Ghaderi, Z., King, B., & Hall, C. M. (2022). Crisis preparedness of hospitality managers: Evidence from Malaysia. *Journal of Hospitality and Tourism Insights*, *5*(2), 292–310. doi:10.1108/JHTI-10-2020-0199

Gilfillan, G. (2018). *Characteristics and use of casual employees in Australia*. Parliament of Australia, Research Paper Series, Canberra.

Gills, B. (2020). Deep restoration: From the great implosion to the great awakening. *Globalizations*, *17*(4), 577–579. Advance online publication. doi:10.1080/14747731.2020.1748364

Gilly, J. P., Kechidi, M., & Talbot, D. (2014). Resilience of organisations and territories: The role of pivot firms. *European Management Journal*, *32*(4), 596–602. doi:10.1016/j.emj.2013.09.004

Giudici, M., & Filimonau, V. (2019). Exploring the linkages between managerial leadership, communication and teamwork in successful event delivery. *Tourism Management Perspectives*, *32*, 100558. doi:10.1016/j.tmp.2019.100558

Glaesser, D. (2006). *Crisis management in the tourism Industry*. Butterworth-Heinemann. doi:10.4324/9780080464596

Godinic, D., Obrenovic, B., & Khudaykulov, A. (2020). Effects of economic uncertainty on mental health in the COVID-19 pandemic context: Social Identity Disturbance, Job Uncertainty and Psychological Well-Being Model. *International Journal of Innovative Economic Development*, *6*(1), 61–74. doi:10.18775/ijied.1849-7551-7020.2015.61.2005

Goods, C., Veen, A., & Barratt, T. (2019). Is your gig any good?' Analysing job quality in the Australian platform-based food-delivery sector. *The Journal of Industrial Relations*, *61*(4), 502–527. doi:10.1177/0022185618817069

Gossling, S., Scott, D., & Hall, C. M. (2021). Pandemics, tourism, and global change: A rapid assessment of COVID-19. *Journal of Sustainable Tourism*, *29*(1), 1–20. doi:10.1080/09669582.2020.1758708

Graf-Vlachy, L., Sun, S., & Zhang, S. X. (2020). Predictors of managers' mental health during the COVID-19 pandemic. *European Journal of Psychotraumatology*, *11*(1), 1834195. doi:10.1080/20008198.2020.1834195 PMID:33244365

Greenhalgh, L., & Rosenblatt, Z. (1984). Job insecurity: Toward conceptual clarity. *Academy of Management Review*, *9*(3), 438–448. doi:10.2307/258284

Hajibaba, H., Gretzel, U., Leisch, F., & Dolnicar, S. (2015). Crisis-resistant tourists. *Annals of Tourism Research*, *53*, 46–60. doi:10.1016/j.annals.2015.04.001

Hall, C. M. (2010). Crisis events in tourism: Subjects of crisis in tourism. *Current Issues in Tourism*, *13*(5), 401–417. doi:10.1080/13683500.2010.491900

Hall, C. M. (2020). Biological invasion, biosecurity, tourism, and globalisation. In D. Timothy (Ed.), *Handbook of globalisation and tourism* (pp. 114–125). Edward Elgar.

Hall, C. M., & Prayag, G. (2020). Earthquakes and tourism: Impacts, responses, and resilience – An introduction. In C. M. Hall & G. Prayag (Eds.), *Tourism and earthquakes*. Channel View.

Hall, C. M., Prayag, G., & Amore, A. (2018). *Tourism and resilience*. Channel View.

Hall, C. M., Scott, D., & Gössling, S. (2020). Pandemics, transformations and tourism: Be careful what you wish for. *Tourism Geographies*, *22*(3), 577–598. doi:10.1080/14616688.2020.1759131

Hancock, A. (2020). Restaurants, hotels and gyms face up to a future of social distancing. *Financial Times*. Available from: https://www.ft.com/content/7c90

Hellgren, J., Sverke, M., & Isaksson, I. (1999). A two-dimensional approach to job insecurity: Consequences for employee attitudes and well-being. *European Journal of Work and Organizational Psychology*, *8*(2), 179–195. doi:10.1080/135943299398311

Henderson, J. C. (2007). Corporate social responsibility and tourism: Hotel companies in Phuket, Thailand, after the Indian Ocean tsunami. *International Journal of Hospitality Management*, *26*(1), 228–239. doi:10.1016/j.ijhm.2006.02.001

Heredia-Colaco, V., & Rodrigues, H. (2021). Hosting in turbulent times: Hoteliers' perceptions and strategies to recover from the Covid-19 pandemic. *International Journal of Hospitality Management*, *94*, 94. doi:10.1016/j.ijhm.2020.102835 PMID:34785842

Herscovitch, L., & Meyer, J. P. (2002). Commitment to organizational change: Extension of a three-component model. *The Journal of Applied Psychology*, *87*(3), 474–487. doi:10.1037/0021-9010.87.3.474 PMID:12090605

Herzberg, F., Mausner, B., & Bloch Snyderman, B. (2005). *The Motivation to Work*. Transaction Publishers.

Heskett, J. L., Jones, T. O., Loveman, G. W., Sasser, W. E., & Schlesinger, L. A. (2008). Putting the service-profit chain to work. *Harvard Business Review*. Available at: https://hbr.org/2008/07/putting-the-service-profit-chain-to-work

Hodari, D., & Sturman, M. C. (2014). Who's in charge now? The decision autonomy of hotel general managers. *Cornell Hospitality Quarterly*, *55*(4), 433–447. doi:10.1177/1938965513518839

Houdmont, J., Kerr, R., & Addley, K. (2012). Psychosocial factors and economic recession: The Stormont study. *Occupational Medicine*, *62*(2), 98–104. doi:10.1093/occmed/kqr216 PMID:22355088

Huang, S., Chen, Z., Liu, H., & Zhou, L. (2017). Job satisfaction and turnover intention in China: The moderating effects of job alternatives and policy support. *Chinese Management Studies*, *11*(4), 689–706. doi:10.1108/CMS-12-2016-0263

Hui, D. S., Azhar, E. I., Madani, T. A., Ntoumi, F., Kock, R., Dar, O., Ippolito, G., Mchugh, T. D., Memish, Z. A., & Drosten, C. (2020). The continuing 2019-nCoV epidemic threat of novel coronaviruses to global health—The latest 2019 novel coronavirus outbreak in Wuhan, China. *International Journal of Infectious Diseases*, *91*, 264–266. doi:10.1016/j.ijid.2020.01.009 PMID:31953166

Humphrey, T., & Nash, D. (2020). *UQ fast tracks nurses in response to COVID-19 pandemic*. https://www.uq.edu.au/news/article/2020/04/uq-fast-tracks-nurses-response-covid-19-pandemic

Hunt, R. (2020). *Marriott CEO: coronavirus is hurting the hotel chain worse than 9/11 or world war II.* Available at: https://www.nasdaq.com/articles/marriott-ceopercent3A-coronavirus-ishurting-the-hotel-chain-worse-than-9-11-or-world-war-ii-2020

Hurrell, J. J. Jr, Nelson, D. L., & Simmons, B. L. (1998). Measuring job stressors and strains: Where we have been, where we are, and where we need to go. *Journal of Occupational Health Psychology*, *3*(4), 368–389. doi:10.1037/1076-8998.3.4.368 PMID:9805282

International Monetary Fund. (2020). *World economic outlook, April 2020. The great lockdown*. Available at: https://www.imf.org/en/Publications/WEO/Issues/2020/04/14/weo-april-2020

Ivkov, M., Blešić, I., Janićević, S., Kovačić, S., Miljković, D., Lukić, T., & Sakuls, D. (2019). *Natural Disasters vs Hotel Industry Resilience: An Exploratory Study among Hotel Managers from Europe*. De Gruyter Open. doi:10.1515/geo-2019-0030

Jayawardena, C., Tew, P. J., Lu, Z., Tolomiczenko, G., & Gellatly, J. (2008). SARS: Lessons in strategic planning for hoteliers and destination marketers. *International Journal of Contemporary Hospitality Management*, *20*(3), 332–346. doi:10.1108/09596110810866145

Jiang, L., & Lavaysse, L. M. (2018). Cognitive and affective job insecurity: A meta-analysis and a primary study. *Journal of Management*, *44*(6), 2307–2342. doi:10.1177/0149206318773853

Jiang, Y., Ritchie, B. W., & Verreynne, M. L. (2019). Building tourism organizational resilience to crises and disasters: A dynamic capabilities view. *International Journal of Tourism Research*, *21*(6), 882–900. doi:10.1002/jtr.2312

Jiang, Y., & Wen, J. (2020). Effects of COVID-19 on hotel marketing and management: A perspective article. *International Journal of Contemporary Hospitality Management*, *32*(8), 2563–2573. doi:10.1108/IJCHM-03-2020-0237

Johansen, B. F., Johansen, W., & Weckesser, N. M. (2016). Emotional stakeholders as "crisis communicators." In social media: The case of the Telenor customer complaints crisis. *Corporate Communications*, *21*(3), 289–308. doi:10.1108/CCIJ-05-2015-0026

Jones, P., & Comfort, D. (2020). The COVID-19 crisis, tourism and sustainable development. *Athens Journal of Tourism.*, *7*(2), 75–86. doi:10.30958/ajt.7-2-1

Kahneman, D. (2011). *Thinking, Fast and Slow*. Doubleday.

Kahneman, D., & Krueger, A. B. (2006). Developments in the measurement of subjective well-being. *The Journal of Economic Perspectives*, *20*(1), 3–24. doi:10.1257/089533006776526030

Kaine, S., & Josserand, E. (2019). The organisation and experience of work in the gig economy. *The Journal of Industrial Relations*, *61*(4), 479–501. doi:10.1177/0022185619865480

Kamalahmadi, M., & Parast, M. M. (2016). A review of the literature on the principles of enterprise and supply chain resilience: Major findings and directions for future research. *International Journal of Production Economics*, *171*, 116–133. doi:10.1016/j.ijpe.2015.10.023

Kanfer, R., Wanberg, C. R., & Kantrowitz, T. M. (2001). Job search and employment: A personality–motivational analysis and meta-analytic review. *The Journal of Applied Psychology*, *86*(5), 837–855. doi:10.1037/0021-9010.86.5.837 PMID:11596801

Karatepe, O. M., Rezapouraghdam, H., & Hassannia, R. (2020). Job insecurity, work engagement and their effects on hotel employees' non-green and nonattendance behaviors. *International Journal of Hospitality Management*, *87*, 1–12. doi:10.1016/j.ijhm.2020.102472

Katona, G. (1975). *Psychological Economics*. Elsevier.

Kaushal, V., & Srivastava, S. (2021). Hospitality and tourism industry amid COVID-19 pandemic: Perspectives on challenges and learnings from India. *International Journal of Hospitality Management*, *92*, 102707. doi:10.1016/j.ijhm.2020.102707 PMID:33024348

Keskin, H., Akgun, A. E., Ayar, H., & Kayman, S. S. (2016). Cyberbullying victimization, counterproductive work behaviours and emotional intelligence at workplace. *Procedia: Social and Behavioral Sciences*, *235*, 281–287. doi:10.1016/j.sbspro.2016.11.031

Khawaja, K. F., Sarfraz, M., Rashid, M., & Rashid, M. (2021). How is COVID-19 pandemic causing employee withdrawal behavior in the hospitality industry? An empirical investigation. *Journal of Hospitality and Tourism Insights*, *5*(3), 687–706. doi:10.1108/JHTI-01-2021-0002

Kichuk, A., Brown, L., & Ladkin, A. (2019). Talent pool exclusion: The hotel employee perspective. *International Journal of Contemporary Hospitality Management*, *31*(10), 3970–3991. doi:10.1108/IJCHM-10-2018-0814

Kiefer, T. (2005). Feeling bad: antecedents and consequences of negative emotions in ongoing Change. *Journal of Organizational Behavior*, *26*(8), 875–897. doi:10.1002/job.339

Killingsworth, M. A. (2021). Experienced well-being rises with income, even above $75,000 per year. *Proceedings of the National Academy of Sciences of the United States of America*, *118*(4), e2016976118. doi:10.1073/pnas.2016976118 PMID:33468644

Kim, J., Kim, J., Lee, S. K., & Tang, L. R. (2020). Effects of epidemic disease outbreaks on financial performance of restaurants: Event study method approach. *Journal of Hospitality and Tourism Management*, *43*, 32–41. doi:10.1016/j.jhtm.2020.01.015

Kiraly, O., Potenza, M. N., Stein, D. J., King, D. L., Hodgins, D. C., Saunders, J. B., Griffiths, M. D., Gjoneska, B., Billieux, J., Brand, M., Abbott, M. W., Chamberlain, S. R., Corazza, O., Burkauskas, J., Sales, C. M. D., Montag, C., Lochner, C., Grünblatt, E., Wegmann, E., ... Demetrovics, Z. (2020). Preventing problematic internet use during the COVID-19 pandemic: Consensus guidance. *Comprehensive Psychiatry*, *100*, 152180. doi:10.1016/j.comppsych.2020.152180 PMID:32422427

Kozul-Wright, R., & Barbosa, N. (2020). This crisis will change the world – for better, or worse. *Tribune Magazine*. https://tribunemag.co.uk/2020/03/coronavirus-will-change-the-world-for-better-or-worse

Kuhnert, K. W., & Vance, R. J. (1992). Job insecurity and moderators of the relation between job insecurity and employee adjustment. In J. C. Quick, L. R. Murphy, & J. J. J. Hurrell (Eds.), *Stress and well-being at work: Assessments and interventions for occupational mental health* (pp. 48–63). American Psychological Association. doi:10.1037/10116-004

Lai, I. K. W., & Wong, J. W. C. (2020). Comparing crisis management practices in the hotel industry between initial and pandemic stages of COVID-19. *International Journal of Contemporary Hospitality Management*, *32*(10), 32. doi:10.1108/IJCHM-04-2020-0325

Latack, J. C., Kinicki, A. J., & Prussia, G. E. (1995). An integrative process model of coping with job loss. *Academy of Management Review*, *20*(2), 311–342. doi:10.2307/258849

Lazarus, R. S., & Folkman, S. (1984). *Stress, Appraisal, and Coping*. Springer Publishing Company.

Lee, A. V., Vargo, J., & Seville, E. (2013). Developing a tool to measure and compare organizations' resilience. *Natural Hazards Review*, *14*(1), 29–41. doi:10.1061/(ASCE)NH.1527-6996.0000075

Lee, C., & Way, K. (2010). Individual employment characteristics of hotel employees that play a role in employee satisfaction and work retention. *International Journal of Hospitality Management*, *29*(3), 344–353. doi:10.1016/j.ijhm.2009.08.008

Lee, S., & Jeong, D. (2017). Job insecurity and turnover intention: Organizational commitment as mediator. *Social Behavior and Personality*, *45*(4), 529–536. doi:10.2224bp.5865

Lehman, W. E., & Simpson, D. D. (1992). Employee substance use and on-the-job behaviors. *The Journal of Applied Psychology*, *77*(3), 309–321. doi:10.1037/0021-9010.77.3.309 PMID:1601823

Lengnick-Hall, C. A., & Beck, T. E. (2009). Resilience capacity and strategic agility: Prerequisites for thriving in a dynamic environment. No. 0059 College of Business, University of Texas at San Antonio.

Lengnick-Hall, C. A., Beck, T. E., & Lengnick-Hall, M. L. (2011). Developing a capacity for organizational resilience through strategic human resource management. *Human Resource Management Review*, *21*(3), 243–255. doi:10.1016/j.hrmr.2010.07.001

Leonidou, L. C., Leonidou, C. N., Fotiadis, T. A., & Zariti, A. (2013). Resources and capabilities as drivers of hotel environmental marketing strategy: Implications for competitive advantage and performance. *Tourism Management*, *35*, 94–110. doi:10.1016/j.tourman.2012.06.003

Levy, S. E., & Park, S.-Y. (2011). An analysis of CSR activities in the lodging industry. *International Journal of Hospitality Management*, *18*(1), 147–154.

Li, B., Yang, J., Zhao, F., Zhi, L., Wang, X., Liu, L., Bi, Z., & Zhao, Y. (2020). Prevalence and impact of cardiovascular metabolic diseases on COVID-19 in China. *Clinical Research in Cardiology; Official Journal of the German Cardiac Society*, *109*(5), 531–538. doi:10.100700392-020-01626-9 PMID:32161990

Liu, C., Zhou, Q., Li, Y., Garner, L. V., Watkins, S. P., Carter, L. J., Smoot, J., Gregg, A. C., Daniels, A. D., Jervey, S., & Albaiu, D. (2020). Research and development on therapeutic agents and vaccines for COVID-19 and related human coronavirus diseases. *ACS Central Science*, *6*(3), 315–331. doi:10.1021/acscentsci.0c00272 PMID:32226821

Liu, C. E., Yuan, X., Zhang, M. N., & Hu, C. H. (2019). Work-related identity discrepancy and work withdrawal behavior: The mediation effect of negative emotion. *International Journal of Business and Social Science*, *10*(7), 229–236. doi:10.30845/ijbss.v10n7p25

Lundberg, C., Gudmundson, A., & Andersson, T. (2009). Herzberg's Two-Factor Theory of work motivation tested empirically on seasonal workers in hospitality and tourism. *Tourism Management*, *30*(6), 890–899. doi:10.1016/j.tourman.2008.12.003

Mair, S. (2020, March 30). What will the world be like after coronavirus? Four possible futures. *The Conversation*. https://theconversation.com/what-will-the-world-be-like-after-c…d= IwAR2wr9pzssSdBSxjaHaWba9-iHSF3flYgZ9BVI1jAx_Y4YlXVAImcJcNdjM

Malik, A., Sinha, S., & Goel, S. (2020). "The "screen"ing of you and me: Effects of COVID-19 on counterproductive work behaviors. *IEEE Engineering Management Review*, *48*(3), 37–43. doi:10.1109/EMR.2020.3010323

Manolis, C., Meamber, L., Winsor, R., & Brooks, C. (2001). Partial employees and consumers. *Marketing Theory*, *1*(2), 225–243. doi:10.1177/147059310100100204

Mao, Y., He, J., Morrisson, A. M., & Coca-Stefaniak, J. A. (2020). Effects of tourism CSR on employee psychological capital in the COVID-19 crisis: From the perspective of conservation of resources theory. *Current Issues in Tourism, 24*(19), 2716–2734. doi:10.1080/13683500.2020.1770706

Maphanga, P. M., & Henama, U. S. (2019). The tourism impact of Ebola in Africa: Lessons on crisis management. *African Journal of Hospitality, Tourism and Leisure, 8*(3). https://www.ajhtl.com/ uploads/7/1/6/3/7163688/ article_59_vol_8_3__2019.pdf

March, H., Saurí, D., & Olcina, J. (2014). Rising temperatures and dwindling water supplies? Perception of climate change among residents of the Spanish Mediterranean tourist coastal areas. *Environmental Management, 53*(1), 181–193. doi:10.100700267-013-0177-7 PMID:24122097

Markey, R., & McIvor, J. (2018). Regulating casual employment in Australia. *The Journal of Industrial Relations, 60*(5), 593–618. doi:10.1177/0022185618778084

MartinsA.RiordanT.DolnicarS. (2020, May 8). *A post-COVID-19 model of tourism and hospitality workforce resilience*. doi:10.31235/osf.io/4quga

Marwa, S. (2012). The criticality of quality management in building corporate resilience. In K. S. Ng (Ed.), *Quality management and practices*. InTech. doi:10.5772/38424

Mathieu, J. E., & Zajac, D. M. (1990). A review and meta-analysis of the antecedents, correlates, and consequences of organizational commitment. *Psychological Bulletin, 108*(2), 171–194. doi:10.1037/0033-2909.108.2.171

McAvoy, A. (2020). *Hawaii looks to restrict lodging reservations to prevent visitor arrivals*. Associated Press. https://skift.com/2020/04/14/hawaii-looks-to-restrict-lodging-reservations-toprevent-visitor-arrivals/

McGinley, S. P., Hanks, L., & Line, N. D. (2017). Constraints to attracting new hotel workers: A study on industrial recruitment. *International Journal of Hospitality Management, 60*, 114–122. doi:10.1016/j.ijhm.2016.10.010

McGuire, D., Germain, M., & Reynolds, K. (2021). Reshaping HRD in light of the COVID-19 pandemic: An ethics of care approach. *Advances in Developing Human Resources, 23*(1), 26–40. doi:10.1177/1523422320973426

McIlvaine, H. (2020). *More hands on deck*. https://insideretail.com.au/news/more-hands-on-deck-woolies-invites-ex-qantas-staff-to-apply-for-jobs-202003

McKibbin, W. J. (2009). *The swine flu outbreak and its global economic impact*. Available at: https:// www.brookings.edu/on-the-record/the-swine-flu-outbreak-and-its-global-economic-impact

McKinsey. (2020). Retrieved April 10, 2022, from https://www.mckinsey.com/featured-insights/coronavirus-leading-through-the-crisis/charting-the-path-to-the-next-norm al/the-earliest-that-us-hotels-return-to-pre-covid-19-revenues-might-be-2022

McKinsey & Company. (2020). *Beyond coronavirus: The path to the next normal*. https://www. mckinsey.com//media/McKinsey/Industries/Healthcare%20Systems%20and%20Services/Our%20Insights/Beyond%20coronavirus%20The%20path%20to%20the%20next%20normal/Beyondcoronavirus-The-path-to-the-next-normal.ashx

McManus, S., Seville, E., Vargo, J., & Brunsdon, D. (2008). Facilitated process for improving organisational resilience. *Natural Hazards Review*, *9*(2), 81–90. doi:10.1061/(ASCE)1527-6988(2008)9:2(81)

Melian-Alzola, L., Fernandez-Monroy, M., & Hidalgo-Penate, M. (2020). Hotels in contexts of uncertainty: Measuring organisational resilience. *Tourism Management Perspectives*, *36*, 100747. doi:10.1016/j.tmp.2020.100747 PMID:33024657

Meyer, J. P., Stanley, D. J., Herscovitch, L., & Topolnytsky, L. (2002). Affective, continuance, and normative commitment to the organization: A meta-analysis of antecedents, correlates, and consequences. *Journal of Vocational Behavior*, *61*(1), 20–52. doi:10.1006/jvbe.2001.1842

Milojevic, D., & Katsadze, B. (2020). *Social Sustainability in COVID-19 Crisis: The case of the hotel industry*. Retrieved March 14, 2022, from https://www.divaportal.org/smash/get/diva2:1441677/FULLTEXT01.pdf

Mirabito, A. M., & Berry, L. L. (2015). You say you want a revolution? Drawing on social movement theory to motivate transformative change. *Journal of Service Research*, *18*(3), 336–350. doi:10.1177/1094670515582037

Miret, M., Caballero, F., Olaya, B., Koskinen, S., Naidoo, N., Tobiasz-Adamczyk, B., Leonardi, M., Haro, J., Chatterji, S., & Ayuso-Mateos, J. (2017). Association of experienced and evaluative wellbeing with health in nine countries with different income levels: A cross-sectional study. *Globalization and Health*, *13*(1), 65. doi:10.118612992-017-0290-0 PMID:28835255

Mohsin, A., Lengler, J., & Kumar, B. (2013). Exploring the antecedents of intentions to leave the job: The case of luxury hotel staff. *International Journal of Hospitality Management*, *35*, 48–58. doi:10.1016/j.ijhm.2013.05.002

Morais-Storz, M., Platou, R., & Norheim, K. B. (2018). Innovation and metamorphosis towards strategic resilience. *International Journal of Entrepreneurial Behaviour & Research*, *24*(1).

Mossoun, A., Pauly, M., Akoua-Koffi, C., Couacy-Hymann, E., Leendertz, S. A. J., Anoh, A. E., Gnoukpoho, A. H., Leendertz, F. H., & Schubert, G. (2015). Contact to non-human primates and risk factors for zoonotic disease emergence in the Taï region, C^ote d'Ivoire. *EcoHealth*, *12*(4), 580–591. doi:10.100710393-015-1056-x PMID:26302959

Muffels, R., & Wilthagen, T. (2013). Flexicurity: A new paradigm for the analysis of labor markets and policies challenging the trade-off between flexibility and security. *Sociology Compass*, *7*(2), 111–112. doi:10.1111oc4.12014

Myers, S. S., Gaffikin, L., Golden, C. D., Ostfeld, R. S., Redford, K. H., Ricketts, T. H., Turner, W. R., & Osofsky, S. A. (2013). Human health impacts of ecosystem alteration. *Proceedings of the National Academy of Sciences of the United States of America*, *110*(47). Advance online publication. doi:10.1073/pnas.1218656110 PMID:24218556

Nelson, D. C., & Nesmith, M. (2003). The impact of safety training on work-related injuries at eating and drinking places. *Journal of Human Resources in Hospitality & Tourism*, *1*(4), 19–32. doi:10.1300/J171v01n04_02

Neuman, J. H., & Keashly, L. (2004). *Development of the Workplace Aggression Research Questionnaire (WAR-Q)*. Preliminary Data from the Workplace Stress and Aggression.

Notelaers, G., De Witte, H., Van Veldhoven, M., & Vermunt, J. K. (2007). Construction and validation of the short inventory to monitor psychosocial hazards. *Medecine du Travail et Ergonomie*, *44*(1), 11–17.

Novelli, M., Burgess, L. G., Jones, A., & Ritchie, B. W. (2018). No Ebola… still doomed'–The Ebola induced tourism crisis. *Annals of Tourism Research*, *70*, 76–87. doi:10.1016/j.annals.2018.03.006 PMID:32572288

Nunn, J. (2020, April 14). Restaurants will never be the same after coronavirus – but that may be a good thing. *The Guardian*. https://www.theguardian.com/commentisfree/2020/apr/14/coronavirus-restaurants-pandemic-workers-communities-prices

O'Neil, A., Nicholls, S. J., Redfern, J., Brown, A., & Hare, D. L. (2020). Mental health and psychosocial challenges in the COVID-19 pandemic: Food for thought for cardiovascular health care professionals. *Heart Lung and Circulation*, *29*(7), 960–963. doi:10.1016/j.hlc.2020.05.002 PMID:32561126

Orchiston, C., Prayag, G., & Brown, C. (2016). Organizational resilience in the tourism sector. *Annals of Tourism Research*, *56*, 145–148. doi:10.1016/j.annals.2015.11.002

Ozbay, G., Sariisik, M., Ceylan, V., & Cakmak, M. (2021). A comparative evaluation between the impact of previous outbreaks and COVID-19 on the tourism industry. *International Hospitality Review*, *35*(2).

Ozdemir, M. A. (2020). What are the economic, psychological and social consequences of the covid-19 crisis on tourism employees? *International Journal of Social, Political and Economic Research*, *7*(4), 1137–1163. doi:10.46291/IJOSPERvol7iss4pp1137-1163

Patriarca, R., Di Gravio, G., Costantino, F., Falegnami, A., & Bilotta, F. (2018). An analytic framework to assess organizational resilience. *Safety and Health at Work*, *9*(3), 265–276. doi:10.1016/j.shaw.2017.10.005 PMID:30370158

Peachey, J. W., Burton, L. J., & Wells, J. E. (2014). Examining the influence of transformational leadership, organizational commitment, job embeddedness, and job search behaviors on turnover intentions in intercollegiate athletics. *Leadership and Organization Development Journal*, *35*(8), 740–755. doi:10.1108/LODJ-10-2012-0128

Pearlin, L. I., & Bierman, A. (2013). Current issues and future directions in research into the stress process. In C. S. Aneshensel, J. Phelan, & A. Bierman (Eds.), *Handbook of the sociology of mental health* (2nd ed., pp. 325–340). Springer. doi:10.1007/978-94-007-4276-5_16

Peteet, J. R. (2000). Cancer and the meaning of work. *General Hospital Psychiatry*, *22*(3), 200–205. doi:10.1016/S0163-8343(00)00076-1 PMID:10880715

Peterson, R. R., & DiPietro, R. B. (2021). Exploring the impact of the COVID-19 pandemic on the perceptions and sentiments of tourism employees: Evidence from a small island tourism economy in the Caribbean. *International Hospitality Review*, *35*(2), 156–170. doi:10.1108/IHR-10-2020-0063

Pforr, C., & Hosie, P. J. (2008). Crisis management in tourism: Preparing for recovery. *Journal of Travel & Tourism Marketing*, *23*(2-4), 249–264. doi:10.1300/J073v23n02_19

Pham, N. T., Thanh, T. V., Tuckova, Z., & Thuy, V. T. N. (2020). The role of green human resource management in driving hotel's environmental performance: Interaction and mediation analysis. *International Journal of Hospitality Management*, *88*, 102392. doi:10.1016/j.ijhm.2019.102392

Pindek, S., Krajcevska, A., & Spector, P. E. (2018). Cyberloafing as a coping mechanism: Dealing with workplace boredom. *Computers in Human Behavior*, *86*, 147–152. doi:10.1016/j.chb.2018.04.040

Politico. (2020, March 19). Coronavirus will change the world permanently. Here's how. *Politico Magazine*. https://www.politico.com/news/magazine/2020/03/19/coronavirus-effect-economylife-society-analysis-covid-135579

Prayag, G. (2018). Symbiotic relationship or not? Understanding resilience and crisis management in tourism. *Tourism Management Perspectives*, *25*, 133–135. doi:10.1016/j.tmp.2017.11.012

Probst, T. M. (2005). Economic stressors. In J. Barling, E. K. Kelloway, & M. R. Frone (Eds.), *Handbook of work stress* (pp. 267–297). Sage. doi:10.4135/9781412975995.n11

Rahi, K. (2019). Indicators to assess organizational resilience–a review of empirical literature. *International Journal of Disaster Resilience in the Built Environment*, *10*(2/3), 85–98. doi:10.1108/IJDRBE-11-2018-0046

Reisel, W. D., Probst, T. M., Chia, S. L., Maloles, C. M., & Konig, C. J. (2010). The effects of job insecurity on job satisfaction, organizational citizenship behavior, deviant behavior, and negative emotions of employees. *International Studies of Management & Organization*, *40*(1), 74–91. doi:10.2753/IMO0020-8825400105

Remeikis, A. (2020). *Australian government won't "jump to a solution" to help casual workers in coronavirus crisis*. Retrieved 16 May, 2022, from The Guardian website: https://www.theguardian.com/world/2020/mar/10/australian-government-warned-not-to-drag-its-feet-on-help-for-casual-workers-in-coronavirus-crisis

Riketta, M. (2002). Attitudinal organizational commitment and job performance: A meta-analysis. *Journal of Organizational Behavior*, *23*(3), 257–266. doi:10.1002/job.141

Riley, M. (2004). Labor Mobility and Market Structure in Tourism. In A. A. Lew, C. M. Hall, & A. M. Williams (Eds.), *A Companion to Tourism* (pp. 135–145). Blackwell Publishing Ltd. doi:10.1002/9780470752272.ch11

Ritchie, B. (2008). Tourism disaster planning and management: From response and recovery to reduction and readiness. *Current Issues in Tourism*, *11*(4), 315–348. doi:10.1080/13683500802140372

Robinson, R. N. S., Martins, A., Solnet, D. J., & Baum, T. (2019). Sustaining precarity: Critically examining tourism and employment. *Journal of Sustainable Tourism*, *27*(7), 1008–1025. doi:10.1080/09669582.2018.1538230

Ross, G. F. (2005). Tourism industry employee work stress- a present and future crisis. *Journal of Travel & Tourism Marketing*, *19*(2-3), 133–147. doi:10.1300/J073v19n02_11

Rosse, J. G., & Hulin, C. L. (1985). Adaptation to work: An analysis of employee health, withdrawal, and change. *Organizational Behavior and Human Decision Processes*, *36*(3), 324–347. doi:10.1016/0749-5978(85)90003-2 PMID:10275698

Ruiz-Martin, C., López-Paredes, A., & Wainer, G. (2018). What we know and do not know about organizational resilience. *International Journal of Production Management and Engineering.*, *6*(1), 11–28. doi:10.4995/ijpme.2018.7898

Ryu, S., Gao, H., Wong, J. Y., Shiu, E. Y. C., Xiao, J., Fong, M. W., & Cowling, B. J. (2020, May). Nonpharmaceutical measures for pandemic influenza in nonhealthcare settings – international travel – related measures. *Emerging Infectious Diseases*, *26*(5), 961–966. doi:10.3201/eid2605.190993

Sabahi, S., & Parast, M. M. (2020). Firm innovation and supply chain resilience: A dynamic capability perspective. *International Journal of Logistics*, *23*(3), 254–269. doi:10.1080/13675567.2019.1683522

Sabatino, M. (2016). Economic crisis and resilience: Resilient capacity and competitiveness of the enterprises. *Journal of Business Research*, *69*(5), 1924–1927. doi:10.1016/j.jbusres.2015.10.081

Santana, G., Hall, M. C., Timothy, D. J., & Duval, D. T. (2003). Crisis management and tourism: Beyond the rhetoric. *Safety and Security in Tourism: Relationships, Management, and Marketing.*, *15*(2-4), 299–321.

Sarfraz, M., Shah, S. G. M., Fareed, Z., & Shahzad, F. (2020). Demonstrating the interconnection of hierarchical order disturbances in CEO succession with corporate social responsibility and environmental sustainability. *Corporate Social Responsibility and Environmental Management*, *27*(6), 27. doi:10.1002/csr.2014

Schouteten, R., & Van Der Vleuten, T. (2013). Organizational Change and Job Satisfaction Among Voluntary and Paid Workers in a Dutch Voluntary Organization. Institute for Management Research, Nijmegen, the Netherlands.

Seville, E., Brunsdon, D., Dantas, A., Le Masurier, J., Wilkinson, S., & Vargo, J. (2008). Organisational resilience: Researching the reality of New Zealand organisations. *Journal of Business Continuity & Emergency Planning*, *2*(3), 258–266. PMID:21339112

Sharma, G. D., Thomas, A., & Paul, J. (2021). Reviving tourism industry post-COVID-19: A resilience based framework. *Tourism Management Perspectives*, *37*, 100786. doi:10.1016/j.tmp.2020.100786 PMID:33391988

Shoss, M. K. (2017). Job insecurity: An integrative review and agenda for future research. *Journal of Management*, *43*(6), 1911–1939. doi:10.1177/0149206317691574

Shropshire, J., & Kadlec, C. (2012). I'm leaving the IT field: The impact of stress, job insecurity, and burnout on IT professionals. *International Journal of Information and Communication Technology Research*, *2*(1), 6–16.

Singapore Tourism Board. (2020). *SG clean quality mark extended to tourism and lifestyle businesses as part of nationwide efforts to uplift sanitation and hygiene*. https://www.stb.gov.sg/content/stb/en/media-centre/media-releases/sg-clean-qualitymarkextendedtotourismandlifestylebusinessesaspar.html.html

Smith, T. D. (2018). An assessment of safety climate, job satisfaction and turnover intention relationships using a national sample of workers from the United States. *International Journal of Occupational Safety and Ergonomics*, *24*(1), 27–34. doi:10.1080/10803548.2016.1268446 PMID:28010625

Snell, D., Gekara, V., & Gatt, K. (2016). *Cross-occupational skill transferability: challenges and opportunities in a changing economy*. https://www.ncver.edu.au/research-and-statistics/publications/all-publications/cross-occupational-skill-transferability-challenges-and-opportunities-in-a-changing-economy

Soeker, M. S., Wegner, L., & Pretorius, B. (2008). I'm going back to work: Back injured clients' perceptions and experiences of their worker roles. *Work (Reading, Mass.)*, *30*(2), 161–170. PMID:18413932

Sogno, A. (2020). COVID-19 crisis forces hoteliers to review their human resources strategies. *HospitalityNet*. Available from: https://www.hospitalitynet.org/opinion/4098660.html

Steiner, J. F., Cavender, T. A., Main, D. S., & Bradley, C. J. (2004). Assessing the impact of cancer on work outcomes: What are the research needs? *Cancer*, *101*(8), 1703–1711. doi:10.1002/cncr.20564 PMID:15386303

Stewart, A., & Stanford, J. (2017). Regulating work in the gig economy: What are the options? *Economic and Labour Relations Review*, *28*(3), 420–437. doi:10.1177/1035304617722461

Storseth, F. (2006). Changes at work and employee reactions: Organizational elements, job insecurity, and short-term stress as predictors for employee health and safety. *Scandinavian Journal of Psychology*, *47*(6), 541–550. doi:10.1111/j.1467-9450.2006.00548.x PMID:17107503

Sundaram, R. M. (2019). A study on growth of tourism industry in Kanyakumari district. *Journal of the Gujarat Research Society*, *21*(16), 720–727.

Sverke, M., Hellgren, J., & Naswall, K. (2002). No security: A meta-analysis and review of job insecurity and its consequences. *Journal of Occupational Health Psychology*, *7*(3), 242–264. doi:10.1037/1076-8998.7.3.242 PMID:12148956

Tausig, M. (2013). The sociology of work and well-being. In C. S. Aneshensel, J. Phelan, & A. Bierman (Eds.), *Handbook of the sociology of mental health* (2nd ed., pp. 433–455). Springer. doi:10.1007/978-94-007-4276-5_21

Tausig, M., & Fenwick, R. (1999). Recession and well-being. *Journal of Health and Social Behavior*, *40*(1), 1–16. doi:10.2307/2676375 PMID:10331318

Taylor, P. L. (2020). This is what the future of hotels looks like. Get ready for shrink wrap and "Health detectors." *Forbes*. Available from: https://www.forbes.com/sites/petertaylor/2020/05/12/this-is-what-the-future-of-hotels-looks-like-get-ready-for-shrink-wrap-and-health-detectors/#3c8011421cae

Tibay, V., Miller, J., Chang-Richards, A. Y., Egbelakin, T., Seville, E., & Wilkinson, S. (2018). Business resilience: A study of Auckland hospitality sector. *Procedia Engineering*, *212*, 1217–1224. doi:10.1016/j.proeng.2018.01.157

Tourism From Zero. (2020). *#TourismFromZero Initiative*. https://tourismfromzero.org/

Tsai, C. H., & Chen, C. W. (2010). An earthquake disaster management mechanism based on risk assessment information for the tourism industry-a case study from the island of Taiwan. *Tourism Management*, *31*(4), 470–481. doi:10.1016/j.tourman.2009.05.008

Tsai, C. H., & Chen, C. W. (2011). Development of a mechanism for typhoon- and floodrisk assessment and disaster management in the hotel industry – A case study of the Hualien area. *Scandinavian Journal of Hospitality and Tourism*, *11*(3), 324–341. doi:10.1080/15022250.2011.601929

Ünsar, S. A. (2011). Effect of motivation on severance tendency: A field research. *Journal of Academics Sight*, *25*, 1–15.

UNWTO. (2020). *Supporting jobs and economies through travel and tourism a call for action to mitigate the socio-economic impact of the COVID-19 and accelerate recovery*. Available at: https://webunwto.s3.eu-west-1.amazonaws.com/s3fs-public/2020-04/COVID19_Recommendations_English_1.pdf

US Bureau of Labor Statistics. (2023). *Labor force statistics from the current population survey*. Available at: www.bls.gov/cps/electronically-mediated-employment.Html

Van Hoye, G., Saks, A. M., Lievens, F., & Weijters, B. (2015). Development and test of an integrative model of job search behaviour. *European Journal of Work and Organizational Psychology*, *24*(4), 544–559. doi:10.1080/1359432X.2014.964214

Vargas-Sanchez, A. (2018). Crisis situations in tourist destinations: How can they be managed? *Enlightening Tourism. A Pathmaking Journal, 8*(1), 47-69.

Verreynne, M. L., Williams, A. M., Ritchie, B. W., Gronum, S., & Betts, K. S. (2019). Innovation diversity and uncertainty in small and medium sized tourism firms. *Tourism Management*, *72*, 257–269. doi:10.1016/j.tourman.2018.11.019

Vigoda, E. (2000). Organizational politics, job attitudes, and work outcomes: Exploration and implications for the public sector. *Journal of Vocational Behavior*, *57*(3), 326–347. doi:10.1006/jvbe.1999.1742

Vinodkumar, M. N., & Bhasi, M. (2010). Safety management practices and safety behaviour: Assessing the mediating role of safety knowledge and motivation. *Accident; Analysis and Prevention*, *42*(6), 2082–2093. doi:10.1016/j.aap.2010.06.021 PMID:20728666

Vranjes, I., Baillien, E., Vandebosch, H., Erreygers, S., & De Witte, H. (2018). When workplace bullying goes online: Construction and validation of the Inventory of Cyberbullying Acts at Work (ICA-W). *European Journal of Work and Organizational Psychology*, *27*(1), 28–39. doi:10.1080/1359432X.2017.1363185

Vujičić, D., Jovičić, A., Lalić, D., & Cvejanov, A. (2014). The relation between job insecurity, job satisfaction and organizational commitment among employees in the tourism sector in Novi Sad. *Economic and Industrial Democracy*, *36*(4), 633–652. doi:10.1177/0143831X14527017

Wan, Y. K., Wong, I. A., & Kong, W. H. (2014). Student career prospect and industry commitment: The roles of industry attitude, perceived social status, and salary expectations. *Tourism Management*, *40*, 1–14. doi:10.1016/j.tourman.2013.05.004

Wang, J., & Ritchie, B. W. (2010). A theoretical model for strategic crisis planning: Factors influencing crisis planning in the hotel industry. *International Journal of Tourism Policy*, *3*(4), 297–317. doi:10.1504/IJTP.2010.040390

Wen, B., Zhou, X., Hu, Y., & Zhang, X. (2020). Role stress and turnover intention of front-line hotel employees: The roles of burnout and service climate. *Frontiers in Psychology*, *11*, 36. doi:10.3389/fpsyg.2020.00036 PMID:32082216

WHO. (2020). Retrieved May 10, 2022 from https://www.who.int/publications/m/it em/covid-19-public-health-emergency-of-international-concern-(pheic)-global-research-and-innovation-forum.

Wolf, S., Hinkel, J., Hallier, M., Bisaro, A., Lincke, D., Ionescu, C., & Klein, R. J. (2013). Clarifying vulnerability definitions and assessments using formalisation. *International Journal of Climate Change Strategies and Management*, *5*(1), 54–70. doi:10.1108/17568691311299363

Wolf, T., Metzing, M., & Lucas, R. (2019). Experienced Well-Being and Labor Market Status: The Role of Pleasure and Meaning. The German Socio-Economic Panel, DIW, Berlin.

Wolfe, N. D., Dunavan, C. P., & Diamond, J. (2007). Origins of major human infectious diseases. *Nature*, *447*(7142), 279–283. doi:10.1038/nature05775 PMID:17507975

World Bank. (2020). *International Tourism, Number of Arrivals*. Retrieved April 4, 2022, from. https://data.worldbank.org/indicator/ST.INT.ARVL

WTTC. (2018). *Impact of the Ebola epidemic on travel & tourism*. WTTC.

Xiang, Y.-T., Yang, Y., Li, W., Zhang, L., Zhang, Q., Cheung, T., & Ng, C. H. (2020). Timely mental health care for the 2019 novel coronavirus outbreak is urgently needed. *The Lancet. Psychiatry*, *7*(3), 228–229. doi:10.1016/S2215-0366(20)30046-8 PMID:32032543

Yang, J.-T., Wan, C.-S., & Fu, Y.-J. (2012). Qualitative examination of employee turnover and retention strategies in international tourist hotels in Taiwan. *International Journal of Hospitality Management*, *31*(3), 837–848. doi:10.1016/j.ijhm.2011.10.001

Section 3

Enabling Future State Career Satisfaction in Hospitality

This section identifies multiple proactive, practical opportunities for hospitality leaders to address fundamental matters catalyzing dissonance within the industry's 21st Century hospitality workforce. This section develops and tests behavioral models as well as evaluates emerging technologies within the framework of career-level job satisfaction.

Chapter 6
Exploring Organizational Commitment of Employees Working at Hotel Front Desks:
A Phenomenological Discovery

ABSTRACT

This study focuses on the various dimensions of organizational commitment for employees working at a hotel front desk. The study also explores how those various dimensions can be leveraged in a positive and engaging way to enhance organizational commitment and job satisfaction while reducing employee burnout and voluntary separation. Following a literature review in this area, multiple interviews were conducted with hotel front desk employees who maintained diversity in tenure, role, and type of hotel where they were working. As a result of these interviews, it was determined that there was a duality of interests that manifested in terms of employees' organizational commitment. Intrinsic motivations appeared with younger employees who were thinking of a longer career pathway for themselves. Extrinsic motivations, such as enjoying a hotel brand's travel-related benefits, were more apparent with older employees. Additional areas of future research are identified based on the results from this qualitative study.

DOI: 10.4018/978-1-6684-2528-2.ch006

INTRODUCTION AND BACKGROUND

How organizations in the hospitality industry attract and retain talent are critical pathways that are becoming increasingly more significant as strategic differentiators for companies in modern eras of globalization and rapid technological change (Grisseman, Plank, & Brunner-Sperdin, 2013). As human resource leaders determine how best to compete for talent, there is a tendency to focus more on transactional aspects of an employee / employer relationship including salary, benefits, and work schedule. However, research has also been conducted that explores additional dimensions that may determine greater success with the challenges of attracting and recruiting talent. These include widespread reported issues from employees including perceived lack of personal achievement in a hospitality role, low commitment to a long-term hospitality career pathway and high turnover rates among peers (Dai, Zhuang, & Huan, 2019). These issues ultimately can have a significant impact on organizational commitment within both the hospitality industry as well as within the specific culture of a local property level (Yao, Qiu, & Wei, 2019). According to the World Tourism Cities Federation, the average turnover rate in the travel industry is 18% but is observed as high as 40% in some places in the world (2018).

Transactional strategies to retain employees in the hospitality industry often manifest as material rewards encompassing such tactics as competitive pay and benefits (Jia, Shaw, & Tsui, 2014). To reduce turnover and increase organizational commitment at an employee level, however, research has determined that developmental rewards are regarded as more impactful over a longer period. These types of rewards include training, advancement opportunities, mentoring, recognition programs and in-role empowerment (Jia et al, 2014). When integrated with material rewards, developmental rewards have proven to significantly increase employee retention by enhancing organizational commitment (Moncarz, Zhao, & Kay, 2009). Therefore, it becomes a salient focus to further explore the dimensions and nature of how organizational inducement can influence employee engagement. The employee – organization relationship (EOR) often is considered to encompass two aspects: What employers expect their employees to contribute to the organization and what incentives employers will use to motivate employees to make these contributions (Guan, Yeh, Chiang, & Huan, 2020). Elements such as these which are provided by the employer are often considered organizational inducements (Hom, Tsui, & Wu, 2009). Organizational inducements are defined by Guan et. al. as "the actions that the organization provides to its employees to motivate them to demonstrate the attitudes and behaviors that the organization expects to see, including material rewards and developmental rewards" (2009, p. 260).

Social exchange theory provides us with context to understand how organizational inducements serve a purpose of catalyzing behaviors from employees that reciprocate rewards provided by the employer (Guan et. al., 2020). Material and developmental reward elements are more frequently present in recent years within the hospitality industry driven by talent shortages and the need for organizations to position themselves as attractive to the workforce. This has led many organizations to formally adapt strategic, and high performance, human resources management practices (Madera, Dawon, Guchait, & Belarmino, 2017; Page, Bently, Teo, & Ladkin, 2018) with the goal of building a high-performance service climate encouraging positive behaviors from employees (Li & Huang, 2017).

One dimension that this study will explore further is the impact of involuntary separations on employees' organization commitment. Organizational commitment is a factor of positive psychology. Seminal research by Kahn on the subject reports that organizational commitment is a result of when an employee integrates their sense of self with that of their work role, ultimately manifesting with three distinct dimensions of engagement: Physical engagement, cognitive engagement, and emotional engagement (1990). Schaufeli, Salanova, Gonzalez-Roma, Bakker. (2002) further defines the phenomenon of organizational commitment as two distinct but interconnected elements of the psychological state which are identified as engagement to burnout with one's job. Within this continuum are three additional cognitive and emotional dimensions identified as absorption, vigor, and dedication. Absorption is further defined as a state of engagement where an employee feels that time passes quickly when at work. This can be translated into feelings of positive or negative dimensions, but the employee does not sense that time is passing slowly on the job (Guan et. al., 2020). Vigor is defined as an employee's strength of commitment and his or her ability to keep toward a goal when faced with some notable degree of challenge. There is an aspect of individual work and self-reliance that is factored into the dimension of vigor. Lastly, dedication is defined as where an employee demonstrates not just a strong engagement with work (like with absorption) but also where the employee demonstrates a high degree of positive enthusiasm for the work being done and the organization it is being done for (Schaufeli et. al., 2002). Understanding the dynamics of how employees capture and process these three psychological dimensions can be a critical element for an organization seeking to understand how to deploy material and developmental rewards effectively. It has been demonstrated that organizational commitment can be negatively impacted by poor management practices, which in turn also impacts turnover, job satisfaction and performance (Karatepe, Beirami, & Bouzari, 2014). It becomes clear, then, that there is value for both academic and practical purposes to better understand these dynamics. For the purposes of management practice, this study focuses on understanding the dynamics of how the notion of involuntary termination can influence and impact the various dimensions of organizational commitment for hotel front desk employees at a variety of property types.

RESEARCH QUESTION AND METHODOLOGY

One of the critical areas of need from a hotel company's perspective is locating and retaining engaged, qualified employees. The literature review revealed that this situation is problematic across all classifications of hotel operations ranging from budget, no-frill hotels to mid-range hotels (both full-service and limited-service properties) and extending to high-end resort and conference properties. Simply no hotel anywhere in the world is spared the challenge of first locating workers, and then retaining trained, skilled workers, who will be effective at providing guest services. The purpose of this study is to engage employees in all hotel classifications to begin the process of better understanding what drives interest on an employee's part in working for the industry, what factors strengthens their organizational commitment and what factors weaken it.

The intent with this study is to initiate scaffolding comprehension of the factors encompassing organizational commitment with a specific segment of hospitality workers: The front desk associate. Frequently considered the hub of a hotel's operation, this employee is often considered the face of the hotel by its guests. Guests will interact with front desk associates at the start of their stay on the property and often encounter them at the end. As a result, guests will engage front desk associates throughout their stay to satisfy a variety of needs, even if those associates working at the front desk coordinate a hotel's response rather than directly address it.

To conduct this study, front desk associates from a variety of hotels were invited to participate in a zoom interview. Employees were identified through each property's human resources function after general leadership had approved researcher engagement with its employees. Hotel properties where associates were employed were classified into three different categories including:

- Budget Hotels, often offering few to no additional services or amenities; Food and Beverage services were usually non-existent at these properties or limited to the reselling of packaged snack food out of the front desk area
- Mid-range hotels, which could be either a limited service (no food and beverage) or a full-service hotel (property has a restaurant on site).
- High-end hotels or resorts. These properties were either in densely populated urban areas and focused on convention attendees or secluded resorts focused on leisure travelers.

30 different individuals were scheduled for open-ended discovery conversations across all three classifications resulting in nearly 100 hours of exchanges. Due to the unexpected consistency of unstructured responses, it was concluded that there may not be significant differences from hotel property to hotel property in how employees working at the front desk determine organizational commitment. To further identify what these factors might be, 3 participants from each of the hotel classification categories were selected for additional follow-up interviews. These follow-up interviews maintained a more structured question and answer session. These additional sessions were transcribed and appear below. Each participant was asked the same 10 questions, which were developed as a result of the original open-ended discovery conversations. These 10 questions are as follows:

1) How long have you been employed in the hospitality sector?
2) What attracted you originally to working in the hospitality sector?
3) What do you enjoy about working in your current role in the hospitality sector?
4) What frustrates you about working in your current role in the hospitality sector?
5) When you learn about layoffs in another industry, how do you feel about your own role?
6) When you learn about layoffs in the hospitality industry, how do you feel about your own role?
7) When you learn about layoffs in your hotel, not necessarily in your area, how do you feel about your own role?

8) When you learn about layoffs in your department, how do you feel about your role?
9) Do you see yourself choosing to stay employed in the hospitality sector?
10) What changes would you like to see that would make it more attractive to stay in the hospitality sector?

Interview Transcripts

Participant 1, Budget Hotel

Q1 | How long have you been employed in the hospitality sector?

I've been working at hotels for 2 years now as a way to earn money. The work is not challenging, but there are a lot of different tasks that have to be done and some of it involves math, which I'm not great at.

Q2 | What attracted you originally to working in the hospitality sector?

I don't have a college degree, so this was work that I could get. There's always a need it seems for people to work in hotels and it wasn't difficult to get hired. The managers are stressed about getting everything done and not having enough people, so it wasn't a long or upsetting process to get hired. I really hate it when it takes weeks or months to go through interviews and there's very little feedback or communication from people who are hiring. That's super stressful. Here, I walked into a hotel that was near where I live that had a "hiring now" sign up, talked to someone within 10 minutes of walking in and was hired on the spot with background and drug checks being done over the next couple of days.

Q3 | What do you enjoy about working in your current role in the hospitality sector?

First, I really liked that I didn't have to wait weeks to get hired. I walked in and had a job offer within an hour. I like that I can be independent at work without someone watching my every move, even right at the beginning. There are a variety of tasks I have to do including checking people in, checking people out, answering questions in person and on the phone, taking payment and making change, stocking the snack bar and selling items and being the center of operations for the hotel. I do enjoy talking to people and learning about where they came from, where they are going and what takes them on the road. We are located right off the interstate, so we get a lot of people who are stopping in just for the night and there are lots of interesting stories. I enjoy hearing about that. Sometimes people are tired or grumpy or just don't want to talk, and they can take that out on you but you learn pretty quickly how to figure out who is in a good mood and who just needs to get to their room quickly.

Q4 | What frustrates you about working in your current role in the hospitality sector?

There's always a lot going on, and I really wish we had a separate phone operator. It can be challenging when you are working to check in a guest in front of you and a phone call or two start coming in. The managers want you to do both, but it's really hard to do both at the same time. If you put the person standing in front of you first, the people on the phone get upset that the phone rang or they were put on hold. I try to excuse myself with the person I'm helping, answer the phone, put the phone on hold, get back to the person in front of me and then get back to the phone. I've heard that there isn't hold music and it's just silent on the phone, which I think makes it more frustrating for the people on hold. I wish the owners would put in hold music or something to let people know they're waiting and we haven't disconnected. If we have a line in front of us it makes it harder. I also don't like that there really isn't any training. If something isn't being done right, we're just told to do it differently and left to figure things out on our own. When I first started, training was someone showing me things for the first day or two, and there were parts that I really struggled with picking up (computers and math, mostly). If I get stuck in the computer system, there's no one to reach out to for help besides the manager on duty, but they have their own stuff going on. I also don't feel like there's any future in this job, it's just a thing to make money now. I know I can do better, and I want to get a degree at some point, but I'm not sure in what or how to go about finding one of those jobs you read about that people say is fulfilling and that they love. This is just a way to pay for life as it is, but it's day to day and not something that is moving me forward in a career or in life.

Q5 | When you learn about layoffs in another industry, how do you feel about your own role?

I sometimes take notice, but often it doesn't seem to impact me at all. We don't have a specific industry or type of person that consistently stays here, a lot of our business is driving from one place to another and they need a place to sleep for a night or two. There are some retirement places nearby, so we often get people who are helping someone move into one of those who need their own place for a night. At any rate, I don't like hearing about layoffs, it usually means bad times are coming but I don't really connect other industries to myself.

Q6 | When you learn about layoffs in the hospitality industry, how do you feel about your own role?

I guess you mean those large corporate hotels? We have a brand, but we are owned independently so our hotel really rises and falls on its own. If our nightly occupancy is high consistently, it really doesn't matter what is happening to corporate hotels or resorts. I don't think the media really covers too much about smaller, budget interstate hotels at least I don't see that kind of story. Layoffs usually are about corporate office employees, though, not the folks at the actual hotels. We aren't directly impacted by that and I tend not to really feel a part of a corporate brand even if that logo is on our sign.

Q7 | When you learn about layoffs in your hotel, not necessarily in your area, how do you feel about your own role?

I don't think that's actually happened here. We don't have too many people working here, maybe 7-8? One guy got fired a few months ago, but he was showing up drunk for work – he was on the overnight shift and I guess he thought nobody would notice or care? I know of everyone and I say hi when I see them, but I work by myself with only 2 other people at any given time, our hotel manager or assistant manager and a housekeeping person. What happens to others doesn't usually worry me too much, but I don't see people getting laid off here. We all do so much, probably more like 2-3 peoples' worth of work that if we lost someone it would be really tough to do everything we need to do for guests. There are days that the hotel is more empty than full, and that bothers me because I know that is how we keep money coming in and without that the hotel won't stay in business.

Q8 | When you learn about layoffs in your department, how do you feel about your role?

We don't really have departments – there's three of us that work the front desk. I am the main daytime person, there's a main nighttime person and a third person who works both. The nighttime person got fired, but they hired someone else. I don't think it's about the hotel downsizing it's more about getting fired if you don't do your job. I do my job, and I take care of guests as best I can. I try not to make trouble for the manager, and I'm pretty self-sufficient. I've made some mistakes with counting change wrong or screwing up the computer, but that was mostly in the first couple of months. I guess if they took away one of the 3 front desk positions and made it 2, it would be something I get stressed about. Not that I would lose my job but having to work more and harder with only 2 people – we are open 24/7 and only having two people to cover that would be nearly impossible I imagine.

Q9 | Do you see yourself choosing to stay employed in the hospitality sector?

I am good at this, but I am wondering what other things are out there in life. There are other types of hotels that seem to have more people, money, resources and different things going on. Like Disneyland resorts, for example, seems to be about more fun than realistic work although I suspect the stuff I do is a part of what their hotel people do. I would like to get a degree and learn more about things I could do that perhaps feel less like working to pay for things and more like I'm enjoying myself. I do like my job, but I also get bored. I do the same things day after day and very little changes. That's work, though, right? And I have to think that I don't like change – we upgraded to a new computer system called a rooms management system that looked and operated completely differently than the one we had when I first got hired. That was a stressful time because we were given some youtube videos and a manual from the computer company that sold us the system on how to operate it. The first few months I was reading the manual while actually checking people in and when I got stuck or crashed the system, it even took my manager a long time to figure things out. I would like to possibly be a manager and I think I would be good at it, I've learned a lot of things and maybe that could be something I could do in the future. I know how to make it better for the workers with training than what we have now, but not sure how I could become a manager – get a college degree, I guess. Our current manager has one. I don't think I have the time or money for that right now though…

Q10 | What changes would you like to see that would make it more attractive to stay in the hospitality sector?

I would like the owners to put more money into the hotel itself – some of the rooms and the lobby are beginning to feel a little run down and tired. Second, I would like to have some opportunities like having them pay for training or classes toward a degree. Maybe not all of it and I would be happy to agree to stay for a longer period of time if they did, to commit to their company. Most times, though, I feel like I'm just another resource to keep the business going to make money for the owners. I like the work and the job is very convenient for me, which is great! I wish also there were some opportunities to plan for the future – college, better job and retirement. I'm not saving much right now and although that time is a long time off, you read about needing to save for when you're not working all the time. I have no idea how to do that and still make ends meet, so an employer helping me understand that all better would be great.

Participant 2, Budget Hotel

Q1 | How long have you been employed in the hospitality sector?

I've worked in the hotel world for 10 years now. I've been at my current location for 1 year and with this company for five.

Q2 | What attracted you originally to working in the hospitality sector?

It seemed like a fun place to work when we would stay in a hotel growing up. People were always cheerful to see us and the hotels were clean and inviting. I started working to pay for my associate's egree and I'd like to get my bachelor's in hotel management, but am working to pay off some other debts before I take on other ones.

Q3 | What do you enjoy about working in your current role in the hospitality sector?

I like that I have a voice at our hotel. We don't have a lot of extra money in the company to do things, but the managers and owners are always open and friendly about listening to what ideas I have and my peers have. For example, I suggested we buy one of those large plastic beverage dispensers that we could use during the summer to provide a free cool drink to people. It was like $20 and then just the process of using the ice machines and water dispensers we already have on site to keep it full. You fill it with ice and water and that is a great little service for people when it's hot outside. I thought it would be cool to have sliced lemon or lime or some sort of fruit in there, but we don't have a kitchen on site so they didn't do that part, but I liked that I got to pitch an idea and then put it in place. Guests really love it also!

Q4 | What frustrates you about working in your current role in the hospitality sector?

The work is really repetitive – how often can you check in or out a guest, answer questions or do the other front desk work without having it get boring? Doesn't take too long! I don't want to do this work forever, and standing on my feet for a whole shift can be tiring – I'd like to try different things. The owners and managers are really good with this company, though, and they do listen so that offsets the monotony of the actual work itself.

Q5 | When you learn about layoffs in another industry, how do you feel about your own role?

I get concerned. We are near a large resort that has a lot of business conferences at it. We really benefit from that because we are less than a ½ a mile from the resort and a lot of people will stay with us rather than the more expensive place. There are a lot of technology conferences that come, especially in the winter and spring to play golf and go to workshops…but if that industry is laying off people like it recently, they won't have those conferences anymore. That will be a problem for my job at that point.

Q6 | When you learn about layoffs in the hospitality industry, how do you feel about your own role?

I am less concerned about this – our hotel rarely markets other than to attach itself to what's going on at the nearby resort. Our best business are the 30-40 conferences that the resort hosts, we are always busy and sometimes sold out then. In-between those, however, we can be pretty quiet. Our business doesn't follow the pattern of the larger industry, so it doesn't make much difference to me if someone is laying someone off.

Q7 | When you learn about layoffs in your hotel, not necessarily in your area, how do you feel about your own role?

I get worried about this, but it's only happened twice in my time at this company. Once was when they had to close a hotel, another one from where I worked. This hotel was affected by construction closing down a major road and re-routing traffic and it just really caused occupancy to fall off. After six months, the hotel was closed and workers were laid off. I get worried when we are really slow – I know it's hard to forecast because we get our business from conference overflow at the nearby resort, and that usually is more of a last minute thing. I can't think of a time, though, where we laid off employees in a specific department only though, like housekeeping. We run very lean on employment and are always begging management to add more people when we are busy. During the slow times, though, we don't bring that up!

Q8 | When you learn about layoffs in your department, how do you feel about your role?

I don't think I've ever been a part of something like that, so I can't really answer. There are five front desk staff and if some of them were laid off because of business cutbacks I would imagine I would feel stressed – first because it might be me and if I survived the cut then I would be stressed at having to figure out how to do what we do with fewer people – that is already hard!

Q9 | Do you see yourself choosing to stay employed in the hospitality sector?

I like working in hotels! I like that the work is easy to describe and do. I have some friends that work in an office and that seems so boring. I am inside all day, I don't have to perform physical labor and I like providing good service to people. I also like that I can say things and be heard by management. If I was working at a place where they didn't care or listen, I wouldn't stay. I've been with this company for a while now because they aren't like that and it's important to listen to your employees when they have ideas.

Q10 | What changes would you like to see that would make it more attractive to stay in the hospitality sector?

I would like our hotel to be more independent in its marketing so that we aren't completely (or nearly completely) dependent on the resort's conference schedule. I think the owners can also invest a bit more in keeping the hotel modern with some better room décor (linens, etc.) and a modern lobby look. I think it would be really cool if we had some of the app-driven operations like letting guests select their own rooms or check themselves in and use their phone to open their doors. I know that all costs money, though, but it seems like that is the future. Putting in a pool would be a good idea – we're not a resort, but that local "staycation" crowd goes every year. Again, though, pools cost money to put in and maintain so I get why we don't have it. I personally would like to get a degree and I know many companies will pay for that for their employees. I don't know how many of the other folks working here would want that but I wish that was something they did for me at least. I was a part of the review by the corporate brand where they came six months ago and evaluated how well we did things to their standard. I would love to do a job like that, but not sure how I could get from where I am to there. It isn't something you can talk about with a manager or owner, since they won't like hearing that someone is thinking about leaving. Why would they help?

Participant 3, Budget Hotel

Q1 | How long have you been employed in the hospitality sector?

I started working here when I began college two years ago.

Q2 | What attracted you originally to working in the hospitality sector?

I don't have a car and I began college in the pandemic, so I needed a job that was flexible with my class schedule and was convenient to walk to. At the time, hotels were beginning to staff up again but nobody wanted to work in one. People were getting money from the government that was as much or more than what they would earn at an entry-level position like this. Also, people were concerned about getting sick. I live in a dorm and there was no way I wasn't going to get sick (which I did within the first semester, but I got better) so this didn't bother me. They were happy to have someone who wanted to work. I don't think there was anything specific about working in a hotel that jumped out at me, other than it was easy to get hired and near campus.

Q3 | What do you enjoy about working in your current role in the hospitality sector?

This hotel is right at the main entrance to campus and there's a lot of cool businesses and restaurants now creating a fun vibe to be a part of. We have a lot of school spirit and put-up decorations with school colors and logos and we can have a lot of fun. We're pretty popular with families and friends of students who come to visit or help students move in and out of dorms each semester, so that kind of "with it" school spirit vibe is attractive to them. We even have our lounge open again where they do game day happy hours or tailgates. There are a couple of large tvs in there and snacks but mostly it's just a place where people can come together and have a good time when the school's football or basketball or whatever team sport is playing. That was something they had before the pandemic, but it was the employees (who, like me, are mostly college students) who really pushed to bring back.

Q4 | What frustrates you about working in your current role in the hospitality sector?

Honestly, I hate the actual work. It's thoughtless, boring and repetitive. I'm only doing it for the money, but I like being able to have fun with people when they're with us. It's like having a bunch of people over for a party. I get that work is work, but it just doesn't engage me much. I'm earning my undergraduate degree in business, and I'm already seeing a lot of opportunities with this hotel to do things better. It is frustrating that I'm not given an opportunity to bring some of that to the job. Like I just finished an accounting class this last semester, and I saw lots of areas of our nightly front desk audit process that is wrong or is done in a way that's really cumbersome. I have ideas on how to do it better, but our general manager likes it how it's done now and won't listen. Another thing that bothers me is that they won't pay for my school. I guess they figure they're paying ME and I can do whatever I want with that money, but I have a friend who works for a large corporate hotel on the other side of town (she has a car) and they pay ½ her tuition as long as she gets As and Bs…she gets paid on top of that also. I get that we're not a corporate hotel, but it would be fantastic if they invested in me. I can help with making it a better business with what I'm learning, so they'd benefit if they had be more involved in the business beyond just my current job, but they haven't been open to that really. I guess this is just a college job and I'll find something better when I'm done with my degree.

Q5 | When you learn about layoffs in another industry, how do you feel about your own role?

I'm studying business, so we hear about this all the time. I get concerned when downsizing or contracting trends start in business because things are connected. We are not a business or a leisure property, we're a budget hotel that has parents, family and friends as its primary customers so as long as the University is enrolling students and has on-campus housing, we will have business. I'm aware of layoffs in other industries, and don't like bad economic times, but it honestly doesn't mean much for this particular job.

Q6 | When you learn about layoffs in the hospitality industry, how do you feel about your own role?

I don't think that's happening right now. I started in the hotel job when things were starting to open back up after all the hotels shut down at the beginning of Covid. Since then, we just can't find enough people to work. We'll hire people, they'll show up for a few shifts and then we never hear from them again – if they even last that long. The managers tell us when people are coming in for interviews so we can meet and greet them since we're at the desk – they want us to give a great first impression. The problem is that a lot of people never even show for their interview! I don't think anyone is even thinking about layoffs because it's so hard just find people.

Q7 | When you learn about layoffs in your hotel, not necessarily in your area, how do you feel about your own role?

I can't really answer this directly, but I remember when my dad was laid off in 2009. It was a really stressful time because the family had to cut out expenses and everyone was stressed and grumpy. It was a change from the routine and schedules we knew. I was a kid at that point, so I remember not having Christmas or birthday presents, not going on summer vacations and things that we had enjoyed previously or that some of my friends still were doing. That lasted for four or five years until my dad found a new job that was like his other one. I think those memories would play a part in how I feel if I was at any job (not just this one) and rumors of layoffs started.

Q8 | When you learn about layoffs in your department, how do you feel about your role?

I don't think my answer is any different here than before other than it would probably be a lot more stressful if it was specific to my area as opposed to others. I don't always have self-confidence about my performance on the job, and feel like I could easily be the target for something like this. It's funny, though, on one hand I don't like the work so not doing it anymore wouldn't be that upsetting. I think it's more about the sense that they don't want you around anymore and – of course – the money. More than anything, I think the word "layoff" has a really negative connotation and (for me, at least) would bring up those bad memories from 12 years ago.

Q9 | Do you see yourself choosing to stay employed in the hospitality sector?

Maybe, if I can get a job within a business function. I want to be able to use my degree and a business degree can get you some really good-paying jobs. Hotels don't always pay well, especially in the operations / property level jobs. I wouldn't want to keep doing what I am doing. I would like to be a leader and in a business function. I think I would be really good at that – taking what I learned in college and combining it with my experiences on the front line in this job so that I can make it better for those who are just starting out and coming up the ranks. You can do that anywhere, of course, in any industry so what I'm thinking isn't just specific to hospitality. However, since I will have hopefully 4 years of experience working in a hotel when I graduate, that will make it easier – in theory - to get the type of job I want in this industry. I'm concerned about the next global crisis, though…hotels seem really susceptible to external factors that impact the business in a negative way. Everyone is expecting climate change to continue, the Russia / Ukraine war and whatever the next pandemic is…plus stuff we can't even anticipate…I may want to get into an industry that doesn't shut down whenever this sort of thing happens.

Q10 | What changes would you like to see that would make it more attractive to stay in the hospitality sector?

I love that you ask this! I hope the owners read your report! I would love for them to say that what we do here compliments what we learn in class and tie it all together a bit more. There's a lot of talk about internships and apprenticeships, and while I don't think that I would want one of those since they're for a limited time, I would love to do more at the hotel to help the hotel with what I'm learning. For example, our general manager doesn't have a business degree and I'm three quarters of the way through mine. Why not have me work, especially in down times on the desk, with business functions like how we operate, how we document our transactions, etc. I would like them to help pay for tuition since they'd be benefitting from me going through classes. Also, this hotel is owned by a company that has six other hotels and a small corporate office – why hire people off the street when you can promote from within with people who are already familiar with the culture, the properties, etc. Having a leadership development program to retain employees after they finish school would be a great thing for us to have. That takes the stress out of job hunting for students working at the hotel (the majority of the employees are students) and the stress out of finding qualified people for the owners. I also like that we get involved with school spirit and tap into the vibe of our location. I think we could do more with that! I'd love for the owners to get a liquor license and turn that lounge into something that could make some money for us with all of the game -day events that we put up in there. I'd also like them to keep investing in their hotel technology and appointments, with refreshed linen and décor (go full school spirit with colors and decorations in the rooms for example) as well as modern ways to run a hotel like using apps to have guests pick their own rooms and check themselves in and out. Another great idea, is to use different rooms for different themes and charge differently based on what's in the room – you could have a football tailgate room with a minibar or different amenities than a standard guest room. Let customers pay more or less depending on what they want out of us and diversify your marketing. I guess it comes down to wanting to be more involved with driving what happens with the business as opposed to the routines of doing the work I currently do.

Participant 1, Mid-Range Hotel

Q1 | How long have you been employed in the hospitality sector?

I've been employed for 1 year, this is a brand new job for me!

Q2 | *W*hat attracted you originally to working in the hospitality sector?

We bid on shifts, so there is some flexibility to when you work and what days you work. That is really important for me since I have kids and am not always available on a regular 9-5 schedule. We are a two income household, so I'm happy to pick up shifts at unusual times that might be more difficult for the hotel to staff. My favorite is the mid-day shift for four hours...I can get my kids to school and then work before being home when school is over.

Q3 | What do you enjoy about working in your current role in the hospitality sector?

I like working with people. Our hotel is a business hotel, our guests are here on business and we are busiest Sunday – Thursday. We are a corporate owned hotel, and a lot of newer technology has been put in place that automates what front desk people traditionally did. We don't answer external phones, we rarely check someone in or out or issue keys, we don't settle guest folios (their bills). That's all fun because we get to do different things – we are responsible for getting the complimentary breakfast or dinner / happy hour food set up after the kitchen staff prepares it. We keep the snack bar selection stocked and charge selected people's rooms. We answer questions from guests about their needs (most often it's about using the WiFi or helping them with toiletry items) and recommend places they can go for lunch. Even though we're at the front desk, we're more like ambassadors for our guests during their stay and that is something I enjoy. I get to use all my "mom skills" and get paid for it! I know you said "front desk" but I want to point out that we are really modern and don't have a desk. We have free standing clear podiums with ipads that we call pods – I love it because we don't put up a barrier between us and the guests like you have in a traditional hotel set up. I feel like I can establish a stronger relationship quicker with someone because we are just two people interacting and they have needs and I'm helping them. It's really a great feeling!

Q4 | What frustrates you about working in your current role in the hospitality sector?

I hate it when we're slow. There is a strong seasonality to our location and when we're in the off season, the time at work drags. I would like to have things to do beyond being a guest ambassador when there are no guests. We've suggested doing things like making outreach calls to recent guests to learn about how they liked (or didn't like) their stay or even calling folks who stayed with us to see about whether they are planning to return to the area and – if they are – perhaps book a reservation for them. So many of our guests say "I'd love to bring my family here and see things" and I think that's a great opportunity for us. There are a lot of tourist-type activities in town, and having a hotel that offers free hot breakfast AND dinner is really economical for guests with kids. The problem is that our corporate protocols won't let us do that as there is a centralized marketing department to do that. I think it would be better if someone that the guest actually met during a prior stay be the one they continue to talk to, but we just aren't allowed. I don't think our company really listens to us – we are heard by our managers when there are things at the property level that they can address. A lot of what frustrates me are limitations placed upon us by people who are in another state, though.

Q5 | When you learn about layoffs in another industry, how do you feel about your own role?

Well, that's happening now but we haven't really seen anything trickle down to our level yet. Our business travelers still say that they are just starting to physically travel to places on business as opposed to zoom meetings or similar, and that they're really happy because it helps them do better. I suppose if a business isn't doing well that it would start cutting back on that kind of an expense, and that would really hurt us as a business and I imagine they would downsize staff at that point.

Q6 | When you learn about layoffs in the hospitality industry, how do you feel about your own role?

My husband is in banking and we got pretty stressed recently when multiple banks closed down. He works for a major bank, and they're doing great, but there's always that thought that if one company in an industry is having a problem, others will soon. When we learned about the banks that closed, it triggered us to review what we're saving, what we have put away already, what upcoming expenses we know about and what we can do to reduce. So I suppose if we started hearing about hotels laying off employees, we might do the same. He makes nearly four times what I make, though, so we might not be as nervous about losing my paycheck!

Q7 | When you learn about layoffs in your hotel, not necessarily in your area, how do you feel about your own role?

There hasn't been any yet while I've been here, but I understand that the last few years involved plenty of layoffs at the hotel. Headcount at the hotel is budgeted for on an annual basis and reviewed each quarter as well. Corporate has to approve all headcount budgets, and that's something negotiated by our managers. It really seems to stress out our manager, he was here throughout the pandemic so this is something he's really nervous about. He always makes a big deal to the staff when headcount budget is approved and that we're all safe for another quarter! I don't know if he would tell us if headcount was reduced so far in advance, but imagine that we would figure it out if he didn't tell us anything…the media has made a huge deal about a worker shortage, so finding another job would probably be easy. I would be upset because I need consistency of a flexible routine like I have here though. That may not be so easy to find, so learning about layoffs would definitely bother me.

Q8 | When you learn about layoffs in your department, how do you feel about your role?

There haven't been any layoffs at my hotel, and certainly not in my department. Quite the opposite – we are always hiring! It's hard to find people who do the job we are doing as a guest ambassador. Most people come in and say, I can do front desk work like answer phones and check people in. We've changed the role at my company and my hotel, so people get confused and not realize that it's more about building relationships with people and learning what they need and providing it as opposed to administrative tasks that repeat over and over. The people I see applying are younger and perhaps less interested or able to do what this role needs now, but I love it! I love being able to help people using skills I can bring that I've developed as a parent.

Q9 | Do you see yourself choosing to stay employed in the hospitality sector?

If I get to keep doing what I'm doing, and we have enough people to keep doing it for, then I love it! I think this is a great opportunity for people like myself who are not just starting out in adulthood but looking for a chance to interact with people, do something impactful but isn't stressful and can be left behind at work when you leave for the day. Getting paid to do that is a bonus! I do like this work and I like the environment I do it in. There's a benefit that I haven't had the opportunity to take advantage of yet, but we are planning to – and that's the travel benefits. As an employee of a corporate hotel network, we can stay at any of the branded hotels our corporation owns and operates for free or nearly free. What a fantastic benefit, and it isn't something that is used to attract employees like myself who want to travel. We have some upcoming family vacations that this will really help us with because we can spend more on the experience and less on lodging – how fantastic! If I stay in this industry as our kids get older and move out, I can see my husband and I doing some personal travel for just the two of us and also enjoying this benefit. It's unique to the hospitality and travel world and I can't imagine why they don't use it to get more employees like myself who are at that stage of their lives.

Q10 | What changes would you like to see that would make it more attractive to stay in the hospitality sector?

I would really like to have a greater say and impact with the vitality and health of business generation at my specific hotel. Specifically, I think that our corporate policies should allow flexibility for a property to complement what a centralized marketing department would do in generating occupancy and room nights. My job is about establishing a connection with our customer and I can't imagine why that is limited only to when they are physically with us. Why not let us do outreach ahead of their stay and begin that relationship early? Why not be the ones to follow-up after and potentially generate new business? Seems like common sense since we're the ones with the relationship with the customer and relationship drives business revenue. Other than that, I really enjoy the flexibility of scheduling and the travel-oriented benefits, which are unique to this type of operation. Seems to be something that could be done to secure employees but I don't see much in the way of that either.

Participant 2, Mid-Range Hotel

Q1 | How long have you been employed in the hospitality sector?

I've been a part – time employee on and off for ten years, but not consecutively. I was laid off between 2020 and 2021 for nearly 9 months and then brought back in May 2021 ahead of the summer travel season once vaccine availability started increasing.

Q2 | What attracted you originally to working in the hospitality sector?

I'm retired, so I was looking for something to do that would supplement my retirement income that would not be too stressful, provide some interaction with others and offer me the ability to travel on a budget. I work for a large corporate – owned hotel and one of our benefits is to stay at other properties within our hotel network (domestically and internationally) for a significantly reduced room rate.

Q3 | What do you enjoy about working in your current role in the hospitality sector?

I really like that the work isn't too difficult and much of it is based on either a consistent operational process or a social interaction. I'm not terribly good with computers, but there's always some folks around (usually younger) who are able to help me with that aspect of the job. I do like interacting with people and that I can leave the work at work when I go home. I'm not looking for additional responsibilities at this point in my life. I have been able to take some trips (financed by the job) where I took advantage of our ability to secure a "pennies on the dollar" rate at some fantastic properties in fantastic locations, which I would really identify as my favorite part of this job.

Q4 | What frustrates you about working in your current role in the hospitality sector?

I tend not to get too involved in any of the business-oriented aspects of what goes on, it just isn't of any interest to me. Most of my peers are frustrated by management decisions or corporate decisions, and it really affects their mental health. I've had a lot of them express admiration and/or envy around my ability to simply not care, but why would I? This isn't a career for me as it may be for them. I'm here to 1) interact with people, 2) get paid to supplement my income and 3) take advantage of the travel benefits. Beyond that, I do what those in charge want me to do. Are there some idiotic decisions being made? Of course! As I discovered in my own career before retirement, if people are involved then idiocy soon follows regardless of context or industry. I am not interested in volunteering because why should I do the same amount of work as I am not, but not get paid for it? Could I find employment that may pay more? Sure, but they don't offer the same travel benefits and so there's an opportunity cost associated with that option. Don't misunderstand, I certainly have ideas (both based on observation and on experience) that would enhance or enrich the hotel property. I also understand and accept that I am not in charge of the operation or the business, and that I am being compensated to execute policy and procedures that others are responsible for. What some of my peers could realize is that they are not judged on whether they agree with how a business elect to do something – if they want to reinvent the world, secure a position that has that responsibility in its job description. Otherwise, recognize that a front-line role is about making what management dreams up a reality. I think the inability of younger people to embrace that perspective can be really disruptive and personally frustrating. Not everything has to be a social platform to correct a perceived injustice, especially if it's centered around how far away a customer has to be greeted (no closer than 5' before management wants us to make eye contact and initiative a friendly greeting) or what by what ring the telephone has to be answered by (no later than the 3rd ring, 1st or 2nd preferred). At the end of the day, I have a clear vision of how I am benefiting from my choice to remain employed with this business in this role, and that tends to dilute and de-prioritize frustrations stemming from events and people outside of that.

Q5 | When you learn about layoffs in another industry, how do you feel about your own role?

I honestly don't care. I try not to follow news in the modern, 24-hour a day news cycle. Little of it is breaking or significant news, with most being rehashed or re-contextualized content. If a company that I'm not employed by announces a layoff, so what? Even more so when it isn't even a hospitality or tourism company, why would that even matter? Again, I'm not here to manage the health of the business so while I understand the potential connections between the hospitality industry and others, from my current point of view it just isn't really a concern on any level.

Q6 | When you learn about layoffs in the hospitality industry, how do you feel about your own role?

Still don't care. Each business is unique and just because one company is experiencing trouble or making a decision about the size of its workforce doesn't mean it's automatically connected to the company I work for. Also, the adage of "don't worry about things you cannot control" is something to mention in response to this question. If corporate decides that headcount at the hotel has to be reduced, and it has nothing to do with my performance or attitude (things I CAN control), than why should I expend energy that leads to worry, stress or discontent on it? Seems silly. Now, this isn't how most of my colleagues approach this question, and that's why I assume it's on your list to ask me about. They WILL worry, and there's a whole lot of politicking that occurs around the "office" so to speak, when layoffs are being rumored. People try to be more valuable in their manager's eyes to avoid the cut. I've been laid off more than once in my lifetime, with the most recent being in April 2020. What could be done to avoid that? Nothing – the hotel closed. Nobody was travelling anywhere. Would all of the stress and effort leading up to that moment been worth it? From my point of view, hardly. In every economic (global or industry level) downturn I've worked through over the last thirty years, I've rarely found that anyone's efforts prior to a layoff meant anything when the proverbial ax fell. If anything, it added to the discourse and discontent someone felt as a result of being laid off after trying so hard to avoid that outcome. It's a lesson you can only learn from actual experience, and an empowering choice on your own. No matter how many people tell you about it, or how it shows up in your research, people can't be told to do it. They have to decide to adopt this perspective on their own.

Q7 | When you learn about layoffs in your hotel, not necessarily in your area, how do you feel about your own role?

I think that it's natural to consider possible outcomes when you learn that your own company will be reducing its headcount, and that isn't exclusive to hospitality. It was something I felt and observed in 2020 when the hotel laid me off. It's also something I felt and observed in others throughout my career. Let me talk about the 2020 experience a bit, since I know you're specifically focusing on hotels and hotel employees. By January of 2020, a viral outbreak on a global scale was beginning to make news. I remember hearing about it and thinking about the earlier SARS outbreaks, the H1N1 influenza outbreak, the Great Recession, 9/11 and the ensuing Gulf and Afghanistan wars and how those all impacted our economy. When I began working, American companies weren't as connected to other countries as we are today. While I know that many younger people feel that criticism of that economic model is not looked upon fondly, my experiences are that a global economy can be a fragile beast. Certainly where hotels are concerned, a viral outbreak in Africa or China can certainly have a significant impact on a hotel's business in the United States. I know that's a lot of context, but ultimately it's my thinking process. I enjoy reflecting and processing, and I recognize that I have the scope of experience to benefit from it. At the end of the day, if layoffs are announced at the hotel, I just simply assume that I will learn of the degree to which it impacts me soon enough and modifying my behavior to change that outcome is a frivolous exercise. That allows me to do my work at work with as little stress as possible. It also lets me go home after my work without any stress at all.

Q8 | When you learn about layoffs in your department, how do you feel about your role?

I think I already answered this in the prior question. A hotel is not an office, and there aren't large groups of people in a department sitting around when layoffs are announced wondering if they'll be the ones getting a pink slip. I've lived through that in the corporate world, on both sides of the equation having received a pink slip (and I'm old enough to have actually gotten the proverbial pink piece of paper) and handed them out as well. I'm past that. I don't feel any different about my role whether its announced that layoffs or imminent or profits are up. I do want to clarify, that I interpret disappointment different than stress or worry. I would absolutely be disappointed in a layoff environment if I lost my job. There are value-added elements to it that I outlined earlier in the interview like the travel benefits that would certainly result in a feeling of loss should I no longer have access to them. However, would I be worried about being laid off? Or stressed about it? Not at all.

Q9 | Do you see yourself choosing to stay employed in the hospitality sector?

I think this is my last job. I'm already in retirement and working to fulfill needs other than those defined by career advancement. I have no aspirations on promotion, upward mobility or career pathways, things that are generating all of the headlines relating to workforce development these days. I don't want to be dismissive of those concepts as they are relevant for a certain population, I just recognize that I'm not in that population. However, in the labor shortage that the United States is experiencing, I believe that there are many others like me who would be willing to work in exchange for similar benefits to what motivates me. It is important that employers understand the characteristics of their labor as deeply as they understand the characteristics of their target market segments because not all employees (or potential employees) are interested in the same things. I couldn't care less about healthcare benefits, I have medicare. I'm not interested in a 401K because I'm already of the age to access my retirement savings. Yet, I am capable of providing the same work and guest services as any other potential employee. Since I am also a consumer of these services when I go on trips, I can perhaps provide BETTER service since I maintain awareness and perspective from both sides of the coin. So it begs the question – perhaps employers need to develop better strategies on what types of people they want to attract as workers?

Q10 | What changes would you like to see that would make it more attractive to stay in the hospitality sector?

The one thing that I guess I would zero in on is...don't cut my travel benefits or flexible scheduling! If those go, I doubt I would continue to remain employed as my primary source of motivation for continuing this relationship would be gone. I have reiterated that several times already, though, so let me provide something new: I would like some better training to be offered. Training today mostly consists of someone demonstrating the functionality of a computer system used in the job, reviewing a desired process to provide services or presenting a performance outcome metric that is quantifying the evaluation of job performance. With the first one especially, but really for all three, I would suggest that hotel management review how adults learn best. In today's world of education, we know about different learning styles, active learning methods and how assessment reinforces learning to increase desired outcomes. Yet, rarely do I find these principles being used when hotel employees are being trained on things. I'm not suggesting this from the perspective of optimizing hotel operations or lowering costs due to more effective training. I'm simply thinking of how it makes the lives of front-line employees so much easier if we are comfortable with the tools we are expected to use to perform the duties we are expected to complete to the standards we are expected to achieve. More effective learning practices embedded with training efforts would certainly achieve that.

Participant 3, Mid-Range Hotel

Q1 | How long have you been employed in the hospitality sector?

I've been involved in the hospitality industry for three years. This is my first year working in a hotel, as I am participating in a college – based program that combines classroom learning and on-the-job experience. My first two years were about taking classes focusing on hotel operations, marketing, human resources, information systems and other related topics. The third year has been about a combination of classroom learning integrated with some specific on-the-job based projects that involve working in various departments within the hotel, rotating through each one. The fourth and final year will be fewer classes with more day-to-day work that has been developed with the University to make sure that we have the learning experience we're supposed to as well as earn the credits we need for graduation. The University has an arrangement with this hotel company where our activities are pre-determined and there are tests we take based on our work experiences. This is transformed then into credits earned and awarded by the University.

Q2 | What attracted you originally to working in the hospitality sector?

I did some career assessments online and as a part of high school career coaching. The service industry is one that I scored highly in. It looks at what you like, what motivates you, your personality characteristics and matches you with an industry that you would do well in. Travel and hospitality was the one where I matched the best, and I chose hotels since there are college programs and you have to travel for work less than in, say, the airline industry.

Q3 | What do you enjoy about working in your current role in the hospitality sector?

I enjoy the variety of tasks. We are a full-service hotel, so we offer our guests a restaurant and bar as well as other amenities within the hotel itself. I have enjoyed rotating through all of the various departments learning how to perform the duties of each. I did not enjoy engineering much as I am not skilled in how to fix things like HVAC units or other things that get supported by that department. I also did not enjoy housekeeping as I don't enjoy cleaning in general. I did really like rooms management, which the front desk is a part of. I enjoyed the variety of tasks but also the ability to interact with guests and serve as the face of the hotel. I also really like that my program has set up a structure to follow with my developing career that extends beyond this initial experience. Even after I graduate from the program, I have a sense of where I am going, what I will accomplish next and how long I can expect before I reach that career milestone. Having less ambiguity in how I spend my professional life during the next 5-10 years is very important to me.

Q4 | What frustrates you about working in your current role in the hospitality sector?

Some of the people there really bother me. I don't understand why someone would work in a job where they don't like what you are supposed to do. I get that it's a paycheck, but there are so many options to earn money now it seems to make more sense to find something you love doing and get employed doing that thing. Hotels are about servicing people, but if you hate people why would you work at a hotel? It seems like a ridiculous question, but there are several employees I've encountered who embody that statement. Another group of people really dislike management or corporate, and I think I can relate more to that group. Sometimes management or corporate do things that seem really counter-productive to guests' needs, the health of the business or the needs of the employees. I try not to speak out too much in this case, because I am also in training for management and have exposure beyond what someone not in my program may experience. I've learned there is more than one side to everything and what is right is not always readily apparent for everyone. I don't like having to hide that the company is paying for my education either – this should be something that is more consistently available for everyone? I think it is, but when I mentioned it early on some people really responded poorly and jealously, so I stopped bringing it up. I think it's great that the company supports training and education, and more folks should take advantage of it!

Q5 | When you learn about layoffs in another industry, how do you feel about your own role?

I haven't paid too much attention to this – I'm focusing on learning about how a hotel operates and how the business of running a hotel is done. My program has a commitment requirement when they pay tuition in that participants have to work for a minimum of two years for the company following graduation.

I guess it makes sense to think about where layoffs at a hotel could start, but this is really beyond what I think about right now.

Q6 | When you learn about layoffs in the hospitality industry, how do you feel about your own role?

There haven't been any really since I started my program. I know that the industry did lay off thousands of people at the start of the COVID pandemic, and I believe that happened with the Great Recession as well. I was pretty young then and only know about it after the fact. I think that learning that other hotel companies are laying off people would worry me but it just isn't something I have personally experienced yet (thankfully) and don't have anything personal to reference.

Q7 | When you learn about layoffs in your hotel, not necessarily in your area, how do you feel about your own role?

I'm pretty sure this would bother me and I would want to do everything I could to convince management that I'm not someone they want to let go! Still, I have boundaries and maintaining a work/life balance is key for me. I realize that I don't want to be let go, but I seems like there's a lot of opportunity everywhere for people with experience and I'm gaining a lot of that. I would be concerned and do what I can to hold onto my job as long as it didn't impact how I want to live outside of work – at that point, I may even start proactively exploring leaving and joining a new company that would fit my values better.

Q8 | When you learn about layoffs in your department, how do you feel about your role?

I don't really have a department, I am moving around to all of the department. I think being a part of this college program would probably keep me safe from something like this (at least for now). I can see, though, that there are some who have such a negative attitude about work, the company, guests, etc. that it would actually be easy to cut them! In fact, it may make for a better work environment for people who aren't cut to get rid of some of those folks – improving the positive culture can truly change the mental health of employees for the better. If you're around someone who is complaining and doesn't do a good job and you see that management doesn't deal with it sends a message, and it isn't one that supports a good culture. If layoffs were occurring and there weren't any negative people on the team where it was happening, that could be really tough. I would hope that the company would support those who are cut with a great severance as well as those who are still employed by bringing in counselors and offering time off or other services to help people process their trauma. Loosing co-workers is traumatic, these are the people you spend a lot of time with. A sudden change can really make things messy for someone's happiness and satisfaction.

Q9 | Do you see yourself choosing to stay employed in the hospitality sector?

Absolutely, I believe I am in this for the long haul! After I complete my program, I hope to apply for an assistant manager role within the company and really get involved with making worthwhile changes! A hotel can be such a fun and fulfilling place to work, and I really feel like I can bring a lot of energy and now experience to that table. There are so many different avenues to follow career-wise in a hotel, whether you stay in operations or sales at a property, or move to a corporate role in marketing, human resources, information technology or sales. Honestly, I think that's one of the neat things about hospitality is that you can keep things fresh by doing different things over time while continuing to reinvent yourself professionally. I've discovered that I really become energized when I get involved with a variety of tasks, so continuing to work in an industry that easily allows that is important.

Q10 | What changes would you like to see that would make it more attractive to stay in the hospitality sector?

I would like to see a better use of social media and technology in improving a guest experience, whether it's at the pre-stay phase (prior to booking even), the stay itself and after the stay. For example, our website now shows static, individual pictures of different rooms at the hotel to help a guest decide what type of room they want to book. Why not have that as a virtual reality-based tour that includes views out the window, the lobby, etc. Also, our website needs to be more mobile friendly. We just added functionality of choosing your room 24 hours before arrival and checking in through the app, which is great but there are more things you could do. I'm focusing on identifying next generation app functionality for a hotel as my senior year project. I hope to be able to develop it during the next year and present it to hotel or corporate leadership before I graduate with possibly being assigned to implement such a project. That way I can keep a foot in the hotel property operation (which I'm already familiar with) and begin to get involved with the corporate strategic part of the business. Another opportunity is to make sure employees are taken care of including building a great culture that allows people to get involved at work using their strengths while not encroaching on what they want to accomplish outside of work.

Participant 1, High End Hotel

Q1 | How long have you been employed in the hospitality sector?

I have been a hotel worker for 11 years. I have been with my current employer for seven years. Prior to that, I was with a different employer in the hotel industry for five years.

Q2 | What attracted you originally to working in the hospitality sector?

I began working at a hotel during high school and just never left! I liked working at a hotel better than flipping burgers or retail or any other job that someone with only a high school diploma can get. Once I started, I got bitten by the hospitality bug and found that I didn't want to do anything else with my life. I started in banquet operations, but really enjoy the front desk more. I like our uniform, which is a tie and jacket – very professional. It makes me feel good to be wearing something professional like that and I really enjoy being able to help guests with what they need when they're with us. We do have a separate concierge, but the front desk is encouraged to also help with those tasks when we aren't busy and I really enjoy helping guests figure out where they want to go for dinner, getting bottles of wine or champagne brought to rooms for special occasions or making sure whatever needs they have are met. I like the audit process of the front desk where you review, balance and cash out operations from the day but I don't like that it happens overnight. I don't mind the work hours so much, but I do miss the guest interaction. Hotels have always been something that are constant and permanent businesses from my perspective, so working at one seems more stable than some other types of employment. I know there have been some bad years during the past decade and a half with recessions and pandemics, but I'm still here and I've never been laid off!

Q3 | What do you enjoy about working in your current role in the hospitality sector?

More than anything, I enjoy interacting with guests. I find that I get a sense of personal satisfaction when a guest is angry or frustrated and I can help resolve that emotion for them. A lot of our guests are tired and upset when they arrive due to issues they faced in getting to us. Airline travel seems especially stressful for many with delayed or canceled flights. Our guests are staying at the hotel primarily for leisure purposes, and sometimes they're anything but relaxed when they arrive. My goal is to turn that around and let them know that whatever has happened is in the past and what's about to happen will be better. Our management likes this approach and has empowered the front desk to offer our guests coupons for a complimentary cocktail or side item with dinner, we can upgrade them to the next classification of room that may have better amenities or view or even offer a slightly discounted room rate. I'm told that there have been financial models built that show when we do this for our guests on the front end, the goodwill and positive emotional energy that we create translates into a significantly higher per capital spend rate by our guests. That's great for the hotel, of course, but what really motivates me is when someone smiles and honestly thanks me for trying to make their day better. That's the best feeling in the world and that's what I love most about my job.

Q4 | What frustrates you about working in your current role in the hospitality sector?

Lately I get frustrated by the lack of commitment to guest satisfaction some employes showcase. It seems to be more with the younger workers than anyone – they're very concerned with the guests being respectful to them and how they are treated. On one hand, I get it – who wants to be yelled at? On the other, it seems to be missing the point. Our job is there to provide hospitality services to the guest and arguing about respect is counterproductive to that outcome. I get frustrated when younger workers say that I need to work on my self-respect because I will allow a guest to vent frustrations rather than insist they be quiet (as some of the newer employees will do). It isn't just a different approach, it's a whole different mindset to the role of the worker and how customers or management are expected to treat them. It's really a newer aspect of the working environment and while I can't fault it's purported outcome, I really disagree with the stand-offish manner in which I observe some people pursuing it. I also find it frustrating that management seems disinterested or powerless to correct that kind of behavior as well. I'm not sure how things changed so much over the past decade, but it's a noticeable difference now from when I started.

Q5 | When you learn about layoffs in another industry, how do you feel about your own role?

I don't really pay attention to this other than what I hear on the news. I don't like hearing about it, so when layoffs are announced I tend not to learn more about what led to that point.

Q6 | When you learn about layoffs in the hospitality industry, how do you feel about your own role?

I don't have influence or power to change how the industry as a whole does with its business. I can't even really make changes to how our own hotel does, let alone the company itself. Focusing on the entire industry is beyond what I can realistically impact so I tend not to.

Q7 | When you learn about layoffs in your hotel, not necessarily in your area, how do you feel about your own role?

Rumor of layoffs are very upsetting, and they seem to be pretty consistent things in employee gossip. They happen in cycles it seems, you won't hear anything for several months and then all of a sudden everyone is whispering about how the company is doing and how layoffs are imminent. 2 out of 3 times it seems that these rumors are false or overstated. Someone might be let go for poor performance, but since that is private information all we know is that someone is gone. That turns into the rumors of layoffs.

Q8 | When you learn about layoffs in your department, how do you feel about your role?

Our department has 12 people, so it's large enough that we could lose 1-2 positions I suppose. The only time it's happened, though, is in May of 2020 when our hotel shut down. We didn't have any bookings at all, nobody was taking vacations. We were past the shelter in place orders but recovery by June was seeming less and less likely. Our staff was slashed by 75% with only front desk employees remaining (bellmen and concierge, also in our department, were eliminated completely). They would only staff one person at a time in an area and we couldn't interact with anyone else during our shift. It was a strange time. I didn't lose my job, but there was a definite sense that if things didn't start improving quickly there wouldn't be a hotel left at all. I think that's the only time I've ever felt anything like that and things did not improve at all for nearly a year. I remember being very interested in vaccine development because it felt like that was the only way that we were going to recover as a business. I lost a few extended family members to the virus, and I vividly remember thinking that life as we knew it was clearly over and I would be out of a job soon. I associate being laid off now with that experience, so if there was ever a notification in the future that it would be my department that was going to be specifically downsized, I imagine I would have a pretty intense reaction emotionally to that news, whether I was directly or indirectly impacted.

Q9 | Do you see yourself choosing to stay employed in the hospitality sector?

I think so, although I probably won't stay forever in hotel operations. I am applying for a leadership development program within the company and I hope that I can transition into a manager role soon. I have a pretty solid understanding of how rooms management and front desk operations work, and I'm eager to be able to take a team and develop their skills. I've read a lot about newer operational trends and what is trending in terms of incorporating technology into the guest experience. I want to be a part of bringing some of that to my company and so I'm really excited about this opportunity as well as additional ones down the road. I'm thankful that our organization has developed so many pathways to train and develop professionally, as well as invest in individuals who are willing to take the time and effort to grow.

Q10 | What changes would you like to see that would make it more attractive to stay in the hospitality sector?

The hospitality sector is one that is always dynamic and changing and that makes it exciting to me career-wise. I feel that there are always going to be unforeseen challenges due to the unpredictability of guests and their needs, but that is what also is attractive – office work without any sort of excitement is super boring. I would like to see more testing of new services, new technology and new initiatives to take place in pilot initiatives localized around one or two properties. This way, even though we are a large company, we can move quickly to determine if something works as well in real life as it does on paper. For example, integrating a concept of the Internet of Things into the rooms is something that I think is a serious strategic differentiator for hoteliers. Much like how we expect appliances and everyday functions in our home to be connected to our home network, we should offer guests the same connected experience when they stay with us. By conducting short, localized tests in specific locations, it minimizes risk to the company and I would like to see that sort of strategy adaptation a part of our culture. Another opportunity would be to engage employees with equity around the company – more than a bonus, employees should become engaged with the company's success and longevity because they have a vested interest. I'm not sure what that might look like, and many employees don't have much financial independence to shoulder downturns in the market, but a bonus that has no connection to one's day to day tasks really isn't a motivator either. I would like to see some innovation occur in this area though.

Participant 2, High End Hotel

Q1 | How long have you been employed in the hospitality sector?

I just joined the company 4 months ago. I retired from my primary career in mid 2020 as a part of an effort by that company to save costs by encouraging early retirement among employees who were within 5 years of that age. I figured, why not – let's get to the part where I am living for myself since everyone was in lockdown due to the pandemic anyway. What I discovered, though, was that I needed some structure to my life that I missed no longer having a professional outlet. After trying some different things, I saw that the local resort was advertising for a part-time front desk clerk that was benefits eligible, specifically travel benefits within the resort brand. My wife and I are starting to plan some trips now that restrictions are being lifted in some places across the world and the notion of being able to use this benefit to stay at places we might not be able to otherwise easily afford was really attractive.

Q2 | What attracted you originally to working in the hospitality sector?

I have travelled extensively in my career and I have stayed at a lot of different hotel types. You could say I'm a master customer and I maintained the highest tier of my favorite brand's customer loyalty program for many, many years. After I retired, and after running out of things to do around the house, I began casting around looking for something to do that would be stimulating but not overly stressful. Walmart greeters are something that a lot of older workers get associated with, but I really didn't want to do that or anything in retail. I was attending a meeting for another association at this gorgeous resort in the area and I noticed that they had a "help wanted" sign on the entrance. I thought about it throughout my meeting and applied for the job afterwards before heading home for the day. I think what attracted me initially was that this resort creates a bubble around its wonderful fantasy world of service and hospitality that is really fantastic to spend time in. It isn't the real world, it's a relaxed space with soft music, high ceilings, gorgeous architecture and sumptuous food. What's not to like about spending more time there? I figured that I had picked up enough about how a hotel operates with my many guest nights throughout my working days that I could leverage that into a job. They thought so also!

Q3 | What do you enjoy about working in your current role in the hospitality sector?

For me, it's like pulling the curtain back on how the magic is created. Hotels like to present themselves as a well-oiled machine that operates effortlessly to exceed guests' needs. The truth is that there is a lot chaos that occurs out of sight of guests to make that appearance become a reality. I think guests are aware of it on some level, but they're coming to this type of resort to buy into the fantasy so there's an easier suspension of disbelief. It isn't manipulation if both sides want it, and I feel that they do! Being a part of the team that makes that magic happen for guests is really stimulating for me. I enjoy having to think outside the box sometimes to solve guests' problems, things that you can't really anticipate with everything ranging from luggage being lost and people showing up without even a toothbrush to room doorknobs coming off and trapping guests inside. We are near wilderness areas, and wildlife can freely walk the property. Not all wildlife is friendly and cuddly, though. Venomous snakes, predatory large cats and scary looking giant spiders are just a few of thing critters that an unsuspecting guest may encounter. Helping navigate all of that for our guests and ensure that they still have a magical experience is what thrills and fulfills me. I can leave a shift exhausted if we're hosting a busy conference with lots of activity with check-in and guests settling down, but it's a satisfied exhaustion knowing that what I did made a difference. Being able to see the immediate results of your work is different than what I experienced in my original career but it's such a welcome change now.

Q4 | What frustrates you about working in your current role in the hospitality sector?

I don't feel like I am connected to the team beyond that we perform the same job functions. Let me explain a bit what I mean by that. Obviously I am separated by age being significantly older than the rest of the team. But it's more than just a difference in age, it's often a difference in values and perspective on what being in a service industry means for its employees. I wholly subscribe to the notion that "we work while others play," but it's not really a mantra for the younger generations employed at the resort. Employees call out sick because they don't want to work on a weekend or they know we have a busy scheduled day with a large conference starting and thousands of people checking in within a short amount of time. Who does that when you're in this business? I've seen employees argue with customers and point out how the customer is wrong, with the employee refusing to do anything until they get an apology. Again, I get that self-respect is important but I don't subscribe to personalizing and internalizing bad behavior from our guests. Guests will conduct themselves poorly when they are either 1) stressed and tired due to things outside of our control or 2) trying to scam the hotel. You have to know which scenario you're dealing with and act accordingly as a hotel employee. More often than not, I find we're dealing with scenario number 1. They aren't mad at us, we're just a convenient target. I don't like it, who does? But if my job is to help create magic for our guests (and it is), I don't find that fighting back and demanding an apology is going to get to the end result you want. I feel like the team is fractured on how to approach this scenario with little support or insight from management. Not being unified with the team on issues like this make the job feel more lonely than perhaps it needs to be. I'm not looking for a social outlet, but I'm also not there for the paycheck per se so some positive engagement is beneficial and looked for.

Q5 | When you learn about layoffs in another industry, how do you feel about your own role?

Couldn't care less, I'm out of the rat race.

Q6 | When you learn about layoffs in the hospitality industry, how do you feel about your own role?

I'm not in this for a long-term career so, again, I want my company and team to do well but it doesn't cast doubt about a future in my role if the industry is laying off people. I'll stay until it's no longer fun or I'm asked to go…

Q7 | When you learn about layoffs in your hotel, not necessarily in your area, how do you feel about your own role?

This would bother me some I imagine, although it isn't something that has taken place in the time I've been on the payroll. Resort employees work together as a team to achieve a common goal of guest satisfaction, even if we're not working together directly. Layoffs are a stressful negative presence in a workplace culture and even if people are being let go in departments outside of yours, the collective culture will feel the loss making the goal of guest services more difficult. Employees who live paycheck to paycheck will not be able to perform their guest service duties if they're too worried about their own livelihood. This kind of thing can be a real killer of culture and once it's gone, its very difficult to recapture.

Q8 | When you learn about layoffs in your department, how do you feel about your role?

I think this would be tough, but not as difficult as the previous scenario. In this one, there's no ambiguity about what is happening – people who were there are now gone, and the remaining team has to pull together to perform its work. With all due respect to anyone who is let go, those remaining can connect and bond stronger than they were before over a common experience. When layoffs occur in another department where you may have less visibility, layoffs can take on an almost mythic quality that drives misinformation and fear throughout all departments.

Q9 | Do you see yourself choosing to stay employed in the hospitality sector?

I plan to stay for as long as it's fun and fulfilling for me and as long as I can retain the travel benefits within the hotel brand. I won't spend my retirement doing a job that is frustrating, unfulfilling or boring. My tolerance for any of those at this stage of the game is extremely low. Likewise, while I am not living paycheck to paycheck, I do have financial motivation invested in using the travel benefits associated with the resort. If those were to ever to no longer be available, I doubt that I would choose to stay.

Q10 | What changes would you like to see that would make it more attractive to stay in the hospitality sector?

While this doesn't affect my own decision to stay or leave, I do feel that the hospitality industry is more fragile than many others in terms of susceptibility to external factors. A recession hits, and people stop travelling and the hotel is in trouble. A pandemic hits, and people stop travelling and the hotel is in trouble. A terrorist attack, and people stop travelling and the hotel is in trouble. While this would be problematic for any industry, compound it with the fact that so many of hotel employees are not well – paid and often live paycheck to paycheck. Any sort of interruption in earnings can really damage one's affection for employment in the industry, and loosing well-trained people is just not something a business can regularly afford to experience. I don't know what the answer is, but the next generation of hotel and resort leaders do need to invest in stepping up their product lines so as to be more resilient to unforeseen external market factors.

Participant 3, High End Hotel

Q1 | How long have you been employed in the hospitality sector?

I've been employed at the hotel for two years now. I graduated in 2020 with a degree in hospitality management but wasn't able to find a job immediately due to the covid pandemic. I was hired in 2021 as a front desk associate but was promoted after my first year to PM Rooms Management Shift Lead, which works the desk but also oversees the concierge, bell staff and guest services teams in the lobby and on the premium concierge floor, which is reserved for frequent guests and those who are gold or platinum levels in our frequent stay program.

Q2 | What attracted you originally to working in the hospitality sector?

I did an internship in high school working at a limited-service hotel, which is really similar to the large conference hotel I work at now except there were fewer people and resources to get things done. It was a great first job because you learned about all aspects of hotel operations. I remember checking people in and then having to plunge their toilets later in the evening. I don't know how to describe it really except that I was bit by the hospitality bug and feel good about my work knowing that I make others feel good about their stay. I don't have to plunge toilets anymore as we have a rooms comfort team to handle in-room issues, but the goal and purpose is really the same: Provide amazing guest service.

Q3 | What do you enjoy about working in your current role in the hospitality sector?

There is always so much activity at the hotel – I'm employed at a high rise modern hotel adjacent to a major convention center. The last year and a half have been crazy busy as every conference is making up for nearly two years of missed time! It has been non-stop conference after conference and there is rarely a week where we aren't near a sold out situation. That's exciting and there's always energy within the hotel, which makes coming to work a very stimulating situation. Now that I'm in a semi - management role, I feel like an orchestra conductor that keeps all of the various parts of the orchestra in synch with one another while also having to play your own instrument (I still work the desk). I am not one to stay idle in my work, I enjoy multi-tasking and consuming as much stimulating content as quickly as possible. This hotel and this job keeps me on my toes and I wouldn't want to work at a job that didn't offer me that.

Q4 | What frustrates you about working in your current role in the hospitality sector?

I don't appreciate employees who won't match me with high energy, a passion for serving others and a knack for solving problems. I caught some employees laughing at a guest the other night because the guest was reporting that their floor may be haunted. Apparently, they had seen some things like lights flickering and experienced cold spots, which have perfectly normal explanations, but this guest was TERRIFIED. I didn't observe the employees working with that guest to be respectful of where she was and realized that addressing what she believed (as opposed to changing her belief) was the real problem that had to be solved. That lack of critical skills and thinking bothered me. Another example? I'm a firm believer in an all-hands-on-deck mentality where everyone on the front desk team is scheduled to work when we are expecting 1,000+ arrivals in a single afternoon, but we have employees always call out. They're not sick, they just don't want to work that hard. It isn't just the front desk where we see this, housekeeping struggles with the same lack of dedication from its team. I'm not necessarily blaming the employee for a larger cultural shift, but it is a business problem that needs to be solved. I don't think management takes it seriously or feels if they convey being annoyed with younger generations (who are unfortunately stereotyped here but I observe older folks on staff sometimes doing the same thing), the problem will resolve on its own. It won't. What this requires I feel is a fundamental redesign of how you engage employees and what can make them care about the outcome of the hotel. Paychecks are what traditionally did that, but my hotel HR classes in college explored alternative means of motivation that involved bonuses for hourly employees, ownership equity in the business, a different kind of evaluation mechanism and more. We don't really have any of that in place with my current company, but I think it's the real answer to how to address worker shortages and apathy.

Q5 | When you learn about layoffs in another industry, how do you feel about your own role?

I would be concerned about this simply because I understand the symbiotic nature of hospitality and other industries. Our bread-and-butter markets are other industries that pay to hold conferences for themselves. If they aren't doing well, expensive conferences are either scaled back or eliminated. That hurts the hotel business, so while I wouldn't immediately be worried about losing my position, I think knowing layoffs were happening in other industries would put me on alert.

Q6 | When you learn about layoffs in the hospitality industry, how do you feel about your own role?

If the hotel industry is laying off workers, it's usually because there is something that is affecting all companies in the industry. I'd be worried and making sure that I was showcasing my worth and value to the organization in highly visible means. I'd encourage the team members I lead to do the same.

Q7 | When you learn about layoffs in your hotel, not necessarily in your area, how do you feel about your own role?

I think if this is happening, I would be brushing off my resume – clearly the hotel is in trouble and while it wouldn't change how I go about performing my job duties, I would also simultaneously do what is needed to take care of my career mobility and earnings.

Q8 | When you learn about layoffs in your department, how do you feel about your role?

Being a manager, I would expect to know about layoffs in the department before it became public knowledge and hope to even be a part of the decision-making process in reducing headcount. Working closely with the associates in a shift-lead capacity would provide valuable insight to leadership making these decisions. If I have no idea that this is happening, then I would most likely assume that I'm being cut and initiative the job hunt process immediately.

Q9 | Do you see yourself choosing to stay employed in the hospitality sector?

Absolutely, this is a perfect industry for me to build a career in. I'm lucky in that I have aligned my education and work experience well thus far, and I know that I want to stay in the hospitality sector and grow as a professional. I've had great experiences thus far and look forward to many, many more.

Q10 | What changes would you like to see that would make it more attractive to stay in the hospitality sector?

I would like a couple of things to be different to really create an amazing work environment. First, do more to create a culture where everyone is engaged and focused on serving guests and not just in receiving the quantitative benefits of the job (salary, discounted travel benefits, healthcare, etc.). Second, I would like to see more structure around leadership development and upward mobility. One thing I got used to in college was structure around attaining my goals. There should be more defined career pathways that include milestone jobs, training, education, etc. so that expectations can be set accordingly. For example, if it will take 4-5 years of experience to become a Rooms Division Director, it is important to communicate that as well as identify the steps you need to take to become eligible. Third, I would revisit how people are rewarded for performance. I think that there is a lot of opportunity to develop a framework that adjusts dynamically based on what some does and how well they do it. Fourth, and this is more for other employees than I, is to offer on-site childcare. Many of our employees have kids and childcare coverage is a source of major stress and discontent with this group. While not all employees would be able to take advantage of this benefit, having on-site childcare would be important for those that need it.

CONCLUSION

There were several consistent themes that manifested themselves across various participants. First, there appeared to be two primary classifications of motivators for employees: Those that were engaged and fulfilled by the prospect of serving guests in a hospitality situation and those that were motivated by the unique benefits of the industry (namely the travel benefits where employees can enjoy significantly reduced room rates throughout properties in a hotel brand's network).

For employees who reported that were motivated by serving guests, the fundamental reasons for their affection for this type of work were varied. Some interview participants described their enjoyment with the unpredictable nature of guest services and others reported that they could observe the results of their work immediately. Employees also often mentioned that while work itself was busy and intense, there was almost universal praise for it being the kind of work that stayed at work. Employees who participated in the interview clearly valued the opportunity to retain a balance between commitments at work and commitments outside of work.

Employees reporting the travel benefits as a primary motivator tended to be older and previously retired. These employees are less motivated by base pay or fringe benefits but want the ability to travel in retirement at reduced rates and are willing to take work where they receive this benefit. With the industry reporting challenges in finding qualified and interested workers, pursuing associates who are similarly positioned in their post-career status may prove to be a unique solution to staffing deficiencies.

The differences in areas of opportunity for the industry were noted between the two groups of employees as well. For employees who were motivated by the prospect of serving guests, the most common areas of opportunity were greater structure for career mobility within a company, greater investment in modernizing properties and additional focus on establishing an employee culture that is focused on providing excellent service. Additionally, many employees who fell into this category expressed concerns that their employers do not offer an accessible mechanism for submitting ideas to leadership on how the business can be improved. Employees in this category tended to have either experience or education related to the industry (and many times, they had both) leading to an observed need to express new ideas with the intended outcome of fixing problems, generating more revenue or getting noticed by leadership. The employees in this category also made note of team members who did not seem engaged with the mission of the hotel and were not interested, or effective, at providing guest services.

Employees who were primarily motivated by travel benefits did not include discussions on career mobility and had less of a focus on modernizing properties when asked about areas of opportunity for the industry. However, this group did note that they observed many disengaged workers on the job and that their departments often had an unsupportive and non-inclusive culture. This group of employees identified as older than other workers at the hotel and felt that they had less in common with their peers as a result.

Finally, both groups of employees did have individuals who believe that hotels would benefit from revisiting how employees are rewarded for their efforts. While specific ideas on how to achieve this were few, participants seem to believe that increased equity in the hotel and its business itself would further motivate employees to provide higher levels of guest services. Increased equity could manifest as a bonus or an alternative form of ownership, but the fundamental idea revolved around that to increase commitment to guest services required transitioning an employee away from simply being in a work-for-hire situation.

Interestingly enough, the literature review had identified that organizational commitment would be impacted with advance awareness of layoffs although this was not reflected by the participants of this study. According to participants, layoffs would – at best – dilute their organizational commitment and they report that in many cases it wouldn't even do that. There seemed to be an understanding among most participants that layoffs outside the hotel industry, in the hotel industry or at their hotel were all situations that were out of their ability to directly influence an outcome. It is possible that the difference in results can be explained by the fact that prior studies had been completed with a largely international audience while the participants of this study were all American citizens. There may be other factors contributing to the difference in how awareness of upcoming layoffs would impact organizational commitment, although those are not revealed in this study.

OPPORTUNITIES FOR FUTURE RESEARCH

There are multiple areas of interest with this study that can be expanded on with future research efforts. First, and foremost, would be the idea of exploring more extensively the notion that employees can be retained by an employer investing in an individual's professional development. Based on the results of this research, the impact on employee retention of creating a detailed career pathway that includes position milestones, required training or educational credentials, and acquired experiences would be a salient topic to explore. Nearly every employee mentioned this as a critical need, even those employees who were older and retired (but working to support their interest in traveling during retirement). Determining which specific elements of a career pathway impact parameters like job satisfaction and organizational, and the degree to which each element influences the identified parameters, is a critical area for a future research effort.

An additional area of research because of this study would be to further explore how representative the phenomenon of locating more workers in hotels among an already retired population. The notion of retired populations willing accept reduced hotel rates within a branded network in exchange for paid, part – time work was a repetitive thread across all three categories of properties studied suggested that this staffing strategy may already be in use by some hotel companies. Still this hiring strategy was not prevalent in the literature review indicating that it may be an untapped strategy. Understanding more about the psychological profile of this population and why it is willing to engage in such an exchange would be of great benefit for nearly any hotel company seeking qualified workers.

A third area of additional research involves a greater understanding of what factors within an organizational culture can strengthen or dilute an individual's commitment to an organization. A common thread among most of this study's participants was displeasure at observing employees who did not appear committed to providing guest services. Additional research should be undertaken to better understand what specific observable actions lead to these perspectives being formed and what impact the different factors have with strengthening or weakening one's organizational commitment. This study seemed to suggest that misalignment of values between employees on how to provide quality guest services could lead to significant dissonance and discord among a working unit. This is obviously an undesirable outcome for a hotel, but additional research would be needed to understand this phenomenon more comprehensively.

REFERENCES

Dai, Y., Zhuang, W., & Huan, T. C. (2019). Engage or quit? The moderating role of abusive supervision between resilience, intention to leave and work engagement. *Tourism Management*, *70*, 69–77. doi:10.1016/j.tourman.2018.07.014

Grissemann, U., Plank, A., & Brunner-Sperdin, A. (2013). Enhancing business performance of hotels: The role of innovation and customer orientation. *International Journal of Hospitality Management*, *33*(1), 347–356. doi:10.1016/j.ijhm.2012.10.005

Guan, X., Yeh, S. S., Chiang, T. Y., & Huan, T. C. (2020). Does organizational inducement foster work engagement in hospitality industry? Perspectives from a moderated mediation model. *Journal of Hospitality and Tourism Management*, *43*, 259–268. doi:10.1016/j.jhtm.2020.04.010

Hom, P. W., Tsui, A. S., Wu, J. B., Lee, T. W., Zhang, A. Y., Fu, P. P., & Li, L. (2009). Explaining employment relationships with social exchange and job embeddedness. *The Journal of Applied Psychology*, *94*(2), 277–297. doi:10.1037/a0013453 PMID:19271791

Jia, L., Shaw, J. D., Tsui, A. S., & Park, T.-Y. (2014). A social-structural perspective on employee organization relationships and team creativity. *Academy of Management Journal*, *57*(3), 869–891. doi:10.5465/amj.2011.0147

Kahn, W. A. (1990). Psychological conditions of personal engagement and disengagement at work. *Academy of Management Journal*, *33*(4), 692–724. doi:10.2307/256287

Karatepe, O. M., Beirami, E., Bouzari, M., & Safavi, H. P. (2014). Does work engagement mediate the effects of challenge stressors on job outcomes? Evidence from the hotel industry. *International Journal of Hospitality Management*, *36*, 14–22. doi:10.1016/j.ijhm.2013.08.003

Li, Y., & Huang, S. (2017). Hospitality service climate, employee service orientation, career aspiration and performance: A moderated mediation model. *International Journal of Hospitality Management*, *67*, 24–32. doi:10.1016/j.ijhm.2017.07.012

Madera, J. M., Dawson, M., Guchait, P., & Belarmino, A. M. (2017). Strategic human resources management research in hospitality and tourism. *International Journal of Contemporary Hospitality Management*, *29*(1), 48–67. doi:10.1108/IJCHM-02-2016-0051

Moncarz, E., Zhao, J., & Kay, C. (2009). An exploratory study of US lodging properties' organizational practices on employee turnover and retention. *International Journal of Contemporary Hospitality Management*, *21*(4), 437–458. doi:10.1108/09596110910955695

Page, S. J., Bentley, T., Teo, S., & Ladkin, A. (2018). The dark side of high performance human resource practices in the visitor economy. *International Journal of Hospitality Management*, *74*, 122–129. doi:10.1016/j.ijhm.2018.02.016

Schaufeli, W. B., Salanova, M., Gonzalez-Roma, V., & Bakker, A. B. (2002). Burnout and engagement in university students. *Journal of Cross-Cultural Psychology*, *33*(5), 464–481. doi:10.1177/0022022102033005003

Yao, T., Qiu, Q., & Wei, Y. (2019). Retaining hotel employees as internal customers: Effect of organizational commitment on attitudinal and behavioral loyalty of employees. *International Journal of Hospitality Management*, *76*, 1–8. doi:10.1016/j.ijhm.2018.03.018

Chapter 7
Adapting a Theoretical Framework to Reduce Employee Turnover Within a Hotel Front Desk Workplace

ABSTRACT

This narrative describes the background, methodology, and results of a recreated study from 2020 which explored dimensions of an employee's trust both with supervisors and one's coworkers in the hospitality industry in South Korea. The study was recreated in 2023 using hotel employees in the United States. Both an employee's trust in their supervisor and in their co-workers were measured by four distinct factors encompassing reliability, considerateness, confidence, and integrity. Additionally, emotional exhaustion was measured using four dimensions while depersonalization was measured using three factors. The 2023 conclusions mirrored those of 2020, with one notable exception: Hypothesis 4, which posited that trust in co-worker support has a negative influence on emotional exhaustion. This variance may be a result of cultural differences or a larger sample in the 2023 study. Study limitations, possible practical application of the findings, and opportunities for additional study are identified at the conclusion of the narrative.

DOI: 10.4018/978-1-6684-2528-2.ch007

INTRODUCTION

The literature review revealed that there are many diverse efforts to explore the factors that influence employee's turnover in a hotel environment. While there are many recent studies focused on this situation, many of these are conducted in an international environment. While these provide great exposure and insight into the multi-faceted phenomenon that drives employee turnover in a hotel environment, there is a need to calibrate for cultural differences between different countries and determine what aspects remain the same and which could be different.

Across multiple studies, researchers agree that an employee's level of trust to receive adequate support from both supervisors and co-workers is a key factor in reducing a decision to seek new employment. Support can be defined as an employee's perception that supervisors and peers will attempt to provide effective comfort and assistance for addressing work-related challenges. Levels and effectiveness of support have been determined to be inversely proportional to an employee's desire to voluntarily separate from an organization.

Han, Quan, Al-Ansi, Chung, Ngah, Ariza-Montes and Vega-Munoz's study of 2020 identified that literature has not previously brought the concept of burnout and its constituents into the framework bridging the association between trust-in-support factors and employee turnover. Their study aimed to fill this gap in literature by demonstrating the importance of trust in support and its role in reducing the burnout phenomenon among hotel employees and explaining their voluntary turnover decision formation in a satisfactory manner. Their research developed a theoretical framework encompassing trust in support groups (supervisor and co-worker) while also defining the factors that comprise the phenomenon of burnout (emotional exhaustion, depersonalization, and reduced personal accomplishment) while clearly illustrating how hotel employee turnover occurs by measuring the strength of associations between trust-in-support dimensions and employee burnout constituents.

The original study was conducted with employees at hotels located in various metropolitan cities in South Korea. As a part of this study, this effort has been recreated with hotel front desk employees located within the continental United States as well as compare results from both studies and determine if differences exist between cultural environments.

BACKGROUND

The idea of quality work being provided in a service-based environment such as the hospitality industry being produced as a byproduct of trust is one that has been explored in both the employee and supervisor relationship (Cheng & O-Yang, 2018; Tsui, Pearce, Porter, & Tripoli, 2002) and in the relationship among co-workers (Born, Akkerman & Thommes, 2016). Trust has been defined as the confidence an individual maintains in the integrity of another person, object, brand or company (Born et. al., 2016). It has been established that in order for companies to provide its customers with services aligned with established prices, there has to be a certain degree of trust among supervisors, co-workers and with leadership of an organization (DeConinck, 2010; Tsui et. al., 2002; Susskind, Kacmar & Borchgrevink, 2003). As such, both in the original study, as well as the newly conducted study, embraced the concept of trust as core dimensional perspectives that were studied independently.

Trust is reviewed in to distinct methods. First, a predictive relationship of trust can be measured in the degree of information and social exchange which is occurring between supervisors and employees (Limpanitgul, Robson, Gould-Williams & Lertthaitrakul, 2013; Susskind et. al., 2003). The intellectual, emotional and social support that an employee perceives to receive from his or her supervisor is a primary component (from the employee's perspective) that establishes the strength (or perception of strength) for this relationship (Born et. al. 2016, DeConinck et. al., 2010; Tsui et. al 2002; Rousseau, Salek, Aubé, & Morin, 2009). Additional studies identified in the literature have demonstrate that when a population maintains a high level of trust in key relationships (such as the one between supervisor and employee or between co-workers), the level of institutional citizenship, defined as one's willingness to complete work, is able to offset some of the negative factors associated with a workplace environment (De Clercq, Azeem, Haq, & Bouckenooghe, 2020). These factors can include distress of a psychological nature, an employee burning out in their role, overall satisfaction one holds with their role, an individual's mental health or well-being, and one's overall commitment to an employer(Chen 7 Shaffer, 2017; Karatepe & Olugbade, 2017). Limpantigul et al (2013) conducted a study in the airline industry which researched the notion that an employee's job attitude (which encompasses one's individual perspective of accomplishment and emotional fulfillment) can be significantly increased when there are high levels of trust among co-workers as well as high levels of trust in one's supervisor. This was discovered to be true even in environments where customer interactions were less than positive and engaging. When this information is aligned with the notion that trust-based relationships can dilute, or even reduce, the severity of burnout an employee may feel (De Clercq et. al., 2020), it helps to establish evidence of a potential linkage between reducing burnout and employee turnover via trust-based relationships.

Burnout is defined as an emotional and psychological level of exhaustion that results from repeated and sustained working environments that are perceived and understood by an employee to be demanding, challenging and unrelenting (Shih, Jiang, Klein & Wang, 2013; Hakanen, Peeters, & Schaufeli, 2018). So and so (16) have established that emotional exhaustion, depersonalization of self in one's role and reduced personal accomplishment are core, critical dimensions of employee burnout (Shih et. al., 2013, Maslach, Schaufeli & Leiter, 2001; Karatepe & Uludag, 2008). Emotional exhaustion occurs when an individual employee or collective team reflect feelings and display behaviors consistent with an' emotionally drained feeling resulting from multiple interactions of a negative or challenging nature with people [Yu, Ariza-Montes, Hernández-Perlines, Vega-Muñoz & Han, 2020; Leiter & Meechan, 1986). The notion of depersonalization reflects diluted or indifferent emotional engagements with others where an individual is perceived to be treated in a manner that ignores or discounts his or her individual characteristics (Karatepe & Uludag, 2008). According to Yu et. al. (2020), reduced personal accomplishment is defined as an individual's perception that he or she is not achieving satisfactory resolution on formally or informally expressed goals within the framework of one's working environment.

Burnout is established to occur more frequently in a service-based industry such as hospitality when compared to other working industries where more tangible work outcomes are defined (Yu et. al., 2020; Tsui et al., 2002; Karatepe & Uludag, 2008; Sirgy, 2019). Additional, recent research has established that front-line hospitality workers can experience significant psychological and mental stress when guest interactions increase, when complaints about provided services (one's "work") are received and when shift – based employee rotations are perceived as excessive or frequent (Yu et. al., 2020; Kim, Kim & Hwang, 2015; Sirgy 2019). Furthermore, the impact of employee burnout on a company's success has been identified through prior research. Shih et al. (2013) explored how work exhaustion, depersonalization and reduced levels of perceived accomplishment are positively correlated with individual burnout, poor quality of work and employee turnover. Kim et al. (2015)

researched how the factors of perceived job stress influenced individual and team behaviors on the job, indicating that qualities of provided service are positively correlated with increases in job stresses. Yu et. al. (2020) demonstrated that job satisfaction is most significantly determined by one's level of burnout concluding that mitigating such burnout can provide positive, measurable results as it relates to quality of services provided.

TESTED CONCEPTUAL MODEL

The conceptual model developed by Han, Quan, Al-Ansi, Chung, Ngah, Ariza-Montes & Vega-Muñoz (2020) is shown in figure 1. As it is identical to the model showcased in the original study, it continues to link trust associated with support provided by a supervisor, and trust associated with support provided by a co-worker. In addition, the model aligns an employee's emotional exhaustion, depersonalization and reduced personal accomplishment as direct predictors of hotel employee turnover. The same nine hypothesis tested in the original study will be recreated for the new sampling of domestic United States hotel front desk employees:

Figure 1. Proposed model and research hypothesis

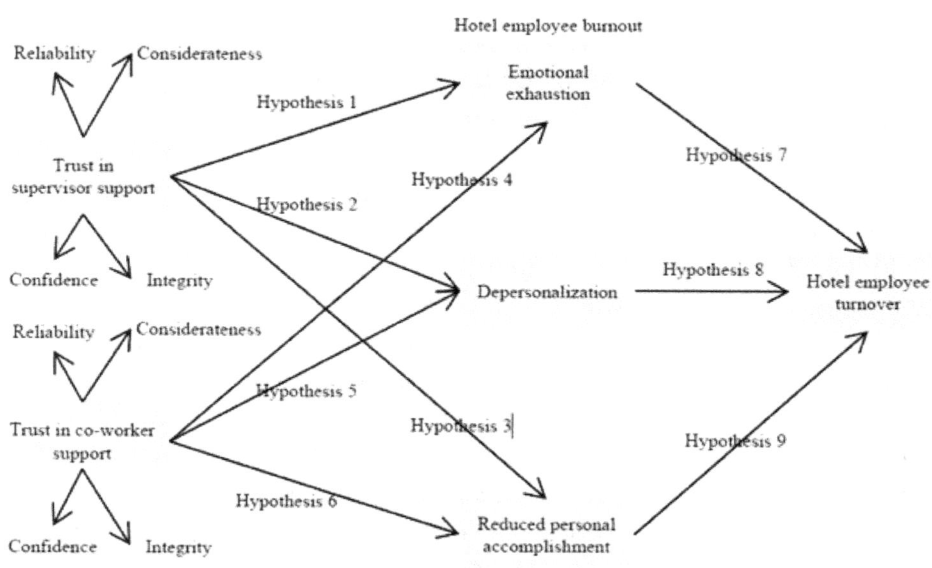

Hypothesis 1 (H1). Trust in supervisor support has a negative influence on emotional exhaustion.
Hypothesis 2 (H2). Trust in supervisor support has a negative influence on depersonalization.
Hypothesis 3 (H3). Trust in supervisor support has a negative influence on reduced personal accomplishment.
Hypothesis 4 (H4). Trust in co-worker support has a negative influence on emotional exhaustion.
Hypothesis 5 (H5). Trust in co-worker support has a negative influence on depersonalization.
Hypothesis 6 (H6). Trust in co-worker support has a negative influence on reduced personal accomplishment.
Hypothesis 7 (H7). Emotional exhaustion has a positive influence on hotel employee turnover.
Hypothesis 8 (H8). Depersonalization has a positive influence on hotel employee turnover.
Hypothesis 9 (H9). Reduced personal accomplishment has a positive influence on hotel employee turnover.

RESEARCH METHODOLOGY

The original study by Han et. al. (2020) was intended to quantify responses of survey respondents using a cross-sectional survey questionnaire featuring a quantitative approach. In general, respondents were asked to evaluate scenarios presented by questions utilizing a 7-point scale ranging from a "1" indicating "strongly disagree" to a "7" indicating "strongly agree." The survey questions are as follows:

Trust in Supervisor Support

1. I can rely on my supervisor. *(reliability)*
2. My supervisor is considerate of subordinate's feelings. *(considerateness)*
3. Supervisors and subordinates have confidence in one another. *(confidence)*
4. My supervisor seems willing to listen to my problems. *(integrity)*

Trust in Co-Worker Support

1. I can rely on those I work with in this group. *(reliability)*
2. We are usually considerate of one another's feelings in this work group. *(considerateness)*
3. We have confidence in one another in this group. *(confidence)*
4. Members of my work group show a great deal of integrity. *(integrity)*

Emotional Exhaustion

1. I feel emotionally drained from my work.
2. I feel used up at the end of the workday.
3. I feel fatigued when I get up in the morning and have to face another day on the job.
4. I feel burned out from my work.

Depersonalization

1. I feel I treat some customers as if they were impersonal objects.
2. I have become more callous towards people since I took this job.
3. I worry that this job is hardening me emotionally.

Reduced Personal Accomplishment

1. I feel very energetic. *
2. I feel exhilarated after working closely with my customers. *
3. I have accomplished many worthwhile things in this job. *

Hotel Employee Turnover

1. It is likely that I will actively look for a new job next year.
2. I often think about quitting.

Note. All measurement items were evaluated from Strongly disagree (1) to Strongly agree (7).
* = Reverse coded

An employee's trust in their supervisor providing support was measured by 4 distinct factors encompassing reliability, considerateness, confidence and integrity. An employee's trust in their co-workers providing support was measured by the same 4 factors previously identified. Emotional exhaustion was measured using four dimensions while depersonalization was measured using three factors. As was the case in the original study, reduced personal accomplishment was measured using three reverse coded factors. Finally, two factors were used to measure hotel employee turnover.

As the original study revised its original draft survey instrument after initial testing and validation with academic and industry experts, no additional modifications or validation were integrated into this iteration of the study.

DATA COLLECTION AND DESCRIPTIVE STATISTICS FOR SAMPLE

To maintain consistency with the original study, data was collected in this original iteration using the same method: a web-based survey. After the researcher gained approval from various hotel leadership about the study, the researcher generated and delivered a survey link via email or mobile device to employees at 18 different hotels located in the United States, with the specific target sample residing within Arizona, Nevada, New Mexico, Colorado, and Utah. As was the case with the original survey, respondents were first presented with instructions to carefully complete the survey instrument.

To be selected, respondents had to be currently working at a front desk in the hotel industry and they needed to be working at a property that could be classified as a budget hotel with few amenities or services, a mid-range hotel (limited or full service) or a high-end hotel or resort. Smaller specialty or boutique properties such as bed and breakfast establishments were not included in the sampling frame. This procedure offered a potential sample of 800 respondents. Through this procedure, the researcher obtained a total of 437 usable responses and these records were retained for data analysis.

Of 437 participants, 59.27% (n=259) of the respondents indicated they were female while 40.73% (n=178) of the respondents indicated that they were male. In reporting marital status, 54.7% reported being single and 45.3% reported being married. In terms of educational achievement, 18.4% reported that they had earned a four-year degree from a university, 36.1% had earned a two year degree from a community college, 4.4% earning a graduate degree (or higher) while 41.1% had earned a high school diploma or equivalent. A majority of respondents reported that their employment status was as full-time workers (77.2%) with the remaining 22.8% identifying as part-time workers. Regarding years of service, 70.2% of respondents indicated less than two years of service with their current employer. This was followed by 13.4% reporting between 2-5 years of service, 11.3% between 6-10 years and 5.1% reporting greater than 10 years of service. For the last demographic variable, respondents reported annual income as follows: About 67.3% reported their income between $25,000 and $39,999. This was followed by 21.9% reporting income of $24,999 or less, 6.7% between $40,000 and $54,999 and 3.3% reporting between $55,000 and $69,999 with .8% reporting annual income in excess of $70,000.

While similar demographic results are observed in this revised study, it is important to note that there are differences among some of these metrics. A comparison in Figure 2 between the original demographics (observed from a South Korean sample) and the updated demographics (from the current sample of several western United States) reveals the following similarities and differences:

Table 1. Demographics comparing the original sample (2020) to the retested sample (2023)

Metric	South Korea	United States
n	280	437
Female	54.60%	59.27%
Male	45.40%	40.73%
Education, High School or less	1.10%	41.10%
Education, 2 Year Degree	23.30%	36.10%
Education, 4 Year Degree	62.00%	18.40%
Education, Graduate Degree	13.60%	4.40%
Status, Full Time	70.70%	77.20%
Status, Part Time	28.90%	22.80%
Tenure, Less Than 2 Years	13.20%	70.20%
Tenure, 2-5 Years	49.6%	13.40%
Tenure, 6-10 years	6.80%	11.30%
Tenure, Greater than 10 years	30.40%	5.10%
Income, Less than $24,999	28.90%	21.90%

continues on following page

Table 1. Continued

Metric	South Korea	United States
Income, \$25,000 - \$39,999	33.60%	67.30%
Income, \$40,000 - \$54,000	27.90%	6.70%
Income, \$55,000 - \$69,999	7.90%	3.30%
Income, Greater than \$70,000	1.80%	0.80%

There are some overall similarities in between the two samples in terms of gender, status and income with significant differences occurring in tenure and education. Most notably, the revised sample in the United States is much newer to the profession than the South Korean sample was and there is – in general – much less formal education reported among the sample in the United States than their counterparts in the original South Korean sample.

RESULTS | CONFIRMATORY FACTOR ANALYSIS (CFA) AND MEASUREMENT MODEL ASSESSMENT

Identical to the original study, SPSS 20 was the tool utilized to complete the descriptive statistical analysis for the collected data. For the confirmatory and hypothesis testing of the new study, the AMOS 20 add-on module for SPSS was utilized, just as it was with the original test. Prior to any analysis occurring, an initial screening process of data was established to determine the normal status of the distribution, any outliers that may be present and other identified missing items.

To ascertain whether the data had a normal distribution or a skew (positive or negative), goodness-of-fit statistics were applied. Goodness-of-fit refers to a statistical test that determines how well the data obtained from the sample aligns with the properties of a normal distribution, which increases the likelihood that it will fit a distribution from a population. Goodness-of-fit statistics for the model were calculated identical to how they were in the original student producing the following results for the new study:

- $X^2 = 411.2642$
- $df = 414$
- $p < 0.001$
- $x^2/df = 1.98$
- Root Mean Square Error of Approximation (RMSEA) = 0.052

- Comparative Fit Index (CFI) = 0.962
- Incremental Fit Index (IFI) = 0.967
- Tucker Lewis Index (TLI) = 0.944

As was the case with the original study, the goodness-of-fit analysis revealed that the statistics of the model were adequate to good, and the new study was slightly better than the original. Table 1 displays the results of the confirmatory factor analysis completed with the 2023 data set:

Table 2. Results of the confirmatory factor analysis (2023 study)

	(1)	(2)	(3)	(4)	(5)	(6)	Mean (Std. Dev.)	CR	AVE
(1) TISS	1.000	-	-	-	-	-	5.211 (1.273)	0.912	0.561
(2) TICWS	0.428 (0.239)	1.000	-	-	-	-	4.937 (1.002)	0.751	0.822
(3) EE	-0.417 (0.152)	-0.337 (0.023)	1.000	-	-	-	5.540 (1.946)	0.849	0.518
(4) DE	-0.144 (0.013)	-0.175 (0.032)	0.617 (0.632)	1.000	-	-	2.391 (0.412)	0.903	0.787
(5) RPA	0.612 (0.045)	0.411 (0.107)	-0.137 (0.054)	-0.273 (0.065)	1.000	-	4.982 (1.294)	0.750	0.785
(6) HET	-0.735 (0.297)	-0.263 (0.044)	0.648 (0.369)	0.571 (0.238)	-0.328 (0.117)	1.000	6.019 (1.107)	0.698	0.861

Notes: For factor columns 1-6, the first number in each cell is the correlation between constructs. The bottom number is the squared correlation. TISS = Trust in Supervisor Support, TICWS = Trust in Co-Worker Support, EE = Emotional Exhaustion, DE = Depersonalization, RPA = Reduced personal accomplishment, HET= Hotel Employee Turnover, CR = Composite reliability, AVE = Average variance extracted.

Composite reliability (CR) is a method to measure scale reliability overall and preferred pairing with confirmatory factor analysis. Comparatively, the 2020 study and the 2023 study provided similar results with all values in the 2023 exceeding the minimum required value of 0.7 (Han et. al., 2020). In addition, the average variance extracted (AVE) would need to have a value of at least, or greater than, 0.5 to be valid. All six factors exceeded this in the 2023, as they did in the 2020 study. Finally, these values were all greater than the between-variable correlations (squared) in the 2023 study (see Table 1) as well as in the 2020 study. This result confirms that the validities of the convergent and discriminant were not an issue of either study.

EQUATION MODELING AND EVALUATION OF PROPOSED FRAMEWORK

To prepare for an evaluation of the eight hypotheses, an identical structural equation model to the 2020 study was created for the 2023 study. It was run using a maximum likelihood estimation approach. This model fulfills the requirements of the goodness-of-fit statistics with the following parameters being calculated:

- $X^2 = 427.9124$
- df = 398
- $p < 0.001$
- $x^2/df = 2.378$
- Root Mean Square Error of Approximation (RMSEA) = 0.079
- Comparative Fit Index (CFI) = 0.981
- Incremental Fit Index (IFI) = 0.947
- Tucker Lewis Index (TLI) = 0.902

In an evaluation of the anticipation ability revealed by the analysis, the variance in hotel employee turnover was 57.13% explained by the conceptual framework. In addition, in the 2023 study the re-tested conceptual framework had 31.56% of the variance for emotional exhaustion, 26.15% of the variance for depersonalization and 19.11% of the variance for personal accomplishment explained by the model's trust-in-support factors and burnout dimensions.

The Beta (β) values and t-values associated with each of the nine hypothesis were realized as follows:

Hypothesis 1 (H1). Trust in supervisor support has a negative influence on emotional exhaustion.
β: -0.527 *t*-value: -5.363 $p < 0.01$

Hypothesis 2 (H2). Trust in supervisor support has a negative influence on depersonalization.
β: -0.453 *t*-value: -3.974 $p < 0.01$

Hypothesis 3 (H3). *Trust in supervisor support has a negative influence on reduced personal* accomplishment.
β: -0.325 *t*-value: -4.417 $p < 0.01$

Hypothesis 4 (H4). Trust in co-worker support has a negative influence on emotional exhaustion.
β: -0.453 *t*-value: -3.974 $p < 0.01$

Hypothesis 5 (H5). Trust in co-worker support has a negative influence on depersonalization.
β: +0.013 *t*-value: +0.032 $p > 0.05$

Hypothesis 6 (H6). *Trust in co-worker support has a negative influence on reduced personal* accomplishment.
β: -0.373 *t*-value: -4.211 $p < 0.01$

Hypothesis 7 (H7). Emotional exhaustion has a positive influence on hotel employee turnover.
β: +0.606 *t*-value: +2.184 $p < 0.01$

Hypothesis 8 (H8). Depersonalization has a positive influence on hotel employee turnover.
β: +0.149 *t*-value: +3.001 $p > 0.05$

Hypothesis 9 (H9). Reduced personal accomplishment has a positive influence on hotel employee turnover.
β: +3.649 *t*-value: +3.089 $p < 0.01$

As was discovered in the 2020 study, the 2023 study observed that trust in supervisor support had both a significant and negative influence on emotional exhaustion (β: -0.527, *t*-value: -5.363, $p < 0.01$), depersonalization (β: -0.453, t-value: -3.974, $p < 0.01$), and reduced personal accomplishment (β: -0.325, *t*-value: -4.417, $p < 0.01$). Ultimately this indicates that as in the 2020 study, the 2023 study also supported Hypotheses 1, 2 and 3.

The hypothesized effect of trust in co-worker support on factors affecting burnout (H4, H5, and H6) was also tested in both studies. Just as in the 2020 study, the 2023 study showed that trust in co-worker support has a significant and negative influence on reduced personal accomplishment (β: -0.373, t-value: -4.211, $p < 0.01$). Also similar, co-worker influence on depersonalization (β: +0.013, t-value: +0.032, $p > 0.05$) was found to not be significant. In a departure from the 2020 study's results, though, co-worker influence on emotional exhaustion (β: -0.453, t-value: -3.974, $p < 0.01$) was found to be significant. Hypotheses 4, not supported in the 2020 study, was supported in the 2023 study. Hypothesis 6 was supported in both studies. Hypothesis 5 was not supported in either study.

Hypothesis 7, 8 and 9 tested the factors of burnout on turnover. The assessed findings in both the 2020 and 2023 studies revealed that emotional exhaustion (β: +0.606, t-value: +2.184, $p < 0.01$) and reduced personal accomplishment (β: +3.649, t-value: +3.089, $p < 0.01$) both exerted a significant and positive effect on employee turnover. Once again, both the 2020 and 2023 studies revealed that depersonalization (β: +0.149, t-value: +3.001, $p > 0.05$) did not have a significant impact on hotel employee turnover. As a result, Hypothesis 7 and Hypothesis 9 were supported in both the 2020 and 2023 studies while Hypothesis 8 was not supported in either study.

As was the case with the 2020 study, a final analysis was undertaken that assessed an indirect effect of research variables to identify indirect associations among study constructs. As before, the 2023 study produced the following goodness-of-fit statistical parameters for this structural model:

- $X^2 = 427.9124$
- df = 398
- $p < 0.001$
- $x^2/df = 2.378$
- Root Mean Square Error of Approximation (RMSEA) = 0.079
- Comparative Fit Index (CFI) = 0.981
- Incremental Fit Index (IFI) = 0.947
- Tucker Lewis Index (TLI) = 0.902

The results of total impact on hotel employee turnover for each factor are as follows:

- β emotional exhaustion = 0.511; $p < 0.01$
- β trust in supervisor support = -0.472; $p < 0.01$
- β reduced personal accomplishment = 0.189; $p < 0.01$
- β trust in co-worker support = 0.021; $p < 0.01$
- β depersonalization = 0.014; $p > 0.05$

DISCUSSION AND IMPLICATIONS

This study was intended to repeat the work of the 2020 study conducted by Han et. al. in further testing an empirical effort to develop a robust conceptual framework that explains hotel employee turnover. The main purpose of doing this additional research is to validate the effectiveness of the model by assessing the results from conducting the same study in a completely different geographic market. The 2023 study was conducted using front-desk hotel employees located in the western United States. The original 2020 study was conducted in South Korea.

In general, the hypothesized relationships between trust in supervisor support, trust in co-worker support, emotional exhaustion, depersonalization and reduced personal accomplishment in the workplace were further explored and found to be generally supported. As with the 2020 study, the 2023 study also validated that the conceptual framework included a sufficient level of prediction power, satisfying a significant threshold for explaining total variance in employee turnover.

One area of difference between the 2020 and 2023 studies was with Hypothesis 4, which explored if there was an impact by trust in co-workers on emotional exhaustion. The results of the 2020 study did not support Hypothesis 4 while the results of the 2023 study did. This may be a result multiple factors including cultural differences or a larger sample in the 2023 study. The 2023 study supporting Hypothesis 4 only strengthens the conclusions of the 2020 study that to reduce turnover among a hotel's employes, leadership should focus on establishing an engaging working environment that enhances trust among both supervisors and co-workers and establishing a working environment where employees have confidence in their supervisors and feel engaged with their co-workers.

The total effect of emotional exhaustion was found to maintain the greatest impact on hotel employee turnover in the 2023 study as well as in the 2020 study. Both studies also recognized that trust in supervisor support had a negative and significant impact on hotel employee turnover while reduced personal accomplishment had a positive and significant impact on hotel employee turnover. Neither the 2020 study or the 2023 study discovered a significant effect on hotel employee turnover as a result of depersonalization. The 2023 study determined that trust in co-worker support had a negative and significant impact on hotel employee turnover, albeit a much weaker one than the other factors. The 2020 study did not determine that trust in co-worker support had a significant impact on hotel employee turnover.

As a validation for the 2020 study, the 2023 study continued to demonstrate that burnout factors such as emotional exhaustion and reduced personal accomplishment will dilute or eliminate trust in supervisor support on employee turnover in a significant way. Employee turnover is maximized when employees feel emotionally exhausted and/or that they are experiencing reduced personal accomplishment in the workplace. While this dynamic is not unique to the hotel industry (Han et. al., 2020), the two studies serve to validate the findings as significant within the hotel industry across two distinct cultural environments.

How this ultimately manifests as practical solutions can reflect the individual interests, experiences and priorities of an individual leader or that of the entire organization. However, it is clear that to reduce hotel employee turnover, trust must be maintained among workers and – most importantly – between employees and their supervisors. Investing in leadership's trust-building skills to establish and maintain engaging and enriching personal relationships among managers and supervisors would seem to be a recommended effort based on the results of both the 2020 and the 2023 study.

LIMITATIONS

As the 2023 study maintained the same sampling, data collection and analysis methodologies, many of the limitations associated with the original study continue to be relevant with the current study. In 2020, the proposed theoretical model was tested using a sample of hotel employees in South Korea. In 2023, the proposed theoretical model was tested using a sample of hotel employees who exclusively work at the front desk at a hotel property at one of four states in the Western United States. The limitation in the 2020 study was that the results of one culture could not be used to represent the dynamics of the industry on a global scale. While the 2023 study now adds insight on how the proposed theoretical model behaves in a new environment, there are only two different cultures which have been tested. Additional research is required to continue to explore similarities and differences among different locations defined by political boundaries, geography, and ethnic cultural values.

Likewise, the original limitation of the 2020 study in focusing exclusively on trust-in-support factors and burnout dimensions to explain hotel employee turnover still exists. As noted in the original study, additional variables such as job satisfaction, commitment, rewards, well being and even workplace aesthetics like green designs could factor into employee turnover yet were not studied in the original study. As the 2023 study had the objective of validation as a primary goal, it was important to repeat the methodologies of sampling, data collection and analysis. As such, this limitation continues to exist in the 2023 study.

CONCLUSION

The vast shortages of employees willing to work in the hospitality industry following the onset of the COVID-19 pandemic were significant and unprecedented. While many maintain a sense of what factors are significant in an employee's decision to voluntarily separate from his or he job, the empirical evidence presented in the 2020 study and now the 2023 validation study reinforce how critical an effective relationship between an employee and her supervisor truly is. With nearly identical results emerging from two distinct cultures being studied, there can be little doubt that trust in one's supervisor as well as trust in one's co-workers can reduce the loss of talent from a hotel operation. Although operational shutdowns were common at the time of the original study, the 2023 study is conducted in an environment where the hospitality industry has recovered nearly all of the jobs lost to the pandemic's arrival and the ensuing decisions to shut down industries in an attempt to mitigate the viral transmission across the United States. There is renewed interest in travel and lodging options three years after the start of the pandemic, and hotels are prospering as a result.

Following on the conclusion identified in the original study, hotel operators and owners should invest in leadership training among their people leaders to equip this group of employees with tools, skills and knowledge on how to create an effective and high-performing culture that reduces voluntary separation. Ensuring that trust is established and maintained, as well as engineering opportunities for employees to secure and acknowledge personal achievements in their work roles is critical to reducing turnover. Through the two studies' efforts to empirically demonstrate the significant and decisive roles of trust-in-support frameworks, there is additional insight into how to retain talent in a labor pool of limited availability.

REFERENCES

Born, M., Akkerman, A., & Thommes, K. (2016). Peer influence on protest participation: Communication and trust between co-workers as inhibitors or facilitators of mobilization. *Social Science Research*, *56*, 58–72. doi:10.1016/j.ssresearch.2015.11.003 PMID:26857172

Chen, Y. P., & Shaffer, M. A. (2017). The influences of perceived organizational support and motivation on self-initiated expatriates' organizational and community embeddedness. *Journal of Business Research*, *52*, 197–208.

Cheng, J. C., & O-Yang, Y. (2018). Hotel employee job crafting, burnout, and satisfaction: The moderating role of perceived organizational support. *International Journal of Hospitality Management*, *72*, 78–85. doi:10.1016/j.ijhm.2018.01.005

De Clercq, D., Azeem, M. U., Haq, I. U., & Bouckenooghe, D. (2020). The stress-reducing effect of coworker support on turnover intentions: Moderation by political ineptness and despotic leadership. *Journal of Business Research*, *111*, 12–24. doi:10.1016/j.jbusres.2020.01.064

DeConinck, J. B. (2010). The effect of organizational justice, perceived organizational support, and perceived supervisor support on marketing employees' level of trust. *Journal of Business Research*, *63*(12), 1349–1355. doi:10.1016/j.jbusres.2010.01.003

Ferrin, D. L., & Dirks, K. T. (2002). Trust in leadership: Meta-analytic findings and implications for research and practice. *The Journal of Applied Psychology*, *87*(4), 611–628. doi:10.1037/0021-9010.87.4.611 PMID:12184567

Hakanen, J. J., Peeters, M. C., & Schaufeli, W. B. (2018). Different types of employee well-being across time and their relationships with job crafting. *Journal of Occupational Health Psychology*, *23*(2), 289–301. doi:10.1037/ocp0000081 PMID:28191997

Han, H., Wei, Q., Al-Ansi, A., Chung, H., Ngah, A. H., Ariza-Montes, A., & Vega-Muñoz, A. (2020). A theoretical framework development for hotel employee turnover: Linking trust in supports, emotional exhaustion, depersonalization, and reduced personal accomplishment at workplace. *Sustainability (Basel)*, *12*(8065), 1–13. doi:10.3390u12198065

Karatepe, O. M., & Olugbade, O. A. (2017). The effects of work social support and career adaptability on career satisfaction and turnover intentions. *Journal of Management & Organization*, *23*(3), 337–355. doi:10.1017/jmo.2016.12

Karatepe, O. M., & Uludag, O. (2008). Role stress, burnout and their effects on frontline hotel employees' job performance: Evidence from Northern Cyprus. *International Journal of Tourism Research*, *10*(2), 111–126. doi:10.1002/jtr.645

Kim, S. S., Kim, J., & Hwang, J. (2015). The effects of mentoring on role stress, job attitude, and turnover intention in the hotel industry. *International Journal of Hospitality Management*, *48*, 68–82. doi:10.1016/j.ijhm.2015.04.006

Leiter, M. P., & Meechan, K. A. (1986). Role Structure and Burnout in the Field of Human Services. *The Journal of Applied Behavioral Science*, *22*(1), 47–52. doi:10.1177/002188638602200107 PMID:10276302

Limpanitgul, T., Robson, M. J., Gould-Williams, J., & Lertthaitrakul, W. (2013). Effects of co-worker support and customer cooperation on service employee attitudes and behaviour: Empirical evidence from the airline industry. *Journal of Hospitality and Tourism Management*, *20*, 23–33. doi:10.1016/j.jhtm.2013.05.004

Maslach, C., Schaufeli, W. B., & Leiter, M. P. (2001). Job Burnout. *Annual Review of Psychology*, *52*(1), 397–422. doi:10.1146/annurev.psych.52.1.397 PMID:11148311

Rousseau, V., Salek, S., Aubé, C., & Morin, E. M. (2009). Distributive justice, procedural justice, and psychological distress: The moderating effect of coworker support and work autonomy. *Journal of Occupational Health Psychology*, *14*(3), 305–317. doi:10.1037/a0015747 PMID:19586224

Shih, S. P., Jiang, J. J., Klein, G., & Wang, E. (2013). Job burnout of the information technology worker: Work exhaustion, depersonalization, and personal accomplishment. *Information & Management*, *50*(7), 582–589. doi:10.1016/j.im.2013.08.003

Sirgy, J. M. (2019). Promoting quality-of-life and well-being research in hospitality and tourism. *Journal of Travel & Tourism Marketing*, *36*(1), 1–13. doi:10.1080/10548408.2018.1526757

Susskind, A. M., Michele Kacmar, K., & Borchgrevink, C. P. (2003). Customer service providers' attitudes relating to customer service and customer satisfaction in the customer-server exchange. *The Journal of Applied Psychology*, *88*(1), 179–187. doi:10.1037/0021-9010.88.1.179 PMID:12675405

Tsui, A. S., Pearce, J. L., Porter, L. W., & Tripoli, A. M. (1997). Alternative approaches to the employee-organization relationship: Does investment in employees pay off? *Academy of Management Journal*, *40*(5), 1089–1121. doi:10.2307/256928

Yu, J., Ariza-Montes, A., Hernández-Perlines, F., Vega-Muñoz, A., & Han, H. (2020). Hotels' eco-friendly physical environment as nature-based solutions for decreasing burnout and increasing job satisfaction and performance. *International Journal of Environmental Research and Public Health*, *17*(17), 6357. doi:10.3390/ijerph17176357 PMID:32882825

Chapter 8
An Analysis of Emerging Future-State Hotel Factors Impacting Job Satisfaction:
An Eye to the Future

ABSTRACT

This narrative explores the historical progression of workforce development through four generally accepted categorical periods of technological disruption and societal transformation referred to as industrial revolutions. The fourth industrial revolution has also catalyzed workforce development creating a concept called the gig economy, which features a workforce that individually contracts with companies, rather than seek permanent employment, to provide goods and services. Next, it evaluates how these different periods of societal change, and the gig economy impacts job satisfaction, insecurity, and engagement for hotel front desk employees. The chapter provides practical recommendations for leadership to minimize these outcomes including a review of Guaxni, a series of cultural values from eastern societies that can have beneficial results when integrated into Western workplaces. Finally, this chapter also evaluates the impact of emerging artificial intelligence (AI) technologies on the job satisfaction, insecurity, and turnover intent of hotel front-desk employees.

DOI: 10.4018/978-1-6684-2528-2.ch008

INTRODUCTION: THE FOUR INDUSTRIAL REVOLUTIONS

For as long as there has been organized civilizations, the concept of work has existed. The history of work is a complex and non-linear discovery that occurs in phases of dramatic and rapid development followed by significant periods of sustaining routines that preserve the status quo. In many cases, both scenarios are identified simultaneously either separated by geography, industry, or both. A review of the history of work that isn't focused on a specific industry or geography can therefore be challenging to assemble and summarize. As such, it isn't the technique this essay will adapt.

Rather, the trajectory of work will be mapped out across four different periods of rapid development that have been identified as industrial revolutions. Each of these phases have been accompanied by significant change in societal norms, cultural values and expectations surrounding work. After all, a study of work and the individuals who seek it is often a study of society. Workers reflect the values of their society, after all, and this continues to be as true in the 21st century as it was at the dawn of time.

The four industrial revolutions have a common element and that is the introduction of disruptive technology that catalyzes a scope and dimension of change that is impactful in how much changes as well as how long the change lasts. In many cases, changes made during one of the four revolutionary periods continue to be intact in modern times. These changes become integrated into everyday life and newer generations who were born after disruption occurred come to know changes as how life should just be having never experienced anything differently. The four industrial revolutions have taken place in a relatively short period of time, spanning less than 400 years. This is not a surprising reflection; Technology is primarily known to be able to increase the speed at which things are done. For example, in 2023, retail banking services are available 24 hours a day, 7 days a week via an app on one's mobile device. One can deposit, transfer, or withdraw money. One can set up new accounts and conduct a variety of other activities that – less than ten years ago – required a visit to a retail branch.

The first industrial revolution is largely thought to start in the mid eighteenth century and is characterized by the mechanization of industries. The invention of the steam engine allowed for significant upscaling of capacity to extract coal which fueled the mechanization of many industries of the day. The most significant disruption was felt in the agriculture industry where mechanization allowed for greater output with less input from a human. The other major impact driving this period was the ability to manufacture an expanded railroad network that provided the means of moving large quantities of goods from one distant location to another. As quaint as it may seem from a modern context, this was truly the foundation of how the modern world operates under a global economic network.

The second industrial revolution occurred nearly a century later at the end of the 19th century. Of the four revolutions, this period is considered the most important of all four. Most innovations associated with modern life were introduced during this period. There were three primary components that allowed the second industrial revolution to transform the world in the way that it did. First, Electricity, gas and oil all were introduced to society as new sources of energy. Second, these sources of energy allowed for innovation in metallurgy and chemical synthesis. Three processes resulted in the development of steel, concrete, and new communication technologies such as the telegraph and telephone. The third component of the second industrial revolution was the invention of the automobile and the airplane. The benchmarks of modern life (energy, construction, communication, and travel) all came to be during this era.

The third industrial revolution is often thought of occurring in the middle of the twentieth century following World War II, but its true date of inception is not as clearly defined as the first and second revolutions are. There is much innovation that began during the war, as the scope and duration of that conflict have long been demonstrated to have been a significant factor contributing to the further development of technology. However, due to wartime dynamics, much of that development was kept out of the public view until after the conclusion of the war so while the post-war period is often associated with the start of the third industrial revolution, that appears to be more of just when the public began benefiting from advancements that had already been underway. Regardless, the revolution is about change in society, and there is no doubt that the post-war period is when that occurred.

The third industrial revolution has its foundation in the harnessing of nuclear energy which helped bring forth the rise in electronics, telecommunications, and computers. These innovations created new industries including space exploration, biotechnology, geographical exploration, and genetics. Increasing the prevalence of automation of tasks across industries to unprecedented levels was largely due to the creation of programable logic controllers and robotic operations, both associated with this phase of development.

The fourth industrial revolution, often referred to as Work 4.0, presents an interesting perspective for reflection. There is some disagreement among societies about whether a new revolution has begun or if dynamics are merely reflecting the continuation of the third. Part of the challenge is that unlike the retrospective qualities of the first three revolutions, 21st century societies are living through the fourth industrial revolution, and it is being shaped and developed in real time. This can easily convolute reflections and evaluations since much of what is interpreted is being based on subjective observations and experiences that occur in real time as opposed to a more objective reflection on historical events.

Nevertheless, there are some aspects to this period of development that can be identified as unique and supportive of the case to define it as a separate new revolution as opposed to a continuation of the last. When innovation is reviewed in the fourth revolution, unifying aspects of velocity, scope and systems impact all support the classification of a distinct revolution. While much attention is often attributed to technology driving this revolution, it is more about how global communities are being connected outside of formal systems like governments. This is the era of connectivity, and the presence and accessibility of the internet has effectively disrupted nearly every industry in every country on the planet. This phase of development has led to unbelievable surges in artificial intelligence, nanotechnology, materials science, energy storage, quantum computing, the Internet of Things, robotics, and digital fabrication efforts. Societal changes being made possible by the advent of technologies are occurring at a rapid pace where cultures are acknowledges changes to its value, norms, and expectations on a regular basis and in real time. This societal advancement is occurring so quickly now that it is fracturing society in what is being adopted and what is being rejected. Societal transformation is occurring in real time on a global scale, and the opportunities and responsibilities associated with innovation are rarely understood before deployment. Truly, the impact that this revolution is having on civilization is so great in scope that it can easily branch into several different foci of narratives, but for the purposes of this essay, it is important to remain focused on the disruptive qualities that this industrial revolution is engendering on labor markets.

This chapter concludes the book-length journey of exploring hotel employee job satisfaction characteristics with a review and analysis of emerging global workplace trends as measured against historical progression while also investigating relevant future state technological disruption. The narrative explores different facets of opportunities in the hospitality industry associated with the gig economy framework, how foreign cultural parameters can be integrated into the work culture at a hospitality organization and the impact of newly developed artificial intelligence technology on hotel employee job insecurity.

BACKGROUND

Automation eliminating existing jobs is a phenomenon that has occurred during all four industrial revolutions. All of the industrial revolutions have had positive and negative impacts on workers. As automation substitutes for labor from one industry to the next, the displacement of workers could prove to be more costly than it is worth, ultimately driving a return to less automated processes. In other cases, lost jobs may become permanently eliminated although technological innovation often provides new opportunities in situations like this. For example, many organizations have begun developing artificial intelligence technology to manage low level customer service interactions (these are affectionally dubbed "chat bots"). While this can be considered a disruptive technology in that it has by and large reduced, if not outright eliminated, the need for a human to answer a customer's call on the phone, there is a modified need in that the chatbot can't do its job if it isn't programmed properly with company – specific qualities. Who is going to train the chatbot? That is the new opportunity, and workers have the opportunity to engage in upskilling to transition if they are interested, open and willing to do so.

Within the hotel industry, technology allows a customer to review options for their stay, secure a reservation, check themselves in, select their specific room, access that room, compete their stay and pay their bill all without ever engaging with a person. While enjoying one's stay, a guest can connect with the Internet of Things in the hotel and control their room's temperature, obtain food and beverage, and resolve minor concerns about their stay (additional towels, set up wake up calls, etc.). What is the opportunity, then, for the future of working in a hotel with that sort of disruptive technology? It does seem bleak at first glance, but there are always alternative pathways and solutions. In this case, there are two primary answers for this that spring to mind.

First, a hospitality worker may have to transition from being one that supports guests directly to one that supports the technology that supports the guests. The sort of automated experience described in the prior paragraph that already exists in many areas of the hospitality industry doesn't just happen. It takes people working to create specific products that are designed, tested, sold, and implemented. It takes post purchase support to modify and optimize technology solutions to ensure that it operates as desired and that it is periodically maintained to ensure good health of the network. It also requires diagnostic and intermediary efforts when disruptive or malicious elements are accidentally (or purposefully) introduced to the network environment.

This transition in skillsets can be challenging for employees who are presently employed in the industry. After doing a job in a specific way using a curated set of skills, being made obsolete by external factors associated with a revolution can be a bitter pill to swallow. Many people aren't capable of that transition without encouragement, and this highlights an often-overlooked aspect of management and leadership skills within a transition: It isn't enough to simply identify an opportunity involving automation technology. Leadership must also identify a pathway for people impacted by automation technology to transition from the world they have existed in to the one that will exist once the new automation technology has been implemented. It is here that an untapped and unrealized opportunity exists for the hotel industry.

A Deeper Dive into the Gig Economy

Tourism is one of the economic activities most affected by changing and uncertain conditions (Hall, 2010; Senbeto & Hon, 2020). This has been evidenced by the COVID-19 pandemic, which has reduced tourism and travel, thus declining hotel occupancy rates (Gössling, Scott, & Hall, 2020; Jiang & Wen, 2020). As such, the hospitality industry – like many others – is looking to remain profitable and in existence through a renewed focus on expense control. One of the ways that has been of interest for many industries is utilizing non-employees to deliver services via a gig economy. The hospitality industry, like many others, has embraced the idea of the gig economy with popular brands such as VRBO and AirBNB. But what is this element of the fourth industrial revolution and how does it operate? The development of the digitally enabled economy has increased existing trends towards self-employment and fragmented work to the detriment of more stable forms of employment. In some cases, fragmentation has been extreme, where small, poorly remunerated, unitary tasks are competitively offered to an internationally fragmented workforce. Altogether, this defines a gig economy that has been both denounced as one of the worst forms of workforce exploitation and heralded as providing ultimate flexibility and freedom. The digitally enabled economy is a new way of framing work and career that has been brought about by the integration of the internet into many elements of life. It is also referred to as the platform economy, the on-demand economy, or the gig economy. The gig economy allows workers to work for themselves when they want to work, as opposed to getting hired for a traditional full time or part time role. The integration of cloud-based applications for many processes within life has created pathways for peer-to-peer delivery of services and goods that historically have exclusively been provided by companies to their customers. Now, an individual can choose to provide contract services to an organization (or a person) and work on their own schedule as one lines up separate gigs that fit within the time that someone wants to contribute to work. The disaggregation of the 'workplace' in both crowdwork and on-demand gig work is significant as it potentially creates a disconnected, individualized experience of work (Kaine & Josserand, 2019).

The fragmentation of work facilitated by gig economy business models that reduce labor costs by deeming workers 'independent contractors' (thereby avoiding employment-related liabilities such as insurances and paid leave) has come under scrutiny around the world (Kaine & Josserand, 2019). It has been argued that such fragmentation reflects a more general trend, now known as the 'fissuring'of work (Weil, 2014) characterized by 'extreme flexibility, shifting of risks to workers and income instability', and that these features 'have long become a reality for a portion of the workforce in current labor markets that goes far beyond the persons employed in the gig economy' (De Stefano, 2016).

Work within that economy has generally become known as 'gig work' and denotes 'task-based' and 'electronically mediated jobs' (US Bureau of Labor Statistics, 2021) that allow for online platform or smartphone app-based connection between those offering to perform services or tasks and those requesting services. Within this broader definition of 'gig work', two categories have been identified: 'crowdwork' and 'work on demand' (De Stefano, 2016).

The first category refers to cloud-based crowdwork that is generally undertaken in a worker's own home and can be further divided into two sub-categories. First, crowd-based platforms trade largely in 'microtasks' that 'co-ordinate the use of human intelligence to perform tasks which computers are unable to execute' (such as Amazon Mechanical Turk). The second sub-category leverages specific professional expertise to deliver work online (Scholz, 2017).

On-demand gig work differs from crowdwork in that it involves 'real-world' rather than virtual tasks (Stewart & Stanford, 2017). Common examples, which are the focus of the various contributions to this special issue, include point-to-point transport and food delivery services. Other examples are handyman and cleaning services – with the variety of services offered through on demand services also expanding into personal care, personal beauty, and pet care services. Three key themes from the extant literature on work in the gig economy. These are:

1) conditions for gig workers (including contract, risk, income, regulation, and resistance),
2) the impact of gig work (on workers' experience, on skills and on job quality) and
3) information, technology, and gig work such as personal information, social media and algorithmic management (Kaine & Josserand, 2019)

The concept of 'contract' is central to research on the conditions of gig workers and is mainly related to five other concepts: employment, employer, employee, terms and independent. Many platforms construct their contracts around self-employment, giving them the capacity to avoid labor regulations applied to direct employees (Howcroft & Bergall-Kareborn, 2019). This situation is compounded by a lack of awareness among workers regarding the status of their contract (MacDonald & Giazitzoglu, 2019).

Research relating to the concept of 'contract' also deals with the design of gig work contracts (Stewart & Standford, 2017) and, to a degree, how to improve these (Byrne & Pecchenino, 2019; Cachon, Daniels, & Lobel, 2017) and the implications of the configuration of contracts as a whole, or of specific clauses. For instance, Stewart and Stanford (2017) conclude that Uber contracts are 'unfair' because they give Uber the right to change terms unilaterally at any time. Other characteristics include dynamic prices and pay rates that aim at eliminating capacity rationing (Cachon et al., 2017). Byrne and Pecchenino (2019) discuss extensively the future value that the firm and the worker can, respectively, derive from a specific contract, contrasting the situation of high-end consultants with that of Uber drivers.

The key focus in terms of 'risk' concerns risks on the workers' side. A first category of risk results from the often-precarious nature of gig work that does not offer the safety net associated with more traditional forms of work (Chen, 2018); in the absence of training, health or retirement benefits, the risk of operation is shifted from the employer to the worker (Bajwa, Gastaldo, &

Ruggiero, 2018). Another source of risk lies in the fact that workers provide capital in the form of tools or equipment, support the fluctuation of business and income, or can be 'deactivated' from an app (Stewart & Stanford, 2017). Given the lack of health insurance benefits or a workplace health and safety programs (Fox, Spicer, & Chosewood, 2018), there is an increased health and well-being risk but also a safety risk, for activities such as ridesharing where customers are not screened or vetted in any significant way (Christie & Ward, 2019).

Risk is also approached in a more subjective manner with research on how employees perceive and tolerate job risk; but there is an objective risk due to a lack of income predictability (Doucette and Brandford, 2019), uncertain project frequency and uncertain work hours (Gandhi, Hidayanto, & Sucahyo, 2018). Foremost, earnings are less than those of their peers in traditional work (Friedman, 2014) with long working hours (Carmody and Fortuin, 2019; Graham and Anwar, 2018).

Sun, Wang & Wan (2019) analyze the daily decisions on whether and how to participate in work depending on hourly income rates. An individual's capacity to earn, for instance in the case of crowd w depends on their online reputation, with no guaranteed weekly or monthly income; also, they need to factor in healthcare costs and savings for leave in their calculation of income (Arenas, Garcia & Ota'Iora, 2018). Low and unpredictable earnings or limited hours mean that gig workers often need to engage in multiple occupations (Doucette and Brandford, 2019) and/or must work at different times than formal work, for instance during weekends, holidays, etc. (Arenas et al., 2018).

Due to being deemed by platforms as self-employed, gig workers will miss out on entitlements and be excluded from the social welfare safety net (Hawley, 2018). This leads to a call for ensuring that gig work does not create a situation where what are considered basic work conditions are denied to workers (Stewart & Stanford, 2017). A key argument is that the development of on-demand gig platforms requires 'regulatory innovation' so that 'the blurring of the relationship between intermediary and worker that has been a central feature of most platform- based business models' does not undermine labor protections (Stewart and Standford, 2017).

When exploring the impact of gig work, the focus is turned to understanding how workers experience their activity, on the skill requirements to be a part of the workforce and on society through the creation (or destruction) of jobs (Gandini, 2018). While Ashford, Caza & Reid (2018) underline that gig workers find themselves energized by the variety of work, overall findings from this stream of research tend to emphasize negative emotions associated with gig work. For instance, gig workers in crowdsourcing platforms can feel devalued by the perception that their work is not considered important (Petriglieri, Ashford & Wrzesniewski., 2019). More generally, they tend to struggle with anxiety linked to precariousness and volatile income flows, leading to what has been described as emotional oscillation (Ashford et al., 2018). Challenges that can contribute to such emotions include poor communication with the platform when issues occur (Carmody and Fortuin, 2019), career uncertainty (Schwartz, 2018) and fear of losing their jobs/gigs (Ashford et al., 2018). Isolation and missing out on the social benefits of an office culture are also an issue although Wood, Lehdonvirta, & Graham (2018) show, for instance, that while face-to-face communication is typically scarce, online communities can contribute to the gig worker experience. As gig workers lack the more stable social connections that characterize traditional work, they must thus exert agency to construct relationships, building ties with other independent workers, clients, supporters, and employers (Ashford et al., 2018).

Gig work is associated with new opportunities to learn, where gig workers develop new skills through gig work (Ashford et al., 2018). In that sense, each contract or each client can bring an opportunity to learn new routines and skills (Ashford et al., 2018), leading to the conclusion that crowd workers may accumulate a rich experience by being exposed to different types of clients and projects (Arenas et al., 2018). One idea is that gig workers should develop portable and adaptable skills (Ashford et al., 2018) by themselves, for instance relying on online training resources (Schwartz, 2018). Furthermore, they should work on relevant and re-deployable skill sets that help them adapt to constantly changing demands (Ashford et al., 2018). The emerging picture is that of on-demand learning to match the on-demand labor needs of platform companies (Means, 2018).

While the benefit of empowerment regarding scheduling, the true experience of the gig worker can be sobering. In addition, there is discussion on the benefit of this employment model within the larger economic context. Whether the gig economy is creating quality jobs, or whether it is creating jobs at all where the question of quality is problematic. In some contexts, the conditions are such that the job quality, as perceived by workers, is very low. For instance, Chen (2018) shows how the work conditions of app-based taxi drivers in China lead workers to qualify their job as a 'life struggle, creating exhaustion and health problems. A more nuanced picture of the work of online workers in Asia and Africa in the form of a trade-off. On the positive side, these jobs offer flexibility, autonomy, task variety and complexity, while the negative characteristics include low pay, social isolation, unsocial and irregular hours, overwork, sleep deprivation and exhaustion (Wood et al., 2019. A positive aspect of gig work is the advantages it presents for different groups such as stay-at-home parents or elder caregivers, even in some instances providing new employment possibilities for the disabled and the elderly (Jiang, Wagner, & Nardi, 2015).

Josserand and Kaine (2019) study the identity work of ride-share drivers in Australia. They show how ride-share drivers struggle to maintain a coherent sense of self when confronted with the discrepancies between their occupational identity and its materiality. Through identity work, drivers tend to accept that their occupation is a trade-off between freedom, material gain and social experience on the one hand and low expectations in terms of conditions, investment requirements, an incentive structure limiting their freedom and an uncertain future on the other. Confronted with this trade-off, drivers construct self-narratives of their identity, which include insisting on a brighter future, the temporary aspect of their activity, being entrepreneurs or disenchantment. An important conclusion

is that overall drivers only partially integrate the rhetoric provided by the gig platforms and conduct identity work that helps them make sense of their activity as temporary or marginal. They thus discard ride sharing as a full-time activity, which raises questions on how platform companies can maintain quality of service in the long run.

Goods, Veen, & Barratt (2019) offer an insightful investigation of the quality of jobs in the bike courier industry in Australia and provide an integrative framework that helps analyze the intricate concept of job quality in terms of individual, labor market and socio-political fit. At an individual level, job quality can be approached with a contextualized subjective lens. Fit resulted from the individual circumstances of workers, meaning that job quality was acceptable for specific categories of workers such as young, temporary migrants with limited command of English. It is important to note that jobs were considered acceptable because most workers had exit strategies.

Burbano's (2021) exploration of the non-pecuniary motivations of gig workers suggests another important research question – how platform 'employers' might influence the drive and commitment of their gig workforce beyond the obvious extrinsic motivator of remuneration for their services. A related question that has not yet been adequately answered is what the emergence of gig work means for skills acquisition and career development. The maintenance of skills has been identified as 'essential' for self-employed knowledge workers (Leighton, 2016), but there is little understanding of how this might vary across different sectors of the gig economy, nor is there much analysis of the preferences of different groups of gig workers around career development.

The gig economy cannot exist in its present form without cloud-based technology that is accessed primarily by mobile devices. The opportunities it presents is largely driven through the convenience of access. Given it is based on platform intermediation, information and information technology play a key role in gig work through three broad categories:

1) the management and usage of personal information,
2) the role of social media and
3) controversial algorithmic management practices (Leighton, 2016)

Algorithmic management, which can be defined as the management of labor by machine, is a key preoccupation for researchers on the gig economy (Goods et al., 2019). Algorithmic management is based on the constant data collection that happens through the rating system and the collection of data on individual workers (Adams, Freedman, & Prassl, 2018).

Algorithmic management covers at least three main functions: first, discipline and control that aims at reinforcing compliance and is based on the panoptic properties of the technologies implemented (Adams et al., 2018; Gandini, 2018; Veen, Barratt, & Goods, 2020); second, performance management, notably through customer ratings but also by providing incentives to drive performance (Adams et al., 2018; Gandini, 2018; Shafiei Gol et al., 2019); and finally, by providing legitimation for decisions to terminate gig workers (Chan, 2019).

Algorithmic management raises several issues such as It points to asymmetries of information that constrain workers' choice and favor the platform companies (Cheng and Foley, 2019; Schwartz, 2018; Veen et. al., 2020). This means that workers lack sufficient information about the performance management and incentive system (Veen et al., 2020). Despite this, research shows that gig workers try to use 'gaming strategies' (Chan and Humphreys, 2018) that are 'cynical efforts to manipulate the rankings data without addressing the underlying condition that is the target of measurement' (Sauder and Espeland, 2009: 76).

The gig economy also relies on the collection of individual information about gig workers. The information can be very extensive and includes such things as customer ratings, skills and capabilities, financial information, but also a picture of criminal records in some activities. This information is not managed or curated by a pool of experts, but created by users themselves, which is a hallmark of the gig economy (Ashford, et al., 2018). For this model to be effective, there must be a management of trust around personal information where the rating is the basis for entrusting anonymous workers with performing a task (Schiek and Gideon, 2018). However, in other contexts, anonymity is not possible or desired where it might raise suspicion from clients (Wood et al., 2018). This is especially the case when personal information is made available to clients to assess the capabilities of workers and their capacity to perform a specific task (Wood et al., 2018).

Ascending in society's acceptance and affinity during the past twenty years is social media, which plays an important role in the gig economy via two main functions: Community building among gig workers and directly facilitating gig work. Social media allows gig workers to share information and communicate; this is especially important since gig work platforms often do not offer such possibilities (Chan, 2019; Chen, 2018; Wang, Tao, & Liang, 2019). Worker-led communities can be very active and share work-related information, such as in the case of ride-share drivers' online forums (Chan, 2019). Beyond being a tool for knowledge exchange, research shows that social media has played a central role in workers' resistance to platform organizations, thus becoming the most important channel for strikes and collective activism (Chen, 2018).

The second possible role of social media platforms is that they can become, at least in some industries, the preferred platform to facilitate gig work (Wang et al., 2019). This is because social media platforms can support the display of relevant and rich information about gig workers (Carr, Hall, & Mason, 2017), thus supporting the signaling of skills and knowledge (Chan, 2019). They also serve a function in identity verification and matching (Ticona and Mateescu, 2018). Professional freelancers and other gig workers already use social media as support for 'self-branding' (Ticona & Mateescu, 2018).

The gig economy has developed around accessibility of cloud-based applications to serve in a disruptive capacity across multiple industries and allowed a peer-to-peer distribution network to arise. Datafication in the tourism and hospitality sector has created new opportunities for business strategy and growth for many organizations. Algorithms are being used to aggregate and analyze data, contributing to the decision-making process (Newell & Marabelli, 2015). Sharing economy platforms are increasingly utilizing algorithms to manage and coordinate extremely large amounts of data on both workers and customers (Cheng and Foley, 2019).

The process goes beyond simple analytics and has replaced some of the tasks that are traditionally managed by human beings, particularly those within the boundary of middle managers (Jarrahi and Sutherland, 2019). In addition to understanding the dynamics that developed the current model, there is value to understand the direction of developmental trajectories. Wu, Zhang, & Li (2019) contribute to a better understanding of what might be the future of management. They investigate how quality of service can be ensured through these new labor control tools, focusing on the combination of incentive pay schemes and platform evaluation systems. They show that these systems impact in a distinct manner across different categories of workers. For example, full-time drivers lost most of the autonomy promised by the platform because of the impact of the bonus systems put in place. This is an important assessment of the strength of algorithmic management and how difficult it is to resist.

Motivating gig employees without having direct organizational authority over performance can be a challenge for many managers (Burbano, 2021). One employer-level characteristic whose influence on traditional employee behavior has been explored in recent years is a firm's charitable giving (Bode, Singh, & Rogan, 2015; Burbano, 2016). Proximity to and participation in charitable activities have been shown to drive the effects of this employer-level characteristic on traditional employee behavior (Bode et al., 2015; Brockner, Senior, & Welch, 2014; Kim, Lee, Lee, & Kim, 2010), making it theoretically unclear whether gig workers (who are physically distant from and do not participate in charitable activities) will in practice be motivated by employer charitable giving. On the other hand, charitable giving could increase gig workers' feeling of affiliation with, and decrease how distant gig workers feel from, their gig employer. This in turn could positively influence gig workers' perceptions about working for their employer (Wiesenfeld, Raghuram, & Garud, 2001; Wiesenfeld, Raghuram, & Garud, 1999) and motivate them (Bolino & Turnley, 2003; Niehoff & Moorman, 1993; Organ & Ryan, 1995; O'Reilly & Chatman, 1986). Gig workers have been shown to respond to employer corporate social responsibility (CSR) more broadly in the form of willingness to accept lower wages (Burbano, 2016), suggesting that motivating effects may dominate, though CSR is a multifaceted construct that includes more than charitable giving (Burbano, 2021).

Field experiments implemented on two online gig labor markets provided support that charitable giving has a positive effect on gig workers' willingness to go beyond what was required for their employer. These studies explored the nonpecuniary motivation of a type of worker—the gig or contingent worker—who is becoming increasingly important for firms. The jobs used in the field experiments were data-entry focused. Future work could explore whether and how effects differ when jobs are of a different type (e.g., more creative and innovative in nature). Extant work examining the strategic human capital management of nontraditional workers such as virtual workers has mainly focused on team- and individual-level characteristics that influence the productivity of these workers (Martins, Gibson, & Maynard, 2004). Research suggests that an employer-level characteristic can influence the productivity of nontraditional workers, and points to the promise of exploring the effects of other types of CSR inputs and other employer-level characteristics on nontraditional workers' productivity. The finding that gig workers who originally feel more distant from their gig employers are more responsive to information about employer charitable giving responds to a call to examine heterogeneous attitudes among virtual workers (Martins et al., 2004).

So, the story of the gig economy becomes a cautionary one in that there may be opportunities to tap into a peer-network to assist with staffing challenges but there are unique challenges to address in the new distribution channels. While the gig economy platforms only constitute a small proportion of total employment, that could change in the decades to come. In addition to operational challenges, it is critical that leadership review the implications for the management of performance and reward of a non-direct workforce (Josserand and Kaine, 2019) before pursuing such a staffing strategy. There are also some associated areas that combine more traditional HR concerns such as recruitment and selection and the efficient allocation of work with the better use of information and data (Cheng and Foley, 2019). Managers could benefit from highlighting their firm's charitable giving activities to gig and contingent workers, particularly if their workers communicate infrequently with and are likely to feel distant to their gig employers or are pro-socially oriented. Though corporate philanthropy programs are commonly highlighted during full-time employee career fairs and other recruiting initiatives, managers note that they are rarely highlighted during the recruiting of gig employees.

Workforce Development in the 4th Industrial Revolution and Career Pathways

Although innovation in technology is what often receives the lion's share of attention with any of the four industrial revolutions, the lasting impact often comes not from technology, but the changes made in society itself. How people change what they do, how they do it, how they consume and process information, how they learn and how they make choices are all behaviors that irrevocably must change as a result of the introduction of disruptive technology. Humans learn new skills and forget old ones. Prior to the second industrial revolution, for example, most people knew how to take care of and ride a horse. With the advent of the automobile, this skill set was lost to many, but new skills were gained including operation of an automobile, knowledge of standardized driving law in a culture and (for some) awareness of how to operate and/or address problems with operation of an internal combustion engine.

Workforce development, therefore, is an overlooked aspect of an industrial revolution and should receive more focus than it gets. It shouldn't be enough to simply say that a new technology has arrived that can do the job a person did, and now that job no longer exists. What happens to the person? What framework exists to support someone' transition from what was to what will be? While there are still many areas of opportunity in this area, the fourth industrial revolution has incorporated this perspective much more prevalent than its predecessors ever did. That said, an optimized strategy for transitioning people still eludes most industries, the hospitality industry included. The major labor shortages of 2021 and 2022 (which, in truth, started long before the COVID-19 pandemic of 2020) are illustrative of a need to develop a better proverbial mousetrap on how to transition the skillsets of a society when disruptive technology arrives. After all, it isn't that there is a shortage of workers per se. It's that there's a shortage of workers with an identified skill set to integrate with the new technology.

Technology isn't just about automation or processing power, it's the conceptual idea of turning inputs into outputs that are sustainable and provide measurable benefits. Falling under the expanded scope of technologies is one of the greatest innovations of the working world, and that is the career pathway. It isn't a wholly new idea, but – like many ideas – builds upon what has existed in the past and adapts and refines it within a new context. The career pathway in its current form is truly a product of its time and society's newly trained need to have access to information, but it's also developed from thousands of years old workforce development processes like apprenticeships.

A career pathway is a strategic map that outlines professional tactics to support an interested party in transitioning from their current state to a desired future state. It is specifically framed within the notion of jobs and how those jobs fit together along a greater continuum that exists for a decade or longer, although the concept could be adapted for a non-professional framework as well. A career pathway integrates milestone steps, tools, opportunities, and roles along its continuum to help frame a journey for someone who may have an interest in an industry but not maintain an awareness of what is needed to engage in work for that industry.

A career pathway is often defined at its terminal points by employable positions – these could be company specific but are more often defined at an industry level. An entry point role that requires minimal skills and experience (which often translates to minimum pay as well) is a requirement, although not every possible user of this pathway will need to engage their journey at this point. A skillfully defined career pathway will have multiple entry points to retain as much flexibility as possible. At the opposite end of the continuum, a career pathway will feature a target or destination role. This is often a position that requires several years to obtain and involves a confluence of education, training, and experience in order to be qualified to fulfill that role. As expected, compensation associated with a target or destination role is often significantly higher.

Between the entry point role and the target or destination role are a strategically outlined sequence of industry accepted training, education, and experiences. These may or may not be distinct elements of the pathway, depending on how an industry provides interested parties opportunities to acquire defined training, education, and experiences. Training could be formal training programs (like an apprenticeship) or could emerge from specific roles that one is recommended to acquire. Similarly, education could emerge from formal degree-based programs or could be integrated into a non-degree bearing experience like workshops, certifications or on the job training. Experiences could be acquired through a paying job, a non-paid academic experience (such as k-12 student teaching experiences being integrated as a part of an undergraduate teacher preparation program) or a company /industry specific development program. Many large corporations have formed internal leadership development initiatives to create pipelines for its next generation of leaders while small organizations often benefit from community sponsored boot camps or seminars coordinated by local government or chambers of commerce.

A career pathway taps into a specific fourth industrial revolution societal identified by many communities that are connected to the global network: A need to have access to information. Historically and traditionally, the process of engineering a lifelong career was one veiled with some opaque context. Candidates were often left to their own devices to determine what they were interested in (often through trial and error), there wasn't a definitive resource outlining for candidates how to acquire the skills, education and experiences needed to secure the destination role they desired, and industry simply didn't recognize any sort of standardized time frame when this should all be accomplished. It left many candidates in the proverbial dark in terms of what they wanted, what they needed to get there and how long it was going to take. This lack of awareness is completely out of alignment with how people were trained to consumer information during the fourth industrial revolution. Access to information via technology means that there is an expectation a consumer can find what one needs before a decision is made, affectionally and colloquially referred to as "googling" something.

The distinct, if not yet meteoric, rise in interest associated with career pathways is a specific response to the misalignment described in the prior paragraph. A career pathway now identifies what you need to do to get to that dream job based on where you are today. It gives you a sense of how long it will take and how much money you can expect to make with each milestone along the way. If engineered properly, there are plenty of on and off ramps that can be easily connected to career pathways in other industries because the age of information is about the age of choice. Let's say an interested party begins the career pathway as a nurse, but once into it decides that there is a better alignment with personal interests, values, and skills in another industry. Connecting two career pathways like you would assemble a jigsaw is a benefit and helps one understand how, for example, healthcare provider training could be leveraged into a career in app development for the healthcare industry (the experiential knowledge associated with being a nurse, doctor or EMT would be a great springboard to become a software engineer when matched with technology development skills landing a position where one now creates an effective app useful for a nurse, doctor or EMT, for example).

So what might this look like for a hotel industry? It could easily take many different forms depending on what career it was defined for. This is the challenge of the career pathway concept. To be useful, it must be simultaneously comprehensive and flexible, which are characteristics that are often at odds with one another. The more specific a pathway is in identifying a mixture of entry points, required training, mandatory experience, and critical education the less flexible it becomes. This is where the power of modern computer processing can really elevate the concept. A career pathway is at its most effective when it is customized to be specific for a single user. Innovations in artificial intelligence and quantum computer processing have led to the development of algorithm based software that creates interactivity between the information itself (options for training, education and experience) and the specific needs of a user. It is in this scenario that an individual can identify their already acquired training, education and experience, as well as professional accomplishments, and have the power of advanced modern technology develop a unique pathway that leverages what has come before into an optimized plan to achieve future goals.

The hospitality industry is no different in that regard, and its employees could stand to benefit from this type of career planning opportunity as much as any industry. In some regards, employees in the industry may receive elevated benefits from such an approach because many workers at the property level in the hotel industry are often in entry-level positions which have historically not provided much context or guidance in forward career mobility. If you are employed as a housekeeper, what is your career plan? If you are working as bell staff or a restaurant server, how do you transition to a higher paying role? In the author's personal experience as well as insight gained through research, the answer is disheartening in that there isn't one. At best, it appears that there are limited energies by the industry that are dedicated to investing in developing front-line hospitality workers. At most, an associate in that role is guided into a low or middle management position at the property level, but pathways to opportunities beyond that are often left undefined. In short, an associate is often left to their own devices to figure out next steps in career mobility. What tends to happen is that career mobility doesn't occur, and an individual remains stagnant in a role. Once stagnant in a role, it is common to stay in the role until voluntary separation (burnout or retirement) or involuntary separation (laid off due to automation) eventually terminates the experience.

Integrating Guaxni into Western Hospitality Culture

As front-line hotel employees are at the center of customer service and service provision, it is vital that managers maintain a positive relationship with their subordinates in order to ensure the quality of service provided to the customers (Wang, Kim, Milne, 2017). As pointed out by Law, Wong, Wang, & Wang (2000), guanxi is a very important contributor to the effectiveness of staff management in China. Guanxi is a sophisticated phenomenon that is deeply rooted in the core of Confucianism. While it is a fundamental element of many eastern cultures, it has its followers in the west. The tents of the philosophy have direct practical application as well – since this meta-analysis is about discovery and innovation around the engagement and retention of front-line hospitality workers, this research has relevancy in this study as well.

Due to the notion that guanxi is aligned philosophically with Confucianism, it is for this reason many researchers have directly adopted the Chinese term in its untranslated form. Guanxi is defined as a relation or relationship (Bian, 1997) to facilitate exchanges of favor between people (Hwang, 1987) or between two or more entities (Chen, Chen, & Huang, 2013). Researchers have also confirmed Guanxi's significant impact on individual and organizational outcomes such as effectiveness of leadership (Chen and Tjosvold, 2006), work performance (Weng, 2014), self-development (Ren and Chadee, 2017) and service performance (Wu, Liu, & Shang, 2018).

Guanxi is a direct Chinese translation of the English word 'relationship' but incorporates subtle connotations defined and originated in Confucian philosophy. There are different dimensions to the core concepts of guanxi, all of which can be considered for integration into a work environment (Wang, Kim and Milne, 2020). Leader–member guanxi (LMG) is based mainly in the locality of the workplace and is a reciprocal exchange for a specific purpose (Fan, 2002) while a direct link between LMG and perceived organizational support on job involvement (Cheng, 2011), employee creativity (Li, Duverger, & Yu, 2018) and career success (Yang and Lau, 2015). LMG is theorized from the perspective of a collectivistic culture, based on a unique set of Confucian ideologies and social identification processes such as hierarchy and rationalism (Farh, Tsui, Xin & Cheng, 1998). The development of LMG is often through family and social ties, shared geographical backgrounds or other similar traits (Chen, Yu, & Son, 2014). LMG often results in more personal and private exchanges, such as sentiment and obligation, between leaders and members (Lin, 1998) and allows mutual access to each party's personal life (Wang, Kim & Milne, 2020).

Employees in the hotel industry have more contact with customers; hence, their performances are easily observed by their customers, which may adversely affect the organization if judged negatively (Hom et al., 2009). As employees' task performance determines the service quality provided to guests, hotels rely on their employees to achieve their business goals and maintain their competitive advantage. There is often a positive correlation displayed between quality of performed tasks in a service environment and employee's level of engagement with their role, which includes their relationship with their supervisor (Wang et. al. 2020). The direct effect of supervisor - employee relations on task performance can be explained as well through social exchange theory. Social exchange theory suggests that the behavior of one person can lead to the expectation that the other person will reciprocate in the same way with an equal amount of exchange (Blau, 1964).

Following this line of reasoning, favorable treatment from the leader can lead to the employee's feelings of obligation to pay back by working hard, which is one means of reciprocation (Wang et. al., 2020). a positive reciprocity occurs when an employee receives a favor from his or her supervisor, which makes the employee feel obliged to return the favor to the supervisor by working harder (Ouyang, 2011). The return of favor is not only deemed compulsory in Confucian culture, but a bigger favor is also often returned to show gratitude. Consequently, high-quality LMG can encourage positive sentiments and obligations from employees, which can lead to their demonstration of a high level of task performance (Wang, et. al, 2020).

LMG is limited to Confucian cultures, which showcases five core values: Benevolence, righteousness, propriety, wisdom and trust (Wang et. al., 2020). In Confucian ideology, the effectiveness of LMG is largely reliant on the leader's virtues and his or her subordinate's followership. When a leader integrates his or her virtues into their leadership, they maintain good quality LMG with every subordinate with virtues such as benevolence and trust in much the same way as a parent. In return, the people around him or her will show the highest levels of followership by working harder and engaging more with their jobs (Chen et. al., 2014). Chou (2002) discussed conceptually the idea that a highly differentiated guanxi between a leader and his or her team members is very likely to elicit negative work outcomes.

A high leader-member guanxi differentiation (LMGD) in a team environment may indicate a lack of virtue from the leader, which may well influence the reciprocation from subordinates and lead to low levels of work engagement. In contrast, low LMGD within a team may be the result of the leader treating their subordinates virtuously, which may encourage subordinates to engage more with their jobs. Atwater and Carmeli (2009) found that manager – employee relations positively influenced employees' feelings of energy. Graves and Luciano (2013) indicated that high quality of leader–member relations enhanced employees' feelings of competence and autonomy, which, in turn, affected their subjective vitality. Xanthopoulou, Baker, Demerouti, and Schaufeli (2009) discovered a positive association between leader–member relations and employees' work engagement and positive emotions.

In Confucianism, a high LMGD in a team environment may also indicate a lack of virtue on the part of the leader, which hinders the reciprocal processes among the employees. In a high-LMGD environment, employees who do not return favors to their leader are likely to demonstrate poorer work performance. When the LMGD is low in a work group, the employees demonstrate higher levels of followership with stronger work performance. The effect of LMG on job dedication was positive only when LMG-P (personal life inclusion) differentiation was low (Chen et al., 2014).

The implications are clearly beneficial for inclusion of such values into a hotel working environment, regardless of the surrounding religious or philosophical context of a host culture, albeit a culture that already adopts Confucianism and guanxi will be more willing to adopt its values into practice (Wang et. al., 2020). Engaged employes are physically, cognitively, and emotionally invested in their work roles, with a high level of psychological safety (Kahn, 1990). Work engagement has gained considerable attention from the service industry, since employees with high level of work engagement can make a big difference in the service provided to customers which in turn offer the organizations a competitive advantage (Leiter and Bakker, 2010). Work engagement is particularly important in the hotel industry, since the willingness to exceed expectations of service can encourage employees to demonstrate more proactive and responsible behavior for delivering quality services to customers (Demerouti, Bakker, Nachreiner & Schaufeli, 2001).

The Impact of Artificial Intelligence (AI) on Job Insecurity for Hotel Employees

Artificial intelligence (AI), which is the human-like intelligence demonstrated by a machine, is one of the major sources of innovation and has rapidly proliferated in various service sectors (Mahroof, 2019; Rust and Huang, 2014). AI is an area of computer sciences where machines perform human-like tasks to enhance business efficiency. AI occurs when systems disseminate large, sophisticated databases (Aghaei, Nematbakhsh, & Farsani, 2012). Using algorithms, AI attempts to resolve human-related problems with the combined efforts of machine efficiency and human characteristics (Lu Cai, & Gursoy., 2019). In this vein, AI enables businesses in various fields to provide their customers with unique experiences by utilizing deep-learning algorithms that study and memorize customers' needs and preferences without human interaction (Lu et al., 2019).

Traditionally, the hotel industry relies heavily on the understanding of interactive communications between service providers and customers (Autor & Dorn, 2013). However, AI enables the hotel industry to restructure its environment by transforming the customer-related data into practical insights, allowing hotels to create new customer experience provided by AI (Ivanov

& Webster, 2017). Chatbots are able to conduct conversations with guests through auditory or textual methods, in order to improve service processes. In addition, customer relations has been reimagined with the use of service robots, such as the concierge robot and the room service robot to further enhance the guests' onsite experience (Ivanov & Webster, 2017). Hilton Worldwide introduced an AI-powered concierge bot called Connie, who recommends local attractions to guests (Hilton, 2016). Marriott International also launched "The Bot Experience", which allows guests to experience their robot attendants, Leo & Cleo, who can deliver room service during guests' stay (Marriott, 2020). Outside of the financial cost associated with the investment in technology solutions, there is little risk for a hotelier choosing to deploy this kind of approach. According to Osawa, Ema, Hattori, Akiya, Kanzaki and Kubo (2017), even if the robot's skill is lesser than guest's expectation, robot-assistance could reduce human workers' emotional labor.

According to Koo, Curtis, and Ryan (2021), specific jobs in the hotel industry such as housekeeping, and maintenance are destined for automation. This is because AI is expected to increase operational efficiency, decrease staffing costs, and improve the customer experience. Other guest service roles, including the front desk and concierge, may be able to share their tasks in part or in whole with AI, depending on the skills the AI provides. Rust and Huang (2014) explained that AI job replacement in the service sector could occur in mechanical and analytical intelligence, while intuitive and empathetic intelligence remains an important part of human employees.

Hotel employees' awareness of AI and robotics significantly influences their turnover intention. Specifically, employees in lower-skilled positions are keenly aware of the high risks that their tasks will be replaced by AI in the near future. Managing employees' perceived job insecurity is critically important since job insecurity plays a vital role in anticipating employees' attitudinal and affective reactions toward the organization such as an employee's job engagement, job satisfaction, job commitment, and turnover intention (Ashford. Lee, & Bobko, 1989; Huang, Chen, and Liu, 2017; Shoss, 2017).

According to Schaufeli and Bakker (2004), employees who are engaged at work experience a positive attitude and emotions at work. In other words, employees who have a high level of work engagement are more likely to provide customers with excellent customer service, and stay in the organization (Lee, 2015; Roberts and Davenport, 2002). On the other hand, employees who experience job insecurity cannot fully engage within their work, because they are preoccupied with their job performance and eventually succumb to negative emotions, such as anxiety and frustration (Kiefer, 2005). Therefore, the extent of employees' job engagement is closely related to their work behavior and is a critical factor in their turnover intention (Saks, 2006). This phenomenon is referred to as self-determination.

Self-determination can be defined as "experiencing a sense of choice in initiating and regulating one's own actions." (Deci, Connell, & Ryan, 1989, p. 580). In other words, self-determination is a quality of human functioning that integrates intrinsic/extrinsic motivations based on one's capacity of choices (Deci and Ryan, 1985). These motivational processes can be influenced by job insecurity, thereby affecting work behavior, such as job performance, organizational behavior, job engagement, turnover intention, and so forth (Urbanaviciute, Lazauskaite-Zabielske, & De Witte, 2018; Shin, Hur, Moon, & Lee, 2019). For example, the findings from Shin et al. (2019)'s study demonstrated that job insecurity induced significant effects on job performance and organizational citizenship behavior, which confirms self-determination theory by positing motivation affecting employees' behavioral reactions to job stressor. Engaged employees provide organizations with benefits such as a lowered absenteeism rate and reduced health insurance costs as they experience greater physical/psychological well-being (Meyer and Gagne, 2008; Ryan & Deci, 2000).

job insecurity causes employees' negative attitudinal responses including increased turnover intention, decreased organizational commitment, and job satisfaction (Ashford et al., 1989).

CONCLUSION

Job insecurity only occurs in situations of involuntary job loss such as fear of losing one's job or ability to mentally cope with the workload. In other words, perceived job insecurity is a result of subjective threat (Greenhalgh & Rosenblatt, 1984). Job insecurity includes two vital elements, namely the severity of threat and powerlessness. The severity of the threat can be determined by the individual's perception of how they might lose their job (Greenhalgh & Rosenblatt (1984), such as the threats of losing a current job/job features when an unexpected event occurs, or threats from various sources, such as promotion opportunities, autonomy in work schedule, and so forth. (Ashford et al., 1989; Greenhalgh & Rosenblatt, 1984).

Moreover, the individual employee feels insecure when the organization introduces new technology, which eventually results in unemployment of less skilled employees (Koo et al., 2021). Likewise, organizational decline and reorganization are the most critical sources impacting a threat to the individual (Greenhalgh, 1983; Karkoulian, Mukaddam, McCarthy, & Messarra. 2013). Powerlessness can transpire when the individual perceives that they have no power to resist threats to continuity, and it is regarded as an essential variable of job insecurity because it deteriorates the individual's experienced threat. Powerlessness could take place when employees notice a lack of protection for their jobs, such as a lack of protection from unions, or unreasonable contracts. In addition, the culture of the company also influences an individual's sense of powerlessness especially when the company provides little support, treats them unfairly, or if individuals have no power/autonomy to make decisions (Greenhalgh and Rosenblatt, 1984). In other words, individuals do not perceive a threat to their jobs if they have enough power to cope with perceived threats (Ashford et al., 1989).

Darvishmotevali, Arasli, & Kilic (2017) investigated the effect of job insecurity on frontline employees' performance in the hotel. Their results indicated that job performance could be mitigated when frontline employees perceived job security and psychological advantages, such as supervisor support and intrinsic motivation, which can eliminate the negative effect of job insecurity on frontline employees' job performance. Job engagement can be referred to as "the simultaneous employment and expression of a person's 'preferred self' in task behaviors that promote connections to work and to others, personal presence (physical, cognitive, and emotional) and active, full performance" (Kahn, 1990, p. 700).

Kahn (1992) later identified that people demonstrate a high level of job engagement when they are physically involved in work, when they are cognitively meticulous, when they are focused and concentrated, when they are attentive, and when they are emotionally committed to their tasks and co-workers in the organization. Disengagement, on the other hand, is when an individual neglects prioritized work and spends time completing meaningless tasks (May, Gilson & Harter., 2004). In this regard, job engagement has been regarded as a motivational trigger as it persistently affects the individuals' work performance, especially when employees are faced with changes at work (Kanfer, 1990; May et al., 2004; Owens, Baker, Sumpter, & Cameron, 2016). Koo et. al. (2021) developed a behavioral model to explain this dynamic, which is featured in Figure 8.1 below:

Figure 1. Turnover intention as it is impacted by perceived job insecurity and perceived job engagement
Source: Koo et al. (2021)

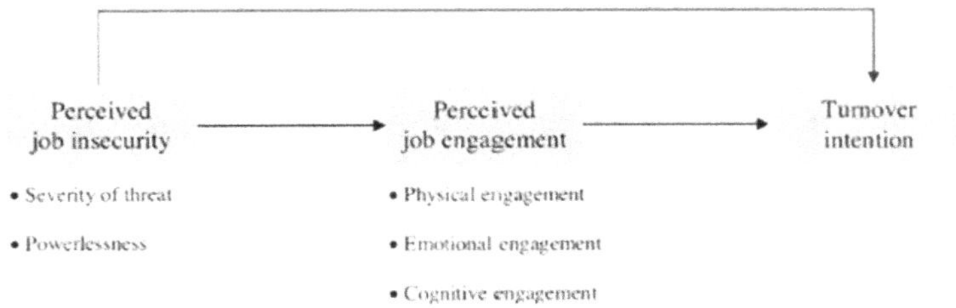

Koo et. al., 2021 successfully conceptualized job insecurity based on a self-determination theory standpoint by empirically testing the model in Figure 1, which uncovered causal relationships among job insecurity, job engagement, and turnover intention. Job insecurity should be viewed by the lens of self-determination theory to explain individuals' intrinsic/ extrinsic motivations created by job insecurity and delineate the impact of job insecurity on affective/attitudinal reactions. Job insecurity has a critical role in anticipating attitudinal and affective reactions. Sub-factors of job insecurity, namely severity of threat and powerlessness, have successfully indicated that there are both direct and indirect effects on job engagement and turnover intention (Koo et. al., 2021).

The severity of threat, which occurs by changes in the current position, tasks, or significance of job, positively affected job engagement. The presence of a perceived threat triggered hotel employees to be more engaged in their work so that they can survive in a new environment. Powerlessness, on the other hand, elicits hotel employees' adverse reaction to their level of job engagement. Powerlessness is related to an individual's conditions or feelings of having no capacity to resist threats to continuity. In other words, hotel employees perceive powerlessness when they realize they do not have enough control over the changes in their workplace, and it negatively affects their enthusiasm to work (Koo et. al., 2021).

Meanwhile, job engagement exerted a negative effect on turnover intention. Job engagement played an important intermediary variable in the relationship between job insecurity (i.e., severity of threat and powerlessness) and turnover intention. The role maintained by an employee does not impact the relationships in the model in either a direct or indirect manner. In other words, hotel employees, whether they are in non-managerial positions or managerial positions, view the new trend and phenomenon with the same thought. Technology is not something that can be ignored for a business to remain competitive in its industry or optimized in its operations (Lu et. al., 2019). Far more effective is for proactive mitigation strategies that will engage and assist employees, front-line and management alike, through the process of mitigating perceived threats, accepting newer processes of completing tasks and integrating technology opportunities in an engaged fashion into their role.

REFERENCES

Adams, A., Freedman, J., & Prassl, J. (2018). Rethinking legal taxonomies for the gig economy. *Oxford Review of Economic Policy*, *34*(3), 475–494. doi:10.1093/oxrep/gry006

Aghaei, S., Nematbakhsh, M. A., & Farsani, H. K. (2012). Evolution of the world wide web: From Web 1.0 to Web 4.0. *International Journal of Web & Semantic Technology*, *3*(1), 1–10. doi:10.5121/ijwest.2012.3101

Arenas, C., Garcia, V.H.M., & Ota´lora, J.E. (2018). Crowdworking as a knowledge management mechanism in the elicitation of missional software requirement. In *Knowledge Management in Organizations. KMO 2018. Communications in Computer and Information Science*. Cham: Springer.

Ashford, S. J., Caza, B. B., & Reid, E. M. (2018). From surviving to thriving in the gig economy: A research agenda for individuals in the new world of work. *Research in Organizational Behavior*, *38*, 23–41. doi:10.1016/j.riob.2018.11.001

Ashford, S. J., Lee, C., & Bobko, P. (1989). Content, causes, and consequences of job insecurity: A theory-based measure and substantive test. *The Academy of Management Annals*, *32*(4), 803–829.

Atwater, L., & Carmeli, A. (2009). Leader–member exchange, feelings of energy, an involvement in creative work. *The Leadership Quarterly*, *20*(3), 264–275. doi:10.1016/j.leaqua.2007.07.009

Autor, D. H., & Dorn, D. (2013). The growth of low-skill service jobs and the polarization of the US labor market. *The American Economic Review*, *103*(5), 1553–1597. doi:10.1257/aer.103.5.1553

Bajwa, U., Gastaldo, D., Di Ruggiero, E., & Knorr, L. (2018). The health of workers in the global gig economy. *Globalization and Health*, *14*(1), 14. doi:10.118612992-018-0444-8

Bian, Y. (1997). Bringing strong ties back in: Indirect ties, network bridges, and job searches in China. *American Sociological Review*, *62*(3), 366–385. doi:10.2307/2657311

Blau, P. M. (1964). Justice in social exchange. *Sociological Inquiry*, *34*(2), 193–206. doi:10.1111/j.1475-682X.1964.tb00583.x

Bode, C., Singh, J., & Rogan, M. (2015). Corporate social initiatives and employee retention. *Organization Science*, *26*(6), 1702–1720. doi:10.1287/orsc.2015.1006

Bolino, M. C., & Turnley, W. H. (2003). Going the extra mile: Cultivating and managing employee citizenship behavior. *The Academy of Management Perspectives*, *17*(3), 60–71. doi:10.5465/ame.2003.10954754

Brockner, J., Senior, D., & Welch, W. (2014). Corporate volunteerism, the experience of self-integrity, and organizational commitment: Evidence from the field. *Social Justice Research*, *27*(1), 1–23. doi:10.100711211-014-0204-8

Burbano, V. C. (2016). Social responsibility messages and worker wage requirements: Field experimental evidence from online labor marketplaces. *Organization Science*, *27*(4), 1010–1028. doi:10.1287/orsc.2016.1066

Burbano, V. C. (2021). Getting gig workers to do more by doing good: Field experimental evidence from online platform labor marketplaces. *Organization & Environment*, *34*(3), 387–412. doi:10.1177/1086026619846455

Byrne, J., & Pecchenino, R. A. (2019). Heigh ho, heigh ho: Flexible labor contracts with real option characteristics. *Business Economics (Cleveland, Ohio)*, *54*(1), 25–34. doi:10.105711369-018-00106-3

Cachon, G. P. K., Daniels, K. M., & Lobel, R. (2017). The role of surge pricing on a service platform with self-scheduling capacity. *Manufacturing & Service Operations Management*, *19*(3), 368–384. doi:10.1287/msom.2017.0618

Carmody, P., & Fortuin, A. (2019). 'Ride-sharing', virtual capital and impacts on labor in Cape Town, South Africa. *African Geographical Review*, *38*(3), 196–208. doi:10.1080/19376812.2019.1607149

Carr, C. T., Hall, R. D., Mason, A. J., & Varney, E. J. (2017). Cueing employability in the gig economy: Effects of task-relevant and task-irrelevant information on Fiverr. *Management Communication Quarterly*, *31*(3), 409–428. doi:10.1177/0893318916687397

Chan, N. K. (2019). "Becoming an expert in driving for Uber": Uber driver/bloggers' performance of expertise and self-presentation on YouTube. *New Media & Society*, *21*(9), 2048–2067. doi:10.1177/1461444819837736

Chan, N. K., & Humphreys, L. (2018). Mediatization of social space and the case of Uber drivers. *Media and Communication*, *6*(2), 29–38. doi:10.17645/mac.v6i2.1316

Chen, C. C., Chen, X. P., & Huang, S. (2013). Chinese guanxi: An integrative review and new directions for future research. *Management and Organization Review*, *9*(1), 167–207. doi:10.1111/more.12010

Chen, J. Y. (2018). Thrown under the bus and outrunning it! The logic of Didi and taxi drivers' labour and activism in the on-demand economy. *New Media & Society*, *20*(8), 2691–2711. doi:10.1177/1461444817729149

Chen, Y., & Tjosvold, D. (2006). Participative leadership by American and Chinese managers in China: The role of relationships. *Journal of Management Studies*, *43*(8), 1727–1752. doi:10.1111/j.1467-6486.2006.00657.x

Chen, Y., Yu, E., & Son, J. (2014). Beyond leader–member exchange (LMX) differentiation: An indigenous approach to leader–member relationship differentiation. *The Leadership Quarterly*, *25*(3), 611–627. doi:10.1016/j.leaqua.2013.12.004

Cheng, C. H. (2011). A study of critical factors of the job involvement for hotel employees—Taking hotels in Taiwan as an example. *International Journal of Hospitality Management*, *30*(4), 990–996. doi:10.1016/j.ijhm.2011.03.001

Cheng, M., & Foley, C. (2019). Algorithmic management: The case of Airbnb. *International Journal of Hospitality Management*, *83*, 33–36. doi:10.1016/j.ijhm.2019.04.009

Chou, L. F. (2002). Guanxi and social networks in Chinese organizations. Indigenous. *Psychological Research in Chinese Societies.*, *18*(1), 175–228.

Christie, N., & Ward, H. (2019). The health and safety risks for people who drive for work in the gig economy. *Journal of Transport & Health*, *13*, 115–127. doi:10.1016/j.jth.2019.02.007

Darvishmotevali, M., Arasli, H., & Kilic, H. (2017). Effect of job insecurity on frontline employee's performance: Looking through the lens of psychological strains and leverages. *International Journal of Contemporary Hospitality Management*, *29*(6), 1724–1744. doi:10.1108/IJCHM-12-2015-0683

De Stefano, V. (2016). "The rise of the "just-in-time workforce": On-demand work, crowdwork and labor protection in the "Gig Economy." *Comparative Labor Law Journal, 37*(3), 471-504.

Deci, E. L., Connell, J. P., & Ryan, R. M. (1989). Self-determination in a work organization. *The Journal of Applied Psychology*, *74*(4), 580–590. doi:10.1037/0021-9010.74.4.580

Deci, E. L., & Ryan, R. M. (1985). *Intrinsic Motivation and Self-determination in Human Behavior*. Plenum. doi:10.1007/978-1-4899-2271-7

Demerouti, E., Bakker, A. B., Nachreiner, F., & Schaufeli, W. B. (2001). The job demands-resources model of burnout. *The Journal of Applied Psychology*, *86*(3), 499–512. doi:10.1037/0021-9010.86.3.499

Doucette, M. H., & Bradford, W. D. (2019). Dual job holding and the gig economy: Allocation of effort across primary and gig job. *Southern Economic Journal*, *85*(4), 1217–1242. doi:10.1002oej.12338

Fan, Y. (2002). Questioning guanxi: Definition, classification and implications. *International Business Review*, *11*(5), 543–561. doi:10.1016/S0969-5931(02)00036-7

Farh, J.-L., Tsui, A. S., Xin, K., & Cheng, B.-S. (1998). The influence of relational demography and guanxi: The Chinese case. *Organization Science*, *9*(4), 471–488. doi:10.1287/orsc.9.4.471

Fox, M. A., Spicer, K., Chosewood, L. C., Susi, P., Johns, D. O., & Dotson, G. S. (2018). Implications of applying cumulative risk assessment to the workplace. *Environment International*, *115*, 115. doi:10.1016/j.envint.2018.03.026

Friedman, G. (2014). Workers without employers: Shadow corporations and the rise of the gig economy. *Review of Keynesian Economics*, *2*(2), 171–188. doi:10.4337/roke.2014.02.03

Gandhi, A., Hidayanto, A., & Sucahyo, Y. (2018). Exploring people's intention to become platform-based gig workers: An empirical qualitative study. In *2018 International Conference on Information Technology Systems and Innovation (ICITSI), 22–26 October, Conference Proceedings* (pp. 266–271). 10.1109/ICITSI.2018.8696017

Gandini, A. (2018). Labour process theory and the gig economy. *Human Relations*, *72*(6), 1039–1056. doi:10.1177/0018726718790002

Goods, C., Veen, A., & Barratt, T. (2019). "Is your gig any good?" Analysing job quality in the Australian platform-based food-delivery sector. *The Journal of Industrial Relations*, *61*(4), 502–527. doi:10.1177/0022185618817069

Gossling, S., Scott, D., & Hall, C.M. (2021). Pandemics, tourism and global change: A rapid assessment of COVID-19. *Journal Sustainable Tourism*, *29*(1), 1–20.

Graham, M., & Anwar, M. (2018). Two models for a fairer sharing economy. In N. Davidson, M. Finck, & J. Infranca (Eds.), *The Cambridge Handbook of the Law of the Sharing Economy* (pp. 328–340). Cambridge University Press. doi:10.1017/9781108255882.025

Graves, L. M., & Luciano, M. M. (2013). Self-determination at work: Understanding the role of leader–member exchange. *Motivation and Emotion*, *37*(3), 518–536. doi:10.100711031-012-9336-z

Greenhalgh, L. (1983). Managing the job insecurity crisis. *Human Resource Management Journal*, *22*(4), 431.

Greenhalgh, L., & Rosenblatt, Z. (1984). Job insecurity: Toward conceptual clarity. *Academy of Management Review*, *9*(3), 438–448. doi:10.2307/258284

Hall, C. M. (2010). Crisis events in tourism: Subjects of crisis in tourism. *Current Issues in Tourism*, *13*(5), 401–417. doi:10.1080/13683500.2010.491900

Hawley, A. J. (2018). Regulating labour platforms, the data deficit. *European Journal of Government and Economics*, *7*(1), 5–23. doi:10.17979/ejge.2018.7.1.4330

Hilton. (2016). *Hilton And IBM Pilot "Connie," The World's First Watson-Enabled Hotel Concierge (March).* Retrieved from: https://newsroom.hilton.com/corporate/news/h

Howcroft, D., & Bergall-Kareborn, B. (2019). A typology of crowdwork platforms. *Work, Employment and Society*, *33*(1), 21–38. doi:10.1177/0950017018760136

Huang, S., Chen, Z., Liu, H., & Zhou, L. (2017). Job satisfaction and turnover intention in China: The moderating effects of job alternatives and policy support. *Chinese Management Studies*, *11*(4), 689–706. doi:10.1108/CMS-12-2016-0263

Hwang, K.-K. (1987). Face and favor: The Chinese power game. *American Journal of Sociology*, *92*(4), 944–974. doi:10.1086/228588

IvanovS. H.WebsterC. (2017). *Adoption of robots, artificial intelligence and service automation by travel, tourism and hospitality companies–a cost-benefit analysis. Artificial Intelligence and Service Automation by Travel, Tourism and Hospitality Companies–A Cost-Benefit Analysis*. Prepared for the International Scientific Conference "Contemporary Tourism – Traditions and Innovations", Sofia University. https://ssrn.com/abstract=3007577

Jarrahi, M. H., & Sutherland, W. (2018). *Algorithmic management and algorithmic competencies: Understanding and appropriating algorithms in gig work*. Paper Presented at the Lecture Notes in Computer Science Iconference 2019.

Jiang, L., Wagner, C., & Nardi, B. (2015). Not just in it for the money: A qualitative investigation of workers' perceived benefits of micro-task crowdsourcing. *2015 48th Hawaii International Conference on System Sciences, 5–8 January Conference Proceedings*, 773–782. 10.1109/HICSS.2015.98

Jiang, Y., & Wen, J. (2020). Effects of COVID-19 on hotel marketing and management: A perspective article. *International Journal of Contemporary Hospitality Management*, *32*(8), 2563–2573. doi:10.1108/IJCHM-03-2020-0237

Josserand, E., & Kaine, S. (2019). Different directions or the same route? The varied identities of ride-share drivers. *The Journal of Industrial Relations*, *61*(4), 549–573. doi:10.1177/0022185619848461

Kahn, W. A. (1990). Psychological conditions of personal engagement and disengagement at work. *Academy of Management Journal*, *33*(4), 692–724. doi:10.2307/256287

Kahn, W. A. (1992). To be fully there: Psychological presence at work. *Human Relations*, *45*(4), 321–349. doi:10.1177/001872679204500402

Kaine, S., & Josserand, E. (2019). The organisation and experience of work in the gig economy. *The Journal of Industrial Relations*, *61*(4), 479–501. doi:10.1177/0022185619865480

Kanfer, R. (1990). Motivation theory and industrial/organizational psychology. In *Handbook of Industrial and Organizational Psychology* (Vol. 1, pp. 75–170). Consulting Psychologists Press.

Karkoulian, S., Mukaddam, W., McCarthy, R., & Messarra, L. C. (2013). Job insecurity: A whirlpool of chronic powerlessness. *Education, Business and Society*, *6*(1), 55–70. doi:10.1108/17537981311314727

Kiefer, T. (2005). Feeling bad: Antecedents and consequences of negative emotions in ongoing Change. *Journal of Organizational Behavior*, *26*(8), 875–897. doi:10.1002/job.339

Kim, H. R., Lee, M., Lee, H. T., & Kim, N. M. (2010). Corporate social responsibility and employee company identification. *Journal of Business Ethics*, *95*(4), 557–569. doi:10.100710551-010-0440-2

Koo, B., Curtis, C., & Ryan, B. (2021). Examining the impact of artificial intelligence on hotel employees through job insecurity perspectives. *International Journal of Hospitality Management*, *95*(1), 102763. doi:10.1016/j.ijhm.2020.102763

Law, K. S., Wong, C.-S., Wang, D., & Wang, L. (2000). Effect of supervisor–subordinate guanxi on supervisory decisions in China: An empirical investigation. *Journal of Human Resource Management.*, *11*(4), 751–765.

Lee, J. J., & Ok, C. M. (2015). Drivers of work engagement: An examination of core self-evaluations and psychological climate among hotel employees. *International Journal of Hospitality Management*, *44*, 84–98. doi:10.1016/j.ijhm.2014.10.008

Leighton, P. (2016). Professional self-employment, new power and the sharing economy: Some cautionary tales from Uber. *Journal of Management & Organization*, *22*(6), 859–874. doi:10.1017/jmo.2016.30

Leiter, M. P., & Bakker, A. B. (2010). Work engagement: introduction. In M. P. Leiter & A. B. Bakker (Eds.), *Work Engagement: A Handbook of Essential Theory and Research* (pp. 1–9). Psychology Press.

Li, Z., Duverger, P., & Yu, L. (2018). Employee creativity trumps supervisor-subordinate guanxi: Predicting prequitting behaviors in China's hotel industry. *Tourism Management*, *69*, 23–37. doi:10.1016/j.tourman.2018.05.004

Lin, N. (1998). Guanxi: a conceptual analysis. In A. Y. So, N. Lin, & D. Poston (Eds.), *The Chinese Triangle of Mainland China, Taiwan, and Hong Kong: Comparative Institutional Analyses* (pp. 153–166). Greenwood Publishing Group.

Lu, L., Cai, R., & Gursoy, D. (2019). Developing and validating a service robot integration willingness scale. *International Journal of Hospitality Management*, *80*, 36–51. doi:10.1016/j.ijhm.2019.01.005

MacDonald, R., & Giazitzoglu, A. (2019). Youth, enterprise and precarity: Or, what is, and what is wrong with, the 'gig economy'? *Journal of Sociology (Melbourne, Vic.)*, *55*(4), 724–740. doi:10.1177/1440783319837604

Mahroof, K. (2019). A human-centric perspective exploring the readiness towards smart warehousing: The case of a large retail distribution warehouse. *International Journal of Information Management*, *45*, 176–190. doi:10.1016/j.ijinfomgt.2018.11.008

Marriott. (2020). *The Bot Experience*. Retrieved from https://www.marriott.com/offe rs/the-bot-experience-1347181

Martins, L. L., Gilson, L. L., & Maynard, M. T. (2004). Virtual teams: What do we know and where do we go from here? *Journal of Management*, *30*(6), 805–835. doi:10.1016/j.jm.2004.05.002

May, D. R., Gilson, R. L., & Harter, L. M. (2004). The psychological conditions of meaningfulness, safety and availability and the engagement of the human spirit at work. *Journal of Occupational and Organizational Psychology*, *77*(1), 11–37. doi:10.1348/096317904322915892

Means, A. J. (2018). Platform learning and on-demand labor: Sociotechnical projections on the future of education and work. *Learning, Media and Technology*, *43*(3), 326–338. doi:10.1080/17439884.2018.1504792

Meyer, J. P., & Gagne, M. (2008). Employee engagement from a self-determination theory perspective. *Industrial and Organizational Psychology: Perspectives on Science and Practice*, *1*(1), 60–62. doi:10.1111/j.1754-9434.2007.00010.x

Newell, S., & Marabelli, M. (2015). Strategic opportunities (and challenges) of algorithmic decision-making: A call for action on the long-term societal effects of 'datification.'. *The Journal of Strategic Information Systems*, *24*(1), 3–14. doi:10.1016/j.jsis.2015.02.001

Niehoff, B. P., & Moorman, R. H. (1993). Justice as a mediator of the relationship between methods of monitoring and organizational citizenship behavior. *Academy of Management Journal*, *36*(3), 527–556. doi:10.2307/256591

O'Reilly, C. A., & Chatman, J. (1986). Organizational commitment and psychological attachment: The effects of compliance, identification, and internalization on prosocial behavior. *The Journal of Applied Psychology*, *71*(3), 492–499. doi:10.1037/0021-9010.71.3.492

Organ, D. W., & Ryan, K. (1995). A meta-analytic review of attitudinal and dispositional predictors of organizational citizenship behavior. *Personnel Psychology*, *48*(4), 775–802. doi:10.1111/j.1744-6570.1995.tb01781.x

Osawa, H., Ema, A., Hattori, H., Akiya, N., Kanzaki, N., & Kubo, A. (2017). Analysis of robot hotel: reconstruction of works with robots. *26th IEEE International Symposium on Robot and Human Interactive Communication*. 10.1109/ROMAN.2017.8172305

Ouyang, Y. (2011). An exploration of LMX and personal guanxi on job performance: The mediating effects of CSR. *Journal of Global Business Issues*, *5*(1), 1–10.

Owens, B. P., Baker, W. E., Sumpter, D. M., & Cameron, K. S. (2016). Relational energy at work: Implications for job engagement and job performance. *The Journal of Applied Psychology*, *101*(1), 35–49. doi:10.1037/apl0000032

Petriglieri, G., Ashford, S. J., & Wrzesniewski, A. (2019). Agony and ecstasy in the gig economy: Cultivating holding environments for precarious and personalized work identities. *Administrative Science Quarterly*, *64*(1), 124–170. doi:10.1177/0001839218759646

Ren, S., & Chadee, D. (2017). Influence of work pressure on proactive skill development in China: The role of career networking behavior and guanxi HRM. *Journal of Vocational Behavior*, *98*, 152–162. doi:10.1016/j.jvb.2016.11.004

Roberts, D. R., & Davenport, T. O. (2002). Job engagement: Why it's important and how to improve it. *Employment Relations Today*, *29*(3), 21–29. doi:10.1002/ert.10048

Rust, R. T., & Huang, M.-H. (2014). The service revolution and the transformation of marketing science. *Marketing Science*, *33*(2), 206–221. doi:10.1287/mksc.2013.0836

Ryan, R. M., & Deci, E. L. (2000). Self-determination theory and the facilitation of intrinsic motivation, social development, and well-being. *The American Psychologist*, *55*(1), 68–78. doi:10.1037/0003-066X.55.1.68

Saks, A. M. (2006). Antecedents and consequences of employee engagement. *Journal of Managerial Psychology*, *21*(7), 600–619. doi:10.1108/02683940610690169

Sauder, M., & Espeland, W. N. (2009). The discipline of rankings: Tight coupling and organizational change. *American Sociological Review*, *74*(1), 63–82. doi:10.1177/000312240907400104

Schaufeli, W. B., & Bakker, A. B. (2004). Job demands, job resources, and their relationship with burnout and engagement: A multi-sample study. *Journal of Organizational Behavior*, *25*(3), 293–315. doi:10.1002/job.248

Scholz, T. (2017). *Uberworked and Underpaid: How Workers are Disrupting the Digital Economy*. Polity Press.

Schwartz, D. (2018). Embedded in the crowd: Creative freelancers, crowdsourced work, and occupational community. *Work and Occupations*, *45*(3), 247–282. doi:10.1177/0730888418762263

Senbeto, D. L., & Hon, A. H. (2020). The impacts of social and economic crises on tourist behaviour and expenditure: An evolutionary approach. *Current Issues in Tourism*, *23*(6), 740–755. doi:10.1080/13683500.2018.1546674

Shin, Y., Hur, W. M., Moon, T. W., & Lee, S. (2019). A motivational perspective on job insecurity: Relationships between job insecurity, intrinsic motivation, and performance and behavioral outcomes. *International Journal of Environmental Research and Public Health*, *16*(10), 1–16. doi:10.3390/ijerph16101812

Shoss, M. K. (2017). Job insecurity: An integrative review and agenda for future research. *Journal of Management*, *43*(6), 1911–1939. doi:10.1177/0149206317691574

Stewart, A., & Stanford, J. (2017). Regulating work in the gig economy: What are the options? *Economic and Labour Relations Review*, *28*(3), 420–437. doi:10.1177/1035304617722461

Sun, H., Wang, H., & Wan, Z. (2019). Model and analysis of labour supply for ride-sharing platforms in the presence of sample self-selection and endogeneity. *Transportation Research Part B: Methodological*, *125*, 76–93. doi:10.1016/j.trb.2019.04.004

Ticona, J., & Mateescu, A. (2018). Trusted strangers: Carework platforms' cultural entrepreneurship in the on-demand economy. *New Media & Society*, *20*(11), 4384–4404. doi:10.1177/1461444818773727

Urbanaviciute, I., Lazauskaite-Zabielske, J., Elst, T. V., & De Witte, H. (2018). Qualitative job insecurity and turnover intention: The mediating role of basic psychological needs in public and private sectors. *Career Development International*, *23*(3), 274–290. doi:10.1108/CDI-07-2017-0117

US Bureau of Labor Statistics. (2021). *Labor force statistics from the current population survey*. Available at: www.bls.gov/cps/electronically-mediated-employment.Html

Veen, A., Barratt, T., & Goods, C. (2020). Platform-capital's 'app-etite' for control: A labour process analysis of food-delivery work in Australia. *Work, Employment and Society*, *34*(3), 388–406. doi:10.1177/0950017019836911

Wang, P. Q., Kim, P. B., & Milne, S. (2017). Leader–member exchange (LMX) and its work outcomes: The moderating role of gender. *Journal of Hospitality Marketing & Management*, *26*(2), 125–143. doi:10.1080/19368623.2016.1185989

Wang, P. Q., Kim, P. B., & Milne, S. (2020). The impacts of leader-member guanxi and its differentiation on hotel employees moderated by Confucian values. *International Journal of Hospitality Management*, *91*(3), 102668. doi:10.1016/j.ijhm.2020.102668

Wang, X., Tao, Z., Liang, L., & Gou, Q. (2019). An analysis of salary mechanisms in the sharing economy: The interaction between streamers and unions. *International Journal of Production Economics*, *214*, 106–124. doi:10.1016/j.ijpe.2019.04.003

Weil, D. (2014). *The Fissured Workplace: Why Work Became So Bad for So Many and What Can Be Done to Improve It*. Harvard University Press. doi:10.4159/9780674726123

Weng, L.-C. (2014). Improving employee job performance through ethical leadership and "guanxi": The moderation effects of supervisor-subordinate guanxi differentiation. *Asia Pacific Management Review.*, *19*(3), 321–345.

Wiesenfeld, B. M., Raghuram, S., & Garud, R. (1999). Communication patterns as determinants of organizational identification in a virtual organization. *Organization Science*, *10*(6), 777–790. doi:10.1287/orsc.10.6.777

Wiesenfeld, B. M., Raghuram, S., & Garud, R. (2001). Organizational identification among virtual workers: The role of need for affiliation and perceived work-based social support. *Journal of Management*, *27*(2), 213–229. doi:10.1177/014920630102700205

Wood, A., Lehdonvirta, V., & Graham, M. (2018). Workers of the Internet unite? Online freelancer organisation among remote gig economy workers in six Asian and African countries. *New Technology, Work and Employment*, *33*(2), 95–112. doi:10.1111/ntwe.12112

Wu, Q., Zhang, H., Li, Z., & Liu, K. (2019). Labor control in the gig economy: Evidence from Uber in China. *The Journal of Industrial Relations*, *61*(4), 574–596. doi:10.1177/0022185619854472

Wu, W., Liu, J., & Shang, X. (2018). Gain without pay causes lazybones' loss: The influence of formal and informal leader–member relationships on customer service performance. *Chinese Management Studies*, *12*(3), 634–657. doi:10.1108/CMS-03-2017-0057

Xanthopoulou, D., Bakker, A. B., Demerouti, E., & Schaufeli, W. B. (2009). Reciprocal relationships between job resources, personal resources, and work engagement. *Journal of Vocational Behavior*, *74*(3), 235–244. doi:10.1016/j.jvb.2008.11.003

Yang, F. X., & Lau, V. M.-C. (2015). Does workplace guanxi matter to hotel career success? *International Journal of Hospitality Management*, *47*, 43–53. doi:10.1016/j.ijhm.2015.03.004

Compilation of References

Aaron, C. (1999). Relationship among five forms of commitment: An empirical assessment. *Journal of Academy of Management Journal.*, *20*(3), 397–409.

Abdel-Halim, A. A. (1981). Effects of role stress-job design-technology interaction on employee work satisfaction. *Academy of Management Journal*, *24*(2), 260–273. doi:10.2307/255840

Abildgaard, J. S., Nielsen, K., & Sverke, M. (2018). Can job insecurity be managed? Evaluating an organizational-level intervention addressing the negative effects of restructuring. *Work and Stress*, *32*(2), 105–123. doi:10.1080/02678373.2017.1367735

Abou Kamar, M. S. (2014). Six-Sigma application in the hotel industry: Is it effective for performance improvement. *Research Journal of Management Sciences*, *3*(12), 1–14.

Ackerlof, G., & Shiller, R. (2009). *Animal Spirits: How Human Psychology Drives the Economy, and Why It Matters for Global Capitalism*. Princeton University Press.

Adams, A., Freedman, J., & Prassl, J. (2018). Rethinking legal taxonomies for the gig economy. *Oxford Review of Economic Policy*, *34*(3), 475–494. doi:10.1093/oxrep/gry006

Aghaei, S., Nematbakhsh, M. A., & Farsani, H. K. (2012). Evolution of the world wide web: From Web 1.0 to Web 4.0. *International Journal of Web & Semantic Technology*, *3*(1), 1–10. doi:10.5121/ijwest.2012.3101

Agyeiwaah, E., Dayour, F., & Zhou, J. Y. (2022). How does employee commitment impact customers' attitudinal loyalty? *Journal of Hospitality and Tourism Insights*, *17*(1), 1–30. doi:10.1108/JHTI-09-2020-0169

Ahmed, M. Z., Ahmed, O., Aibao, Z., Hanbin, S., Siyu, L., & Ahmad, A. (2020). Epidemic of COVID-19 in China and associated psychological problems. *Asian Journal of Psychiatry*, *51*, 102092. doi:10.1016/j.ajp.2020.102092 PMID:32315963

Akgunduz, Y., & Eryilmaz, G. (2018). Does turnover intention mediate the effects of job insecurity and co-worker support on social loafing? *International Journal of Hospitality Management*, *68*, 41–49. doi:10.1016/j.ijhm.2017.09.010

Akorede, S. (2018). *Three things to learn from Google's workplace culture*. Retrieved from https://www.entrepreneur.com/article/317582

Akova, O., Cetin, G., & Cifci, I. (2015). The relation between demographic factors and the turnover intention in pre-opening hotel businesses. *Procedia: Social and Behavioral Sciences*, *207*, 377–384. doi:10.1016/j.sbspro.2015.10.177

Al-Ayed, S. I. (2019). The impact of strategic human resource management on organizational resilience: An empirical study on hospitals. *Verslas: teorija ir praktika*, *20*(1), 179–186.

Allan, B. A., Autin, K. L., & Duffy, R. D. (2014). Examining social class and work meaning within the psychology of working framework. *Journal of Career Assessment*, *22*(4), 543–561. doi:10.1177/1069072713514811

Allen, T., Murray, K. A., Zambrana-Torrelio, C., Morse, S. S., Rondinini, C., Di Marco, M., Breit, N., Olival, K. J., & Daszak, P. (2017). Global hotspots and correlates of emerging zoonotic diseases. *Nature Communications*, *8*(1), 1124. doi:10.103841467-017-00923-8 PMID:29066781

Allvin, M., Mellner, C., Movitz, F., & Aronsson, G. (2013). The diffusion of flexibility: Estimating the incidence of low-regulated working conditions. *Nordic Journal of Working Life Studies*, *3*(3), 99–116. doi:10.19154/njwls.v3i3.3013

Ammon, C. E. (2002). Spanish flu epidemic in 1918 in Geneva, Switzerland. *Eurosurveillance*, *7*(12), 190–192. doi:10.2807/esm.07.12.00391-en PMID:12631986

Anderson, K. L., & Mounts, N. S. (2012). Searching for the self: An identity control theory approach to triggers of occupational exploration. *The Journal of Genetic Psychology*, *173*(1), 90–111. doi:10.1080/00221325.2011.573027 PMID:22428377

Andrews, S. (2007). History of Hotels and Motels. In Introduction To Tourism and Hospitality Industry (reprint ed.). New Delhi: Tata McGraw-Hill Education.

Arenas, C., Garcia, V.H.M., & Ota´lora, J.E. (2018). Crowdworking as a knowledge management mechanism in the elicitation of missional software requirement. In *Knowledge Management in Organizations. KMO 2018. Communications in Computer and Information Science*. Cham: Springer.

Ariza-Montes, A., Arjona-Fuentes, J. M., Han, H., & Law, R. (2018). Work environment and well-being of different occupational groups in hospitality: Job Demand–control–support model. *International Journal of Hospitality Management*, *73*, 1–11. doi:10.1016/j.ijhm.2018.01.010

Ariza-Montes, A., Hern'andez-Perlines, F., Han, H., & Law, R. (2019). Human dimension of the hospitality industry: Working conditions and psychological well-being among European servers. *Journal of Hospitality and Tourism Management*, *41*, 138–147. doi:10.1016/j.jhtm.2019.10.013

Arnold, H. J., & Feldman, D. C. (1982). A multivariate analysis of the determinants of job turnover. *The Journal of Applied Psychology*, *67*(3), 350–360. doi:10.1037/0021-9010.67.3.350

Artz, B., & Kaya, I. (2014). Job insecurity and job satisfaction in the United States: The case of public sector union workers. *Industrial Relations Journal*, *45*(2), 103–120. doi:10.1111/irj.12044

Ashford, S. J., Caza, B. B., & Reid, E. M. (2018). From surviving to thriving in the gig economy: A research agenda for individuals in the new world of work. *Research in Organizational Behavior*, *38*, 23–41. doi:10.1016/j.riob.2018.11.001

Ashford, S. J., Lee, C., & Bobko, P. (1989). Content, causes, and consequences of job insecurity: A theory-based measure and substantive test. *The Academy of Management Annals*, *32*(4), 803–829.

Ashforth, B. E., Kreiner, G. E., & Fugate, M. (2000). All in a day's work: Boundaries and micro role transitions. *Academy of Management Review*, *25*(3), 472–491. doi:10.2307/259305

Attila, A. T. (2016). The impact of the hotel industry on the competitiveness of tourism destinations in Hungary. *Journal of Competitiveness*, *8*(4), 85–104. doi:10.7441/joc.2016.04.06

Atwater, L., & Carmeli, A. (2009). Leader–member exchange, feelings of energy, an involvement in creative work. *The Leadership Quarterly*, *20*(3), 264–275. doi:10.1016/j.leaqua.2007.07.009

Autor, D. H., & Dorn, D. (2013). The growth of low-skill service jobs and the polarization of the US labor market. *The American Economic Review*, *103*(5), 1553–1597. doi:10.1257/aer.103.5.1553

Ayse, B. E., & Alexander, E. E. (2018). Alleviating job stress to improve service employee work affect: The influence of rewarding. *Service Business*, *12*(1), 121–141. doi:10.100711628-017-0340-y

Babakus, E., Yavas, U., & Karatepe, O. M. (2017). Work engagement and turnover intentions: Correlates and customer orientation as a moderator. *International Journal of Contemporary Hospitality Management*, *29*(6), 1580–1598. doi:10.1108/IJCHM-11-2015-0649

Bacharach, S. B., Bamberger, P., & Conley, S. (1991). Work-home conflict among nurses and engineers: Mediating the impact of role stress on burnout and satisfaction at work. *Journal of Organizational Behavior*, *12*(1), 39–53. doi:10.1002/job.4030120104

Bajrami, D. D., Terzic, A., Petrovic, M., Radovanovic, M., Tretiakova, T., & Hadoud, A. (2021). Will we have the same employees in hospitality after all? The impact of COVID-19 on employees' work attitudes and turnover intentions. *International Journal of Hospitality Management*, 94. PMID:34785836

Bajwa, U., Gastaldo, D., Di Ruggiero, E., & Knorr, L. (2018). The health of workers in the global gig economy. *Globalization and Health*, *14*(1), 14. doi:10.118612992-018-0444-8

Baker, M. A., & Kim, K. (2020). Dealing with customer incivility: The effects of managerial support on employee psychological well-being and quality-of-life. *International Journal of Hospitality Management*, *87*, 102503. doi:10.1016/j.ijhm.2020.102503

Bambacas, M., & Kulik, T. C. (2013). Job embeddedness in China: How HR practices impact turnover intentions. *International Journal of Human Resource Management*, *24*(10), 1933–1952. doi:10.1080/09585192.2012.725074

Bambra, C., Egan, M., Thomas, S., Petticrew, M., & Whitehead, M. (2007). The psychosocial and health effects of workplace reorganization: A systematic review of task restructuring interventions. *Journal of Epidemiology and Community Health*, *61*(12), 1028–1037. doi:10.1136/jech.2006.054999 PMID:18000123

Bandura, A. (1989). Human agency in social cognitive theory. *The American Psychologist*, *44*(9), 1175–1184. doi:10.1037/0003-066X.44.9.1175 PMID:2782727

Bandura, A. (1991). Social cognitive theory of self-regulation. *Organizational Behavior and Human Decision Processes*, *50*(2), 248–287. doi:10.1016/0749-5978(91)90022-L

Barling, J., Dupre, K. E., & Kelloway, E. K. (2009). Predicting workplace aggression and violence. *Annual Review of Psychology*, *60*(1), 671–692. doi:10.1146/annurev.psych.60.110707.163629 PMID:18793089

Barling, J., & Kelloway, K. E. (1996). Job insecurity and health: The moderating role of workplace control. *Stress Medicine*, *12*(4), 253–259. doi:10.1002/(SICI)1099-1700(199610)12:4<253::AID-SMI710>3.0.CO;2-2

Barton, L. (1994). Crisis management: Preparing for and managing disasters. *The Cornell Hotel and Restaurant Administration Quarterly*, *35*(2), 59–65. doi:10.1177/001088049403500219

Baum, T. (2002). Skills and training for the hospitality sector: A review of issues. *Journal of Vocational Education and Training*, *54*(3), 343–364. doi:10.1080/13636820200200204

Baum, T., & Hai, N. T. T. (2020). Hospitality, tourism, human rights and the impact of COVID-19. *International Journal of Contemporary Hospitality Management*, *32*(7), 2397–2407. doi:10.1108/IJCHM-03-2020-0242

Bec, A., McLennan, B., & Moyle, C. L. (2018). Resilient and sustainable communities. *Sustainability (Basel)*, *10*(12), 4810. doi:10.3390u10124810

Becker, W. J., & Cropanzano, R. (2015). Good acting requires a good cast: A meso-level model of deep acting in work teams. *Journal of Organizational Behavior*, *36*(2), 232–249. doi:10.1002/job.1978

Beehr, T. A., & Newman, J. E. (1978). Job stress, employee health, and organizational effectiveness: A facet analysis, model, and literature review. *Personnel Psychology*, *31*(4), 665–669. doi:10.1111/j.1744-6570.1978.tb02118.x

Bennett, H., & Durkin, M. (2000). The effect of organizational change on employee psychological attachment: An exploratory study. *Journal of Managerial Psychology*, *15*(2), 126–147. doi:10.1108/02683940010310328

Berger, P. L., & Luckmann, T. (1966). *The Social Construction of Reality: A Treatise in the Sociology of Knowledge*. Anchor Books.

Berry, L., Mirabito, A.M., & Baun, W. (2010). What's the hard return on employee wellness programs? *Harvard Business Review, 88*, 1-9.

Bian, Y. (1997). Bringing strong ties back in: Indirect ties, network bridges, and job searches in China. *American Sociological Review*, *62*(3), 366–385. doi:10.2307/2657311

Biddle, B. J. (1986). Recent developments in role theory. *Annual Review of Sociology*, *12*(1), 67–92. doi:10.1146/annurev.so.12.080186.000435

Billing, T. K., Bhagat, R., Babakus, E., Srivastava, B., Shin, M., & Brew, F. (2014). Work–family conflict in four national contexts: A closer look at the role of individualism–collectivism. *International Journal of Cross Cultural Management*, *14*(2), 139–159. doi:10.1177/1470595813502780

Birdir, K. (2002). General manager turnover and root causes. *International Journal of Contemporary Hospitality Management*, *14*(1), 43–47. doi:10.1108/09596110210415123

Blau, P. M. (1964). Justice in social exchange. *Sociological Inquiry*, *34*(2), 193–206. doi:10.1111/j.1475-682X.1964.tb00583.x

Blau, P. M. (1986). *Exchange and power in social life* (2nd ed.). Routledge.

Bode, C., Singh, J., & Rogan, M. (2015). Corporate social initiatives and employee retention. *Organization Science*, *26*(6), 1702–1720. doi:10.1287/orsc.2015.1006

Bolino, M. C., & Turnley, W. H. (2003). Going the extra mile: Cultivating and managing employee citizenship behavior. *The Academy of Management Perspectives*, *17*(3), 60–71. doi:10.5465/ame.2003.10954754

Born, M., Akkerman, A., & Thommes, K. (2016). Peer influence on protest participation: Communication and trust between co-workers as inhibitors or facilitators of mobilization. *Social Science Research*, *56*, 58–72. doi:10.1016/j.ssresearch.2015.11.003 PMID:26857172

Bosman, J., Rothmann, S., & Buitendach, J. H. (2005). Job insecurity, burnout and work engagement: The impact of positive and negative affectivity. *SA Journal of Industrial Psychology*, *31*(4), 48–56. doi:10.4102ajip.v31i4.199

Bouaziz, F., & Hachicha, Z. S. (2018). Strategic human resource management practices and organizational resilience. *Journal of Management Development*, *37*(7), 537–551. doi:10.1108/JMD-11-2017-0358

Brockner, J. (1988). The effects of work layoffs on survivors: Research, theory, and practice. In B. M. Staw & L. L. Cummings (Eds.), *Research in organizational behavior* (Vol. 10). JAI Press.

Brockner, J., Senior, D., & Welch, W. (2014). Corporate volunteerism, the experience of self-integrity, and organizational commitment: Evidence from the field. *Social Justice Research*, *27*(1), 1–23. doi:10.100711211-014-0204-8

Brown, J. (2019). *Employee orientation: Keeping new employees on board*. Retrieved from https://www.thebalancecareers.com/employee-orientation-keeping-new-employees-on-board-1919035

Browne, A., St-Onge Ahmad, S., Beck, C. R., & Nguyen-Van-Tam, J. S. (2016). The roles of transportation and transportation hubs in the propagation of influenza and coronaviruses: A systematic review. *Journal of Travel Medicine*, *23*(1), tav002. doi:10.1093/jtm/tav002 PMID:26782122

Brown, N. A., Orchiston, C., Rovins, J. E., Feldmann-Jensen, S., & Johnston, D. (2018). An integrative framework for investigating disaster resilience within the hotel sector. *Journal of Hospitality and Tourism Management*, *36*, 67–75. doi:10.1016/j.jhtm.2018.07.004

Brown, N. A., Rovins, J. E., Feldmann-Jensen, S., Orchiston, C., & Johnston, D. (2019). Measuring disaster resilience within the hotel sector: An exploratory survey of Wellington and Hawke's bay, New Zealand hotel staff and managers. *International Journal of Disaster Risk Reduction*, *33*, 108–121. doi:10.1016/j.ijdrr.2018.09.014

Brown, S. P., & Peterson, P. A. (1993). Antecedents and consequences of salesperson job satisfaction: Meta-analysis and assessment of causal effects. *JMR, Journal of Marketing Research*, *30*(1), 63–77. doi:10.1177/002224379303000106

Buick, I., & Thomas, M. (2001). Why do middle managers in hotels burn out? *International Journal of Contemporary Hospitality Management*, *13*(6), 304–309. doi:10.1108/EUM0000000005968

Buranyi. (2020, April 10). The WHO v coronavirus: Why it can't handle the pandemic. *The Guardian*. https://www.theguardian.com/news/2020/apr/10/world-health-organization-who-vcoronavirus-why-it-cant-handle-pandemic

Burbano, V. C. (2016). Social responsibility messages and worker wage requirements: Field experimental evidence from online labor marketplaces. *Organization Science*, *27*(4), 1010–1028. doi:10.1287/orsc.2016.1066

Burbano, V. C. (2021). Getting gig workers to do more by doing good: Field experimental evidence from online platform labor marketplaces. *Organization & Environment*, *34*(3), 387–412. doi:10.1177/1086026619846455

Bureau of Labor Statistics. (2023). *Labor force statistics from the current population survey*. Available at: www.bls.gov/cps/electronically-mediated-employment.Html

Burgard, S. A., & Kalousova, L. (2015). Effects of the Great Recession: Health and well-being. *Annual Review of Sociology*, *41*(1), 181–201. doi:10.1146/annurev-soc-073014-112204

Burke, R. J., & Nelson, D. (1998). Mergers and acquisitions, downsizing, and privatization: A North American perspective. In M. K. Gowing, J. D. Kraft, & J. C. Quick (Eds.), *The new organizational reality: Downsizing, restructuring, and revitalization* (pp. 21–54). American Psychological Association. doi:10.1037/10252-001

Burkle, F. M. Jr. (2006). Globalization and disasters: Issues of public health, state capacity and political action. *Journal of International Affairs*, *59*(2), 231–265.

Byrne, J., & Pecchenino, R. A. (2019). Heigh ho, heigh ho: Flexible labor contracts with real option characteristics. *Business Economics (Cleveland, Ohio)*, *54*(1), 25–34. doi:10.105711369-018-00106-3

Cachon, G. P. K., Daniels, K. M., & Lobel, R. (2017). The role of surge pricing on a service platform with self-scheduling capacity. *Manufacturing & Service Operations Management*, *19*(3), 368–384. doi:10.1287/msom.2017.0618

Cain, L., Busser, J., & Kang, H. J. (2018). Executive chefs' calling: Effect on engagement, work-life balance and life satisfaction. *International Journal of Contemporary Hospitality Management*, *30*(5), 2287–2307. doi:10.1108/IJCHM-02-2017-0105

Caldwell, S. D., Herold, D. M., & Fedor, D. B. (2004). Towards an understanding of the relationships between organizational change, individual differences, and changes in person-environment fit: Across-level study. *The Journal of Applied Psychology*, *89*(5), 868–882. doi:10.1037/0021-9010.89.5.868 PMID:15506866

Calgaro, E., Lloyd, K., & Dominey-Howes, D. (2014). From vulnerability to transformation: A framework for assessing the vulnerability and resilience of tourism destinations. *Journal of Sustainable Tourism*, *22*(3), 341–360. doi:10.1080/09669582.2013.826229

Cameron, K. S., Freeman, S. J., & Mishra, A. K. (1993). Downsizing and redesigning organizations. In G. P. Huber & W. H. Glick (Eds.), *Organizational change and redesign* (pp. 19–65). Oxford University Press. doi:10.1093/oso/9780195072853.003.0002

Caplan, S., & Whittemore, R. (2013). Barriers to treatment engagement for depression among Latinas. *Issues in Mental Health Nursing*, *34*(6), 412–424. doi:10.3109/01612840.2012.762958 PMID:23805926

Carmody, P., & Fortuin, A. (2019). 'Ride-sharing', virtual capital and impacts on labor in Cape Town, South Africa. *African Geographical Review*, *38*(3), 196–208. doi:10.1080/19376812.2019.1607149

Carnevale, J. B., & Hatak, I. (2020). Employee adjustment and well-being in the era of COVID-19: Implications for human resource management. *Journal of Business Research*, *116*, 183–187. doi:10.1016/j.jbusres.2020.05.037 PMID:32501303

Carr, C. T., Hall, R. D., Mason, A. J., & Varney, E. J. (2017). Cueing employability in the gig economy: Effects of task-relevant and task-irrelevant information on Fiverr. *Management Communication Quarterly*, *31*(3), 409–428. doi:10.1177/0893318916687397

Carver, C. S., & Scheier, M. F. (1990). Origins and functions of positive and negative affect. *Psychological Review*, *97*(1), 19–35. doi:10.1037/0033-295X.97.1.19

Casey, D., & Sieber, S. (2016). Employees, sustainability and motivation: Increasing employee engagement by addressing sustainability and corporate social responsibility. *Research in Hospitality Management*, *6*(1), 69–76. doi:10.2989/RHM.2016.6.1.9.1297

Cavanaugh, M. A., Boswell, W. R., Roehling, M. V., & Boudreau, J. W. (2000). An empirical examination of self-reported work stress among U.S. managers. *The Journal of Applied Psychology*, *85*(1), 65–74. doi:10.1037/0021-9010.85.1.65 PMID:10740957

Chang, C. L., McAleer, M., & Ramos, V. (2020). A charter for sustainable tourism after COVID-19. *Sustainability (Basel)*, *12*(3671), 1–4. doi:10.3390u12093671

Chan, N. K. (2019). "Becoming an expert in driving for Uber": Uber driver/bloggers' performance of expertise and self-presentation on YouTube. *New Media & Society*, *21*(9), 2048–2067. doi:10.1177/1461444819837736

Chan, N. K., & Humphreys, L. (2018). Mediatization of social space and the case of Uber drivers. *Media and Communication*, *6*(2), 29–38. doi:10.17645/mac.v6i2.1316

Chartered Institute of Personnel and Development. (2007a). *Trade Unions: a short history. Chartered Institute of Personnel and Development*. Retrieved February 4, 2022, from https://www.cipd.co.uk/subjects/empreltns/tradunin/tradunihist.htm?IsSrchRes=1

Chartered Institute of Personnel and Development. (2007b). Work–life balance: Who benefits? *Chartered Institute of Personnel and Development*. Retrieved February 4, 2022, from https://www.cipd.co.uk/subjects/wrkgtime/wrktmewrklfbal/worklifeba.htm?IsSrchRes=1

Chen, C. C., Chen, X. P., & Huang, S. (2013). Chinese guanxi: An integrative review and new directions for future research. *Management and Organization Review*, *9*(1), 167–207. doi:10.1111/more.12010

Cheng, C. H. (2011). A study of critical factors of the job involvement for hotel employees—Taking hotels in Taiwan as an example. *International Journal of Hospitality Management*, *30*(4), 990–996. doi:10.1016/j.ijhm.2011.03.001

Cheng, G. H. L., & Chan, D. K. S. (2008). Who suffers more from job insecurity? A meta-analytic review. *Applied Psychology*, *57*(2), 271–303. doi:10.1111/j.1464-0597.2007.00312.x

Cheng, J. C., & O-Yang, Y. (2018). Hotel employee job crafting, burnout, and satisfaction: The moderating role of perceived organizational support. *International Journal of Hospitality Management*, *72*, 78–85. doi:10.1016/j.ijhm.2018.01.005

Cheng, M., & Foley, C. (2019). Algorithmic management: The case of Airbnb. *International Journal of Hospitality Management*, *83*, 33–36. doi:10.1016/j.ijhm.2019.04.009

Cheng, Y., Huang, H. Y., Li, P. R., & Hsu, J. H. (2011). Employment insecurity, workplace justice and employees' burnout in Taiwanese employees: A validation study. *International Journal of Behavioral Medicine*, *18*(4), 391–401. doi:10.100712529-011-9152-y PMID:21380932

Chen, H., & Ayoun, B. (2019). Is negative workplace humor really all that "negative"? Workplace humor and hospitality employees' job embeddedness. *International Journal of Hospitality Management*, *79*(May), 41–49. doi:10.1016/j.ijhm.2018.12.010

Chen, H., Ayoun, B., & Eyoun, K. (2018). Work-family conflict and turnover intentions: A study comparing China and U.S. hotel employees. *Journal of Human Resources in Hospitality & Tourism*, *17*(2), 247–269. doi:10.1080/15332845.2017.1406272

Chen, J. Y. (2018). Thrown under the bus and outrunning it! The logic of Didi and taxi drivers' labour and activism in the on-demand economy. *New Media & Society*, *20*(8), 2691–2711. doi:10.1177/1461444817729149

Chen, J., Wang, L., & Tang, N. (2016). Half the sky: The moderating role of cultural collectivism in job turnover among Chinese female workers. *Journal of Business Ethics*, *133*(3), 1–12. doi:10.100710551-014-2395-1

Chen, P. J., & Choi, Y. (2008). Generational differences in work values: A study of hospitality management. *International Journal of Contemporary Hospitality Management*, *20*(6), 595–615. doi:10.1108/09596110810892182

Chen, Y. P., & Shaffer, M. A. (2017). The influences of perceived organizational support and motivation on self-initiated expatriates' organizational and community embeddedness. *Journal of Business Research*, *52*, 197–208.

Chen, Y., & Tjosvold, D. (2006). Participative leadership by American and Chinese managers in China: The role of relationships. *Journal of Management Studies*, *43*(8), 1727–1752. doi:10.1111/j.1467-6486.2006.00657.x

Chen, Y., Yu, E., & Son, J. (2014). Beyond leader–member exchange (LMX) differentiation: An indigenous approach to leader–member relationship differentiation. *The Leadership Quarterly*, *25*(3), 611–627. doi:10.1016/j.leaqua.2013.12.004

Chew, E. Y. T., & Jahari, S. A. (2014). Destination image as a mediator between perceived risks and revisit intention: A case of post-disaster Japan. *Tourism Management*, *40*, 382–393. doi:10.1016/j.tourman.2013.07.008

Chiang, C. F., & Hsieh, T. S. (2012). The impacts of perceived organizational support and psychological empowerment on job performance: The mediating effects of organizational citizenship behavior. *International Journal of Hospitality Management*, *31*(1), 180–190. doi:10.1016/j.ijhm.2011.04.011

Chiang, C. F., & Jang, S. (2008). The antecedents and consequences of psychological empowerment: The case of Taiwan's hotel companies. *Journal of Hospitality & Tourism Research (Washington, D.C.)*, *32*(1), 40–61. doi:10.1177/1096348007309568

Chien, G. C., & Law, R. (2003). The impact of the Severe Acute Respiratory Syndrome on hotels: A case study of Hong Kong. *International Journal of Hospitality Management*, *22*(3), 327–332. doi:10.1016/S0278-4319(03)00041-0 PMID:32287842

Chinazzi, M., Davis, T. J., Ajelli, M., Gioannini, C., Litvinova, M., Merler, S., Pastore y Piontti, A., Mu, K., Rossi, L., Sun, K., Viboud, C., Xiong, X., Yu, H., Halloran, M. E., Longini, I. M. Jr, & Vespignani, A. (2020). The effect of travel restrictions on the spread of the 2019 novel coronavirus (COVID-19) outbreak. *Science*, *368*(6489), 395–400. doi:10.1126cience.aba9757 PMID:32144116

Chirumbolo, A., & Areni, A. (2010). Job insecurity influence on job performance and mental health: Testing the moderating effect of the need for closure. *Economic and Industrial Democracy*, *31*(2), 195–214. doi:10.1177/0143831X09358368

Choi, H. M., Mohammad, A. A. A., & Kim, W. G. (2019). Understanding hotel frontline employees' emotional intelligence, emotional labor, job stress, coping strategies and burnout. *International Journal of Hospitality Management*, *82*, 199–208. doi:10.1016/j.ijhm.2019.05.002

Choi, Y. G., Kwon, J., & Kim, W. (2013). Effects of attitudes vs experience of workplace fun on employee behaviors: Focused on Generation Y in the hospitality industry. *International Journal of Contemporary Hospitality Management*, *25*(3), 410–427. doi:10.1108/09596111311311044

Chou, L. F. (2002). Guanxi and social networks in Chinese organizations. Indigenous. *Psychological Research in Chinese Societies.*, *18*(1), 175–228.

Christie, N., & Ward, H. (2019). The health and safety risks for people who drive for work in the gig economy. *Journal of Transport & Health*, *13*, 115–127. doi:10.1016/j.jth.2019.02.007

Chung, H., & van Oorschot, W. (2011). Institutions versus market forces: Explaining the employment insecurity of European individuals during (the beginning of) the financial crisis. *Journal of European Social Policy*, *21*(4), 287–301. doi:10.1177/0958928711412224

Cimbaljević, M., Nedeljković-Knežević, M., Demirović-Bajrami, D., Dunjić, M., El Bilali, H., & Rančić-DemirDemir, M. (2020). How do job-related constructs determine employee turnover? Serbian hotels example. *Journal of the Geographical Institute "Jovan Cvijic"*, *70*(2), 129–143.

Coch, L., & French, J. R. P. Jr. (1948). Overcoming Resistance to Change. *Human Relations*, *1*(4), 512–532. doi:10.1177/001872674800100408

Cohen, J. (2002). I/Os in the know offer insights on generation X workers. *Monitor on Psychology*, *33*(2), 66–67.

Conway, J. M., & Lance, C. E. (2010). What reviewers should expect from authors regarding common method bias in organizational research. *Journal of Business and Psychology*, *25*(3), 325–334. doi:10.100710869-010-9181-6

Coombs, W. T., & Laufer, D. (2018). Global crisis management–current research and future directions. *Journal of International Management*, *24*(3), 199–203. doi:10.1016/j.intman.2017.12.003

Cooper, C. L., & Marshall, J. (1976). Occupational sources of stress: A review of the literature relating to coronary heart disease and mental ill-health. *Journal of Occupational Psychology*, *49*(1), 11–28. doi:10.1111/j.2044-8325.1976.tb00325.x

Corley, K. G. (2004). Defined by our strategy or our culture? Hierarchical differences in perceptions of organizational identity and change. *Human Relations*, *57*(9), 1145–1177. doi:10.1177/0018726704047141

Cottini, E., & Ghinetti, P. (2018). Employment insecurity and employees' health in Denmark. *Health Economics*, *27*(2), 426–439. doi:10.1002/hec.3580 PMID:28868624

Cotton, J. L., & Tuttle, J. M. (1986). Employee turnover: A meta-analysis and review with implications for research. *Academy of Management Review*, *11*(1), 55–70. doi:10.2307/258331

Coverman, S. (1989). Role overload, role conflict and stress: Addressing consequences of multiple role demands. *Social Forces*, *67*(4), 965–982. doi:10.2307/2579710

Cox, T., Griffiths, A., Barlowe, C., Randall, R., Thomson, L., & Rial-Gonzalez, E. (2000). Organisational interventions for work stress: A risk management approach. *HSE Contract Research Report*, *286*, 68.

Crawford, E. R., LePine, J. A., & Rich, B. L. (2010). Linking job demands and resources to employee engagement and burnout: A theoretical extension and meta-analytic test. *The Journal of Applied Psychology*, *95*(5), 834–848. doi:10.1037/a0019364 PMID:20836586

Creed, P. A., Wamelink, T., & Hu, S. (2015). Antecedents and consequences to perceived career goal–progress discrepancies. *Journal of Vocational Behavior*, *87*, 43–53. doi:10.1016/j.jvb.2014.12.001

Creed, P., Tilbury, C., Buys, N., & Crawford, M. (2011). The career aspirations and action behaviours of Australian adolescents in out-of-home-care. *Children and Youth Services Review*, *33*(9), 1720–1729. doi:10.1016/j.childyouth.2011.04.033

Cunliffe, B. (1969). *Roman Bath*. Society of Antiquaries of London. doi:10.26530/20.500.12657/37345

Daft, R. L. (2005). Types of Planned Change. In R. L. Draft (Ed.), *Management* (6th ed., p. 387). Thomas South Western.

Dai, Y., Zhuang, W., & Huan, T. C. (2019). Engage or quit? The moderating role of abusive supervision between resilience, intention to leave and work engagement. *Tourism Management*, *70*, 69–77. doi:10.1016/j.tourman.2018.07.014

Dalal, R. S. (2005). A meta-analysis of the relationship between organizational citizenship behavior and counterproductive work behavior. *The Journal of Applied Psychology*, *90*(6), 1241–1255. doi:10.1037/0021-9010.90.6.1241 PMID:16316277

Dalton, D. R., & Todor, W. D. (1993). Turnover, transfer, absenteeism: An interdependent Perspective. *Journal of Management*, *19*(2), 193–219. doi:10.1177/014920639301900202

Darvishmotevali, M., Arasli, H., & Kilic, H. (2017). Effect of job insecurity on frontline employee's performance: Looking through the lens of psychological strains and leverages. *International Journal of Contemporary Hospitality Management*, *29*(6), 1724–1744. doi:10.1108/IJCHM-12-2015-0683

Davidson, L. P. (2005). "A Service Machine": Hotel Guests and the Development of an Early-Twentieth-Century Building Type. *Perspectives in Vernacular Architecture*, *10*, 113–129. https://www.jstor.org/stable/3514344

Davies, W. (2020, March 24). The last global crisis didn't change the world. But this one could. *The Guardian*. https://www.theguardian.com/commentisfree/2020/mar/24/coronavirus-crisischange-world-financial-global-capitalism

Davy, J. A., Kinicki, A. J., & Scheck, C. L. (1997). A test of job security's direct and mediated effects on withdrawal cognitions. *Journal of Organizational Behavior*, *18*(4), 323–349. doi:10.1002/(SICI)1099-1379(199707)18:4<323::AID-JOB801>3.0.CO;2-#

Dayour, F., Adongo, C. A., Amuquandoh, F. E., & Adam, I. (2021). Managing the COVID-19 crisis: Coping and post-recovery strategies for hospitality and tourism businesses in Ghana. *Journal of Hospitality and Tourism Insights.*, *4*(4), 373–392.

De Clercq, D., Azeem, M. U., Haq, I. U., & Bouckenooghe, D. (2020). The stress-reducing effect of coworker support on turnover intentions: Moderation by political ineptness and despotic leadership. *Journal of Business Research*, *111*, 12–24. doi:10.1016/j.jbusres.2020.01.064

de Jong, T., Wiezer, N., de Weerd, M., Nielsen, K., Mattila-Holappa, P., & Mockałło, Z. (2016). The impact of restructuring on employee well-being: A systematic review of longitudinal studies. *Work and Stress*, *30*(1), 91–114. doi:10.1080/02678373.2015.1136710

De Stefano, V. (2016). "The rise of the "just-in-time workforce": On-demand work, crowdwork and labor protection in the "Gig Economy." *Comparative Labor Law Journal, 37*(3), 471-504.

De Witte, H. (2005). Job insecurity: Review of the international literature on definitions, prevalence, antecedents and consequences. *SA Journal of Industrial Psychology*, *31*(4), 1–6. doi:10.4102ajip.v31i4.200

De Witte, H., De Cuyper, N., Handaja, Y., Sverke, M., Näswall, K., & Hellgren, J. (2010). Associations between quantitative and qualitative job insecurity and well-being. *International Studies of Management & Organization*, *40*(1), 40–56. doi:10.2753/IMO0020-8825400103

De Witte, H., Vander Elst, T., & De Cuyper, N. (2015). Job insecurity, health and well-being. In J. Vuori, R. Blonk, & R. Price (Eds.), *Sustainable Working Lives. Aligning Perspectives on Health, Safety and Well-Being* (pp. 109–128). Springer.

Deci, E. L., Connell, J. P., & Ryan, R. M. (1989). Self-determination in a work organization. *The Journal of Applied Psychology*, *74*(4), 580–590. doi:10.1037/0021-9010.74.4.580

Deci, E. L., & Ryan, R. M. (1985). *Intrinsic Motivation and Self-determination in Human Behavior*. Plenum. doi:10.1007/978-1-4899-2271-7

Deci, E. L., & Ryan, R. M. (2004). *Handbook of Self-determination Research*. The University of Rochester Press.

DeConinck, J. B. (2010). The effect of organizational justice, perceived organizational support, and perceived supervisor support on marketing employees' level of trust. *Journal of Business Research*, *63*(12), 1349–1355. doi:10.1016/j.jbusres.2010.01.003

Deery, M., & Jago, L. (2009). A framework for work-life balance practices: Addressing the needs of the tourism industry. *Tourism and Hospitality Research*, *9*(2), 97–108. doi:10.1057/thr.2009.4

Degoey, P. (2000). Contagious justice: Exploring the social construction of justice in organization. In B. M. Staw & R. I. Sutton (Eds.), Research in Organizational Behavior. JAI Press. doi:10.1016/S0191-3085(00)22003-0

Dekker, S. W. A., & Schaufeli, W. B. (1995). The effects of job insecurity on psychological health and withdrawal: A longitudinal study. *Australian Psychologist*, *30*(1), 57–63. doi:10.1080/00050069508259607

Demerouti, E., Bakker, A. B., Nachreiner, F., & Schaufeli, W. B. (2001). The job demands-resources model of burnout. *The Journal of Applied Psychology*, *86*(3), 499–512. doi:10.1037/0021-9010.86.3.499 PMID:11419809

Densten, I. L. (2001). Re-thinking burnout. *Journal of Organizational Behavior, 22*(8), 833–847. doi:10.1002/job.115

Desclaux, A., Badji, D., Ndione, A. G., & Sow, K. (2017). Accepted monitoring or endured quarantine? Ebola contacts' perceptions in Senegal. *Social Science & Medicine, 178*, 38–45. doi:10.1016/j.socscimed.2017.02.009 PMID:28192745

Devaux, C. A., Mediannikov, O., Medkour, H., & Raoult, D. (2019). Infectious disease risk across the growing human-non human primate interface: A review of the evidence. *Frontiers in Public Health, 7*, 305. doi:10.3389/fpubh.2019.00305 PMID:31828053

Diener, E. (2009). Subjective well-being. In E. Diener (Ed.), Social Indicators Research Series: Vol. 37. *The Science of Well-Being*. Springer. doi:10.1007/978-90-481-2350-6_2

Dik, B. J., & Duffy, R. D. (2009). Calling and vocation at work: Definitions and prospects for research and practice. *The Counseling Psychologist, 37*(3), 424–450. doi:10.1177/0011000008316430

Dimitropoulos, P. E. (2018). Profitability determinants of the Greek hospitality industry: the crisis effect. In Innovative Approaches to Tourism and Leisure. Springer.

Dolnicar, S. (2019). A review of research into paid online peer-to-peer accommodation: Launching the Annals of Tourism Research curated collection on peer-to-peer accommodation. *Annals of Tourism Research, 75*, 248–264. doi:10.1016/j.annals.2019.02.003

Doucette, M. H., & Bradford, W. D. (2019). Dual job holding and the gig economy: Allocation of effort across primary and gig job. *Southern Economic Journal, 85*(4), 1217–1242. doi:10.1002oej.12338

Druce, C. (2007). Green Regime will Bring in the Business. *CatererSearch.* http://www.caterersearch.com/Articles/2007/10/25/316825/Green-regime- 39will-bring-in-the-business39.htm

Dube, K., Nhamo, G., & Chikodzi, D. (2020). COVID-19 cripples global restaurant and hospitality industry. *Current Issues in Tourism*, 1–4.

Duchek, S., Raetze, S., & Scheuch, I. (2019). *The role of diversity in organizational resilience: A theoretical framework*. Business Research. doi:10.100740685-019-0084-8

Duffy, R. D., & Autin, K. L. (2013). Disentangling the link between perceiving a calling and living a calling. *Journal of Counseling Psychology, 60*(2), 219–227. doi:10.1037/a0031934 PMID:23438413

Duffy, R. D., Bott, E. M., Allan, B. A., Torrey, C. L., & Dik, B. J. (2012). Perceiving a calling, living a calling, and job satisfaction: Testing a moderated, multiple mediator model. *Journal of Counseling Psychology, 59*(1), 50–59. doi:10.1037/a0026129 PMID:22059426

Duffy, R. D., & Dik, B. J. (2013). Research on calling: What have we learned and where are we going? *Journal of Vocational Behavior, 83*(3), 428–436. doi:10.1016/j.jvb.2013.06.006

Duffy, R. D., Dik, B. J., Douglass, R. P., England, J. W., & Velez, B. L. (2018). Work as a calling: A theoretical model. *Journal of Counseling Psychology*, *65*(4), 423–429. doi:10.1037/cou0000276 PMID:29999369

Duffy, R. D., Dik, B. J., & Steger, M. F. (2011). Calling and work-related outcomes: Career commitment as a mediator. *Journal of Vocational Behavior*, *78*(2), 210–218. doi:10.1016/j.jvb.2010.09.013

Duffy, R. D., Douglass, R. P., Autin, K. L., & Allan, B. A. (2014). Examining predictors and outcomes of a career calling among undergraduate students. *Journal of Vocational Behavior*, *85*(3), 309–318. doi:10.1016/j.jvb.2014.08.009

Duncan, L. E., & Agronick, G. S. (1995). The intersection of life stage and social events: Personality and life outcomes. *Journal of Personality and Social Psychology*, *69*(3), 558–568. doi:10.1037/0022-3514.69.3.558 PMID:7562395

Duncan, T., Scott, D. G., & Baum, T. (2013). The mobilities of hospitality work: An exploration of issues and debates. *Annals of Tourism Research*, *41*, 1–19. doi:10.1016/j.annals.2012.10.004

Duxbury, L., Higgins, C., & Lee, C. (1994). Work-Family Conflict: A Comparison by Gender, Family Type, and Perceived Control. *Journal of Family Issues*, *15*(3), 449–466. doi:10.1177/019251394015003006

Dysvik, A., & Kuvaas, B. (2010). Exploring the relative and combined influence of mastery approach goals and work intrinsic motivation on employee turnover intention. *Personnel Review*, *39*(5), 622–638. doi:10.1108/00483481011064172

Eisenberger, R., Huntington, R., Hutchison, S., & Sowa, D. (1986). Perceived organizational support. *The Journal of Applied Psychology*, *71*(3), 500–507. doi:10.1037/0021-9010.71.3.500

Eisner, S. P. (2005). Managing generation Y. *S.A.M. Advanced Management Journal*, *70*(4), 4–15.

Elrehail, H., Harazneh, I., Abuhjeeleh, M., Alzghoul, A., Alnajdawi, S., & Ibrahim, H. M. H. (2019). Employee satisfaction, human resource management practices and competitive advantage: The case of Northern Cyprus. *European Journal of Management and Business Economics*, *29*(2), 125–149. doi:10.1108/EJMBE-01-2019-0001

Elshaer, A. M., & Marzouk, A. M. (2019). *Labor in the tourism and hospitality industry: skills, ethics, issues, and rights*. CRC Press. doi:10.1201/9780429465093

Elshaer, I. A., & Saad, S. K. (2016). Political instability and tourism in Egypt: Exploring survivors' attitudes after downsizing. *Journal of Policy Research Tourism Events.*, *9*(1), 3–22.

Elshaer, I. A., & Saad, S. K. (2017). Political instability and tourism in Egypt: Exploring survivors' attitudes after downsizing. *Journal of Policy Research in Tourism, Leisure & Events*, *9*(1), 3–22. doi:10.1080/19407963.2016.1233109

Emen, J. (2020). Hospitality industry facing potentially devastating coronavirus impact. *Barron's*. Available at: https://barrons.com/articles/hospitality-industry-facing-potentially-devastatingcoronavirus-impact-01584118579

Employers and work–life balance. (2008). Work–Life Balance: Introduction. Employers for Work–Life Balance. *The Work foundation*. Retrieved February 4, 2022, from http://www.employersforwork–lifebalance.org.uk/work/definition.htm

Erdil, O., & Müceldili, B. (2014). The effects of envy on job engagement and turnover intention. *Procedia: Social and Behavioral Sciences*, *150*, 447–454. doi:10.1016/j.sbspro.2014.09.050

Etehadi, B., & Karatepe, O. M. (2019). The impact of job insecurity on critical hotel employee outcomes: The mediating role of self-efficacy. *Journal of Hospitality Marketing & Management*, *28*(6), 665–689. doi:10.1080/19368623.2019.1556768

Evans, A., & Vernon, K. (2007). Work–Life Balance in Hong Kong: Case Studies. *Community Business*.

Evans, N., & Elphick, S. (2005). Models of crisis management: An evaluation of their value for strategic planning in the international travel industry. *International Journal of Tourism Research*, *7*(3), 135–150. doi:10.1002/jtr.527

Eyoun, K., Chen, H., Ayoun, B., & Khliefat, A. (2020). The relationship between purpose of performance appraisal and psychological contract: Generational differences as a moderator. *International Journal of Hospitality Management*, *86*, 1–8. doi:10.1016/j.ijhm.2020.102449

Fan, Y. (2002). Questioning guanxi: Definition, classification and implications. *International Business Review*, *11*(5), 543–561. doi:10.1016/S0969-5931(02)00036-7

Farh, J.-L., Tsui, A. S., Xin, K., & Cheng, B.-S. (1998). The influence of relational demography and guanxi: The Chinese case. *Organization Science*, *9*(4), 471–488. doi:10.1287/orsc.9.4.471

Faulkner, B. (2001). Towards a framework for tourism disaster management. *Tourism Management*, *22*(2), 135–147. doi:10.1016/S0261-5177(00)00048-0

Fedor, D. B., Caldwell, S., & Herold, D. M. (2006). The effects of organizational changes on employee commitment: A multilevel investigation. *Personnel Psychology*, *59*(1), 1–29. doi:10.1111/j.1744-6570.2006.00852.x

Ferrin, D. L., & Dirks, K. T. (2002). Trust in leadership: Meta-analytic findings and implications for research and practice. *The Journal of Applied Psychology*, *87*(4), 611–628. doi:10.1037/0021-9010.87.4.611 PMID:12184567

Filimonau, V., & De Coteau, D. (2020). Tourism resilience in the context of integrated destination and disaster management (DM2). *International Journal of Tourism Research*, *22*(2), 202–222. doi:10.1002/jtr.2329

Filimonau, V., Derqui, B., & Matute, J. (2020). The COVID-19 pandemic and organisational commitment of senior hotel managers. *International Journal of Hospitality Management*, *91*, 102659. doi:10.1016/j.ijhm.2020.102659 PMID:32904709

Flum, H., & Blustein, D. L. (2000). Reinvigorating the study of vocational exploration: A framework for research. *Journal of Vocational Behavior*, *56*(3), 380–404. doi:10.1006/jvbe.2000.1721

Fogarty, T. J., Singh, J., Rhoads, G. K., & Moore, R. K. (2000). Antecedents and consequences of burnout in accounting: Beyond the role stress model. *Behavioral Research in Accounting*, *12*, 31–67.

Folkman, S. (1984). Personal control and stress and coping processes: A theoretical analysis. *Journal of Personality and Social Psychology*, *46*(4), 839–852. doi:10.1037/0022-3514.46.4.839 PMID:6737195

Ford, R. C., McLaughlin, F. S., & Newstrom, J. W. (2005). Creating and sustaining fun work environments in hospitality and service organizations. *Journal of Human Resources in Hospitality & Tourism*, *4*(1), 11–30. doi:10.1300/J171v04n01_02

Fox, M. A., Spicer, K., Chosewood, L. C., Susi, P., Johns, D. O., & Dotson, G. S. (2018). Implications of applying cumulative risk assessment to the workplace. *Environment International*, *115*, 115. doi:10.1016/j.envint.2018.03.026

Freudenberger, H. J. (1974). Staff burn-out. *The Journal of Social Issues*, *30*(1), 159–165. doi:10.1111/j.1540-4560.1974.tb00706.x

Friedman, G. (2014). Workers without employers: Shadow corporations and the rise of the gig economy. *Review of Keynesian Economics*, *2*(2), 171–188. doi:10.4337/roke.2014.02.03

Frone, M. R. (2018). What happened to the employed during the Great Recession? A U.S. population study of net change in employee insecurity, health, and organizational commitment. *Journal of Vocational Behavior*, *107*, 246–260. doi:10.1016/j.jvb.2018.05.001 PMID:31303656

Gandhi, A., Hidayanto, A., & Sucahyo, Y. (2018). Exploring people's intention to become platform-based gig workers: An empirical qualitative study. In *2018 International Conference on Information Technology Systems and Innovation (ICITSI), 22–26 October, Conference Proceedings* (pp. 266–271). 10.1109/ICITSI.2018.8696017

Gandini, A. (2018). Labour process theory and the gig economy. *Human Relations*, *72*(6), 1039–1056. doi:10.1177/0018726718790002

Gaunt, R., & Benjamin, O. (2007). Job insecurity, stress and gender. *Community Work & Family*, *10*(3), 341–355. doi:10.1080/13668800701456336

Ghaderi, Z., King, B., & Hall, C. M. (2022). Crisis preparedness of hospitality managers: Evidence from Malaysia. *Journal of Hospitality and Tourism Insights*, *5*(2), 292–310. doi:10.1108/JHTI-10-2020-0199

Gilfillan, G. (2018). *Characteristics and use of casual employees in Australia*. Parliament of Australia, Research Paper Series, Canberra.

Gills, B. (2020). Deep restoration: From the great implosion to the great awakening. *Globalizations*, *17*(4), 577–579. Advance online publication. doi:10.1080/14747731.2020.1748364

Gilly, J. P., Kechidi, M., & Talbot, D. (2014). Resilience of organisations and territories: The role of pivot firms. *European Management Journal*, *32*(4), 596–602. doi:10.1016/j.emj.2013.09.004

Giudici, M., & Filimonau, V. (2019). Exploring the linkages between managerial leadership, communication and teamwork in successful event delivery. *Tourism Management Perspectives*, *32*, 100558. doi:10.1016/j.tmp.2019.100558

Glaesser, D. (2006). *Crisis management in the tourism Industry*. Butterworth-Heinemann. doi:10.4324/9780080464596

Godinic, D., Obrenovic, B., & Khudaykulov, A. (2020). Effects of economic uncertainty on mental health in the COVID-19 pandemic context: Social Identity Disturbance, Job Uncertainty and Psychological Well-Being Model. *International Journal of Innovative Economic Development*, *6*(1), 61–74. doi:10.18775/ijied.1849-7551-7020.2015.61.2005

Goh, E., & Jie, F. (2019). To waste or not to waste: Exploring motivational factors of generation Z hospitality employees towards food wastage in the hospitality industry. *International Journal of Hospitality Management*, *80*, 126–135. doi:10.1016/j.ijhm.2019.02.005

Goods, C., Veen, A., & Barratt, T. (2019). Is your gig any good?' Analysing job quality in the Australian platform-based food-delivery sector. *The Journal of Industrial Relations*, *61*(4), 502–527. doi:10.1177/0022185618817069

Gordon, C. (1976). Development of evaluated role identities. *Annual Review of Sociology*, *2*(1), 405–433. doi:10.1146/annurev.so.02.080176.002201

Gossling, S., Scott, D., & Hall, C.M. (2021). Pandemics, tourism and global change: A rapid assessment of COVID-19. *Journal Sustainable Tourism*, *29*(1), 1–20.

Gossling, S., Scott, D., & Hall, C. M. (2021). Pandemics, tourism, and global change: A rapid assessment of COVID-19. *Journal of Sustainable Tourism*, *29*(1), 1–20. doi:10.1080/09669582.2020.1758708

Gowing, M. K., Kraft, J. D., & Campbell, Q. J. (Eds.). (1998). *The new organizational reality: Downsizing, restructuring, and revitalization*. American Psychological Association. doi:10.1037/10252-000

Graf-Vlachy, L., Sun, S., & Zhang, S. X. (2020). Predictors of managers' mental health during the COVID-19 pandemic. *European Journal of Psychotraumatology*, *11*(1), 1834195. doi:10.1080/20008198.2020.1834195 PMID:33244365

Graham, M., & Anwar, M. (2018). Two models for a fairer sharing economy. In N. Davidson, M. Finck, & J. Infranca (Eds.), *The Cambridge Handbook of the Law of the Sharing Economy* (pp. 328–340). Cambridge University Press. doi:10.1017/9781108255882.025

Grandey, A. A., & Cropanzano, R. (1999). The conservation of resource model applied to work-family conflict and strain. *Journal of Vocational Behavior*, *54*(2), 350–370. doi:10.1006/jvbe.1998.1666

Graves, L. M., & Luciano, M. M. (2013). Self-determination at work: Understanding the role of leader–member exchange. *Motivation and Emotion*, *37*(3), 518–536. doi:10.100711031-012-9336-z

Greenhalgh, L. (1983). Managing the job insecurity crisis. *Human Resource Management Journal*, *22*(4), 431.

Greenhalgh, L., & Rosenblatt, Z. (1984). Job insecurity: Toward conceptual clarity. *Academy of Management Review*, *9*(3), 438–448. doi:10.2307/258284

Greenhaus, J. H., & Beutell, N. J. (1985). Sources of conflict between work and family roles. *Academy of Management Review*, *10*(1), 76–88. doi:10.2307/258214

Grissemann, U., Plank, A., & Brunner-Sperdin, A. (2013). Enhancing business performance of hotels: The role of innovation and customer orientation. *International Journal of Hospitality Management*, *33*(1), 347–356. doi:10.1016/j.ijhm.2012.10.005

Groth, P. (1986). Living Downtown: The History of Residential Hotels in the United States. University of California Press.

Gursoy, D., Maier, T. A., & Chi, C. G. (2008). Generational differences: An examination of work values and generational gaps in the hospitality workforce. *International Journal of Hospitality Management*, *27*(3), 448–458. doi:10.1016/j.ijhm.2007.11.002

Gustin, M., & Weaver, P. (1996). Are hotels prepared for the environmental consumer? *The Cornell Hotel and Restaurant Administration Quarterly*, *20*(2), 1–14.

Gutek, B. A., Searle, S., & Klepa, L. (1991). Rational versus gender role expectations for work–family conflict. *The Journal of Applied Psychology*, *76*(4), 560–568. doi:10.1037/0021-9010.76.4.560

Hajibaba, H., Gretzel, U., Leisch, F., & Dolnicar, S. (2015). Crisis-resistant tourists. *Annals of Tourism Research*, *53*, 46–60. doi:10.1016/j.annals.2015.04.001

Hakanen, J. J., Peeters, M. C., & Schaufeli, W. B. (2018). Different types of employee well-being across time and their relationships with job crafting. *Journal of Occupational Health Psychology*, *23*(2), 289–301. doi:10.1037/ocp0000081 PMID:28191997

Hall, C. M. (2010). Crisis events in tourism: Subjects of crisis in tourism. *Current Issues in Tourism*, *13*(5), 401–417. doi:10.1080/13683500.2010.491900

Hall, C. M. (2020). Biological invasion, biosecurity, tourism, and globalisation. In D. Timothy (Ed.), *Handbook of globalisation and tourism* (pp. 114–125). Edward Elgar.

Hall, C. M., & Prayag, G. (2020). Earthquakes and tourism: Impacts, responses, and resilience – An introduction. In C. M. Hall & G. Prayag (Eds.), *Tourism and earthquakes*. Channel View.

Hall, C. M., Prayag, G., & Amore, A. (2018). *Tourism and resilience*. Channel View.

Hall, C. M., Scott, D., & Gössling, S. (2020). Pandemics, transformations and tourism: Be careful what you wish for. *Tourism Geographies*, *22*(3), 577–598. doi:10.1080/14616688.2020.1759131

Hammer, L. B., Neal, M. B., Newsom, J. T., Brockwood, K. J., & Colton, C. L. (2005). A longitudinal study of the effects of dual-earner couples' utilization of family friendly workplace supports on work and family outcomes. *The Journal of Applied Psychology*, *90*(4), 799–810. doi:10.1037/0021-9010.90.4.799 PMID:16060797

Hancock, A. (2020). Restaurants, hotels and gyms face up to a future of social distancing. *Financial Times*. Available from: https://www.ft.com/content/7c90

Han, H., & Hyun, S. S. (2019). Green indoor and outdoor environment as nature-based solution and its role in increasing customer/employee mental health, well-being, and loyalty. *Business Strategy and the Environment*, *28*(4), 629–641. doi:10.1002/bse.2269

Han, H., Wei, Q., Al-Ansi, A., Chung, H., Ngah, A. H., Ariza-Montes, A., & Vega-Muñoz, A. (2020). A theoretical framework development for hotel employee turnover: Linking trust in supports, emotional exhaustion, depersonalization, and reduced personal accomplishment at workplace. *Sustainability (Basel)*, *12*(8065), 1–13. doi:10.3390u12198065

Hartley, J., Jacobson, D., Klandermans, B., & van Vuuren, T. (1991). *Job insecurity: Coping with jobs at risk*. Sage.

Hawley, A. J. (2018). Regulating labour platforms, the data deficit. *European Journal of Government and Economics*, *7*(1), 5–23. doi:10.17979/ejge.2018.7.1.4330

Heaney, C. A., Israel, B. A., & House, J. S. (1994). Chronic job insecurity among automobile workers: Effects on job satisfaction and health. *Social Science & Medicine*, *38*(10), 1431–1437. doi:10.1016/0277-9536(94)90281-X PMID:8023192

Hellgren, J., Sverke, M., & Isaksson, I. (1999). A two-dimensional approach to job insecurity: Consequences for employee attitudes and well-being. *European Journal of Work and Organizational Psychology*, *8*(2), 179–195. doi:10.1080/135943299398311

Henderson, J. C. (2007). Corporate social responsibility and tourism: Hotel companies in Phuket, Thailand, after the Indian Ocean tsunami. *International Journal of Hospitality Management*, *26*(1), 228–239. doi:10.1016/j.ijhm.2006.02.001

Heredia-Colaco, V., & Rodrigues, H. (2021). Hosting in turbulent times: Hoteliers' perceptions and strategies to recover from the Covid-19 pandemic. *International Journal of Hospitality Management*, *94*, 94. doi:10.1016/j.ijhm.2020.102835 PMID:34785842

Herscovitch, L., & Meyer, J. P. (2002). Commitment to organizational change: Extension of a three-component model. *The Journal of Applied Psychology*, *87*(3), 474–487. doi:10.1037/0021-9010.87.3.474 PMID:12090605

Herzberg, F., Mausner, B., & Bloch Snyderman, B. (2005). *The Motivation to Work*. Transaction Publishers.

Heskett, J. L., Jones, T. O., Loveman, G. W., Sasser, W. E., & Schlesinger, L. A. (2008). Putting the service-profit chain to work. *Harvard Business Review*. Available at: https://hbr.org/2008/07/putting-the-service-profit-chain-to-work

Hill, N., Seo, M. G., Kang, J., & Taylor, M. (2012). Building employee commitment to change across organizational levels: The influence of hierarchical distance and direct managers' transformational leadership. *Organization Science*, *23*(3), 758–777. doi:10.1287/orsc.1110.0662

Hilton. (2016). *Hilton And IBM Pilot "Connie," The World's First Watson-Enabled Hotel Concierge (March)*. Retrieved from: https://newsroom.hilton.com/corporate/news/h

Hinkin, T. R., & Tracey, J. B. (2010). What makes it so great? An analysis of human resources practices among Fortune's best companies to work for. *Cornell Hospitality Quarterly*, *51*(2), 158–170. doi:10.1177/1938965510362487

Hirschi, A., Keller, A. C., & Spurk, D. M. (2018). Living one's calling: Job resources as a link between having and living a calling. *Journal of Vocational Behavior*, *106*, 1–10. doi:10.1016/j.jvb.2017.12.001

Hitt, M. A., Keats, B. W., Harback, H. F., & Nixon, R. D. (1994). Rightsizing building and maintaining strategic leadership: A long-term competitiveness. *Organizational Dynamics*, *23*(2), 18–32. doi:10.1016/0090-2616(94)90066-3

HKIHRM. (2007a). Hong Kong reports the highest staff turnover in Asia. Hong Kong Institute of Human Resource Management.

HKIHRM. (2007b). Job vacancy and employee turnover rates stayed high in 2006. Hong Kong Institute of Human Resource Management.

Hodari, D., & Sturman, M. C. (2014). Who's in charge now? The decision autonomy of hotel general managers. *Cornell Hospitality Quarterly*, *55*(4), 433–447. doi:10.1177/1938965513518839

Hofstede, G. (1984). The cultural relativity of the quality of life concept. *Academy of Management Review*, *9*(3), 389–398. doi:10.2307/258280

Hofstede, G., & Bond, M. H. (1984). Hofstede's culture dimensions: An independent validation using Rokeach's value survey. *Journal of Cross-Cultural Psychology*, *15*(4), 417–433. doi:10.1177/0022002184015004003

Holijevac, I. A. (2003). A vision of tourism and the hotel industry in the 21st Century. *International Journal of Hospitality Management*, *22*(2), 129–134. doi:10.1016/S0278-4319(03)00021-5

Holman, D., & Axtell, C. (2015). Can job redesign interventions influence a broad range of employee outcomes by changing multiple job characteristics? A quasi-experimental study. *Journal of Occupational Health Psychology*, *21*(3), 284–295. doi:10.1037/a0039962 PMID:26641482

Hom, P. W., Tsui, A. S., Wu, J. B., Lee, T. W., Zhang, A. Y., Fu, P. P., & Li, L. (2009). Explaining employment relationships with social exchange and job embeddedness. *The Journal of Applied Psychology*, *94*(2), 277–297. doi:10.1037/a0013453 PMID:19271791

Houdmont, J., Kerr, R., & Addley, K. (2012). Psychosocial factors and economic recession: The Stormont study. *Occupational Medicine*, *62*(2), 98–104. doi:10.1093/occmed/kqr216 PMID:22355088

Howard, A. (1995). *The changing nature of work*. Jossey-Bass.

Howcroft, D., & Bergall-Kareborn, B. (2019). A typology of crowdwork platforms. *Work, Employment and Society*, *33*(1), 21–38. doi:10.1177/0950017018760136

Hsieh, Y. C., Pearson, T., Chang, H. C., & Uen, J. F. (2004). Spillover between work and personal life for lodging manager. *Journal of Human Resources in Hospitality & Tourism*, *3*(2), 61–83. doi:10.1300/J171v03n02_03

Huang, G.-H., Wellman, N., Ashford, S. J., Lee, C., & Wang, L. (2017). Deviance and exit: The organizational costs of job insecurity and moral disengagement. *The Journal of Applied Psychology*, *102*(1), 26–42. doi:10.1037/apl0000158 PMID:27618406

Huang, S., Chen, Z., Liu, H., & Zhou, L. (2017). Job satisfaction and turnover intention in China: The moderating effects of job alternatives and policy support. *Chinese Management Studies*, *11*(4), 689–706. doi:10.1108/CMS-12-2016-0263

Hughes, J. C., & Rog, E. (2008). Talent management: A strategy for improving employee recruitment, retention and engagement within hospitality organizations. *International Journal of Contemporary Hospitality Management*, *20*(7), 743–757. doi:10.1108/09596110810899086

Hui, C., & Lee, C. (2000). Moderating effects of organizational-based self-esteem on organization uncertainty: Employee response relationships. *Journal of Management*, *26*(2), 215–232. doi:10.1177/014920630002600203

Hui, C., Lee, C., & Wang, H. (2015). Organizational inducements and employee citizenship behavior: The mediating role of perceived insider status and the moderating role of collectivism. *Human Resource Management*, *54*(3), 439–456. doi:10.1002/hrm.21620

Hui, D. S., Azhar, E. I., Madani, T. A., Ntoumi, F., Kock, R., Dar, O., Ippolito, G., Mchugh, T. D., Memish, Z. A., & Drosten, C. (2020). The continuing 2019-nCoV epidemic threat of novel coronaviruses to global health—The latest 2019 novel coronavirus outbreak in Wuhan, China. *International Journal of Infectious Diseases*, *91*, 264–266. doi:10.1016/j.ijid.2020.01.009 PMID:31953166

Humphrey, T., & Nash, D. (2020). *UQ fast tracks nurses in response to COVID-19 pandemic*. https://www.uq.edu.au/news/article/2020/04/uq-fast-tracks-nurses-response-covid-19-pandemic

Hunt, R. (2020). *Marriott CEO: coronavirus is hurting the hotel chain worse than 9/11 or world war II.* Available at: https://www.nasdaq.com/articles/marriott-ceopercent3A-coronavirus-ishurting-the-hotel-chain-worse-than-9-11-or-world-war-ii-2020

Hurrell, J. J. Jr, Nelson, D. L., & Simmons, B. L. (1998). Measuring job stressors and strains: Where we have been, where we are, and where we need to go. *Journal of Occupational Health Psychology*, *3*(4), 368–389. doi:10.1037/1076-8998.3.4.368 PMID:9805282

Hurst, J. L., & Good, L. K. (2009). Generation Y and career choice: The impact of retail career perceptions, expectations and entitlement perceptions. *Career Development International*, *14*(6), 570–593. doi:10.1108/13620430910997303

Hu, S., Creed, P. A., & Hood, M. (2017). Career goal revision in response to negative feedback. *Journal of Counseling Psychology*, *64*(3), 335–345. doi:10.1037/cou0000193 PMID:28165259

Hu, S., Hood, M., & Creed, P. A. (2018). Negative career feedback and career outcomes: The mediating roles of self-regulatory processes. *Journal of Vocational Behavior*, *106*, 180–191. doi:10.1016/j.jvb.2018.02.002

Hwang, K. K. (1987). Face and favor: The Chinese power game. *American Journal of Sociology*, *92*(4), 944–974. doi:10.1086/228588

Ibrahim, S. N. H., Suan, C. L., & Karatepe, O. M. (2019). The effects of supervisor support and self-efficacy on call center employees' work engagement and quitting intentions. *International Journal of Manpower*, *40*(4), 688–703. doi:10.1108/IJM-12-2017-0320

Inoue, A., Kawakami, N., Eguchi, H., & Tsutsumi, A. (2018). Interaction effect of job insecurity and role ambiguity on psychological distress in Japanese employees: A cross-sectional study. *International Archives of Occupational and Environmental Health*, *91*(4), 391–402. doi:10.100700420-018-1288-5 PMID:29327214

International Monetary Fund. (2020). *World economic outlook, April 2020. The great lockdown.* Available at: https://www.imf.org/en/Publications/WEO/Issues/2020/04/14/weo-april-2020

Ito, J. K., & Brotheridge, C. M. (2007). Exploring the predictors and consequences of job insecurity's components. *Journal of Managerial Psychology*, *22*(1), 40–64. doi:10.1108/02683940710721938

Ivanoa, M., Ivanov, S., & Magnini, V. (2016). *The Routledge Handbook of Hotel Chain Management*. doi:10.4324/9781315752532

IvanovS. H.WebsterC. (2017). *Adoption of robots, artificial intelligence and service automation by travel, tourism and hospitality companies–a cost-benefit analysis. Artificial Intelligence and Service Automation by Travel, Tourism and Hospitality Companies–A Cost-Benefit Analysis*. Prepared for the International Scientific Conference "Contemporary Tourism – Traditions and Innovations", Sofia University. https://ssrn.com/abstract=3007577

Iverson, R. (1996). Employee acceptance of organizational change: The role of organizational commitment. *International Journal of Human Resource Management*, *7*(1), 122–128. doi:10.1080/09585199600000121

Ivkov, M., Blešić, I., Janićević, S., Kovačić, S., Miljković, D., Lukić, T., & Sakuls, D. (2019). *Natural Disasters vs Hotel Industry Resilience: An Exploratory Study among Hotel Managers from Europe*. De Gruyter Open. doi:10.1515/geo-2019-0030

Jacobson, D. (1991). Toward a theoretical distinction between the stress components of the job insecurity and job loss experiences. In S. B. Bacharach (Ed.), *Research in the sociology of organizations* (Vol. 9, pp. 1–19). JAI Press.

Jahoda, M. (1982). *Employment and unemployment*. University Press.

Jarrahi, M. H., & Sutherland, W. (2018). *Algorithmic management and algorithmic competencies: Understanding and appropriating algorithms in gig work*. Paper Presented at the Lecture Notes in Computer Science Iconference 2019.

Jayawardena, C., Tew, P. J., Lu, Z., Tolomiczenko, G., & Gellatly, J. (2008). SARS: Lessons in strategic planning for hoteliers and destination marketers. *International Journal of Contemporary Hospitality Management*, *20*(3), 332–346. doi:10.1108/09596110810866145

Jeaheng, Y., Al-Ansi, A., & Han, H. (2019). Halal-friendly hotels: Impact of halal-friendly attributes on guest purchase behaviors in the Thailand hotel industry. *Journal of Travel & Tourism Marketing*, *36*(6), 729–746. doi:10.1080/10548408.2019.1631940

Jia, L., Shaw, J. D., Tsui, A. S., & Park, T.-Y. (2014). A social-structural perspective on employee organization relationships and team creativity. *Academy of Management Journal*, *57*(3), 869–891. doi:10.5465/amj.2011.0147

Jiang, L., Wagner, C., & Nardi, B. (2015). Not just in it for the money: A qualitative investigation of workers' perceived benefits of micro-task crowdsourcing. *2015 48th Hawaii International Conference on System Sciences, 5–8 January Conference Proceedings*, 773–782. 10.1109/HICSS.2015.98

Jiang, L., & Lavaysse, L. M. (2018). Cognitive and affective job insecurity: A meta-analysis and a primary study. *Journal of Management*, *44*(6), 2307–2342. doi:10.1177/0149206318773853

Jiang, Y., Ritchie, B. W., & Verreynne, M. L. (2019). Building tourism organizational resilience to crises and disasters: A dynamic capabilities view. *International Journal of Tourism Research*, *21*(6), 882–900. doi:10.1002/jtr.2312

Jiang, Y., & Wen, J. (2020). Effects of COVID-19 on hotel marketing and management: A perspective article. *International Journal of Contemporary Hospitality Management*, *32*(8), 2563–2573. doi:10.1108/IJCHM-03-2020-0237

Jick, T. D. (1985). As the axe falls: Budget cuts and the experience of stress in organizations. In T. A. Beehr & R. S. Bhagat (Eds.), *Human stress and cognition in organizations: An integrated perspective* (pp. 83–114). Wiley.

Johansen, B. F., Johansen, W., & Weckesser, N. M. (2016). Emotional stakeholders as "crisis communicators." In social media: The case of the Telenor customer complaints crisis. *Corporate Communications*, *21*(3), 289–308. doi:10.1108/CCIJ-05-2015-0026

Jones, D. A., & Skarlicki, D. P. (2013). How perceptions of fairness can change: A dynamic model of organizational justice. *Organizational Psychology Review*, *3*(2), 138–160. doi:10.1177/2041386612461665

Jones, E., Chonko, L., Rangarajan, D., & Roberts, J. (2007). The role of overload on job attitudes, turnover intentions, and salesperson performance. *Journal of Business Research*, *60*(7), 663–671. doi:10.1016/j.jbusres.2007.02.014

Jones, J. R., & Harter, J. K. (2005). Race effects on the employee engagement: Turnover intention relationship. *Journal of Leadership & Organizational Studies*, *11*(2), 78–88. doi:10.1177/107179190501100208

Jones, P., & Comfort, D. (2020). The COVID-19 crisis, tourism and sustainable development. *Athens Journal of Tourism.*, *7*(2), 75–86. doi:10.30958/ajt.7-2-1

Josserand, E., & Kaine, S. (2019). Different directions or the same route? The varied identities of ride-share drivers. *The Journal of Industrial Relations*, *61*(4), 549–573. doi:10.1177/0022185619848461

Judge, T. A., Thoresen, C. J., Pucik, V., & Welbourne, T. M. (1999). Managerial coping with organizational change: A dispositional perspective. *The Journal of Applied Psychology*, *84*(1), 107–122. doi:10.1037/0021-9010.84.1.107 PMID:17227155

Jung, H. S., Jung, Y. S., & Yoon, H. H. (2021). COVID-19: The effects of job insecurity on the job engagement and turnover intent of deluxe hotel employees and the moderating role of generational characteristics. *International Journal of Hospitality Management*, *92*, 92. doi:10.1016/j.ijhm.2020.102703 PMID:33041428

Jung, H. S., & Yoon, H. H. (2016). What does work mean to hospitality employees? The effects of meaningful work on employees' organizational commitment: The mediating role of job engagement. *International Journal of Hospitality Management*, *53*, 59–68. doi:10.1016/j.ijhm.2015.12.004

Jung, H. S., Yoon, H. H., & Kim, Y. J. (2012). Effects of culinary employees' role stress on burnout and turnover intention in hotel industry: Moderating effects on employees' tenure. *Service Industries Journal*, *32*(13), 2145–2165. doi:10.1080/02642069.2011.574277

Kahn, A. E. (1988). Surprises of Airline Deregulation. *The American Economic Review*, *78*(2), 316–322.

Kahneman, D. (2011). *Thinking, Fast and Slow*. Doubleday.

Kahneman, D., & Krueger, A. B. (2006). Developments in the measurement of subjective well-being. *The Journal of Economic Perspectives*, *20*(1), 3–24. doi:10.1257/089533006776526030

Kahn, R. L., Wolfe, D. M., Quinn, R. P., Snoek, J. D., & Rosenthal, R. A. (1964). *Occupational Stress: Studies in Role Conflict and Ambiguity*. John Wiley & Sons.

Kahn, W. A. (1990). Psychological conditions of personal engagement and disengagement at work. *Academy of Management Journal*, *33*(4), 692–724. doi:10.2307/256287

Kahn, W. A. (1992). To be fully there: Psychological presence at work. *Human Relations*, *45*(4), 321–349. doi:10.1177/001872679204500402

Kaine, S., & Josserand, E. (2019). The organisation and experience of work in the gig economy. *The Journal of Industrial Relations*, *61*(4), 479–501. doi:10.1177/0022185619865480

Kamalahmadi, M., & Parast, M. M. (2016). A review of the literature on the principles of enterprise and supply chain resilience: Major findings and directions for future research. *International Journal of Production Economics*, *171*, 116–133. doi:10.1016/j.ijpe.2015.10.023

Kaminsky, S. E., & Behrend, T. S. (2015). Career choice and calling: Integrating calling and social cognitive career theory. *Journal of Career Assessment*, *23*(3), 383–398. doi:10.1177/1069072714547167

Kanfer, R. (1990). Motivation theory and industrial/organizational psychology. In *Handbook of Industrial and Organizational Psychology* (Vol. 1, pp. 75–170). Consulting Psychologists Press.

Kanfer, R., Wanberg, C. R., & Kantrowitz, T. M. (2001). Job search and employment: A personality–motivational analysis and meta-analytic review. *The Journal of Applied Psychology*, *86*(5), 837–855. doi:10.1037/0021-9010.86.5.837 PMID:11596801

Kang, H. J. A., & Busser, J. A. (2018). Impact of service climate and psychological capital on employee engagement: The role of organizational hierarchy. *International Journal of Hospitality Management*, *75*, 1–9. doi:10.1016/j.ijhm.2018.03.003

Kang, H. J., Cain, L., & Busser, J. A. (2021). The impact of living a calling on job outcomes. *International Journal of Hospitality Management*, *95*, 95. doi:10.1016/j.ijhm.2021.102916

Karatepe, O. M. (2013). The effects of work overload and work-family conflict on job embeddedness and job performance: The mediation of emotional exhaustion. *International Journal of Contemporary Hospitality Management*, *25*(4), 614–634. doi:10.1108/09596111311322952

Karatepe, O. M., Beirami, E., Bouzari, M., & Safavi, H. P. (2014). Does work engagement mediate the effects of challenge stressors on job outcomes? Evidence from the hotel industry. *International Journal of Hospitality Management*, *36*, 14–22. doi:10.1016/j.ijhm.2013.08.003

Karatepe, O. M., & Olugbade, O. A. (2017). The effects of work social support and career adaptability on career satisfaction and turnover intentions. *Journal of Management & Organization*, *23*(3), 337–355. doi:10.1017/jmo.2016.12

Karatepe, O. M., Rezapouraghdam, H., & Hassannia, R. (2020). Job insecurity, work engagement and their effects on hotel employees' non-green and nonattendance behaviors. *International Journal of Hospitality Management*, *87*(May), 1–12. doi:10.1016/j.ijhm.2020.102472

Karatepe, O. M., & Uludag, O. (2008). Role stress, burnout and their effects on frontline hotel employees' job performance: Evidence from Northern Cyprus. *International Journal of Tourism Research*, *10*(2), 111–126. doi:10.1002/jtr.645

Karkoulian, S., Mukaddam, W., McCarthy, R., & Messarra, L. C. (2013). Job insecurity: A whirlpool of chronic powerlessness. *Education, Business and Society*, *6*(1), 55–70. doi:10.1108/17537981311314727

Karl, K., Peluchette, J., Hall-Indiana, L., & Harland, L. (2005). Attitudes toward workplace fun: A three-sector comparison. *Journal of Leadership & Organizational Studies*, *12*(2), 1–17. doi:10.1177/107179190501200201

Katona, G. (1975). *Psychological Economics*. Elsevier.

Kaushal, V., & Srivastava, S. (2021). Hospitality and tourism industry amid COVID-19 pandemic: Perspectives on challenges and learnings from India. *International Journal of Hospitality Management*, *92*, 102707. doi:10.1016/j.ijhm.2020.102707 PMID:33024348

Kelly, T., & Barrett, M. (2011). The leading causes and potential consequences of occupational stress: A study of Irish trainee accountants. *Irish Accounting Review, 18*(2), 31–55. doi:10.52399/001c.27033

Kerpelman, J. L., Pittman, J. F., & Lamke, L. K. (1997). Toward a microprocess perspective on adolescent identity development: An identity control theory approach. *Journal of Adolescent Research, 12*(3), 325–346. doi:10.1177/0743554897123002

Keskin, H., Akgun, A. E., Ayar, H., & Kayman, S. S. (2016). Cyberbullying victimization, counterproductive work behaviours and emotional intelligence at workplace. *Procedia: Social and Behavioral Sciences, 235*, 281–287. doi:10.1016/j.sbspro.2016.11.031

Kets de Vries, M. F. R., & Balazs, K. (1997). The downside of downsizing. *Human Relations, 50*(1), 11–50. doi:10.1177/001872679705000102

Keyes, C. L. M., Shmotkin, D., & Ryff, C. D. (2002). Optimizing well-being: The empirical encounter of two traditions. *Journal of Personality and Social Psychology, 82*(6), 1007–1022. doi:10.1037/0022-3514.82.6.1007 PMID:12051575

Khawaja, K. F., Sarfraz, M., Rashid, M., & Rashid, M. (2021). How is COVID-19 pandemic causing employee withdrawal behavior in the hospitality industry? An empirical investigation. *Journal of Hospitality and Tourism Insights, 5*(3), 687–706. doi:10.1108/JHTI-01-2021-0002

Kichuk, A., Brown, L., & Ladkin, A. (2019). Talent pool exclusion: The hotel employee perspective. *International Journal of Contemporary Hospitality Management, 31*(10), 3970–3991. doi:10.1108/IJCHM-10-2018-0814

Kiefer, T. (2005). Feeling bad: antecedents and consequences of negative emotions in ongoing Change. *Journal of Organizational Behavior, 26*(8), 875–897. doi:10.1002/job.339

Kieselbach, T., Armgarth, E., Bagnara, S., Elo, A.-L., Jefferys, S., Joling, C., & Rogovsky, N. (2009). *Health in Restructuring: Innovative Approaches and Policy Recommendations (HIRES)*. Universität Bremen.

Killingsworth, M. A. (2021). Experienced well-being rises with income, even above $75,000 per year. *Proceedings of the National Academy of Sciences of the United States of America, 118*(4), e2016976118. doi:10.1073/pnas.2016976118 PMID:33468644

Kim, B. C. P., Murrmann, S. K., & Lee, G. (2009). Moderating effects of gender and organizational level between role stress and job satisfaction among hotel employees. *International Journal of Hospitality Management, 28*(4), 612–619. doi:10.1016/j.ijhm.2009.04.001

Kim, B. C., Lee, G., & Carlson, K. D. (2010). An examination of the nature of the relationship between leader-member-exchange (LMX) and turnover intent at different organizational levels. *International Journal of Hospitality Management, 29*(4), 591–597. doi:10.1016/j.ijhm.2009.10.025

Kim, H. R., Lee, M., Lee, H. T., & Kim, N. M. (2010). Corporate social responsibility and employee company identification. *Journal of Business Ethics, 95*(4), 557–569. doi:10.100710551-010-0440-2

Kim, J. (2015). What increases public employees' turnover intention? *Public Personnel Management, 44*(4), 496–519. doi:10.1177/0091026015604447

Kim, J. (2018). The contrary effects of intrinsic and extrinsic motivation on burnout and turnover intention in the public sector. *International Journal of Manpower, 39*(3), 486–500. doi:10.1108/IJM-03-2017-0053

Kim, J. J., Lee, Y., & Han, H. (2019). Exploring competitive hotel selection attributes among guests: An importance of performance analysis. *Journal of Travel & Tourism Marketing, 36*(9), 998–1011. doi:10.1080/10548408.2019.1683484

Kim, J., Kim, J., Lee, S. K., & Tang, L. R. (2020). Effects of epidemic disease outbreaks on financial performance of restaurants: Event study method approach. *Journal of Hospitality and Tourism Management, 43*, 32–41. doi:10.1016/j.jhtm.2020.01.015

Kim, S. M., Um, K. H., Kim, H. Y., & Kim, Y. H. (2016). Hospital career management systems and their effects on the psychological state and career attitudes of nurses. *Service Business, 10*(1), 87–112. doi:10.100711628-014-0257-7

Kim, S. S., Kim, J., & Hwang, J. (2015). The effects of mentoring on role stress, job attitude, and turnover intention in the hotel industry. *International Journal of Hospitality Management, 48*, 68–82. doi:10.1016/j.ijhm.2015.04.006

Kim, T. T., Paek, S., Chang, H. C., & Lee, G. (2012). Frontline service employees' customer-related social stressors, emotional exhaustion, and service recovery performance: Customer orientation as a moderator. *Service Business, 6*(4), 503–526. doi:10.100711628-012-0164-8

Kipkebut, D. J. (2013). The effects of demographic characteristics on organizational commitment, job satisfaction and turnover intentions: The case of employees in Kenyan universities. *Journal of Organizational Human Behavior, 2*(1), 20–33.

Kiraly, O., Potenza, M. N., Stein, D. J., King, D. L., Hodgins, D. C., Saunders, J. B., Griffiths, M. D., Gjoneska, B., Billieux, J., Brand, M., Abbott, M. W., Chamberlain, S. R., Corazza, O., Burkauskas, J., Sales, C. M. D., Montag, C., Lochner, C., Grünblatt, E., Wegmann, E., ... Demetrovics, Z. (2020). Preventing problematic internet use during the COVID-19 pandemic: Consensus guidance. *Comprehensive Psychiatry, 100*, 152180. doi:10.1016/j.comppsych.2020.152180 PMID:32422427

Klein Hesselink, D. J., & van Vuuren, T. (1999). Job flexibility and job insecurity: The Dutch case. *European Journal of Work and Organizational Psychology, 8*(2), 273–293. doi:10.1080/135943299398366

Kong, H., Wang, S., & Fu, X. (2015). Meeting career expectations: Can it enhance job satisfaction of generation Y? *International Journal of Contemporary Hospitality Management, 27*(1), 147–168. doi:10.1108/IJCHM-08-2013-0353

Konovsky, M., & Folger, R. (1987). Relative effects of procedural and distributive justice on employee attitudes. *Representative Research in Social Psychology, 17*, 15–24.

Koo, B., Curtis, C., & Ryan, B. (2021). Examining the impact of artificial intelligence on hotel employees through job insecurity perspectives. *International Journal of Hospitality Management*, *95*(1), 102763. doi:10.1016/j.ijhm.2020.102763

Korsgaard, M. A., Schweiger, D. M., & Sapienza, H. U. (1995). Building commitment, attachment, and trust in top management teams: The role of procedural justice. *Academy of Management Journal*, *3*(8), 60–84. doi:10.2307/256728

Kotler, P., Bowen, J. T., Makens, J., & Baloglu, S. (2017). *Marketing for Hospitality and Tourism*. Prentice Hall.

Kotter, J., & Schelsinger, A. A. (1979). Choosing strategies for change. *Harvard Business Review*, *57*(2), 102–121. PMID:10240501

Kowske, B. J., Rasch, R., & Wiley, J. (2010). Millennials' (lack of) attitude problem: An empirical examination of generational effects on work attitudes. *Journal of Business and Psychology*, *25*(2), 265–279. doi:10.100710869-010-9171-8

Kozlowski, S., Chao, G., Smith, E., & Hedlund, J. (1993). Organizational downsizing: Strategies, interventions and research implications. In C. L. Cooper & I. T. Robertson (Eds.), *International review of industrial and organizational psychology* (Vol. 8, pp. 263–332). Wiley.

Kozul-Wright, R., & Barbosa, N. (2020). This crisis will change the world – for better, or worse. *Tribune Magazine*. https://tribunemag.co.uk/2020/03/coronavirus-will-change-the-world-for-better-or-worse

Krausz, M., Koslowsky, M., & Eiser, A. (1998). Distal and proximal influences on turnover intentions and satisfaction: Support for a withdrawal progression theory. *Journal of Vocational Behavior*, *52*(1), 59–71. doi:10.1006/jvbe.1996.1565

Krok, D. (2015). The role of meaning in life within the relations of religious coping and psychological well-being. *Journal of Religion and Health*, *54*(6), 2292–2308. doi:10.100710943-014-9983-3 PMID:25524414

Kuhnert, K. W., & Vance, R. J. (1992). Job insecurity and moderators of the relation between job insecurity and employee adjustment. In J. C. Quick, L. R. Murphy, & J. J. J. Hurrell (Eds.), *Stress and well-being at work: Assessments and interventions for occupational mental health* (pp. 48–63). American Psychological Association. doi:10.1037/10116-004

Kuo, B. C. H. (2013). Collectivism and coping: Current theories, evidence, and measurements of collective coping. *International Journal of Psychology*, *48*(3), 374–388. doi:10.1080/00207594.2011.640681 PMID:22335198

Kusluvan, S., Kusluvan, Z., Ilhan, I., & Buyruk, L. (2010). The human dimension: A review of human resources management issues in the tourism and hospitality industry. *Cornell Hospitality Quarterly*, *51*(2), 171–214. doi:10.1177/1938965510362871

Lai, I. K. W., & Wong, J. W. C. (2020). Comparing crisis management practices in the hotel industry between initial and pandemic stages of COVID-19. *International Journal of Contemporary Hospitality Management*, *32*(10), 32. doi:10.1108/IJCHM-04-2020-0325

Lamsa, A. M., & Savolainem, T. (2000). The nature of managerial commitment to strategic change. *Leadership and Organization Development Journal, 21*(6), 297–306. doi:10.1108/01437730010372822

Lapalme, M., Stamper, C. L., Simard, G., & Tremblay, M. (2009). Bringing the outside in: Can "external" workers experience insider status? *Journal of Organizational Behavior, 30*(7), 919–940. doi:10.1002/job.597

Latack, J. C., Kinicki, A. J., & Prussia, G. E. (1995). An integrative process model of coping with job loss. *Academy of Management Review, 20*(2), 311–342. doi:10.2307/258849

Latham, G. P., & Locke, E. A. (1991). Self-regulation through goal setting. *Organizational Behavior and Human Decision Processes, 50*(2), 212–247. doi:10.1016/0749-5978(91)90021-K

Law, K. S., Wong, C.-S., Wang, D., & Wang, L. (2000). Effect of supervisor–subordinate guanxi on supervisory decisions in China: An empirical investigation. *Journal of Human Resource Management., 11*(4), 751–765.

Lazarus, R. S., & Folkman, S. (1984). *Stress, Appraisal, and Coping*. Springer Publishing Company.

Lee, A. V., Vargo, J., & Seville, E. (2013). Developing a tool to measure and compare organizations' resilience. *Natural Hazards Review, 14*(1), 29–41. doi:10.1061/(ASCE)NH.1527-6996.0000075

Lee, C., & Way, K. (2010). Individual employment characteristics of hotel employees that play a role in employee satisfaction and work retention. *International Journal of Hospitality Management, 29*(3), 344–353. doi:10.1016/j.ijhm.2009.08.008

Lee, J. J., & Ok, C. M. (2015). Drivers of work engagement: An examination of core self-evaluations and psychological climate among hotel employees. *International Journal of Hospitality Management, 44*, 84–98. doi:10.1016/j.ijhm.2014.10.008

Lee, S., & Jeong, D. (2017). Job insecurity and turnover intention: Organizational commitment as mediator. *Social Behavior and Personality, 45*(4), 529–536. doi:10.2224bp.5865

Lehman, W. E., & Simpson, D. D. (1992). Employee substance use and on-the-job behaviors. *The Journal of Applied Psychology, 77*(3), 309–321. doi:10.1037/0021-9010.77.3.309 PMID:1601823

Leighton, P. (2016). Professional self-employment, new power and the sharing economy: Some cautionary tales from Uber. *Journal of Management & Organization, 22*(6), 859–874. doi:10.1017/jmo.2016.30

Leiter, M. P., & Bakker, A. B. (2010). Work engagement: introduction. In M. P. Leiter & A. B. Bakker (Eds.), *Work Engagement: A Handbook of Essential Theory and Research* (pp. 1–9). Psychology Press.

Leiter, M. P., & Meechan, K. A. (1986). Role Structure and Burnout in the Field of Human Services. *The Journal of Applied Behavioral Science, 22*(1), 47–52. doi:10.1177/002188638602200107 PMID:10276302

Lengnick-Hall, C. A., & Beck, T. E. (2009). Resilience capacity and strategic agility: Prerequisites for thriving in a dynamic environment. No. 0059 College of Business, University of Texas at San Antonio.

Lengnick-Hall, C. A., Beck, T. E., & Lengnick-Hall, M. L. (2011). Developing a capacity for organizational resilience through strategic human resource management. *Human Resource Management Review*, *21*(3), 243–255. doi:10.1016/j.hrmr.2010.07.001

Lent, R. W., Ireland, G. W., Penn, L. T., Morris, T. R., & Sappington, R. (2017). Sources of self-efficacy and outcome expectations for career exploration and decision making: A test of the social cognitive model of career self-management. *Journal of Vocational Behavior*, *99*, 107–117. doi:10.1016/j.jvb.2017.01.002

Leonidou, L. C., Leonidou, C. N., Fotiadis, T. A., & Zariti, A. (2013). Resources and capabilities as drivers of hotel environmental marketing strategy: Implications for competitive advantage and performance. *Tourism Management*, *35*, 94–110. doi:10.1016/j.tourman.2012.06.003

Levy, S. E., & Park, S.-Y. (2011). An analysis of CSR activities in the lodging industry. *International Journal of Hospitality Management*, *18*(1), 147–154.

Li, B., Yang, J., Zhao, F., Zhi, L., Wang, X., Liu, L., Bi, Z., & Zhao, Y. (2020). Prevalence and impact of cardiovascular metabolic diseases on COVID-19 in China. *Clinical Research in Cardiology; Official Journal of the German Cardiac Society*, *109*(5), 531–538. doi:10.100700392-020-01626-9 PMID:32161990

Limpanitgul, T., Robson, M. J., Gould-Williams, J., & Lertthaitrakul, W. (2013). Effects of co-worker support and customer cooperation on service employee attitudes and behaviour: Empirical evidence from the airline industry. *Journal of Hospitality and Tourism Management*, *20*, 23–33. doi:10.1016/j.jhtm.2013.05.004

Lim, V. K. G. (1996). Job insecurity and its outcomes: Moderating effects of workbased and nonwork-based social support. *Human Relations*, *2*(2), 171–194. doi:10.1177/001872679604900203

Ling, Y., & Poweli, G. N. (2001). Work-family conflict in contemporary China: Beyond an American-based model. *International Journal of Cross Cultural Management*, *1*(3), 357–373. doi:10.1177/147059580113006

Lin, N. (1998). Guanxi: a conceptual analysis. In A. Y. So, N. Lin, & D. Poston (Eds.), *The Chinese Triangle of Mainland China, Taiwan, and Hong Kong: Comparative Institutional Analyses* (pp. 153–166). Greenwood Publishing Group.

Linton, R. (1945). *The Cultural Background of Personality*. Appleton-Century-Crofts.

Lin, Y. T., & Liu, N. C. (2016). High performance work systems and organizational service performance: The roles of different organizational climates. *International Journal of Hospitality Management*, *55*, 118–128. doi:10.1016/j.ijhm.2016.04.005

Little, L. M., Simmons, B. L., & Nelson, D. L. (2007). Health among leaders: Positive and negative affect, engagement and burnout, forgiveness and revenge. *Journal of Management Studies*, *44*(2), 243–260. doi:10.1111/j.1467-6486.2007.00687.x

Liu, A. (2019). Making joy a priority at work. *Harvard Business Review*. Retrieved from https://hbr.org/2019/07/making-joy-a-priority-at-work

Liu, C. E., Yuan, X., Zhang, M. N., & Hu, C. H. (2019). Work-related identity discrepancy and work withdrawal behavior: The mediation effect of negative emotion. *International Journal of Business and Social Science*, *10*(7), 229–236. doi:10.30845/ijbss.v10n7p25

Liu, C., Zhou, Q., Li, Y., Garner, L. V., Watkins, S. P., Carter, L. J., Smoot, J., Gregg, A. C., Daniels, A. D., Jervey, S., & Albaiu, D. (2020). Research and development on therapeutic agents and vaccines for COVID-19 and related human coronavirus diseases. *ACS Central Science*, *6*(3), 315–331. doi:10.1021/acscentsci.0c00272 PMID:32226821

Li, Y., & Huang, S. (2017). Hospitality service climate, employee service orientation, career aspiration and performance: A moderated mediation model. *International Journal of Hospitality Management*, *67*, 24–32. doi:10.1016/j.ijhm.2017.07.012

Li, Z., Duverger, P., & Yu, L. (2018). Employee creativity trumps supervisor-subordinate guanxi: Predicting prequitting behaviors in China's hotel industry. *Tourism Management*, *69*, 23–37. doi:10.1016/j.tourman.2018.05.004

Lo Presti, A., & Nonnis, M. (2012). Moderated effects of job insecurity on work engagement and distress. *TPM*, *19*(2), 97–113.

Luk, C. Y. (2006). Work–life balance in Hong Kong's financial sector. *CSR Asia Weekly*, *2*(11). Retrieved May 5, 2022, from http://www.csr-asia.com/ index.php?p=6001

Lu, L., Cai, R., & Gursoy, D. (2019). Developing and validating a service robot integration willingness scale. *International Journal of Hospitality Management*, *80*, 36–51. doi:10.1016/j.ijhm.2019.01.005

Lu, L., Lu, A. C. C., Gursoy, D., & Neale, N. R. (2016). Work engagement, job satisfaction, and turnover intentions: A comparison between supervisors and line-level employees. *International Journal of Contemporary Hospitality Management*, *28*(4), 737–761. doi:10.1108/IJCHM-07-2014-0360

Lundberg, C., Gudmundson, A., & Andersson, T. (2009). Herzberg's Two-Factor Theory of work motivation tested empirically on seasonal workers in hospitality and tourism. *Tourism Management*, *30*(6), 890–899. doi:10.1016/j.tourman.2008.12.003

Lunenburg, F. (2010). Approaches to managing organizational change. *International Journal of Scholarly Academic Intellectual Diversity*, *12*(1), 1–10.

MacDermid, S. M., Barnett, R., Crosby, F., Greenhaus, J. H., Koblenz, M., & Marks, S. R. (2000). *The Measurement of Work/Life Tension: Recommendations of a Virtual Think Tank*. Alfred P. Sloan Foundation.

MacDonald, R., & Giazitzoglu, A. (2019). Youth, enterprise and precarity: Or, what is, and what is wrong with, the 'gig economy'? *Journal of Sociology (Melbourne, Vic.)*, *55*(4), 724–740. doi:10.1177/1440783319837604

Madera, J. M., Dawson, M., Guchait, P., & Belarmino, A. M. (2017). Strategic human resources management research in hospitality and tourism. *International Journal of Contemporary Hospitality Management*, *29*(1), 48–67. doi:10.1108/IJCHM-02-2016-0051

Madigan, M., Norton, J., & Testa, I. (1999). The quest for work life balance. *Rogers Media*. Available at https://www.benefitscanada.com/content/legacy/content/ 1999/html

Ma, E., & Qu, H. (2011). Social exchanges as motivators of hotel employees' organizational citizenship behavior: The proposition and application of a new three-dimensional framework. *International Journal of Hospitality Management*, *30*(3), 680–688. doi:10.1016/j.ijhm.2010.12.003

Maheshwari, S., & Vohra, V. (2015). Identifying critical HR practices impacting employee perception and commitment during organizational change. *Journal of Organizational Change Management*, *28*(5), 872–894. doi:10.1108/JOCM-03-2014-0066

Mahroof, K. (2019). A human-centric perspective exploring the readiness towards smart warehousing: The case of a large retail distribution warehouse. *International Journal of Information Management*, *45*, 176–190. doi:10.1016/j.ijinfomgt.2018.11.008

Mair, S. (2020, March 30). What will the world be like after coronavirus? Four possible futures. *The Conversation*. https://theconversation.com/what-will-the-world-be-like-after-c… d= IwAR2wr9pzssSdBSxjaHaWba9-iHSF3flYgZ9BVI1jAx_Y4YlXVAImcJcNdjM

Malik, A., Sinha, S., & Goel, S. (2020). "The "screen"ing of you and me: Effects of COVID-19 on counterproductive work behaviors. *IEEE Engineering Management Review*, *48*(3), 37–43. doi:10.1109/EMR.2020.3010323

Manolis, C., Meamber, L., Winsor, R., & Brooks, C. (2001). Partial employees and consumers. *Marketing Theory*, *1*(2), 225–243. doi:10.1177/147059310100100204

Mansour, S., & Tremblay, D. G. (2016). Workload, generic and work–family specific social supports and job stress: Mediating role of work–family and family–work conflict. *International Journal of Contemporary Hospitality Management*, *28*(8), 1778–1804. doi:10.1108/IJCHM-11-2014-0607

Mao, Y., He, J., Morrisson, A. M., & Coca-Stefaniak, J. A. (2020). Effects of tourism CSR on employee psychological capital in the COVID-19 crisis: From the perspective of conservation of resources theory. *Current Issues in Tourism*, *24*(19), 2716–2734. doi:10.1080/13683500.2020.1770706

Maphanga, P. M., & Henama, U. S. (2019). The tourism impact of Ebola in Africa: Lessons on crisis management. *African Journal of Hospitality, Tourism and Leisure*, *8*(3). https://www.ajhtl.com/ uploads/7/1/6/3/7163688/article_59_vol_8_3__2019 pdf

March, H., Saurí, D., & Olcina, J. (2014). Rising temperatures and dwindling water supplies? Perception of climate change among residents of the Spanish Mediterranean tourist coastal areas. *Environmental Management*, *53*(1), 181–193. doi:10.100700267-013-0177-7 PMID:24122097

Markey, R., & McIvor, J. (2018). Regulating casual employment in Australia. *The Journal of Industrial Relations*, *60*(5), 593–618. doi:10.1177/0022185618778084

Markovits, Y., Boer, D., & van Dick, R. (2014). Economic crisis and the employee: The effects of economic crisis on employee job satisfaction, commitment and self-regulation. *European Management Journal*, *32*(3), 413–422. doi:10.1016/j.emj.2013.09.005

Marks, S. R., & Macdermid, S. (1996). Multiple roles and the self: A theory of role balance. *Journal of Marriage and Family*, *58*(2), 417–432. doi:10.2307/353506

Marriott. (2020). *The Bot Experience*. Retrieved from https://www.marriott.com/offe rs/the-bot-experience-1347181

Marriott, J. W. Jr, & Brown, K. A. (1997). *The Spirit to Serve: The Marriott's Way*. Harper Business.

MartinsA.RiordanT.DolnicarS. (2020, May 8). *A post-COVID-19 model of tourism and hospitality workforce resilience*. doi:10.31235/osf.io/4quga

Martins, L. L., Gilson, L. L., & Maynard, M. T. (2004). Virtual teams: What do we know and where do we go from here? *Journal of Management*, *30*(6), 805–835. doi:10.1016/j.jm.2004.05.002

Marwa, S. (2012). The criticality of quality management in building corporate resilience. In K. S. Ng (Ed.), *Quality management and practices*. InTech. doi:10.5772/38424

Maslach, C., & Jackson, S. E. (1984). Burnout in organizational settings. *Applied Social Psychology Annual*, *5*, 133–153.

Maslach, C., Schaufeli, W. B., & Leiter, M. P. (2001). Job Burnout. *Annual Review of Psychology*, *52*(1), 397–422. doi:10.1146/annurev.psych.52.1.397 PMID:11148311

Masterson, S. S., & Stamper, C. L. (2003). Perceived organizational membership: An aggregate framework representing the employee-organization relationship. *Journal of Organizational Behavior*, *24*(5), 473–490. doi:10.1002/job.203

Mathieu, C., Fabi, B., Lacoursière, R., & Raymond, L. (2015). The role of supervisory behavior, job satisfaction and organizational commitment on employee turnover. *Journal of Management & Organization*, *22*(1), 113–129. doi:10.1017/jmo.2015.25

Mathieu, J. E., & Zajac, D. M. (1990). A review and meta-analysis of the antecedents, correlates, and consequences of organizational commitment. *Psychological Bulletin*, *108*(2), 171–194. doi:10.1037/0033-2909.108.2.171

Matteson, M. T., & Ivancevich, J. M. (1987). *Controlling work stress: Effective human resource and management strategies*. Jossey-Bass.

Mattiasson, I., Lindgarde, F., Nilsson, J. A., & Theorell, T. (1990). Threat of unemployment and cardiovascular risk factors: Longitudinal study of quality of sleep and serum cholesterol concentration in men threatened with redundancy. *BMJ (Clinical Research Ed.)*, *301*(6750), 461–466. doi:10.1136/bmj.301.6750.461 PMID:2207398

Mauno, S., De Cuyper, N., Tolvanen, A., Kinnunen, U., & Mäkikangas, A. (2014). Occupational well-being as a mediator between job insecurity and turnover intention: Findings at the individual and work department levels. *European Journal of Work and Organizational Psychology*, *23*(3), 381–393. doi:10.1080/1359432X.2012.752896

May, D. R., Gilson, R. L., & Harter, L. M. (2004). The psychological conditions of meaningfulness, safety and availability and the engagement of the human spirit at work. *Journal of Occupational and Organizational Psychology*, *77*(1), 11–37. doi:10.1348/096317904322915892

McAvoy, A. (2020). *Hawaii looks to restrict lodging reservations to prevent visitor arrivals*. Associated Press. https://skift.com/2020/04/14/hawaii-looks-to-restrict-lodging-reservations-toprevent-visitor-arrivals/

McDowell, T. (2004). *Fun at work: Scale development, confirmatory factor analysis, and links to organizational outcomes* [Unpublished doctoral dissertation]. Alliant International University, San Diego, CA.

McGinley, S. P., Hanks, L., & Line, N. D. (2017). Constraints to attracting new hotel workers: A study on industrial recruitment. *International Journal of Hospitality Management*, *60*, 114–122. doi:10.1016/j.ijhm.2016.10.010

McGuire, D., Germain, M., & Reynolds, K. (2021). Reshaping HRD in light of the COVID-19 pandemic: An ethics of care approach. *Advances in Developing Human Resources*, *23*(1), 26–40. doi:10.1177/1523422320973426

McIlvaine, H. (2020). *More hands on deck*. https://insideretail.com.au/news/more-hands-on-deck-woolies-invites-ex-qantas-staff-to-apply-for-jobs-202003

McKibbin, W. J. (2009). *The swine flu outbreak and its global economic impact*. Available at: https:// www.brookings.edu/on-the-record/the-swine-flu-outbreak-and-its-global-economic-impact

McKinsey & Company. (2020). *Beyond coronavirus: The path to the next normal*. https:// www. mckinsey.com//media/McKinsey/Industries/Healthcare%20Systems%20and%20 Services/Our%20Insights/Beyond%20coronavirus%20The%20path%20to%20the%20 next%20normal/Beyondcoronavirus-The-path-to-the-next-normal.ashx

McKinsey. (2020). Retrieved April 10, 2022, from https://www.mckinsey.com/featured-insights/coronavirus-leading-through-the-crisis/charting-the-path-to-the-next-norm al/ the-earliest-that-us-hotels-return-to-pre-covid-19-revenues-might-be-2022

McKnight, D. H., Ahmad, S., & Schroeder, R. G. (2001). When do feedback, incentive control and autonomy improve morale? The importance of employee-management relationship closeness. *Journal of Managerial Issues*, *13*(4), 466–482.

McLarney, C., & Aujla, S. (2020). The Effects of Organizational Change on Employee Commitment. *The IUP Journal of Organizational Behavior.*, *19*(1), 7–22.

McLean Parks, J., Kidder, D. L., & Gallagher, D. G. (1998). Fitting square pegs into round holes: Mapping the domain of contingent work arrangements onto the psychological contract. *Journal of Organizational Behavior, 19*(S1), 697–730. doi:10.1002/(SICI)1099-1379(1998)19:1+<697::AID-JOB974>3.0.CO;2-I

McManus, S., Seville, E., Vargo, J., & Brunsdon, D. (2008). Facilitated process for improving organisational resilience. *Natural Hazards Review, 9*(2), 81–90. doi:10.1061/(ASCE)1527-6988(2008)9:2(81)

Means, A. J. (2018). Platform learning and on-demand labor: Sociotechnical projections on the future of education and work. *Learning, Media and Technology, 43*(3), 326–338. doi:10.1080/17439884.2018.1504792

Melian-Alzola, L., Fernandez-Monroy, M., & Hidalgo-Penate, M. (2020). Hotels in contexts of uncertainty: Measuring organisational resilience. *Tourism Management Perspectives, 36*, 100747. doi:10.1016/j.tmp.2020.100747 PMID:33024657

Mesmer-Magnus, J. R., DeChurch, L. A., & Wax, A. (2012). Moving emotional labor beyond surface and deep acting: A discordance–congruence perspective. *Organizational Psychology Review, 2*(1), 6–53. doi:10.1177/2041386611417746

Meyer, J. P., & Allen, N. J. (1984). Testing the 'side-bet theory' of organizational commitment: Some methodological considerations. *The Journal of Applied Psychology, 69*(3), 372–378. doi:10.1037/0021-9010.69.3.372

Meyer, J. P., & Allen, N. J. (1990). The measurement and antecedents of affective, continuance and normative commitment to the organization. *Journal of Occupational Psychology, 63*(1), 1–18. doi:10.1111/j.2044-8325.1990.tb00506.x

Meyer, J. P., & Allen, N. J. (1991). A three-component conceptualization of organizational commitment. *Human Resource Management Review, 1*(1), 61–89. doi:10.1016/1053-4822(91)90011-Z

Meyer, J. P., & Gagne, M. (2008). Employee engagement from a self-determination theory perspective. *Industrial and Organizational Psychology: Perspectives on Science and Practice, 1*(1), 60–62. doi:10.1111/j.1754-9434.2007.00010.x

Meyer, J. P., & Herscovitch, L. (2001). Commitment in the workplace: Toward a general model. *Human Resource Management Review, 11*(3), 299–326. doi:10.1016/S1053-4822(00)00053-X

Meyer, J. P., Stanley, D. J., Herscovitch, L., & Topolnytsky, L. (2002). Affective, continuance, and normative commitment to the organization: A meta-analysis of antecedents, correlates, and consequences. *Journal of Vocational Behavior, 61*(1), 20–52. doi:10.1006/jvbe.2001.1842

Michel, J. W., Tews, M. J., & Allen, D. G. (2019). Fun in the workplace: A review and expanded theoretical perspective. *Human Resource Management Review, 29*(1), 98–110. doi:10.1016/j.hrmr.2018.03.001

Milojevic, D., & Katsadze, B. (2020). *Social Sustainability in COVID-19 Crisis: The case of the hotel industry.* Retrieved March 14, 2022, from https://www.divaportal.org/smash/get/diva2:1441677/FULLTEXT01.pdf

Mirabito, A. M., & Berry, L. L. (2015). You say you want a revolution? Drawing on social movement theory to motivate transformative change. *Journal of Service Research, 18*(3), 336–350. doi:10.1177/1094670515582037

Miret, M., Caballero, F., Olaya, B., Koskinen, S., Naidoo, N., Tobiasz-Adamczyk, B., Leonardi, M., Haro, J., Chatterji, S., & Ayuso-Mateos, J. (2017). Association of experienced and evaluative wellbeing with health in nine countries with different income levels: A cross-sectional study. *Globalization and Health, 13*(1), 65. doi:10.118612992-017-0290-0 PMID:28835255

Mitchell, T. R., Holtom, B. C., Lee, T. W., Sablynski, C. J., & Erez, M. (2001). Why people stay: Using job embeddedness to predict voluntary turnover. *Academy of Management Journal, 44*(6), 1102–1121. doi:10.2307/3069391

Mohapatra, A. K., Saxena, A., Joshi, D., & Chaturvedi, N. (2017). Does job security matter for generation Y? A behavioral analysis. *Pacific Business Review International, 10*(5), 92–98.

Mohsin, A., Lengler, J., & Kumar, B. (2013). Exploring the antecedents of intentions to leave the job: The case of luxury hotel staff. *International Journal of Hospitality Management, 35*, 48–58. doi:10.1016/j.ijhm.2013.05.002

Moncarz, E., Zhao, J., & Kay, C. (2009). An exploratory study of US lodging properties' organizational practices on employee turnover and retention. *International Journal of Contemporary Hospitality Management, 21*(4), 437–458. doi:10.1108/09596110910955695

Montani, F., Courcy, F., & Vandenberghe, C. (2017). Innovating under stress: The role of commitment and leader-member exchange. *Journal of Business Research, 77*, 1–13. doi:10.1016/j.jbusres.2017.03.024

Mor Barak, M. E., & Levin, A. (2002). Outside of the corporate mainstream and excluded from the work community: A study of diversity, job satisfaction and well-being. *Community Work & Family, 5*(2), 133–157. doi:10.1080/13668800220146346

Morais-Storz, M., Platou, R., & Norheim, K. B. (2018). Innovation and metamorphosis towards strategic resilience. *International Journal of Entrepreneurial Behaviour & Research, 24*(1).

Moran, J., & Brightman, B. K. (2001). Leading organizational change. *Career Development International, 6*(2), 111–118.

Mossoun, A., Pauly, M., Akoua-Koffi, C., Couacy-Hymann, E., Leendertz, S. A. J., Anoh, A. E., Gnoukpoho, A. H., Leendertz, F. H., & Schubert, G. (2015). Contact to non-human primates and risk factors for zoonotic disease emergence in the Taï region, C^ote d'Ivoire. *EcoHealth, 12*(4), 580–591. doi:10.100710393-015-1056-x PMID:26302959

Mowday, R. T. (1996). Reflections on the study and relevance of organizational commitment. *Human Resource Management Review, 8*(4), 387–401. doi:10.1016/S1053-4822(99)00006-6

Muffels, R., & Wilthagen, T. (2013). Flexicurity: A new paradigm for the analysis of labor markets and policies challenging the trade-off between flexibility and security. *Sociology Compass, 7*(2), 111–112. doi:10.1111oc4.12014

Mulki, J. P., Jaramillo, J. F., & Locander, W. B. (2008). Effect of ethical climate on turnover intention: Linking attitudinal and stress theory. *Journal of Business Ethics*, *78*(4), 559–574. doi:10.100710551-007-9368-6

Myers, S. S., Gaffikin, L., Golden, C. D., Ostfeld, R. S., Redford, K. H., Ricketts, T. H., Turner, W. R., & Osofsky, S. A. (2013). Human health impacts of ecosystem alteration. *Proceedings of the National Academy of Sciences of the United States of America*, *110*(47). Advance online publication. doi:10.1073/pnas.1218656110 PMID:24218556

Nella, D., Panagopoulou, E., Galanis, N., Montgomery, A., & Benos, A. (2015). Consequences of job insecurity on the psychological and physical health of Greek civil servants. *BioMed Research International*, *2015*, 1–9. doi:10.1155/2015/673623 PMID:26557687

Nelson, B. (1999). *Low cost ways to build employee commitment.* Nelson Motivation Inc. Available at https://www.inc.com/articles/1999/12/16412.html

Nelson, D. C., & Nesmith, M. (2003). The impact of safety training on work-related injuries at eating and drinking places. *Journal of Human Resources in Hospitality & Tourism*, *1*(4), 19–32. doi:10.1300/J171v01n04_02

Netemeyer, R. G., Boles, J. S., & McMurrian, R. (1996). Development and validation of work–family conflict and family–work conflict scales. *The Journal of Applied Psychology*, *81*(4), 400–410. doi:10.1037/0021-9010.81.4.400

Neuman, J. H., & Keashly, L. (2004). *Development of the Workplace Aggression Research Questionnaire (WAR-Q)*. Preliminary Data from the Workplace Stress and Aggression.

Newell, S., & Marabelli, M. (2015). Strategic opportunities (and challenges) of algorithmic decision-making: A call for action on the long-term societal effects of 'datification.'. *The Journal of Strategic Information Systems*, *24*(1), 3–14. doi:10.1016/j.jsis.2015.02.001

Niehoff, B. P., & Moorman, R. H. (1993). Justice as a mediator of the relationship between methods of monitoring and organizational citizenship behavior. *Academy of Management Journal*, *36*(3), 527–556. doi:10.2307/256591

Nielsen, K. (2013). Review article: How can we make organizational interventions work? Employees and line managers as actively crafting interventions. *Human Relations*, *66*(8), 1029–1050. doi:10.1177/0018726713477164

Nielsen, K., Fredslund, H., Christensen, K. B., & Albertsen, K. (2006). Success or failure? Interpreting and understanding the impact of interventions in four similar worksites. *Work and Stress*, *20*(3), 272–287. doi:10.1080/02678370601022688

Nielsen, K., & Randall, R. (2012). The importance of employee participation and perceptions of changes in procedures in a teamworking intervention. *Work and Stress*, *26*(2), 91–111. doi:10.1080/02678373.2012.682721 PMID:22745519

Niesen, W., De Witte, & Battistelli, A. (2014). An explanatory model of job insecurity and innovative work behavior: insights from social exchange and threat rigidity theory. In Contemporary Occupational Health Psychology: Global Perspectives on Research and Practice (vol. 3). John Wiley & Sons Limited.

Niesen, W., Hootegem, A. V., Handaja, Y., Battistelli, A., & De Witte, H. (2018). Quantitative and qualitative job insecurity and idea generation: The mediating role of psychological contract breach. *Scandinavian Journal of Work and Organizational Psychology.*, *3*(1), 1–14. doi:10.16993jwop.36

Noer, D. (1993). *Healing the wounds: Overcoming the trauma of layoffs and revitalizing downsized organizations*. Jossey-Bass.

Notelaers, G., De Witte, H., Van Veldhoven, M., & Vermunt, J. K. (2007). Construction and validation of the short inventory to monitor psychosocial hazards. *Medecine du Travail et Ergonomie*, *44*(1), 11–17.

Novelli, L. Jr, Kirkman, B. L., & Shapiro, D. L. (1995). Effective implementation of organizational change: An organizational justice perspective. In C. L. Cooper & D. M. Rousseau (Eds.), *Trends in Organizational Behavior* (Vol. 2, pp. 15–36). Wiley.

Novelli, M., Burgess, L. G., Jones, A., & Ritchie, B. W. (2018). No Ebola… still doomed'– The Ebola induced tourism crisis. *Annals of Tourism Research*, *70*, 76–87. doi:10.1016/j.annals.2018.03.006 PMID:32572288

Nunn, J. (2020, April 14). Restaurants will never be the same after coronavirus – but that may be a good thing. *The Guardian*. https://www.theguardian.com/commentisfree/2020/apr/14/coronavirus-restaurants-pandemic-workers-communities-prices

O' Neill, J. W., & Davis, K. (2011). Work stress and well-being in the hotel industry. *International Journal of Hospitality Management*, *30*(2), 385–390. doi:10.1016/j.ijhm.2010.07.007 PMID:23794780

O'Neil, A., Nicholls, S. J., Redfern, J., Brown, A., & Hare, D. L. (2020). Mental health and psychosocial challenges in the COVID-19 pandemic: Food for thought for cardiovascular health care professionals. *Heart Lung and Circulation*, *29*(7), 960–963. doi:10.1016/j.hlc.2020.05.002 PMID:32561126

O'Reilly, C. A., & Chatman, J. (1986). Organizational commitment and psychological attachment: The effects of compliance, identification, and internalization on prosocial behavior. *The Journal of Applied Psychology*, *71*(3), 492–499. doi:10.1037/0021-9010.71.3.492

Ogbeide, G.-C. (2013). Perception of Green Hotels in the 21st Century. *Journal of Tourism Insights*, *3*(1), 1.

Orchiston, C., Prayag, G., & Brown, C. (2016). Organizational resilience in the tourism sector. *Annals of Tourism Research*, *56*, 145–148. doi:10.1016/j.annals.2015.11.002

Organ, D. W., & Ryan, K. (1995). A meta-analytic review of attitudinal and dispositional predictors of organizational citizenship behavior. *Personnel Psychology*, *48*(4), 775–802. doi:10.1111/j.1744-6570.1995.tb01781.x

Osawa, H., Ema, A., Hattori, H., Akiya, N., Kanzaki, N., & Kubo, A. (2017). Analysis of robot hotel: reconstruction of works with robots. *26th IEEE International Symposium on Robot and Human Interactive Communication*. 10.1109/ROMAN.2017.8172305

Ouyang, Y. (2011). An exploration of LMX and personal guanxi on job performance: The mediating effects of CSR. *Journal of Global Business Issues*, *5*(1), 1–10.

Owens, B. P., Baker, W. E., Sumpter, D. M., & Cameron, K. S. (2016). Relational energy at work: Implications for job engagement and job performance. *The Journal of Applied Psychology*, *101*(1), 35–49. doi:10.1037/apl0000032

Ozbay, G., Sariisik, M., Ceylan, V., & Cakmak, M. (2021). A comparative evaluation between the impact of previous outbreaks and COVID-19 on the tourism industry. *International Hospitality Review*, *35*(2).

Ozdemir, M. A. (2020). What are the economic, psychological and social consequences of the covid-19 crisis on tourism employees? *International Journal of Social, Political and Economic Research*, *7*(4), 1137–1163. doi:10.46291/IJOSPERvol7iss4pp1137-1163

Page, K. M., & Vella-Brodrick, D. A. (2009). The "what," "why" and "how" of employee wellbeing: A new model. *Social Indicators Research*, *90*(3), 441–458. doi:10.100711205-008-9270-3

Page, S. J., Bentley, T., Teo, S., & Ladkin, A. (2018). The dark side of high performance human resource practices in the visitor economy. *International Journal of Hospitality Management*, *74*, 122–129. doi:10.1016/j.ijhm.2018.02.016

Parish, J. T., Cadwallader, S., & Busch, P. (2008). Want to, need to, ought to: Employee commitment to organizational change. *Journal of Organizational Change Management*, *21*(1), 32–52. doi:10.1108/09534810810847020

Park, J., & Gursoy, D. (2012). Generation effects on work engagement among US hotel employees. *International Journal of Hospitality Management*, *31*(4), 1195–1202. doi:10.1016/j.ijhm.2012.02.007

Patriarca, R., Di Gravio, G., Costantino, F., Falegnami, A., & Bilotta, F. (2018). An analytic framework to assess organizational resilience. *Safety and Health at Work*, *9*(3), 265–276. doi:10.1016/j.shaw.2017.10.005 PMID:30370158

Peachey, J. W., Burton, L. J., & Wells, J. E. (2014). Examining the influence of transformational leadership, organizational commitment, job embeddedness, and job search behaviors on turnover intentions in intercollegiate athletics. *Leadership and Organization Development Journal*, *35*(8), 740–755. doi:10.1108/LODJ-10-2012-0128

Pearce, J. L., & Randel, A. E. (2004). Expectations of organizational mobility, workplace social inclusion, and employee job performance. *Journal of Organizational Behavior*, *25*(1), 81–98. doi:10.1002/job.232

Pearlin, L. I., & Bierman, A. (2013). Current issues and future directions in research into the stress process. In C. S. Aneshensel, J. Phelan, & A. Bierman (Eds.), *Handbook of the sociology of mental health* (2nd ed., pp. 325–340). Springer. doi:10.1007/978-94-007-4276-5_16

Perry-Smith, J. E. (2006). Social yet creative: The role of social relationships in facilitating individual creativity. *Academy of Management Journal*, *49*(1), 85–101. doi:10.5465/amj.2006.20785503

Peteet, J. R. (2000). Cancer and the meaning of work. *General Hospital Psychiatry*, *22*(3), 200–205. doi:10.1016/S0163-8343(00)00076-1 PMID:10880715

Peterson, R. R., & DiPietro, R. B. (2021). Exploring the impact of the COVID-19 pandemic on the perceptions and sentiments of tourism employees: Evidence from a small island tourism economy in the Caribbean. *International Hospitality Review*, *35*(2), 156–170. doi:10.1108/IHR-10-2020-0063

Petriglieri, G., Ashford, S. J., & Wrzesniewski, A. (2019). Agony and ecstasy in the gig economy: Cultivating holding environments for precarious and personalized work identities. *Administrative Science Quarterly*, *64*(1), 124–170. doi:10.1177/0001839218759646

Pfefferbaum, B., & North, C. S. (2020). Mental health and the Covid-19 pandemic. *The New England Journal of Medicine*, *383*(6), 510–512. doi:10.1056/NEJMp2008017 PMID:32283003

Pfeffer, J. (1994). *Competitive Advantage Through People*. Harvard Business School Press. doi:10.2307/41165742

Pfeffer, J. (1998). *The human equation: Building profits by putting people first*. Harvard University Press.

Pforr, C., & Hosie, P. J. (2008). Crisis management in tourism: Preparing for recovery. *Journal of Travel & Tourism Marketing*, *23*(2-4), 249–264. doi:10.1300/J073v23n02_19

Pham, N. T., Thanh, T. V., Tuckova, Z., & Thuy, V. T. N. (2020). The role of green human resource management in driving hotel's environmental performance: Interaction and mediation analysis. *International Journal of Hospitality Management*, *88*, 102392. doi:10.1016/j.ijhm.2019.102392

Pindek, S., Krajcevska, A., & Spector, P. E. (2018). Cyberloafing as a coping mechanism: Dealing with workplace boredom. *Computers in Human Behavior*, *86*, 147–152. doi:10.1016/j.chb.2018.04.040

Pocock, B. (2005). Work–life 'balance' in Australia: Limited progress, dim prospects. *Asia Pacific Journal of Human Resources*, *43*(2), 198–209. doi:10.1177/1038411105055058

Podsakoff, P. M., MacKenzie, S. B., Lee, J.-Y., & Podsakoff, N. P. (2003). Common method biases in behavioral research: A critical review of the literature and recommended remedies. *The Journal of Applied Psychology*, *88*(5), 879–903. doi:10.1037/0021-9010.88.5.879 PMID:14516251

Podsakoff, P. M., MacKenzie, S. B., & Podsakoff, N. P. (2012). Sources of method bias in social science research and recommendations on how to control it. *Annual Review of Psychology*, *63*(1), 539–569. doi:10.1146/annurev-psych-120710-100452 PMID:21838546

Politico. (2020, March 19). Coronavirus will change the world permanently. Here's how. *Politico Magazine*. https://www.politico.com/news/magazine/2020/03/19/coronavirus-effect-economylife-society-analysis-covid-135579

Pozner, B. Z., & Randolph, W. A. (1980). Moderators of role stress among hospital personnel. *The Journal of Psychology*, *105*(2), 215–224. doi:10.1080/00223980.1980.9915154 PMID:7400988

Praskova, A., Hood, M., & Creed, P. A. (2014). Testing a calling model of psychological career success in Australian young adults: A longitudinal study. *Journal of Vocational Behavior*, *85*(1), 125–135. doi:10.1016/j.jvb.2014.04.004

Prayag, G. (2018). Symbiotic relationship or not? Understanding resilience and crisis management in tourism. *Tourism Management Perspectives*, *25*, 133–135. doi:10.1016/j.tmp.2017.11.012

Probst, T. M. (2005). Economic stressors. In J. Barling, E. K. Kelloway, & M. R. Frone (Eds.), *Handbook of work stress* (pp. 267–297). Sage. doi:10.4135/9781412975995.n11

Qu, H., & Zhao, X. (2012). Employees' work–family conflict moderating life and job satisfaction. *Journal of Business Research*, *65*(1), 22–28. doi:10.1016/j.jbusres.2011.07.010

Rafiq, M., Wu, W., Chin, T., & Nasir, M. (2019). The psychological mechanism linking employee work engagement and turnover intention: A moderated mediation study. *Work (Reading, Mass.)*, *62*(4), 615–628. doi:10.3233/WOR-192894 PMID:31104045

Rahi, K. (2019). Indicators to assess organizational resilience–a review of empirical literature. *International Journal of Disaster Resilience in the Built Environment*, *10*(2/3), 85–98. doi:10.1108/IJDRBE-11-2018-0046

Reisel, W. D., Probst, T. M., Chia, S. L., Maloles, C. M., & Konig, C. J. (2010). The effects of job insecurity on job satisfaction, organizational citizenship behavior, deviant behavior, and negative emotions of employees. *International Studies of Management & Organization*, *40*(1), 74–91. doi:10.2753/IMO0020-8825400105

Remeikis, A. (2020). *Australian government won't "jump to a solution" to help casual workers in coronavirus crisis*. Retrieved 16 May, 2022, from The Guardian website: https://www.theguardian.com/world/2020/mar/10/australian-government-warned-not-to-drag-its-feet-on-help-for-casual-workers-in-coronavirus-crisis

Ren, S., & Chadee, D. (2017). Influence of work pressure on proactive skill development in China: The role of career networking behavior and guanxi HRM. *Journal of Vocational Behavior*, *98*, 152–162. doi:10.1016/j.jvb.2016.11.004

Rifkin, J. (1995). *The end of work: The decline of the global labor force and the dawn of the post-market era*. Putnam.

Riketta, M. (2002). Attitudinal organizational commitment and job performance: A meta-analysis. *Journal of Organizational Behavior*, *23*(3), 257–266. doi:10.1002/job.141

Riley, M. (2004). Labor Mobility and Market Structure in Tourism. In A. A. Lew, C. M. Hall, & A. M. Williams (Eds.), *A Companion to Tourism* (pp. 135–145). Blackwell Publishing Ltd. doi:10.1002/9780470752272.ch11

Ritchie, B. (2008). Tourism disaster planning and management: From response and recovery to reduction and readiness. *Current Issues in Tourism*, *11*(4), 315–348. doi:10.1080/13683500802140372

Rizzo, J. R., House, R. J., & Lirtzman, S. I. (1970). Role conflict and ambiguity in complex organizations. *Administrative Science Quarterly*, *15*(2), 150–163. doi:10.2307/2391486

Roberts, D. R., & Davenport, T. O. (2002). Job engagement: Why it's important and how to improve it. *Employment Relations Today*, *29*(3), 21–29. doi:10.1002/ert.10048

Robinson, R. N. S., Martins, A., Solnet, D. J., & Baum, T. (2019). Sustaining precarity: Critically examining tourism and employment. *Journal of Sustainable Tourism*, *27*(7), 1008–1025. doi:10.1080/09669582.2018.1538230

Rosa, H. (2013). *Social acceleration: A new theory of modernity*. Columbia University Press. doi:10.7312/rosa14834

Rosenblatt, Z., & Ruvio, A. (1996). A test of a multidimensional model of job insecurity: The case of Israeli teachers. *Journal of Organizational Behavior*, *17*(S1), 587–605. doi:10.1002/(SICI)1099-1379(199612)17:1+<587::AID-JOB825>3.0.CO;2-S

Roskies, E., & Louis-Guerin, C. (1990). Job insecurity in managers: Antecedents and consequences. *Journal of Organizational Behavior*, *11*(5), 345–359. doi:10.1002/job.4030110503

Rosse, J. G., & Hulin, C. L. (1985). Adaptation to work: An analysis of employee health, withdrawal, and change. *Organizational Behavior and Human Decision Processes*, *36*(3), 324–347. doi:10.1016/0749-5978(85)90003-2 PMID:10275698

Ross, G. F. (2005). Tourism industry employee work stress- a present and future crisis. *Journal of Travel & Tourism Marketing*, *19*(2-3), 133–147. doi:10.1300/J073v19n02_11

Rousseau, V., Salek, S., Aubé, C., & Morin, E. M. (2009). Distributive justice, procedural justice, and psychological distress: The moderating effect of coworker support and work autonomy. *Journal of Occupational Health Psychology*, *14*(3), 305–317. doi:10.1037/a0015747 PMID:19586224

Ruiz-Martin, C., López-Paredes, A., & Wainer, G. (2018). What we know and do not know about organizational resilience. *International Journal of Production Management and Engineering.*, *6*(1), 11–28. doi:10.4995/ijpme.2018.7898

Rust, R. T., & Huang, M.-H. (2014). The service revolution and the transformation of marketing science. *Marketing Science*, *33*(2), 206–221. doi:10.1287/mksc.2013.0836

Ryan, R. M., & Deci, E. L. (2000). Self-determination theory and the facilitation of intrinsic motivation, social development, and well-being. *The American Psychologist*, *55*(1), 68–78. doi:10.1037/0003-066X.55.1.68 PMID:11392867

Ryan, R. M., & Deci, E. L. (2001). On happiness and human potentials: A review of research on hedonic and eudaimonic well-being. *Annual Review of Psychology*, *52*(1), 141–166. doi:10.1146/annurev.psych.52.1.141 PMID:11148302

Ryder, N. B. (1965). The cohort as a concept in the study of social change. *American Sociological Review*, *30*(6), 843–861. doi:10.2307/2090964 PMID:5846306

Ryff, C. D. (1989). Happiness is everything, or is it? Explorations on the meaning of psychological well-being. *Journal of Personality and Social Psychology*, *57*(6), 1069–1081. doi:10.1037/0022-3514.57.6.1069

Ryu, S., Gao, H., Wong, J. Y., Shiu, E. Y. C., Xiao, J., Fong, M. W., & Cowling, B. J. (2020, May). Nonpharmaceutical measures for pandemic influenza in nonhealthcare settings – international travel – related measures. *Emerging Infectious Diseases*, *26*(5), 961–966. doi:10.3201/eid2605.190993

S'ahin, F. (2011). The effect of gender on the relationship between leader-member exchange and intention to quit. *Ege Academic Review*, *11*(2), 277–288.

Sabahi, S., & Parast, M. M. (2020). Firm innovation and supply chain resilience: A dynamic capability perspective. *International Journal of Logistics*, *23*(3), 254–269. doi:10.1080/13675567.2019.1683522

Sabatino, M. (2016). Economic crisis and resilience: Resilient capacity and competitiveness of the enterprises. *Journal of Business Research*, *69*(5), 1924–1927. doi:10.1016/j.jbusres.2015.10.081

Saks, A. M. (2006). Antecedents and consequences of employee engagement. *Journal of Managerial Psychology*, *21*(7), 600–619. doi:10.1108/02683940610690169

Santana, G., Hall, M. C., Timothy, D. J., & Duval, D. T. (2003). Crisis management and tourism: Beyond the rhetoric. *Safety and Security in Tourism: Relationships, Management, and Marketing.*, *15*(2-4), 299–321.

Sarabahksh, M., Carson, D., & Lindgren, E. (1989). Hospitality managers' stress and quality of life: Recommendations for change. *Hospitality Education & Research Journal*, *13*(3), 239–245. doi:10.1177/109634808901300324

Sarfraz, M., Shah, S. G. M., Fareed, Z., & Shahzad, F. (2020). Demonstrating the interconnection of hierarchical order disturbances in CEO succession with corporate social responsibility and environmental sustainability. *Corporate Social Responsibility and Environmental Management*, *27*(6), 27. doi:10.1002/csr.2014

Sauder, M., & Espeland, W. N. (2009). The discipline of rankings: Tight coupling and organizational change. *American Sociological Review*, *74*(1), 63–82. doi:10.1177/000312240907400104

Schaubroeck, J., Cotton, J. L., & Jennings, K. R. (1989). Antecedents and consequences of role stress: A covariance structure analysis. *Journal of Organizational Behavior*, *10*(1), 35–58. doi:10.1002/job.4030100104

Schaufeli, W. B., & Bakker, A. B. (2004, May). with burnout and engagement: A multi-sample study. *Journal of Organizational Behavior*, *25*(3), 293–315. doi:10.1002/job.248

Schaufeli, W. B., Bakker, A. B., & Salanova, M. (2006). The measurement of work engagement with a short questionnaire: A cross-national study. *Educational and Psychological Measurement*, *66*(4), 701–716. doi:10.1177/0013164405282471

Schaufeli, W. B., Salanova, M., Gonzalez-Roma, V., & Bakker, A. B. (2002). Burnout and engagement in university students. *Journal of Cross-Cultural Psychology*, *33*(5), 464–481. doi:10.1177/0022022102033005003

Schminke, M., Cropanzano, R., & Rupp, D. E. (2002). Organization structure and fairness perceptions: The moderating effects of organizational level. *Organizational Behavior and Human Decision Processes*, *89*(1), 881–905. doi:10.1016/S0749-5978(02)00034-1

Schneider, B. (1975). Organizational climates: An essay. *Personnel Psychology*, *28*(4), 447–479. doi:10.1111/j.1744-6570.1975.tb01386.x

Schneider, B., White, S. S., & Paul, M. C. (1998). Linking service climate and customer perceptions of service quality: Test of a causal model. *The Journal of Applied Psychology*, *83*(2), 150–163. doi:10.1037/0021-9010.83.2.150 PMID:9577232

Scholz, T. (2017). *Uberworked and Underpaid: How Workers are Disrupting the Digital Economy*. Polity Press.

Schouteten, R., & Van Der Vleuten, T. (2013). Organizational Change and Job Satisfaction Among Voluntary and Paid Workers in a Dutch Voluntary Organization. Institute for Management Research, Nijmegen, the Netherlands.

Schuman, H., & Scott, J. (1989). Generations and collective memories. *American Sociological Review*, *54*(3), 359–381. doi:10.2307/2095611

Schwartz, D. (2018). Embedded in the crowd: Creative freelancers, crowdsourced work, and occupational community. *Work and Occupations*, *45*(3), 247–282. doi:10.1177/0730888418762263

Schweiger, D. M., & Denisi, A. S. (1991). Communication with employees following a merger: A longitudinal field experiment. *Academy of Management Journal*, *34*(1), 110–135. doi:10.2307/256304

Semmer, N. K. (2011). Job stress interventions and organization of work. In J. C. Quick & L. E. Tetrick (Eds.), *Handbook of occupational health psychology* (pp. 299–318). American Psychological Association.

Senbeto, D. L., & Hon, A. H. (2020). The impacts of social and economic crises on tourist behaviour and expenditure: An evolutionary approach. *Current Issues in Tourism*, *23*(6), 740–755. doi:10.1080/13683500.2018.1546674

Seville, E., Brunsdon, D., Dantas, A., Le Masurier, J., Wilkinson, S., & Vargo, J. (2008). Organisational resilience: Researching the reality of New Zealand organisations. *Journal of Business Continuity & Emergency Planning*, *2*(3), 258–266. PMID:21339112

Shah, N., Irani, Z., & Sharif, A. (2017). Big data in an HR context: Exploring organizational change readiness, employee attitudes and behaviors. *Journal of Business Research*, *70*(3), 366–378. doi:10.1016/j.jbusres.2016.08.010

Sharma, G. D., Thomas, A., & Paul, J. (2021). Reviving tourism industry post-COVID-19: A resilience based framework. *Tourism Management Perspectives*, *37*, 100786. doi:10.1016/j.tmp.2020.100786 PMID:33391988

Shih, S. P., Jiang, J. J., Klein, G., & Wang, E. (2013). Job burnout of the information technology worker: Work exhaustion, depersonalization, and personal accomplishment. *Information & Management, 50*(7), 582–589. doi:10.1016/j.im.2013.08.003

Shin, I., & Jeung, C. W. (2019). Uncovering the turnover intention of proactive employees: The mediating role of work engagement and the moderated mediating role of job autonomy. *International Journal of Environmental Research and Public Health, 16*(5), 1–16, 843. doi:10.3390/ijerph16050843 PMID:30857145

Shin, Y., Hur, W. M., Moon, T. W., & Lee, S. (2019). A motivational perspective on job insecurity: Relationships between job insecurity, intrinsic motivation, and performance and behavioral outcomes. *International Journal of Environmental Research and Public Health, 16*(10), 1–16. doi:10.3390/ijerph16101812

Shoss, M. K. (2017). Job insecurity: An integrative review and agenda for future research. *Journal of Management, 43*(6), 1911–1939. doi:10.1177/0149206317691574

Shropshire, J., & Kadlec, C. (2012). I'm leaving the IT field: The impact of stress, job insecurity, and burnout on IT professionals. *International Journal of Information and Communication Technology Research, 2*(1), 6–16.

Sibiya, M., Buitendach, J. H., Kanengoni, H., & Bobat, S. (2014). The prediction of turnover intention by means of employee engagement and demographic variables in a telecommunications organization. *Journal of Psychology in Africa, 24*(2), 131–143. doi:10.1080/14330237.2014.903078

Siemsen, E., Roth, A., & Oliveira, P. (2010). Common method bias in regression models with linear, quadratic, and interaction effects. *Organizational Research Methods, 13*(3), 456–476. doi:10.1177/1094428109351241

Singapore Tourism Board. (2020). *SG clean quality mark extended to tourism and lifestyle businesses as part of nationwide efforts to uplift sanitation and hygiene*. https://www.stb.gov.sg/content/stb/en/media-centre/media-releases/sg-clean-qualitymarkextendedtotourismandlifestylebusinessesaspar.html.html

Singh, J. (1993). Boundary role ambiguity: Facets, determinants, and impacts. *Journal of Marketing, 57*(2), 11–31. doi:10.1177/002224299305700202

Sirgy, J. M. (2019). Promoting quality-of-life and well-being research in hospitality and tourism. *Journal of Travel & Tourism Marketing, 36*(1), 1–13. doi:10.1080/10548408.2018.1526757

Smith, T. D. (2018). An assessment of safety climate, job satisfaction and turnover intention relationships using a national sample of workers from the United States. *International Journal of Occupational Safety and Ergonomics, 24*(1), 27–34. doi:10.1080/10803548.2016.1268446 PMID:28010625

Smollan, R. K. (2016). The personal costs of organizational change: A qualitative study. *Public Performance & Management Review, 39*(1), 223–247. doi:10.1080/15309576.2016.1071174

Snell, D., Gekara, V., & Gatt, K. (2016). *Cross-occupational skill transferability: challenges and opportunities in a changing economy*. https://www.ncver.edu.au/research-and-statistics/publications/all-publications/cross-occupational-skill-transferability-challenges-and-opportunities-in-a-changing-economy

Sobieralski, J. B. (2020). COVID-19 and airline employment: Insights from historical uncertainty shocks to the industry. *Transportation Research Interdisciplinary Perspectives*, *5*(100123), 1–9. doi:10.1016/j.trip.2020.100123 PMID:34173453

Soeker, M. S., Wegner, L., & Pretorius, B. (2008). I'm going back to work: Back injured clients' perceptions and experiences of their worker roles. *Work (Reading, Mass.)*, *30*(2), 161–170. PMID:18413932

Sofat, K., Kiran, R., & Kaushik, S. (2015). Management of organizational change and its impact on commitment: A study of select Indian IT companies. *International Global Business and Management Research Journal.*, *7*(3), 69–87.

Sogno, A. (2020). COVID-19 crisis forces hoteliers to review their human resources strategies. *HospitalityNet*. Available from: https://www.hospitalitynet.org/opinion/4098660.html

Sparrow, P. (1998). The pursuit of multiple and parallel organizational flexibilities: Reconstituting jobs. *European Journal of Work and Organizational Psychology*, *7*(1), 79–95. doi:10.1080/135943298398970

Spreitzer, G. M. (1995). Psychological empowerment in the workplace: Dimensions, measurement, and validation. *Academy of Management Journal*, *38*(5), 1442–1465. doi:10.2307/256865

Spreitzer, G. M., & Porath, C. (2012). Creating sustainable performance. *Harvard Business Review*, *90*(1), 92–99. PMID:22299508

Stamper, C. L., & Masterson, S. S. (2002). Insider or outsider? How employee perceptions of insider status affect their work behavior. *Journal of Organizational Behavior*, *23*(8), 875–894. doi:10.1002/job.175

Staufenbiel, T., & Konig, C. J. (2010). A model for the effects of job insecurity on performance, turnover intention, and absenteeism. *Journal of Occupational and Organizational Psychology*, *83*(1), 101–117. doi:10.1348/096317908X401912

Staw, B. M., Sandelands, L. E., & Dutton, J. E. (1981). Threat rigidity effects in organizational behavior: A multilevel analysis. *Administrative Science Quarterly*, *26*(4), 501–524. doi:10.2307/2392337

Steger, M. F. (2012). Making meaning in life. *Psychological Inquiry*, *23*(4), 381–385. doi:10.1080/1047840X.2012.720832

Steiner, J. F., Cavender, T. A., Main, D. S., & Bradley, C. J. (2004). Assessing the impact of cancer on work outcomes: What are the research needs? *Cancer*, *101*(8), 1703–1711. doi:10.1002/cncr.20564 PMID:15386303

Stewart, A., & Stanford, J. (2017). Regulating work in the gig economy: What are the options? *Economic and Labour Relations Review*, *28*(3), 420–437. doi:10.1177/1035304617722461

Stiglbauer, B., Selenko, E., Batinic, B., & Jodlbauer, S. (2012). On the link between job insecurity and turnover intentions: Moderated mediation by work involvement and well-being. *Journal of Occupational Health Psychology*, *17*(3), 354–364. doi:10.1037/a0028565 PMID:22746370

Storseth, F. (2006). Changes at work and employee reactions: Organizational elements, job insecurity, and short-term stress as predictors for employee health and safety. *Scandinavian Journal of Psychology*, *47*(6), 541–550. doi:10.1111/j.1467-9450.2006.00548.x PMID:17107503

Stryker, S. (1968). Identity salience and role performance: The relevance of symbolic interaction theory for family research. *Journal of Marriage and Family*, *30*(4), 558–564. doi:10.2307/349494

Stum, D. L. (2001). Maslow revisited: Building the employee commitment pyramid. *Strategy and Leadership*, *29*(4), 4–9. doi:10.1108/10878570110400053

Sundaram, R. M. (2019). A study on growth of tourism industry in Kanyakumari district. *Journal of the Gujarat Research Society*, *21*(16), 720–727.

Sun, H., Wang, H., & Wan, Z. (2019). Model and analysis of labour supply for ride-sharing platforms in the presence of sample self-selection and endogeneity. *Transportation Research Part B: Methodological*, *125*, 76–93. doi:10.1016/j.trb.2019.04.004

Susskind, A. M., Michele Kacmar, K., & Borchgrevink, C. P. (2003). Customer service providers' attitudes relating to customer service and customer satisfaction in the customer-server exchange. *The Journal of Applied Psychology*, *88*(1), 179–187. doi:10.1037/0021-9010.88.1.179 PMID:12675405

Susskind, A., & Verma, R. (2011). Hotel guests' reactions to guest room sustainability initiatives. *Cornell Hospitality Report*, *11*(6), 1.

Sverke, M., Gallagher, D. G., & Hellgren, J. (2000). Alternative work arrangements: Job stress, well-being and pro-organizational attitudes among employees with different employment contracts. In K. Isaksson, C. Hogstedt, C. Eriksson, & T. Theorell (Eds.), *Health effects of the new labour market* (pp. 145–167). Plenum.

Sverke, M., & Hellgren, J. (2002). The nature of job insecurity: Understanding employment uncertainty on the brink of a new millennium. *Applied Psychology*, *51*(1), 23–42. doi:10.1111/1464-0597.0077z

Sverke, M., Hellgren, J., & Naswall, K. (2002). No security: A meta-analysis and review of job insecurity and its consequences. *Journal of Occupational Health Psychology*, *7*(3), 242–264. doi:10.1037/1076-8998.7.3.242 PMID:12148956

Sverke, M., Låstad, L., Hellgren, J., Richter, A., & Näswall, K. (2019). A meta-analysis of job insecurity and employee performance: Testing temporal aspects, rating source, welfare regime, and union density as moderators. *International Journal of Environmental Research and Public Health*, *16*(14), 1–29. doi:10.3390/ijerph16142536 PMID:31315198

Tabacchi, M. H., Krone, C., & Farber, B. (1990). A support system to mitigate manager burnout. *The Cornell Hotel and Restaurant Administration Quarterly*, *31*(3), 32–37. doi:10.1177/001088049003100310

Tanova, C., & Holtom, B. C. (2008). Using job embeddedness factors to explain voluntary turnover in four European countries. *International Journal of Human Resource Management*, *19*(9), 1553–1568. doi:10.1080/09585190802294820

Tausig, M. (2013). The sociology of work and well-being. In C. S. Aneshensel, J. Phelan, & A. Bierman (Eds.), *Handbook of the sociology of mental health* (2nd ed., pp. 433–455). Springer. doi:10.1007/978-94-007-4276-5_21

Tausig, M., & Fenwick, R. (1999). Recession and well-being. *Journal of Health and Social Behavior*, *40*(1), 1–16. doi:10.2307/2676375 PMID:10331318

Taylor, P. L. (2020). This is what the future of hotels looks like. Get ready for shrink wrap and "Health detectors." *Forbes*. Available from: https://www.forbes.com/sites/petertaylor/2020/05/12/this-is-what-the-future-of-hotels-looks-like-get-ready-for-shrink-wrap-and-health-detectors/#3c8011421cae

Teoh, M. W., Wang, Y., & Kwek, A. (2019). Coping with emotional labor in high stress hospitality work environments. *International Journal of Contemporary Hospitality Management*, *28*, 883–904.

Tetrick, L. E., & LaRocco, J. M. (1987). Understanding, prediction, and control as moderators of the relationships between perceived stress, satisfaction, and psychological well-being. *The Journal of Applied Psychology*, *72*(4), 538–543. doi:10.1037/0021-9010.72.4.538 PMID:3680098

Tews, M. J., Michel, J. W., & Allen, D. G. (2014). Fun and friends: The impact of workplace fun and constituent attachment on turnover in a hospitality context. *Human Relations*, *67*(8), 923–946. doi:10.1177/0018726713508143

Tews, M. J., Michel, J. W., & Noe, R. A. (2017). Does fun promote learning? The relationship between fun in the workplace and informal learning. *Journal of Vocational Behavior*, *98*, 46–55. doi:10.1016/j.jvb.2016.09.006

Tews, M. J., Michel, J. W., & Stafford, K. (2013). Does fun pay? The impact of workplace fun on employee turnover and performance. *Cornell Hospitality Quarterly*, *54*(4), 370–382. doi:10.1177/1938965513505355

Tian, A. W., Cordery, J., & Gamble, J. (2016). Staying and performing: How human resource management practices increase job embeddedness and performance. *Personnel Review*, *45*(5), 947–968. doi:10.1108/PR-09-2014-0194

Tian, Q., Zhang, L., & Zou, W. (2014). Job insecurity and counterproductive behavior of casino dealers: The mediating role of affective commitment and moderating role of supervisor support. *International Journal of Hospitality Management*, *40*, 29–36. doi:10.1016/j.ijhm.2014.03.005

Tibay, V., Miller, J., Chang-Richards, A. Y., Egbelakin, T., Seville, E., & Wilkinson, S. (2018). Business resilience: A study of Auckland hospitality sector. *Procedia Engineering*, *212*, 1217–1224. doi:10.1016/j.proeng.2018.01.157

Ticona, J., & Mateescu, A. (2018). Trusted strangers: Carework platforms' cultural entrepreneurship in the on-demand economy. *New Media & Society*, *20*(11), 4384–4404. doi:10.1177/1461444818773727

Timms, C., Brough, P., O'Driscoll, M., Kalliath, T., Siu, O. L., Sit, C., & Lo, D. (2015). Flexible work arrangements, work engagement, turnover intentions and psychological health. *Asia Pacific Journal of Human Resources*, *53*(1), 83–103. doi:10.1111/1744-7941.12030

Tourism From Zero. (2020). *#TourismFromZero Initiative*. https://tourismfromzero.org/

Trang, H. L. T., Lee, J. S., & Han, H. (2019). How do green attributes elicit pro-environmental behaviors in guests? The case of green hotels in Vietnam. *Journal of Travel & Tourism Marketing*, *36*(1), 14–28. doi:10.1080/10548408.2018.1486782

Triandis, H. C., Bontempo, R., Villareal, M. J., Asai, M., & Lucca, N. (1988). Individualism and collectivism: Cross-cultural perspectives on self-ingroup relationships. *Journal of Personality and Social Psychology*, *54*(2), 323–338. doi:10.1037/0022-3514.54.2.323

Tsai, C. H., & Chen, C. W. (2010). An earthquake disaster management mechanism based on risk assessment information for the tourism industry-a case study from the island of Taiwan. *Tourism Management*, *31*(4), 470–481. doi:10.1016/j.tourman.2009.05.008

Tsai, C. H., & Chen, C. W. (2011). Development of a mechanism for typhoon- and floodrisk assessment and disaster management in the hotel industry – A case study of the Hualien area. *Scandinavian Journal of Hospitality and Tourism*, *11*(3), 324–341. doi:10.1080/15022250.2011.601929

Tsai, C., Horng, J., Liu, C., & Hu, D. (2015). Work environment and atmosphere: The role of organizational support in the creative performance of tourism and hospitality organizations. *International Journal of Hospitality Management*, *46*, 26–35. doi:10.1016/j.ijhm.2015.01.009

Tsaur, S.-H., Hsu, F.-S., & Lin, H. (2019). Workplace fun and work engagement in tourism and hospitality: The role of psychological capital. *International Journal of Hospitality Management*, *81*, 131–140. doi:10.1016/j.ijhm.2019.03.016

Tsui, A. S., Pearce, J. L., Porter, L. W., & Tripoli, A. M. (1997). Alternative approaches to the employee-organization relationship: Does investment in employees pay off? *Academy of Management Journal*, *40*(5), 1089–1121. doi:10.2307/256928

Ünsar, S. A. (2011). Effect of motivation on severance tendency: A field research. *Journal of Academics Sight*, *25*, 1–15.

UNWTO. (2020). *Supporting jobs and economies through travel and tourism a call for action to mitigate the socio-economic impact of the COVID-19 and accelerate recovery*. Available at: https://webunwto.s3.eu-west-1.amazonaws.com/s3fs-public/2020-04/COVID19_Recommendations_English_1.pdf

Urbanaviciute, I., Lazauskaite-Zabielske, J., Elst, T. V., & De Witte, H. (2018). Qualitative job insecurity and turnover intention: The mediating role of basic psychological needs in public and private sectors. *Career Development International*, *2*(3), 274–290. doi:10.1108/CDI-07-2017-0117

US Bureau of Labor Statistics. (2021). *Labor force statistics from the current population survey*. Available at: www.bls.gov/cps/electronically-mediated-employment.Html

US Bureau of Labor Statistics. (2023). *Labor force statistics from the current population survey*. Available at: www.bls.gov/cps/electronically-mediated-employment.Html

Vahtera, J., Kivimaki, M., & Pentti, J. (1997). Effect of organizational downsizing on health of employees. *Lancet*, *350*(9085), 1124–1128. doi:10.1016/S0140-6736(97)03216-9 PMID:9343499

Vallen, G. K. (1993). "Organizational climate and burnout. *The Cornell H.R. AQ*, (February), 54–59.

Van Hoye, G., Saks, A. M., Lievens, F., & Weijters, B. (2015). Development and test of an integrative model of job search behaviour. *European Journal of Work and Organizational Psychology*, *24*(4), 544–559. doi:10.1080/1359432X.2014.964214

Vandenberghe, C., De Keyser, V., Vlerick, P., & D'hoore, W. (2004). Organizational changes, employee stress, and customer satisfaction: Emergence of the flexihealth concept. *Belgian Science Policy*, *46*, 8–19.

Vargas-Sanchez, A. (2018). Crisis situations in tourist destinations: How can they be managed? *Enlightening Tourism. A Pathmaking Journal, 8*(1), 47-69.

Vaziri, H., Benson, G. S., & Salazar Campo, M. (2019). Hardworking coworkers: A multilevel cross-national look at group work hours and work–family conflict. *Journal of Organizational Behavior*, *40*(6), 676–692. doi:10.1002/job.2361

Veen, A., Barratt, T., & Goods, C. (2020). Platform-capital's 'app-etite' for control: A labour process analysis of food-delivery work in Australia. *Work, Employment and Society*, *34*(3), 388–406. doi:10.1177/0950017019836911

Verreynne, M. L., Williams, A. M., Ritchie, B. W., Gronum, S., & Betts, K. S. (2019). Innovation diversity and uncertainty in small and medium sized tourism firms. *Tourism Management*, *72*, 257–269. doi:10.1016/j.tourman.2018.11.019

Vigoda, E. (2000). Organizational politics, job attitudes, and work outcomes: Exploration and implications for the public sector. *Journal of Vocational Behavior*, *57*(3), 326–347. doi:10.1006/jvbe.1999.1742

Vinodkumar, M. N., & Bhasi, M. (2010). Safety management practices and safety behaviour: Assessing the mediating role of safety knowledge and motivation. *Accident; Analysis and Prevention*, *42*(6), 2082–2093. doi:10.1016/j.aap.2010.06.021 PMID:20728666

Vranjes, I., Baillien, E., Vandebosch, H., Erreygers, S., & De Witte, H. (2018). When workplace bullying goes online: Construction and validation of the Inventory of Cyberbullying Acts at Work (ICA-W). *European Journal of Work and Organizational Psychology*, *27*(1), 28–39. doi:10.1080/1359432X.2017.1363185

Vujičić, D., Jovičić, A., Lalić, D., & Cvejanov, A. (2014). The relation between job insecurity, job satisfaction and organizational commitment among employees in the tourism sector in Novi Sad. *Economic and Industrial Democracy*, *36*(4), 633–652. doi:10.1177/0143831X14527017

Wagner, J. A. III. (1995). Studies of individualism-collectivism: Effects on cooperation in groups. *Academy of Management Journal*, *38*(1), 152–173. doi:10.2307/256731

Wang, D., Tsui, A. S., Zhang, Y., & Ma, L. (2003). Employment relationships and firm performance: Evidence from an emerging economy. *Journal of Organizational Behavior*, *24*(5), 511–535. doi:10.1002/job.213

Wang, H. J., Lu, C. Q., & Siu, O. L. (2015). Job insecurity and job performance: The moderating role of organizational justice and the mediating role of work engagement. *The Journal of Applied Psychology*, *100*(4), 1249–1258. doi:10.1037/a0038330 PMID:25402953

Wang, J., & Ritchie, B. W. (2010). A theoretical model for strategic crisis planning: Factors influencing crisis planning in the hotel industry. *International Journal of Tourism Policy*, *3*(4), 297–317. doi:10.1504/IJTP.2010.040390

Wang, P. Q., Kim, P. B., & Milne, S. (2017). Leader–member exchange (LMX) and its work outcomes: The moderating role of gender. *Journal of Hospitality Marketing & Management*, *26*(2), 125–143. doi:10.1080/19368623.2016.1185989

Wang, P. Q., Kim, P. B., & Milne, S. (2020). The impacts of leader-member guanxi and its differentiation on hotel employees moderated by Confucian values. *International Journal of Hospitality Management*, *91*(3), 102668. doi:10.1016/j.ijhm.2020.102668

Wang, X., Tao, Z., Liang, L., & Gou, Q. (2019). An analysis of salary mechanisms in the sharing economy: The interaction between streamers and unions. *International Journal of Production Economics*, *214*, 106–124. doi:10.1016/j.ijpe.2019.04.003

Wang, Y. C., Ryan, B., & Yang, C. E. (2019). Employee brand love and love behaviors: Perspectives of social exchange and rational choice. *International Journal of Hospitality Management*, *77*, 458–467. doi:10.1016/j.ijhm.2018.08.009

Wan, Y. K., Wong, I. A., & Kong, W. H. (2014). Student career prospect and industry commitment: The roles of industry attitude, perceived social status, and salary expectations. *Tourism Management*, *40*, 1–14. doi:10.1016/j.tourman.2013.05.004

Ware, J. E., & Sherbourne, D. (1992). The MOS 36-Items Short-Form Health (SF36): Conceptual Framework and Item Selection. *Medical Care*, *30*(6), 473–483. doi:10.1097/00005650-199206000-00002 PMID:1593914

Wei, L., Liu, J., Chen, Y., & Wu, L. (2010). Political skill, supervisor-subordinate guanxi and career prospects in Chinese firms. *Journal of Management Studies*, *47*(3), 437–454. doi:10.1111/j.1467-6486.2009.00871.x

Weil, D. (2014). *The Fissured Workplace: Why Work Became So Bad for So Many and What Can Be Done to Improve It*. Harvard University Press. doi:10.4159/9780674726123

Wen, B., Zhou, X., Hu, Y., & Zhang, X. (2020). Role stress and turnover intention of front-line hotel employees: The roles of burnout and service climate. *Frontiers in Psychology*, *11*, 36. doi:10.3389/fpsyg.2020.00036 PMID:32082216

Weng, L.-C. (2014). Improving employee job performance through ethical leadership and "guanxi": The moderation effects of supervisor-subordinate guanxi differentiation. *Asia Pacific Management Review.*, *19*(3), 321–345.

WHO. (2020). Retrieved May 10, 2022 from https://www.who.int/publications/m/it em/covid-19-public-health-emergency-of-international-concern-(pheic)-global-research-and-innovation-forum.

Wiesenfeld, B. M., Raghuram, S., & Garud, R. (1999). Communication patterns as determinants of organizational identification in a virtual organization. *Organization Science*, *10*(6), 777–790. doi:10.1287/orsc.10.6.777

Wiesenfeld, B. M., Raghuram, S., & Garud, R. (2001). Organizational identification among virtual workers: The role of need for affiliation and perceived work-based social support. *Journal of Management*, *27*(2), 213–229. doi:10.1177/014920630102700205

Wiezer, N., Nielsen, K., Pahkin, K., Widerszal-Bazyl, M., De Jong, T., Mattila-Holappa, P., & Mockałło, Z. (2011). *Exploring the link between restructuring and employee well-being*. Central Institute for Labour Protection-National Research Institute.

Wim, J. N. M., & Gijs, B. (1998). Employee commitment in changing organizations: An exploration. *Journal of European Industrial Training*, *22*(6), 243–248. doi:10.1108/03090599810224701

Wiste, P. M., & Li, M. (2017). Component hotel: The continued evolution of urban hotel design in the 21st century. *International Journal of Hospitality and Event Management*, *1*(4), 325–332. doi:10.1504/IJHEM.2016.082165

Witt, L. A. (1991). Exchange ideology as a moderator of job attitudes-organizational citizenship behaviors relationships. *Journal of Applied Social Psychology*, *21*(18), 1490–1501.

Wolf, T., Metzing, M., & Lucas, R. (2019). Experienced Well-Being and Labor Market Status: The Role of Pleasure and Meaning. The German Socio-Economic Panel, DIW, Berlin.

Wolfe, N. D., Dunavan, C. P., & Diamond, J. (2007). Origins of major human infectious diseases. *Nature*, *447*(7142), 279–283. doi:10.1038/nature05775 PMID:17507975

Wolf, S., Hinkel, J., Hallier, M., Bisaro, A., Lincke, D., Ionescu, C., & Klein, R. J. (2013). Clarifying vulnerability definitions and assessments using formalisation. *International Journal of Climate Change Strategies and Management*, *5*(1), 54–70. doi:10.1108/17568691311299363

Wong, S. C., & Ko, A. (2009). Exploratory study of understanding hotel employees' perception on work-life balance issues. *International Journal of Hospitality Management*, *28*(2), 195–203. doi:10.1016/j.ijhm.2008.07.001 PMID:32287852

Wood, A., Lehdonvirta, V., & Graham, M. (2018). Workers of the Internet unite? Online freelancer organisation among remote gig economy workers in six Asian and African countries. *New Technology, Work and Employment*, *33*(2), 95–112. doi:10.1111/ntwe.12112

Woodworth, R. M., & Mandelbaum, R. (2010). Seventy-Five Years of U.S. Hotel Revenues, Expenses, and Profits. *Cornell Hospitality Quarterly*, *51*(1), 20–26. doi:10.1177/1938965509356774

World Bank. (2020). *International Tourism, Number of Arrivals*. Retrieved April 4, 2022, from. https://data.worldbank.org/indicator/ST.INT.ARVL

Wrosch, C., Scheier, M. F., Miller, G. E., Schulz, R., & Carver, C. S. (2003). Adaptive self-regulation of unattainable goals: Goal disengagement, goal reengagement, and subjective well-being. *Personality and Social Psychology Bulletin*, *29*(12), 1494–1508. doi:10.1177/0146167203256921 PMID:15018681

Wrzesniewski, A., McCauley, C., Rozin, P., & Schwartz, B. (1997). Jobs, careers, and callings: People's relations to their work. *Journal of Research in Personality*, *31*(1), 21–33. doi:10.1006/jrpe.1997.2162

WTTC. (2018). *Impact of the Ebola epidemic on travel & tourism*. WTTC.

Wu, Q., Zhang, H., Li, Z., & Liu, K. (2019). Labor control in the gig economy: Evidence from Uber in China. *The Journal of Industrial Relations*, *61*(4), 574–596. doi:10.1177/0022185619854472

Wu, W., Liu, J., & Shang, X. (2018). Gain without pay causes lazybones' loss: The influence of formal and informal leader–member relationships on customer service performance. *Chinese Management Studies*, *12*(3), 634–657. doi:10.1108/CMS-03-2017-0057

Xanthopoulou, D., Bakker, A. B., Demerouti, E., & Schaufeli, W. B. (2009). Reciprocal relationships between job resources, personal resources, and work engagement. *Journal of Vocational Behavior*, *74*(3), 235–244. doi:10.1016/j.jvb.2008.11.003

Xiang, Y.-T., Yang, Y., Li, W., Zhang, L., Zhang, Q., Cheung, T., & Ng, C. H. (2020). Timely mental health care for the 2019 novel coronavirus outbreak is urgently needed. *The Lancet. Psychiatry*, *7*(3), 228–229. doi:10.1016/S2215-0366(20)30046-8 PMID:32032543

Xiao, W., Zhou, L., Wu, Q., Zhang, Y., Miao, D., Zhang, J., & Peng, J. (2014). Effects of person-vocation fit and core self-evaluation on career commitment of medical university students: The mediator roles of anxiety and career satisfaction. *International Journal of Mental Health Systems*, *8*(1), 8. doi:10.1186/1752-4458-8-8 PMID:24555701

Xinhua, G. (2020). Does organizational inducement foster work engagement in hospitality industry? Perspectives from a moderated mediation model. *Journal of Hospitality and Tourism Management*, *43*, 259–268. doi:10.1016/j.jhtm.2020.04.010

Xu, S., Wang, Y., Ma, E., & Wang, R. (2020). Hotel employees' fun climate at work: Effects on work-family conflict and employee deep acting through a collective perspective. *International Journal of Hospitality Management*, *91*, 102666. doi:10.1016/j.ijhm.2020.102666 PMID:32934433

Yang, F. X., & Lau, V. M.-C. (2015). Does workplace guanxi matter to hotel career success? *International Journal of Hospitality Management*, *47*, 43–53. doi:10.1016/j.ijhm.2015.03.004

Yang, J.-T., Wan, C.-S., & Fu, Y.-J. (2012). Qualitative examination of employee turnover and retention strategies in international tourist hotels in Taiwan. *International Journal of Hospitality Management*, *31*(3), 837–848. doi:10.1016/j.ijhm.2011.10.001

Yanti, S., & Dahlan, J. (2017). The effects of organizational culture, leadership behavior, and job satisfaction on employee organizational commitment. *Journal of Positive Management*, *8*(4), 80–96. doi:10.12775/JPM.2017.132

Yao, T., Qiu, Q., & Wei, Y. (2019). Retaining hotel employees as internal customers: Effect of organizational commitment on attitudinal and behavioral loyalty of employees. *International Journal of Hospitality Management*, *76*, 1–8. doi:10.1016/j.ijhm.2018.03.018

Yao, X., Lee, T. W., & Mitchell, T. R. (2004). Job embeddedness: Current research and future directions. In R. Griffeth & P. Hom (Eds.), *Understanding employee retention and turnover* (pp. 153–187). Information Age.

Yu, J., Ariza-Montes, A., Hernández-Perlines, F., Vega-Muñoz, A., & Han, H. (2020). Hotels' eco-friendly physical environment as nature-based solutions for decreasing burnout and increasing job satisfaction and performance. *International Journal of Environmental Research and Public Health*, *17*(17), 6357. doi:10.3390/ijerph17176357 PMID:32882825

Zemke, R., Raines, C., & Filipczak, B. (2000). Generations at Work: Managing the Cash of Veterans, Boomers, Xers, and Nexters in Your Workplace. Amacom.

Zhang, X., & Bartol, K. M. (2010). Linking empowering leadership and employee creativity: The influence of psychological empowerment, intrinsic motivation, and creative process engagement. *Academy of Management Journal*, *53*(1), 107–128. doi:10.5465/amj.2010.48037118

Zhao, X., & Ghiselli, R. (2016). Why do you feel stressed in a "smile factory"? Hospitality job characteristics influence work–family conflict and job stress. *International Journal of Contemporary Hospitality Management*, *28*(2), 305–326. doi:10.1108/IJCHM-08-2014-0385

Zhao, X., & Mattila, A. S. (2013). Examining the spillover effect of frontline employees' work–family conflict on their affective work attitudes and customer satisfaction. *International Journal of Hospitality Management*, *33*, 310–315. doi:10.1016/j.ijhm.2012.10.001

Zheng, X., Zhu, W., Zhao, H., & Zhang, C. (2015). Employee well-being in organizations: Theoretical model, scale development, and cross-cultural validation. *Journal of Organizational Behavior*, *36*(5), 621–644. doi:10.1002/job.1990

Zuo, J., Jin, X.-H., & Flynn, L. (2012). Social sustainability in construction-an explorative study. *International Journal of Construction Management*, *12*(2), 51–63. doi:10.1080/15623599.2012.10773190

About the Author

Mark Vitale has been with the University of Phoenix for over 22 years as both faculty and staff. He is currently serving in the University's Workforce Solutions Group where he leads efforts to align internal resources of the university with customized needs for various workforce sectors. He has created unique educational and upskilling solutions that develop employee satisfaction through establishing career pathways for various industries including business, information technology, healthcare administration, nursing, education criminal justice. Previously, Dr. Vitale led the University of Phoenix Southern Arizona Campus. He teaches Statistics, Leadership and Marketing courses for the University and has served as a peer evaluator for regional and programmatic accreditors. Prior to his tenure in higher education, Dr. Vitale enjoyed a successful career in tourism and hospitality marketing with fortune 500 companies such as the Walt Disney Company and Westin Hotels. Dr. Vitale has a Doctorate in Organizational Systems and Transformational Leadership from Capella University as well as a Bachelor of Science in Biochemistry, and a Master of Business Administration in Marketing from The University of Arizona. He has published and presented original research on workforce development as well as leading cross-organizational teams to develop the architecture for multiple registered apprenticeship frameworks including for law enforcement, commercial pilots, and k-12 teachers. Dr. Vitale currently serves on several boards and leadership councils in Southern Arizona related to workforce development including being the current Chairman of the Board for the Pima County Workforce Investment Board. He has served on board for 8 years and has been leading its efforts as chair for 4. He has also been appointed to multiple state committees tasked with optimizing economic development, education, and workforce development efforts in the State of Arizona. In his free time, Dr. Vitale has a passion for aviation and is a commercially licensed pilot (with multi-engine and instrument ratings) as well as a certified flight instructor with over 1,500 logged flight hours.

Index

A

C

D

E

F

G

H

I

J

L

N

O

P

Q

R

S

T

V

W

www.ingramcontent.com/pod-product-compliance
Lightning Source LLC
LaVergne TN
LVHW080339011026
849161LV00009B/2127